Prais

"One of the best books I have read in qualitative research. I wish I had this book when I was a doctoral student or in the early stages of my academic career. Not only is it good for those in doctoral programs, it is appropriate for mentoring those in the early stages of the journey to tenure."

—Mark Malisa, *University of West Florida*

"Lahman's text is both a sound guide to the practical elements of qualitative inquiry, as well as a compelling overview of the eclectic, ethical, and engaged landscape of the contemporary field. This book is a true invitation to emerging researchers, calling for them to both create strong work and to dream new practices into being."

—Jake Burdick, *Purdue University*

Writing and Representing Qualitative Research

To O,

For my memories of a home full of books, reading and writing, how your beard felt against my cheek as you read a last bedtime story—trusting, to quote your poetry, that you have "absconded to a last home place."

Writing and Representing Qualitative Research

Maria K. E. Lahman

University of Northern Colorado

Los Angeles | London | New Delhi
Singapore | Washington DC | Melbourne

FOR INFORMATION:

SAGE Publications, Inc.
2455 Teller Road
Thousand Oaks, California 91320
E-mail: order@sagepub.com

SAGE Publications Ltd.
1 Oliver's Yard
55 City Road
London EC1Y 1SP
United Kingdom

SAGE Publications India Pvt. Ltd.
B 1/I 1 Mohan Cooperative Industrial Area
Mathura Road, New Delhi 110 044
India

SAGE Publications Asia-Pacific Pte. Ltd.
18 Cross Street #10-10/11/12
China Square Central
Singapore 048423

.

Acquisitions Editor: Helen Salmon
Product Associate: Yumna Samie
Production Editor: Megha Negi
Copy Editor: QuADS Prepress Pvt. Ltd
Typesetter: C&M Digitals (P) Ltd.
Cover Designer: Janet Kiesel
Marketing Manager: Victoria Velasquez

Printed in the United States of America

Library of Congress Cataloging-in-Publication Data

Names: Lahman, Maria K. E., author.

Title: Writing and representing qualitative research / Maria K. E. Lahman, University of Northern Colorado, USA.

Description: Thousand Oaks, California : SAGE Publishing, [2022] | Includes bibliographical references and index.

Identifiers: LCCN 2021011515 | ISBN 9781544348483 (paperback) | ISBN 9781544348506 (epub) | ISBN 9781544348513 (epub) | ISBN 9781544348490 (pdf)

Subjects: LCSH: Qualitative research. | Social sciences—Research.

Classification: LCC H62 .L2467 2022 | DDC 808.06/6001—dc23
LC record available at https://lccn.loc.gov/2021011515

This book is printed on acid-free paper.

SUSTAINABLE FORESTRY INITIATIVE   Certified Sourcing   www.sfiprogram.org   SFI-00756

21 22 23 24 25 10 9 8 7 6 5 4 3 2 1

• Detailed Contents •

PART II • AESTHETIC REPRESENTATIONS OF QUALITATIVE RESEARCH   175

Chapter 7 • Autoethnography: A Kaleidoscope of Knowing   177

• Preface •

An Essential Worker

Amazon, door to door—
Buffered by groceries delivered to my car—
Campus now in my home and yours—
Delivering education during destruction—
    I come to realize writers are a sort of
Essential worker—capturing the conditions of those with
    no time to write.
From my chair, over a computer screen, I watch a
    blue jay, peanut in beak, watch me—
"Greedy robber," I hear someone in my childhood memories say,
    but I love the flash of blue against barren winter
    and rascal, jaunty eye,
Howling time for health workers—some clap, some ring bells, but in
    Colorado, the rugged West, we coyote yowl—exhilaration and pride
      in this moment vibrating through the community
      sinks to shame as the same ideals carry
Insidious death throughout the region.
Joy, juxtaposed against death still lurks, somewhere?
    I wish for her, in the
    constrained COVID lives of my children.
    Does she skirt around the house waiting for
    the right time to place a light
Kiss on their heads, and then the peals of child
Laughter will ring out again? What does it say about me, in a
Moment of pain I'll think, I need to write that—like when my youngest
    one at Thanksgiving bowed her head and said, "I am thankful we are
Not dead."

Oh, post-

Pandemic world, what will we be?

Questions

Rage.

Summers past, I could dig dirt, deadhead spent flowers, mow a swath,

    drifting away from death for a while, in an academic's head—

Too soon, fall and the panic-pedagogy, Pandemic

University—fifty percent occupancy, then twenty-five, ten—

    squatters holding that noble land, signifying we will

    be back someday in full force from

Virtual teaching—vaccinated, with vim and vigour—

Writing the world into being, we touch Death's hem

    and for a moment know the unknowable.

Xaroncharoo government causes such a

Yearning for a time we now know never existed—when we were not

Zoombies, peering through screens, with each stroke of the keyboard

    writing death into existence.

I had quite a different preface prior to the COVID-19 pandemic. Reengaging with this text during the pandemic brought an added sense of urgency to research writing. The vital nature of research writing is apparent in every consultation with student researchers who are bringing to light issues of social justice, essential workers, white privilege, mental health during isolation, and grief—students on the cusp of graduating, fledging into the unknown, post-pandemic university.

• Acknowledgments •

A huge thanks to Helen Salmon, Megan O'Heffernan, Liz Cruz, Yumna Samie, Megha Negi, and Shamila Swamy, who got this book to the finish line during a time of pandemic. A profound thanks to the invisible teams behind them at SAGE who brought, and are still bringing, all aspects of this writing into being—the text editor, creators of the table of contents and indexes (the unsung heroes of all textbooks), copy editors, cover designers, teams in the production, marketing, accounting, technology, legal, custodial, and facilities departments, and others who my ignorance of publishing cause me not to name.

SAGE and I are grateful for feedback from the following reviewers during the development of this text:

- Aideen Murphy, *Neumann University*

- Ann Armstrong, *Northcentral University*

- Bianca Wolf, *University of Puget Sound*

- Jake Burdick, *Purdue University*

- Jasmine Ulmer, *Wayne State University*

- Kirsten Brown, *Edgewood College*

- Mark Malisa, *University of West Florida*

- Melissa Freeman, *University of Georgia*

- Robert L. A. Hancock, *University of Victoria*

- Simone Elias, *Abilene Christian University*

- Suha Tanim, *University of South Carolina*

Along with SAGE's team, my thanks go to Becky De Oliveira, who despite her own busy writing schedule proofread the roughest version of all the chapters of this book, allowing my writing to achieve a professional sheen before review, and then proofread the whole book again, joined by Beth Stover for this round. I appreciate how you both teach the teacher.

I thank all of the contributors to this book. My writing and representing would not be possible without you. More important, your research and that of all the other researchers and research participants I have been privileged to peek over the shoulder of, into worlds I previously had not entered—without these multiple and varied experiences, I would not be able to think and interact with future researchers and writers the way I do. I carry your wisdom and the wisdom imparted to you by participants in your research forward to each future researcher I encounter. It is a gift that gives in ways we cannot fully comprehend.

As I write this, I'm thinking of the Mennonite teachers and professors who first taught me the craft of writing—Vivian Beachy (she would have used a colon), James Bomberger, Jean Janzen, Jay Landis, Lee Snyder, and Caroll Yoder, thank you! And to all the writing teachers I won't name who were tasked with teaching me writing yet did not love reading or writing—I am sorry education has set you up in such an impossible situation. My advice is—tread lightly among others' words, using a supportive green pen, for you may be marking away some future writer's drafts and psyche.

My deepest gratitude to my parents, Omar and Anna Kathryn Eby, for creating a storied home in telling, reading, and writing. Dad, every time I told you about my book, your response was so full of pleasure and pride that sometimes I told you just to cheer myself up. I wish I could tell you one more time. Mom, I wish you could have held a book of mine.

My brother, Lawrence, who first taught me the power of visuals and lyrics, as he penned a comic strip about the family spaniel and chickens and labored over lyrics for guitar compositions—you have a story to write.

My sister, Katrina, may not recall that when I first gave her a business card, after my master's degree, she tossed it back on the table as she left the room saying, "I won't keep one until it says PhD." It had never occurred to me that I could get a PhD. Thanks—it was a clear moment in my story toward that first big step.

Thanks to my children, who in the context of our lives and with unusual intensity during our COVID bubble, live every aspect of my writing journey— groaning at the hours of work, sharing satisfaction with a sentence or an occasional paragraph that seems just right.

Kate, who writes fascinating stories in her head—keep considering putting them to paper.

Martin, one of my favorite authors and critics—keep writing and publishing.

Brent, would anyone seek to be partnered with a writer? I doubt I would. Thanks for all the times you push on for our family when I need time to think and for understanding that much of my writing occurs while staring out a window at birds in the feeder, digging in the garden, late in the night, or mumbling to a computer screen.

• About the Author •

Maria K. E. Lahman is a professor at the University of Northern Colorado, Colorado, USA, where she is a qualitative research methodologist in the Department of Applied Statistics and Research Methods, College of Education and Behavioral Sciences. A Mennonite, Maria's first forays in formal writing were within the context of social justice and peace building, which she continually challenges herself to weave into her pedagogy and writing. Her scholarship is focused on writing and representing qualitative research, with an emphasis on aesthetic accounts, young children, mothering, culturally responsive research, and creating ethical solutions within culturally complex contexts.

Writing Qualitative Research Essentials

I hate writing. I love having written.

—Dorothy Parker (The New York Times, 2016)

This book is groundbreaking due to *foundational areas in qualitative writing* (e.g., journal articles, dissertations), *aesthetic representations* (e.g., poetry, autoethnography), *transparency in publication, promotion of our research accounts*, and *reflexivity* essentials being addressed in one practical and engaging text based on real experiences. Part I of this book is foundational in nature. I frame Part I with a discussion of the daunting and hidden nature of writing, and my goal through this book to help writers complete and publish their research accounts. My goal is to support researchers as they *Publish and Persevere*. I explain the practical nature of the first half of the book regarding writing, dealing with writer's block, the politics of research writing, manuscripts, dissertations, publication, and promotion of research accounts. The idea that writers must understand the traditional writing form, in this case the qualitative research thematic article, to persevere and/or break the form is proposed.

Through the first six chapters, I cover the foundational qualitative writing essentials.

Chapter 1, "Introduction," is where I lay out what prompted me to write this book and describe the gap I am filling between the information available on writing up qualitative research for course projects and dissertations and the resources on disseminating research to wider audiences. I describe the literary influences framing the book and advocate for qualitative writers to draw on these creative forms. Finally, I provide the path for the book and review features that have been developed from qualitative researchers' first-hand experiences to support readers' writing growth. In Chapter 2, "Why, What, and How We Write," I remind writers of the various reasons *why* we represent data, including (1) needing to publish and persevere, (2) believing that research can cause change for good, and (3) expecting that varied representations may allow the reader and writer to grow in understanding. I overview *what* qualitative researchers have historically and contemporarily written. Building on those who have written about qualitative writing, I center the book firmly in this context both in this chapter and throughout the text. Finally, I detail *how* successful writers ensure that they are productive— including time management and writers' groups. In Chapter 3, "Start Writing!" I assume that the readers of this text have analyzed qualitative data and have access to an analyzed data set. Then, I challenge researchers to represent the data set in different ways so they can deeply consider the importance of their representation choices. I advocate for creating a road map or chart of what we are writing and where we are in the process as a way of keeping the writing process organized. I cover ways to hone the craft of writing—pulling on top nonfiction writing experts. Chapter 4, "Qualitative Dissertations: The Three Rules" (disclaimer—there aren't any rules!), is where I review how to form the traditional five chapters of the qualitative dissertation while detailing other dissertation forms that may be available to the student, such as article manuscripts, plays, research poetry, and visuals. I also feature a discussion on the politics and process of the dissertation since this context must be negotiated for a successful outcome. Finally, I review the changes some are advocating for in the area of dissertations. Chapter 5, "Writing the Qualitative Journal Article: Of Rice Cakes, Tortillas, Bread, and Butter," opens with a review of the basic form of qualitative writing, the thematic article. I review the sections in this type of article, with suggestions on how to write them. I explain what a qualitative methodological article is and encourage more qualitative researchers to make contributions in this area. In Chapter 6, "Publish and Persevere: The Publication Process," I fill a gap that occurs for some after course work or when a dissertation has been completed. In this chapter, the publication process for an article and a book are described step-by-step, with examples of ups and downs presented throughout. Providing transparency regarding the publication process is my goal in this chapter.

Samuel Johnson reminded us that "the only end of writing is to enable readers better to enjoy life or better to endure it." As researchers, we should extend these words to research writing, which is no small thing; and in addition, if we could learn to love research writing—the turn of a phrase, a powerful allusion, the moment when your breath catches at a participant's words—what a difference this would make in a profession comprising readers and writers.

1

Introduction

The universe is made of stories, not of atoms.

—Muriel Rukeyser (n.d.)

H as research occurred if it hasn't been written (represented) and disseminated? Some have argued that it has not (e.g., Wolcott, 1994). This perspective is based on the point of view that research is conducted to create impact, facilitate change, and add to knowledge, so a portrayal of research that is disseminated is necessary. Therefore, my primary purpose in this book is to consider *why* and *how* qualitative researchers portray research and how these portrayals may best be disseminated.

In this chapter, I

- discuss why I wrote this book,
- describe my attempt to ground the book in literary and artistic perspectives,
- lay out the path of the book,
- highlight each chapter, and
- detail key features of the book.

I tell my family I have signed a contract for a book with SAGE. I am elated but also full of trepidation. Both of my children respond, "Oh, no!"

"What?" I tease them, exaggerating my outrage. "'Oh, no!' What does that mean?" But I knew what they meant. The first and only book I have written so far was a daunting experience in many ways—the newness and the time constraints, as well as the shifts in my eyesight and overall health that came from sitting and looking at a screen too long.

Later, at a celebratory dinner—for me at least—while eating Japanese noodles and dumplings, it occurs to my daughter Kate, 8 years old, to ask, "What is this book about?"

"How to write," I reply.

"What? [again] You are writing a book about writing?" We all laugh at Kate's genuine incredulity. My children thought it was odd enough to write a book about how to be ethical, but now Kate's astonished tone wipes out an entire genre of writing, the how-to-write books—how to write murder mysteries, poems, theses, dissertations, children's storybooks, and so on.

In what follows, I lay out my reasons for writing this book, both as a defense and as an offense of sorts. I write this book first and foremost for the graduate student and assistant professor I once was and in memory of how profoundly lonely and out of step I felt when it came to writing research. Coming from a literary home with a father who was an English, literature, and journalism professor at a liberal arts college, I had the naive notion that I would just combine what I knew from the humanities with what I wanted to accomplish in higher education as an educator and social science researcher. My belief that I could write in the manner of educational nonfiction writers such as Kidder (e.g., 1989) and Paley (e.g., 2009) for my dissertation seemed to draw blank looks or, more disappointingly, lectures on how we cannot learn from an "*n* of 1" or from a research participant who is a remarkably positive figure. I was told, "Dissertations aren't about the Mother Teresas of the world, because who could be like them?" These assertions came from people I respected, so I began to feel unsure of myself and of a knowledge source I had always learned through—stories.

My mother, a white woman born to Mennonite missionaries in colonized East Africa, was a storyteller. When asked a yes or no question, Mom would settle into long narratives from which the asker would need to make sense of what the point was. These narratives were enchanting to people unless you were an impatient daughter who wanted a quick yes. Yet I am thankful that as I grew older I was able to appreciate the stories and yearn to have had more opportunities to record them prior to her death. I know I am also a story-teller and find myself ending the ones I tell when I teach, which I sense may have been too long, with a crisp "So the point is . . . "—summarizing for non-"storied" students the main nugget I want them to extract. Indeed, while most reviewers of my texts appreciate my storytelling, there are reviewers, including of this text, who want me to get to the point quicker—charts, tables, the gist, have been provided in this book for these readers since I know time is valuable. Yet, paradoxically, in a book that includes organization and time management strategies, I call for times when qualitative researchers can drift, slow down, take a break from listening and writing up others' stories to tell their own stories. What it would have meant to me as an unsure Mennonite at a state university if someone had slowed down and really listened to the story that I, as a fledgling researcher, was trying to tell.

My father, an author and English professor, was a storyteller and writer. When he told stories, Mom would shush any of our comments, and he was allowed to hold court like traditional professors did as though on a dais behind a podium. No one interrupted—not when he wrote stories either; and he was a great storyteller. Toward the end of his life, dementia took from him the one thing these great professors held in common, the ability to hold a vast group of listeners' and readers' attention without the use of whiteboards, PowerPoint, SMART boards, or Zoom. So we told his stories back to him, and at times, he knew when it was the right point to cry, chuckle, or boom with laughter.

My initial writing experiences are what led me to create a course focused on writing and representing qualitative research when I received a position as an assistant professor in qualitative methodology. I wanted students to avoid the isolation I felt and the consistent message that my way of thinking about and representing the world was inferior. I wanted to create a sense of community for students where they could try new writing ideas in a safe environment and grow and thrive as a result. This book emerges from that story. Twenty years later, I like to think the writing experience I had in graduate school is no longer as common for today's students. Yet for those who are in the midst of anything reminiscent of my early experience, this text can be a resource, a comfort, and, perhaps, an inspiration, reminding them that they are not alone. We must continue to ask ourselves as academics, researchers, teachers, and mentors what we risk, as "primary arbiters of knowledge," when we cut off or relegate certain ways of seeing and knowing to a lower-level status or completely exclude them from the academy.

Second, I write this book to emphasize the connection between qualitative portrayals of research and the need to disseminate research, thereby making it transparent and accessible. As instructors, we make a mistake when we concentrate solely on writing research proposals, course research papers, or dissertations while excluding assignments and discussions of manuscripts for the purpose of publication. Students who go on to be professors will no longer be writing course papers or dissertations; they will maintain their place in higher education through the writing and publication of research articles. The lack of concentration on research manuscripts can have profound repercussions for the type of academic position a new professor may receive and ultimately for their chances at tenure. There need to be ample opportunities for students to learn how to craft and refine course work and dissertations into journal articles—no easy feat. The primary graduate qualitative research writing focus needs to be on (a) a publishable manuscript; (b) the thesis and dissertation form, including conversion to a journal manuscript; (c) understanding and participating in the publication process, and building on this foundation; and (d) other ways to represent and disseminate research. Given the lack of emphasis in some students' degrees on publication, I write this book for graduate students, untenured professors, and professors venturing into qualitative research for the first time.

Readers who are in the position, as I am now, to represent qualitative research aesthetically, may wonder at my emphasis on the traditional qualitative journal manuscript. From my experience, as someone who teaches and consults across all areas of the social, psychological, educational, and even some business sciences, I have found that most students and untenured professors will need to concentrate on the traditional qualitative manuscript form. Once the traditional form is mastered, they are well positioned to critique, expand, and break the form.

Third, I write this book in celebration! Over my career, the variety of ways qualitative data are represented has burgeoned. There is much to celebrate and discuss. In this book, I have the privilege to feature the research of my current and former students portrayed through literary, performative, and artistic accounts, such as poetry, visuals, personal accounts, plays, song, sand trays, music, art, videos, collage, quilts, websites, posters, charts, infographics, rants, and more. I am confident, even as I write, that someone is considering representing research in a new way to help us engage with and understand our world.

Literary Framing

Throughout this book, I draw on literary worlds when possible. Researchers can learn from professional artists who spend all of their time writing and representing. Researchers with positions such as mine only spend part of their time on scholarship, and much of this time is not engaged in direct writing experiences. Given the demands to teach, assess, advise, consult, serve internally and externally, and secure funds, in reality, many academics likely feel they are not able to spend significant amounts of time on the actual writing of research. Therefore, we have much we could learn from those who spend most of their time writing. Challenging the conventions of academia to revitalize our writing by engaging with literary and artistic works and wisdom will only improve our ability to represent and disseminate qualitative research.

The heavy and diverse workload in academia and the simultaneous demand for scholarly publication are the primary reason the traditional writing form has served the academy so well. After it is learned, this form can be efficiently pounded out over and over with new literature, variables, and results inserted. However, the form has become deified as a way to distinguish academics as elite knowledge brokers. Aspects of writing such as adherence to American Psychological Association (APA) style are dogmatically applied, to the point that it seems the application of an academic style guide is mistaken for or privileged over the ability to have research ideas, conduct research, and write it up in an accessible and impactful way. Adherence to academic style guides is seen as a mark of quality and excellence when by nonfiction writing standards it is not (e.g., Zinsser, 2006). This is the tyranny of the scientific paper form and style guides. (Note my rebellious use of exclamation marks in this text!)

Researchers need to consider and draw on other forms of writing. Literary authors, for example, have a deep desire to be published so others can engage with their writing. Readers may know some famous stories of writing persistence, such as the example of the woman who wanted to write but was so busy rearing her children that she did not submit her first novel manuscript to a publisher until she was in her 40s. Twenty-six rejections later, her book was published, changing the face of science fiction forever and creating a literary icon—a female child protagonist, awkward with braces and thick glasses, who draws on themes of redemption, quantum physics, and love—to defend the universe from our deepest fears. The woman was Madeline L'Engle; the book, *A Wrinkle in Time* (1962). Tony Hillerman's book agent is infamously reported to have told him to "get rid of the Indian stuff" (Spizer, 2003). Hillerman persisted and published more than 18 mysteries with Native American protagonists, which were made into several movies. I believe we, as qualitative researchers, can learn from the persistence of literary and journalist writers who have dedicated their lives to writing. As Faulkner said, "Read everything—trash, classics, good and bad, and see how they do it. Just like a carpenter who works as an apprentice and studies the master. Read! You'll absorb it. Then write. If it is good, you'll find out" (Stein, 1956).

Path of the Book

Beginning writers must appreciate the prerequisites if they hope to become writers. You pay your dues—which takes years.

—Alex Haley

Part I: Writing Qualitative Research Essentials consists of six chapters, including a syllabus for a qualitative research writing course (Appendix A) in which the foundational and traditional aspects of writing qualitative research is covered. In Chapter 1, "Introduction," the daunting and hidden nature of writing is explored. I also describe the goal of this book, which is to make the qualitative research writing[1] and publication process more transparent and accessible. The idea that one must understand the traditional writing form—for qualitative researchers, this is the thematic article—in order to break it or build on it is proposed. In Chapter 2, "Why, What, and How We Write," I remind writers of the various reasons *why* we represent data, including (a) the imperative to publish (or perish), (b) the belief that research can cause change for good, and

---

[1] A word about the words "write," "writers," and "writing." At all times when I use the word "write," I also mean "represent" and "representing," as in "How do qualitative researchers represent research findings?" I use the word "writers" and "researchers" interchangeably since in this text I am focusing solely on qualitative research writing. I believe the word "write" reads smoothly and have chosen to use this word in all the chapters except Chapter 9, which is about visuals and visual research.

(c) the idea that varied representations may allow the reader and writer to grow. I give an overview of *what* qualitative researchers have historically and contemporarily written. Finally, I detail *how* successful writers ensure productivity. I advocate for reading multiple examples of the research writing style writers are working with as foundational to writing.

In Chapter 3, "Start Writing!" I assume that readers have analyzed qualitative data and have access to an analyzed data set. Then I challenge researchers to represent the same data set or parts of the same data set in different ways. Having done so, they should step away from the representations and then reengage, considering what each rendition has to offer. Ideally, if the researcher had access to other researchers to help with this process, the reflexivity could be even more powerful. To illustrate representing data in multiple ways, I draw on the three data representations in *A Thrice-Told Tale* (Wolf, 1992), my own publications with coauthors (Ku et al., 2008; Lahman et al., 2011), and Erin Patchett's research conducted during her doctoral course work represented in three pieces (see Appendix B). I cover ways to hone the craft of writing—drawing on examples from top nonfiction writing experts—in areas such as first sentences, style, diction, tone, and structure.

In Chapter 4, "Qualitative Dissertations: The Three Rules," I review how to form the traditional five chapters of the qualitative dissertation while giving tips and pointers on the politics and process of writing a dissertation. I detail other dissertation forms that may be available to the student and then highlight examples of qualitative dissertations that illustrate the breadth of possible aesthetic representations, including plays, research poetry, and visuals.

Chapter 5, "Writing the Qualitative Journal Article: Of Rice Cakes, Tortillas, Bread and Butter," opens with a review of the primary form of qualitative research writing, the thematic article. I explain what a qualitative methodological article is and challenge qualitative researchers to engage in this type of representation, since it allows readers a glimpse of what occurs in the background of research and thus enhances others' research abilities and methodological understandings.

In Chapter 6, "Publish and Persevere: The Publication Process," I fill a gap that occurs for some after course work or the dissertation has been completed. Novices are often guided through the research and writing process for a course paper, but publishing may remain a mystery. Through this chapter, I offer a step-by-step overview of the publication process for an article and a book, with examples of the ups and downs prospective authors experience presented throughout. Making the publication process transparent is my goal in this chapter. Text boxes from student authors are included.

Part 2: Aesthetic Representations of Qualitative Research consists of four chapters, in which aesthetic forms of qualitative writing and reflexivity are proposed and advocated for. In Chapter 7, "Autoethnography: A Kaleidoscope of Knowing," I discuss a hallmark of alternative and aesthetic representations, autoethnography, and detail it as a methodology. Some ways in which autoethnography may be positioned, including he*art*felt, critical, and multivoiced, are detailed, with examples provided. The process I followed to write autoethnographies on loss is described in an effort to make this form transparent and accessible to more writers.

Chapter 8, "Poemish Research Representations" is where I describe the primary form I use to explore participants' and my own experiences. I cover what research poetry is, research poets' potential contributions to the field, and how to write research poetry. Examples of research poetry—transcription, autoethnographic, literature review, archival, formed, collage, and more—are presented, along with text boxes from students engaging with research poetry.

I explore the idea of what an image is in Chapter 9, "Visuals in Qualitative Research Representation: In the Blink of an Eye." Research representations that use visual data within a traditional qualitative article and representations that rely primarily on visuals are explored. Representations discussed include collage, photography, video, and art. Considerations in visual representation including quality of images for reproduction purposes, copyright, dissemination, and image as sacred are forwarded. Throughout the chapter, visuals created by qualitative researchers are featured.

In Chapter 10, "Reflecting Reflexivity in Research Representations," I consider the role of reflexivity in research representations, reviewing the scant and superficial nature of reflexivity accounts in our final research products. Considering the reflexive experiences of a student researching people who are homeless, I advocate for *raw reflexivity* with deeper, more vulnerable representations.

I close the book with an epilogue, where I revisit the idea that research and researchers' *becoming* is supported by the concepts of *ish* and *good enough* from children's literature (Reynolds, 2004) and portraiture (Lawrence-Lightfoot & Davis, 1997), respectively. These ideas are further developed as I attempt to advocate for a space where researchers feel safe to attempt new forms of representation without yet being experts.

Features of the Book

In this text, I address the primary qualitative writing challenges for novices and provide resources for sage writers through engaging materials created for lifelong learners. Many successful research scholars received their primary training in quantitative research, and their experience is in writing quantitative research results. The curious mind of the academic, a desire to assist students in expanding research areas, and a wish to portray data in engaging ways cause some of these scholars to seek new, qualitative understandings. This desire to extend research and representation understandings may be seen in the colleagues who audit my courses, attend workshops on qualitative research, and consult on qualitative research issues. This book is for all researchers who desire to engage deeply with writing qualitative research.

Features of the book include first-person *narrative interludes* (Lather, 2012)—integrated into the chapters and indicated by italics—about the reflexive personal writing experiences I have had. The purpose of these writings is not explicated for the reader, with the intention that both the writer (myself) and the reader continue to mull over the interlude. (I present these when I teach as a way of demonstrating the learning and strength that can occur when we, as teachers and scholars, are willing to be vulnerable. Writing and publishing can be a confusing and lonely endeavor.)

Qualitative research writing vignettes from other writers are offset in *text boxes*. These narratives are first-person accounts written by researchers—many of whom were graduate students at the time of the writings—regarding real-life writing challenges they have encountered and how these were negotiated. I am thankful to these generous and candid writers for the learning they provide here.

 I have developed a second set of text boxes, denoted with a writing quill, dedicated to honing writing. These contain practical writing information (e.g., how to write an abstract), ideas for improving writing, or ways to challenge ingrained scholarly writing conventions that may no longer be useful. The writing text boxes are in response to a qualitative reviewer of a manuscript of mine who wrote, "You cannot even write well enough to be published in *The New Yorker*." I gasped while laughing aloud when reading this review. If I could write well enough to be featured in *The New Yorker* magazine, along with the top U.S. writers of our time, I might have a different career. It is this type of academic arrogance around what constitutes scholarship that I wish to counteract through the writing suggestions in this book.

Each chapter has a joke bubble signified by a laughing emoji. I find humor, even the unsophisticated humor in these bubbles, to be such an important part of successful scholarly writing. I'll also point out academic humorists who can give a writer in a hard spot a moment of levity. We have to know how to gently laugh with others, at ourselves, at the field—not mocking or with derision but with genuine pleasure in our foibles as a way of strengthening ourselves to go back into the solitary fray that always must occur at some point in writing. The first joke follows.

Why did the writer get so cold?

They were always around multiple drafts.

Each chapter ends with *The Gist*, which includes a summary of takeaway points and next action steps. There is a list of *reflexive questions* researchers should ask themselves before, during, and after writing, along with suggestions for ways to engage with the questions in a reflexive manner. *Resources* for further reading and *reflexive activities* that could occur on your own, in a writers' group, or during a course and face-to-face or virtually are shared.

The *appendices* have been developed to provide rich extensions to the text. An *example of a student's work* in representing qualitative data in several ways is included. *Reflexive activities* for group or personal use are detailed. A template of the *syllabus* for the writing qualitative research course I teach and suggestions for a *qualitative research poster* presentation layout are shared.

The Gist

With the invaluable help of graduate students and colleagues who are willing to be transparent about hidden areas of qualitative writing, I have crafted a book that will be a resource and perhaps an inspiration for qualitative researchers at many and varied points in their writing careers. Let us now stop reading about the goals of the book and get on with the goal at hand—writing and publishing—for as Eva Young said, "To think too long about doing a thing often becomes its undoing" (cited in Colegrove, 2004).

Reflexive Questions

1. Who are the literary authors whose work you have enjoyed?
   a. Go back and review these authors' work, and try to identify what it is you appreciate about them.
   b. Create a list of what you could draw on from their work in your research writing.
   c. For published authors, revisit a traditional qualitative research article and/or data set. How might you use this work to explore literary possibilities for a different type of representation?

2. Who are literary authors who have been recommended to you as someone you should read?
   a. Create a list of these authors, and start to read one of their works today or in the near future.

3. What present writing goals would you like to accomplish?
   a. What are possible impediments to your goals?
   b. How can you reduce or remove these impediments?

4. What future writing goals would you like to accomplish?
   a. What are the smaller goals within the future goals that must be accomplished first? Consider creating a list of the smaller goals that will lead toward this larger one.
   b. What are possible impediments to your goals?
   c. How can you reduce or remove these impediments?

2

Why, What, and How We Write

A WORD is dead

When it is said,

Some say.

I say it just

Begins to live

That day.

—Emily Dickinson

If a word when it is *said* begins to live, as Dickinson proclaimed, then when a word is *written*—read, read aloud, quoted, and discussed—it is living its life, just as we are. The point of this book is to assist qualitative researchers in helping the words of research participants and their own words to live full, impactful lives. Researchers want to improve the world for all, and words are researchers' partners in this endeavor.

In this chapter, I

- consider *why* qualitative researchers represent data—including to publish or perish, believing research can cause change for good, and

(Continued)

(Continued)

the expectation that representations may allow the reader and writer to grow;

- provide an overview of *what* qualitative researchers write historically and contemporarily; and

- detail *how* successful writers ensure they are productive, including *drifting*, blocking out writing time as sacred, participating in a writers' group, and writing every day (e.g., snack writing), even when there is no time to write.

Why Do We Write?

Professors, if they did not understand this initially, quickly find out that their primary activity is writing—prospectuses, teaching materials, feedback, grants, conference presentations, reports, evaluations, research plans, research results, articles, book chapters, books, poetry, vitae, dossiers, emails, blogs, posts, tweets, and more. Karen Golden-Biddle and Karen Locke (2007) succinctly state, "We are at the core a profession of text writers" (p. 9). What we are writing varies from being high stakes to low stakes, professional to casual, but it is an always present and ongoing aspect of who we are and how we are perceived as professionals.

Scholars have argued throughout the history of higher education over what constitutes research scholarship. The answer changes over time and depends both on the larger field of which we are a part and on what the local everyday judges of our writing believe scholarship is—or are willing to "allow" as scholarly writing. Unfortunately, this discussion is contentious and littered with racial, class, gender, orientation, and other issues of power, with the outcome often limiting access to resources for certain types of researchers—with potentially devastating results. I want to acknowledge this possibility and will weave in suggestions on how to negotiate the process of deciding what constitutes research throughout this text.

When I was an assistant professor, I attended a well-known qualitative researcher's training session. I asked how they helped colleagues understand and value their research representations. I was told that the researcher never bothered with this issue because it was their colleagues' problem, not theirs— such a disappointing answer for someone who felt as out of their depth as I did. The ability to not bother with the important issue of what constitutes scholarship signals the power and privilege of some full professors, but most of us do need to consider what our colleagues or, in the case of students, professors' value, or risk leaving academia.

The question of what constitutes research and scholarship, along with the daunting and unpredictable nature of the writing and publishing process, is reflected in the professional admonishment "publish or perish." This phrase, while true, has become overused, and its threatening tone is unhelpful. I advocate for rephrasing it as "publish and persevere"! I address this area first to get it over with since, while there is truth in the adage, degree attainment or job security should not be the only reason a researcher writes. If as researchers we are to find amity in and lifelong dedication to research, it will be through a belief that research can bring about change and cause understanding for the good. How we represent research may allow for broader and deeper understandings.

The major point of this book is to move readers towards a clear understanding of the writing and publication process. Of this, Jessica Smartt Gullion (2016) writes, "Many graduate programs make the assumption . . . that students already know how to write. . . . Graduate programs are more likely to train students to be researchers, not to be writers" (p. xi). Smartt Gullion goes on to point out that this is an issue not just for students but also for early-career professionals. "I've met many new faculty who have minimal experience writing for publication . . . who spend the first year or two on their tenure track floundering" (p. xii). I agree and feel that struggling with writing as a professor is kept hidden since public knowledge of this struggle would be seen as exposing oneself as a potential failure. Instead, increased transparency would allow for more support and success. With increased success, writers may develop a deeper appreciation for qualitative writing and the possibilities it holds for enhancing research and providing a satisfying and meaningful career, rather than feeling lost and at odds with the writing and publication process.

Having addressed perishing or persevering, another primary reason why qualitative researchers conduct research and publish is that we believe our work can have an impact for the betterment of humanity and the world. Postmodernism and critical studies have allowed us a glimpse of how idealistic and naive this statement is, but even the most critical perspectives would seem to be striving toward some type of hope for humanity's ability to change for the better.

However, having advocated for qualitative research and transformation, I want to emphasize that on any given day the only good thing I am sure of in research is that the writing I have engaged in and the representations of life I have crafted allow me personally to grow. As I engage with the craft of other qualitative researchers, research participants' experiences, and my personal struggle to write and represent, I am always becoming.

What Do We Write?

What do we, as qualitative researchers, write? The contemporary short answer is anything and everything. It is an exciting time to be a qualitative researcher, thanks to the hard work of those who have come before us, such as Norman Denzin, Yvonna Lincoln, Egon Guba, Laurel Richardson, Carolyn Ellis, Arthur Bochner, and more. However, this freedom has not always existed, and it is still not the case in many fields or at certain universities.

In the history of research, while "empirical" means raw observations—which clearly includes qualitative research—qualitative research, if it was even considered at all, was "preresearch"—a footnote or window dressing employed to underscore quantitative results with colorful quotes or engaging scenarios. More recently, qualitative methodology courses, texts, and dissertations may be seen in a wide and diverse array of fields from nursing to counseling to business. Qualitative dissertations with traditional formatting are burgeoning (e.g., Rennie et al., 2002), and alternative formats are seen more frequently. Journals dedicated solely to qualitative research, such as *The Qualitative Report, The Journal of Qualitative Inquiry, International Journal of Qualitative Research Methods, Qualitative Health*, and *Journal of Autoethnography*, to name a few, are thriving. Journals dedicated to academic disciplines accept qualitative research at increasing rates (see a partial list of qualitative journals and journals that accept qualitative accounts in the resources section at the end of Chapter 4). Qualitative researchers have taken to the internet and may be read in blogs (e.g., Lim, 2016), tweets (e.g., @antonioabush, @WriteNThrive, @lahman_maria), Facebook posts (e.g., https://www.facebook.com/DQRDW, YouTube videos (e.g., Weaver-Hightower, 2014; see https://www.youtube.com/playlist?list=PLJlmnEV4K0nOZ72XT2s6JcrGImJnJmqSh), and other online platforms.

What Do Novices Write?

A novice is a new writer who is just beginning to engage in their field and develop a sense of what type of qualitative writing they are expected to publish or a published research writer new to qualitative forms. According to Richard Bach, "a professional writer is an amateur who didn't quit." I think Bach's quotable quote gets at the importance of persistence and being able to change and adapt along with our fields of study. Some early writing will include research proposals and papers for courses, conference papers, and conference talks to practitioners about research. Setting up a clear expectation from the start that presentation and publication should be a goal for all novice researchers allows students to hone their abilities as researchers who publish as they move through the graduate school process. Learning the publication process should not be saved for after the dissertation has been completed—under the intense pressure of an academic job. All prospective professors have a dissertation publication; it is the other publications that help set researchers apart.

A primary way novices represent data is through the dissertation. The dissertation is a form that can help a field to grow or become stultifying. To encourage growth, see if your advisor and dissertation committee would be supportive of adding qualitative elements to your dissertation. Or if the dissertation is a traditional qualitative report such as grounded theory or phenomenology, would the committee support the addition of aesthetic elements such as visuals or research poetry? The dissertation is such a lengthy document that there is often room to try different types of representations. (See an extended discussion of this in Chapter 4, in the section "Innovative Dissertations.")

While a student researcher may be new to what academia traditionally sees as "scholarship," this does not mean they arrive without highly specialized skill sets. Part of advising is getting to know students' areas of expertise and helping them reflect on what they might bring to research data representation. For instance, I am currently teaching two writing teachers, a graphic designer, a zine (magazine) developer, a mindfulness expert, a podcaster, a videographer, a historian, and a disc jockey. What might their interests, experiences, and skills bring to research representation?

Increasingly, graduate students are coming to academia with advanced skills in social media, which can easily be applied to educational social media (ESM)—websites and apps (applications) that allow scholars, researchers, and educators to create and share content in a similar manner to how social networking on the internet occurs. These media skills often outshine any that the faculty graduate students work with may have. We need to advocate for an increase in the validation of ESM as a reputable and necessary outlet for research. The primary way this occurs is by citing ESM, as I have throughout this book. A central argument for representing research through ESM is open access to knowledge, which is framed by a critical equity perspective. Clearly, the answer to what novices are writing is a blooming, full-flowered reply.

How Do We Write?

In composing, as a general rule, run a pen through every other word you have written; you have no idea what vigor it will give your style.

—Sydney Smith

2.1 HOW DO WE WRITE?
MARGARET SEBASTIAN

I woke up this morning from a dream about writing. I hadn't written anything in seven days and I felt like I had something to say. But instead of writing, I started laundry, made breakfast, took a shower, did my hair, picked out clothes for the week, listened to an interview with my favorite comedian, and then read a book on my phone. Three hours have passed, and I'm still thinking I may write something today. Finally, I pick up a sweater, my coat, and my pre-packed book bag with all my articles, and I leave my apartment for the library.

It's terribly quiet in the library. I sit near a window to take in the sun and the fun everyone else is having outside—still haven't written one word. I laugh at myself because I hid my cell phone in my car so I wouldn't text anyone, yet I am searching for it to see what time it is. I finally open up my computer to an

(Continued)

(Continued)

empty page. I write one sentence, and I feel inadequate—like I have no idea what I'm talking about and if I did, someone already wrote it better than me—so I start reading articles about my topic. After about seven or so articles, I realize I could indeed write about the same topic with my own words and from my perspective. Instead of writing, I then look over all the references, find the ones that fit with my research, and look them up.

After another hour, I still have only one sentence.

I look at the screensaver quote my mentor told me to focus on: "What is the easiest thing you can write about right now as if you were talking to your daddy? How would he understand your topic? Would your argument make sense to him? Write it cohesively."

I look outside and see children playing on the playground swings, laughing and smiling.

I write 500 words without looking up again.

Source: Reproduced with permission from Margaret L. Sebastian.

Where would a writer never want to live?

A writer's block. (Vick, 2018)

Read, Read, Read

The greatest part of a writer's time is spent in reading, in order to write.

—Samuel Johnson

How do we learn to write? When I teach qualitative writing, I tell students, "I am asking you a trick question: How do we learn to write?" Invariably, the answer I am given is "by writing." This is certainly partly true, but the answer I want to emphasize first is that writing is learned by reading. Read, read, and *read*—read anything and everything. Dick Meyer (2008) says if you live in the United States, "Statistically, if you're reading this sentence, you're an oddball. The average American spends three minutes a day reading a book. At this moment, you and I are engaged in an essentially antiquated interaction. Welcome, fellow Neanderthal" (p. 87)! I assume academics read more, but if we take a candid moment to self-assess what type of media we read and how much we read, the answer for many busy scholars is "not much"—unless we are giving evaluative feedback (e.g., the weekend I wrote this, I was reading and evaluating 450 pages for three students). Given the predictable format of much of research writing, we often do not read a research article in its entirety—let alone a journal issue—but reach into it for specific aspects we can use, such as the literature review, research design, or findings.

William Faulkner (n.d.) pointed out to writers that reading all sorts of material is important: "Read, read, read. Read everything—trash, classics, good and bad, and see how they do it. Just like a carpenter who works as an apprentice and studies the master. Read! You'll absorb it. Then write." This is certainly also true for qualitative writers. While qualitative researchers, especially novices, should read traditional qualitative accounts to get a sense of the genre, reading anything and everything is also important. For instance, reading James McBride's memoir of his mother and himself, *The Color of Water* (1996), helped me to begin thinking about powerful ways to use italics in qualitative writing. Reading a journalist, memoirist, and Pulitzer Prize winner, Rick Bragg, helped me begin to think of speaking directly to the reader, as well as to consider the use of imperatives and admonishments. Bragg (1997) tells readers directly, "Listen to her" (p. 29) and then, with the readers' attention riveted, quotes from his mother in a compelling way.

Write, Write, Write

Linked closely to reading is a need to practice writing in order to be a successful writer. As Faulkner pointed out in the earlier quote, it is helpful for a writer to think of themselves as an apprentice, at first imitating the masters and then perhaps moving on to breaking existing forms and creating new forms. For qualitative research writers, much of this traditional writing will involve exploring how writers have found ways to convey copious amounts of data through journal articles limited to a word count of 6,000 to 8,000 words or a page count of 30 pages including references.

Opportunities should be provided for research writing in graduate course work, but if you find yourself in the unenviable position of being a student who receives little to no feedback, seek out writing mentorship wherever you can find it. Graduate schools and conferences will often have workshops, mentors, or weekend writing intensives. The university may have a writing center, with documents that guide novices through all aspects of research writing. The drawback is these resources are often formed around traditional ideas of scientific writing. Finding a successful student to engage with who is more advanced in course work than you can also be of help.

Revise, Revise, Revise

Writing and revision should be addressed together because the work of writing for some is really in the revisions. Some writers (myself included) find that ideas come easily and the real problem is having too many ideas. However, rewriting these many ideas may be a difficult task. For some other writers, coming up with the ideas is the harder part and rewriting not as irksome. Either way it helps to reflect on your preference and find ways to improve on weaknesses. For example, early on I realized I had too many ideas and could distract myself with the latest one. I also had figured out how to write conference proposals that would be accepted and found oral talks and conference papers stimulating and successful experiences. However, conference talks were not translating into publications in journals. I made two rules for myself. First, if I had a new research or writing idea, I would put it in a file of ideas, which helped me to set it aside mentally. Second, if the conference paper I had written did not move into a journal article, I did not attend the next conference. This combination of acknowledging my ideas yet setting them aside for later and rewarding myself with a conference experience was quite successful for me.

The central focus of revision for most qualitative research forms[1] is coherence, cohesion, and conciseness. William Zinsser (2006) believed that organization of a lengthy article is an "untaught and underestimated skill," comparing it to the way one might "put the jigsaw puzzle together" (p. 254). He went on to say, "Ask them to try something more extensive—an article or a book—and their sentences leach out all over the floor like marbles" (p. 254).

As you revise carefully, check to see that all the pieces of your work are coherent—meaning consistent and well reasoned. Consider the cohesion of your writing as the backbone of the work. Are the title, abstract, purpose, research questions, literature, theory, methodology, and findings working together? Are there tangents of thought, rabbit holes in the literature, jumps and breaks that seem to belong to a different manuscript? Finally, cut out unnecessary words, pare back superfluous paragraphs, and edit yourself before others do it for you or, worse yet, throw up their hands in disgust at your rambling rhetoric. Zinsser (2006), calling this type of revision "fighting clutter" or "the weeds of writing," advises writers to

> look for clutter in . . . writing and prune it ruthlessly. Be grateful for everything you can throw away. Reexamine every sentence . . . put on paper. . . . Can any thought be expressed with more economy? Is anything pompous . . . pretentious or faddish? . . . Simplify, simplify. (p. 16)

---

[1]Qualitative writers working in innovative forms will at times push back against coherence and a sense of a unified whole with the argument that smoothing out the research creates a false sense of an objective research experience. Innovative writing in and of itself does not mean, however, that the writer will not work to have coherence and cohesiveness; unfortunately, all of us, due to space constraints, need to be concise.

This is hard work—this level of revision is like scrubbing the grout between shower tiles until it shines—which I seldom fully achieve.

Make Writing Time Sacred (and What to Do When You Don't)

I only write when I am inspired. Fortunately, I am inspired at 9 o'clock every morning.

—William Faulkner

This quote by Faulkner illuminates a truth the literature makes clear—engaging with writing consistently is a fruitful way to write. In the text *How to Write a Lot*, the idea of writing time as sacred underscores the need to keep the time protected in an honored way (Silvia, 2007). This makes sense to me since when I step away from writing for too long I start to lose the thread of what I was doing and may not even recall a section of what I had written. This, of course, is where the use of abstracts, headings, tables of contents, and outlines allows writers to pick up where they left off. These are the signposts of our work for future readers that also allow us to check for organization and clarity of thought. Nonetheless, I have never been able to write on a daily basis. I have a deep sympathy for graduate students, so I do not hold research/writing days as sacred when it comes to scheduling a defense. I also continue to look at dissertation drafts when I am off contract from the university. However, I have become increasingly adept at saying no to unproductive work invitations (always presented as opportunities) that eat into my writing time.

I do get up and write when I have insomnia. This usually means I will write for one or two hours before I start to feel tired again. Ideally, I wake up early before my family begins to stir and then set my laptop aside for important family morning routines, knowing I have already accomplished several hours of writing. Also, when I have an intense writing project, such as an upcoming conference paper or book deadline, I lug my laptop with me *everywhere* and write as I wait to pick up kids for carpool or for sporting events to end. I have even written an entire research manuscript backstage during a children's theater production and made final revisions of this chapter hunkered down in my car keeping an eye on the nearby sledding hill to monitor my children for social distancing COVID safety and sledding safety. While this is not sacred writing time, it is writing as an ever-present activity and is only sustainable for several months at a time. It is dissertation deadline–type writing.

Drifting

The afternoon sun was getting low as the Rat rowed gently homeward in a dreamy mood, murmuring poetry to himself.

—Kenneth Grahame (1908, p. 15)

In a chapter where I am advocating for ways to stay engaged with writing, *drifting* may seem a strange interlude. Yet I find drifting to be a vital companion state to writing. For me, drifting usually occurs when I have set aside all devices and am absorbed in some wholly different task, such as gardening, chauffeuring or waiting for children, or simply watching birds congregate at the feeder. Jasmine Ulmer (2018), in an article on how to develop qualitative writing, writes of the importance of disengaging from writing, using the enticing phrase "not writing." "A . . . literal approach to not writing involves moving away from writing altogether. Given . . . demands . . . of productivity, not writing can appear to be a professional liability. . . . Viable options do not include writing all of the time or writing none of the time" (p. 730).

Thinking about drifting brought to my mind the book by Grahame (1908), *The Wind in the Willows*, in which the industrious Mole, always tunneling below ground, encounters the outdoor world of the water Rat and relaxation in nature for the first time: "The Mole never heard a word. . . . Absorbed in the new life he was entering upon, he trailed a paw in the water and dreamed long waking dreams" (pp. 7–8). Ulmer (2018) writes of not writing, saying she does not make a deliberate plan not to write in order to become inspired: "Inevitably, though, it is the escape from writing and the attempt to *not* write that somehow lead to more writing" (p. 730). Describing this as a possible aspect of a "Slow Ontology," Ulmer (2017) goes on to say, "In writing a Slow Ontology, researchers might create writing that is not unproductive, but is differently productive" (p. 201).

I imagine psychologists, activity, and mindfulness experts would tell us it is the time we have taken for self-care, refilling our reservoir, that allows for this to occur. Yet writers would know that this is not the full picture because when we are at our lowest, depleted, even in the deepest despair, ideas for writing arrive inexplicably, with a hint, a nudge, or a bolt— hackneyed but true. While not an ideal setting for drifting, I find a somewhat related form may occur at a laptop when we stop writing to stare off into the distance for some time. If possible, position yourself so when you do move into the writer's daze your gaze is not on stacks of dirty dishes, piles of laundry, or the concrete blocks of a university wall but instead on photos of those you love, a window with a view, or an arrangement of meaningful mementos. It's healthy disengagement—drifting—that leads to more writing.

Motivation and Distraction

As you hone your ability to be a productive writer, it is important to consider what motivates you and what distracts you. The answers may be light irritants (e.g., noises on your street) or the deeply emotional problem of feeling incapable. Make a list of all the ways you are distracted. Then mark which distractions you can control and how to go about addressing them.

Distraction	How to Address
Device notifications	Turn off when writing
Neighbor's barking dog	Wear headphones
Messy house	Move to a different location, tidy for 10 minutes a day
Worrying about outcome of writing	Talk to advisor, deep breathing, make list of worries, then set aside

Similarly, make a list of all the healthy ways you motivate yourself. After you have achieved a small to large accomplishment, what could you do as a "reward"?

Accomplishment	Motivations
After a 20-minute writing period	– Five-minute walk – Fresh tea – Check social media for 5 minutes – Five-minute phone call
After a lengthy, productive writing period	– Go to a movie – Get take-out – Zoom call – Take a run
After a major draft is completed	– Take a day off – Attend a campus sport or theater event – Share with your writers' group

A colleague and I who started working at our university at the same time had both decided as graduate students that we would work on writing our dissertations over a weekend and then go to the last movie matinee on Sunday as a reward. We went to the movie by ourselves, in our own university town, and later laughed imagining how much more fun the reward would have been if we'd known each other and been friends at the time! (It might be hard now to imagine what a big reward going to the movies was in our current era of binge movie streaming!)

Timing and Organization

Ideas for using time wisely and for organization can be a huge help, but they also have the potential for distraction. I find that when I try a new timing idea it works to move me into sustained writing—the sort of writing where I emerge befuddled since I have been working for such a long period of time. This is the most productive writing for me. Some possible strategies for achieving this follow.

Time of Day. *Determine what time of day you are most productive, and if at all possible, shift fresh, first-draft writing to that time of day. If you have a deadline looming or a lengthy writing project, you will have to write at other times of the day also. Writing a dissertation taught me that all my ideas about writing only when I was "fresh" and "focused" are totally false. We can write whenever we need to, but there is no doubt that we write much better at certain times of the day than at others.*

Twenty Minutes. *When you are unable to find larger blocks of time for writing, as is frequently the case for me, consider using the "writing 20 minutes a day" strategy. This is an idea that has support from writers who discuss how to sustain writing (e.g., Cordell, 2014). There is some disagreement as to whether you should keep going once you get going if you have the momentum and time; however, I would say use your best judgment in that area.*

Pomodoro Technique. *In the advanced qualitative writing course I teach, I invite students to share ideas for making the most of their time or organization techniques they are trying or have had success with. Several years ago, a student shared the idea of the Pomodoro technique—which calls for us to work smarter, not harder (Cirillo, n.d.). Since then, Pomodoro has had a huge surge in popularity, with websites, apps, and imitators using terms such as "marinara time." The Pomodoro technique involves working in 25-minute stints, with a 5-minute break in between and then a longer break after four Pomodoro work periods. In theory, this works for writing also. Other time utilization ideas include The Power Hour (DiCarlo, n.d.), the 33.33 minutes rule coined by Eugene Schwartz, and the 5-minute rule devised by Kevin Systrom, the CEO of Instagram. All of these time ideas have in common (a) no interruptions, (b) intense focus, and (c) a brief break under the premise that people will work better when more focused. I also think that part of the Pomodoro technique's success is tying the idea into the striking visual of a tomato cooking timer, which for me evokes food and savory smells—of course, any timer could be used. (For more information about the technique, see Cirillo, n.d.)*

Snack Writing. *Snack writing is an idea promoted by Maria Gardiner and Hugh Kearns (2011). For more writing ideas, you can follow Gardiner @ithinkwell and Kearns @ithinkwellHugh on Twitter. Snack writing lies somewhere between shorter, 20-minute writing ideas and what Kearns refers to as "binge writing"—long blocks of writing that are infrequent. To take advantage of snack writing, identify one- to two-hour blocks of time that occur in your week. These may be at unconventional times—I snack write in the car and have the added benefit of being first in line for school pickup by arriving early after my last appointment. Ideally, snack writing would occur three* *to five times a week. As I move toward a deadline, this is the primary technique I have tended to use daily—even before I found a name for it. I also take snack writing a step further by turning off the internet and all alerts on my laptop.*

One Sentence. *A final type of writing was shared with me by a student with regard to a well-thought-of colleague's advising strategy. I asked about a student and was told, "Oh, they are groaning in the lab over their computer." Startled, I wanted to know what was going on.*

"They have to write one sentence for their advisor."

"One sentence?"

"Yeah, when they start working on the dissertation, they have to meet with their advisor once a week and have at least one sentence written."

Intrigued, I tried to look this idea up and grilled my colleague about it. It is of note that I did not find any information on this style of writing, but I think it is related to the writing advice that suggests you stare at the computer screen until something starts to happen. If all else is failing, this is worth a shot.

Writers' Retreat

When you are having a hard time starting a writing project or have a deadline looming, a writers' retreat may be a partial answer. This could include grant-funded writing opportunities, professional retreats where writers are offered either seclusion or some engagement with other writers, online retreats (e.g., Virtual Writing Retreat @vwr_pgr), and university graduate school writers' camps, or perhaps you could do a retreat on your own or with a friend who is also writing. Go to the mountains or to the beach for a weekend of writing. For me, writing works best when my family goes somewhere and I am able to be in my own home with a minimum of travel or fuss. However, these opportunities are few and far between and may backfire at times, with the writer ending up feeling even more pressure to produce or a sense of isolation, so consider carefully what works best for you.

Writing Courses and Conferences

Courses and conferences for writers abound in the area of literary writing. For qualitative research writers, these are less frequent, but they do exist. I have had the opportunity to attend a writers' conference and found that the other writers' work stimulated multiple ideas for qualitative research writing, from autoethnographic and poetic representation ideas to research ideas. The autoethnography I excerpted in Chapter 7 of this book, "Lemon Tree," was an idea I acquired at a writer's conference. Due to the associated costs, try to take advantage of any opportunity to attend a writers' conference offered by your graduate school or university. Don't set your hopes for the course too high, but taking the opportunity to see that you are not alone and to create a network of fellow writers can be invaluable.

Reading About Writing

There are many books on how to write and even a few on how to write qualitative research (e.g., Anzul et al., 2003; Golden-Biddle & Locke, 2007; Holliday, 2007). If you are not receiving much feedback on your writing or feel you are well into the graduate degree process and still not sure what you are doing, you might consider investing in a few of these books. I suggest finding a nonfiction writing book and a qualitative research writing book (e.g., this volume; Wa-Mbaleka, 2014) or a book chapter that works for you. For nonfiction, I still prefer Zinsser (2006) but am sure this text would not work for all students. Check out the writing books at a library first, or look them over at a bookstore so you do not spend money on a text that doesn't work for you. See the resources at the end of this chapter for book ideas.

Writers' Groups

Writers' groups in higher education usually consist of informal groups of students who may band together for an assignment or formalize their group as they work toward longer pieces of writing, such as a thesis or dissertation. I have heard these groups can be a source of support, not only in dealing with the writing process but also in facing the daunting challenge of degree attainment. Some students have continued to write with group members as they moved into their first professor position.

Student writing groups can also waste time through too much socializing, complaining, undermining others, and providing a false sense of productivity. When I was a doctoral student, I was invited to join a writing group with other students who were dynamic and engaging. However, I had to curtail the amount of time we spent together since the group did little writing and mostly socialized and complained. While I completely understand the need for venting, I already had venues for that in my life and really needed a writing group. My support system finally crystalized into a group of just three fellow students who supported one another in the areas of transitioning to more sophisticated technology, getting through statistics classes, writing, and editing. One member of the group is the person who tipped me off about the amazing job I now have as a qualitative research professor.

There are various types of writers' groups in academia. What may be harder to find is a group that is healthy and produces consistent results. To help graduate students start to consider how a writing group might be a supportive part of their writing experience, I form writers' groups in the qualitative research writing course I teach. Each group consists of three to four students depending on the size of the course. Students may privately indicate course members they wish to be in a group with and anyone they do not want to be in a group with. However, I encourage working in an interdisciplinary group since many students have only had the opportunity to receive feedback on their writing from people who are aligned with them in beliefs and training. Most students tell me I can group them with any other student in the class.

Feedback to a Writers' Group. *At the outset, I require that the groups create a calendar of who will submit what and when. Students must use the internet for communicating feedback and editing—Google Docs, email, or the course platform—and provide feedback using technology (e.g., the Comment function and Track Changes). These requirements are intended to get students up to speed with writing with remote others. Each group creates guidelines for how feedback will be given. For example, a group indicated they would give feedback with the sandwich method. The bread is the positive components of the feedback, and the filling is feedback regarding areas to consider and changes needed—positive feedback first, then constructive criticism, then positive feedback. Other groups have created specific criteria. At the start of each meeting, update other members regarding what you have written since the last meeting. End each group by taking a few minutes to write down and then share with other members writing objectives or goals for the next meeting.*

Forming a Writers' Group. *Writing groups vary in terms of frequency from meeting once a week to twice a month for two to three hours. While a writers' group needs only two members, three to four works well in case someone cannot keep up with commitments for a while and to add a diverse perspective. Each member needs to be comfortable taking their turn to contribute a piece of writing and committing to provide feedback to everything that is submitted. (To read more about writers' groups, see Durst, 1992; Elbow, 1973; Grant et al., 2010.)*

2.2 SCHRODINGER'S RULES OF CRITIQUING

Maria Lahman, with thanks to Holly Lisle (n.d.) for condensing this advice

1. Critique the *writing*, not the writer. Avoid phrasing critiques by starting with the word "you," as in, "You are . . . "; reworded, this would be "The dissertation is . . . " or "The manuscript should. . . ."

2. Share what works along with what seems not to work.

3. Understand that feedback is not about how *you* would write. It is about how *they* could write.

4. Be aware that writing is personal.

5. Be conscious of your writing biases. If you plan to share a bias in a critique, be sure to say it is a bias; otherwise, avoid bias in critiques.

iStock.com/Big_Ryan

Possible Types of Writers' Groups

Lisle (n.d.) identified the possible types of writers' groups. I have rewritten this slightly to fit academia.

Colleagues or Friends. This is a group of writers all working at about the same level. It may literally be formed from friendships that already existed or developed from a collegial writers' group into friendships.

Instructor and Students. This group is put together by a professional writer and is open to beginners. This is designed as a teaching group, with the pro as the teacher. As you can imagine, this group can be terrible or effective depending on the instructor. In an academic context, this type of group often occurs when an experienced professor as part of their university "service" requirement mentors new professors in publication or when a graduate school sponsors student writing groups. If you have someone who loves to teach, who is genuinely interested in seeing the members of the group get published, and whose work appeals to you enough that you think you could learn from them, then an instructor and students group will be effective. If, however, your existence in the group is solely to provide an ego boost for the instructor, then you end up with an unhealthy situation. Lisle cautions that an unhealthy master and serf dynamic occurs when the group is more about boosting the instructor's ego, which can result in group members just listening to stories or excerpts from the instructor's current writing rather than getting help to achieve success. I would add that this can also occur when the instructor forces people into a narrow mold.

Sharks and Fish. Any writers' group can turn into sharks and fish if it becomes a "clique" that tears newcomers' and those not in the popular groups' writing apart. Avoid this group at all costs even if they seem to welcome you. If you are being invited to speak poorly of others' work when they are not present, this is a sure sign the same is happening to you when you are not present.

2.3 CREATING WRITERS' GROUP GUIDELINES

MARIA LAHMAN

The following is the guidance I give writers' groups in my writing course to assist in the creation of the group "rules." I ask the groups to create a set of criteria. Midway through the semester, after we have read scholars' suggestions for qualitative criteria, we revisit the criteria and see if there is anything they would change. I find the criteria are consistently too detailed for creative pieces or too general for traditional thematic qualitative journal articles. I ask that the following occur or be addressed:

iStock.com/Big_Ryan

- The author should provide the target journal's writing guide with the manuscript being reviewed when possible.

- When submitting a piece of writing to be critiqued, the author should provide a paragraph explaining the purpose of the manuscript, who the audience will be, and areas they have questions about.

- When does writing need to be submitted to the group to have time for all to provide a thorough critique by the next meeting?

- How will the writing be shared with the group (email, Google Docs, etc.)?

- What criteria should be used?

- What format should the oral critique take?

The Gist: Get on With It

I find television very educating. Every time somebody turns on the set,

I go into the other room and read a book.

—Groucho Marx

Marx underscores the need to always be reading as we are writing; as writers, we should dwell in the land of words. In this chapter. I presented *why, what,* and *how* qualitative researchers write and included ideas to enhance motivation and reduce distractions. We need to get on with the important task of writing. "We need to stop waiting and get writing," writes Nicolas Cole (n.d.), who describes himself as a digital writer. He goes on to say,

> All through college, I watched the majority of my peers wait to write. They were waiting to feel inspired, waiting to see what the teacher thought of their last piece, waiting for some outside nod of approval instead of just getting on with it and putting pencil to paper (or fingers to keys).

Good writing occurs from persistent work.

Reflexive Questions

1. What are some early writing experiences you had?
   a. Which, if any, experiences were positive or negative?
   b. How does this recollection of early writing affect your writing today?

2. What are more recent writing experiences you have had?

   a. Which, if any, experiences were positive or negative?

   b. How does this recollection of writing affect your writing today?

3. What negative writing experience(s) have you had?

   a. How do these experiences affect your writing today?

4. What positive writing experience(s) have you had?

   a. How do these experiences affect your writing today?

5. How, where, and when do you tend to write? Make a list of the best conditions. Now look at the list critically (a partner or group helps a lot with this). What changes should you consider making?

6. Why do you need to write?

7. What do you need to write?

8. What have you written?

9. Have you ever tried a time or motivation technique to encourage your writing?

   a. How did it work for you?

   b. Which motivation technique could you try from the list in this chapter?

Reflexive Activities

1. *How do we write?* Take a moment and consider what the writing process resembles for you. Look at the reflexive questions above to help with this process. For example, do you feel you write best when up against a deadline? A strength of this type of writing is the ability to keep writing under pressure. While this writing style works for course deadlines and some areas of academic writing in general, initial submission of journal manuscripts does not have a deadline—an exception to this is the call for special journal issues. The thought that writing under pressure brings about great results may be a habit that has been formed in deadline-intense contexts or by people who tend to procrastinate. It is hard to believe that extra time to read over a piece of writing multiple times for polishing it is not beneficial. Once you have identified the different ways you write, question these ways and look for areas that are strengths and areas that are potential weaknesses.

2. *Experienced writers:* Review the writing you have published, considering what aspects of it might work well in qualitative writing and what aspects won't transfer.

Review any of your publications that have qualitative data as part of the study—perhaps a survey with open-ended questions at the end. How might the qualitative data have been represented in a stand-alone article?

Review any qualitative data you have, even if they are partially published in a thematic article. How might the data be represented in different forms? Choose a few forms to experiment with. Read a chapter from the second half of this book in the areas you decide to try. Show the outcome to a colleague or friend. What works for you? What doesn't? What works for the field you publish in? What doesn't?

3. *Positive/negative writing experiences:* Choose a positive and a negative writing experience to write up into a short anecdote or story. Put the writings away for a while—perhaps two weeks. When you read them again, ask what resonates with you. Consider doing this writing activity with a few other writers. What resonates for you about the others' writings? What might you tell the "you" who existed at the time of the story? How might the story be different if it occurred now?

Resources

Articles About Writing

Wolcott, H. F. (2002). Writing up qualitative research . . . better. *Qualitative Health Research, 12*(1), 91–103. https://doi.org/10.1177/1049732302012001007

Books Qualitative Writers Have Written About Writing

Allen, M. (2016). *Essentials of publishing qualitative research.* Routledge. https://doi.org/10.4324/9781315429298

Anzul, M., Downing, M., Ely, M., & Vinz, R. (2003). *On writing qualitative research: Living by words.* Routledge. https://doi.org/10.4324/9780203451427

Durst, R. K. (1992). A writer's community: How teachers can form writing groups. In K. L. Dahl (Ed.), *Teacher as writer: Entering the professional conversation,* (pp. 261–271). National Council of Teachers of English.

Golden-Biddle, K., & Locke, K. (2007). *Composing qualitative research* (2nd ed.). Sage.

Holliday, A. (2016). *Doing and writing qualitative research* (3rd ed.). Sage. https://doi.org/10.4135/9781446287958

Smartt Gullion, J. (2016). *Writing ethnography.* Sense.

Wa-Mbaleka, S. (2014). *Publish or perish: Fear no more.* CentralBooks.

Wolcott, H. F. (2009). *Writing up qualitative research* (3rd ed.). Sage. https://doi.org/10.4135/9781452234878

Writers' Groups Resources

Durst, R. K. (1992). A writer's community: How teachers can form writing groups. In K. L. Dahl (Ed.), *Teacher as writer: Entering the professional conversation* (pp. 261–271). National Council of Teachers of English.

Lisle, H. (n.d.). *The good, the bad, and the ugly or how to choose a writers group.* https://hollylisle.com/the-good-the-bad-and-the-ugly-or-how-to-choose-a-writers-group/

Writers' Group on Facebook: https://www.facebook.com/groups/members writersgroup/

"This group is for those interested in the craft of writing. All are encouraged to help one another through problem spots in their writing, bounce ideas off other members, and talk about the latest news affecting the industry/craft."

Writer's Relief, Inc.—List of Writing Groups by State or Region: writersrelief .com/writing-groups-for-writers/

Writing Conferences and Courses

Top Ten Writing Conferences in North America: https://www.writermag .com/improve-your-writing/conferences-residencies-retreats/top-10-writing-conferences-north-america/

Pennsylvania Writers Conference: https://www.wilkes.edu/academics/ graduate-programs/masters-programs/creative-writing-ma-mfa/pennsylvania-writers-conference/index.aspx

South Hampton Writers Conference: https://www.stonybrook.edu/commcms/ writers/about.php

Southern Writers/Southern Writing Graduate Conference: https://call-for-papers.sas.upenn.edu/cfp/2018/01/28/southern-writerssouthern-writing-graduate-conference-2018

Writing Internet Resources

Cox, J. (2018, November 12). *What is the writing cooperative?* https:// writingcooperative.com/what-is-the-writing-cooperative-do-not-publish-54901adf5325

Handley, A. (n.d.). *9 Qualities of good writing.* http://annhandley.com/ 9-qualities-of-good-writing/#.WsqE5dPwbVo

William, D. K. (2020, August 7). *8 Brainstorming strategies for generating new writing ideas.* The Web Writer Spotlight. http://webwriterspotlight .com/8-brainstorming-strategies-for-generating-new-writing-ideas

Write to Done—Unmissable Articles on Writing: https://writetodone.com/

Start Writing!

People on the outside think there's something magical about writing, that you go up in the attic at midnight and cast the bones and come down in the morning with a story, but it isn't like that. You sit in back of the typewriter and you work, and that's all there is to it.

—Harlan Ellison (in Hult, 2015, p. 329)

At this point, readers have read enough about writing and need to just Start Writing! There is a fine line between spending useful time reading about the craft of writing and using reading as a delaying tactic that puts off the hard work that is writing. My father was reluctant to talk about his writing. He claimed, "There are those who talk about writing and those who write." He was firmly in the latter category. Even as I write this family story, I nervously wonder if I am talking about my writing too much instead of just *writing*.

In this chapter,

- I assume the writer has analyzed qualitative data and has access to a raw data set or a data set they are willing to rewrite, and

- I challenge writers to represent the same data set in different ways.

- Having met that challenge, writers should step away from the representations and then reengage with each representation and

(Continued)

(Continued)

> consider what each gains or loses. If you have access to other writers to help with this process, the reflexivity could be even more powerful.
>
> - I draw on the text *A Thrice-Told Tale* (Wolf, 1992), my journal publications, and a student's research writing, placed in the appendices, to illustrate different representations of the same data set.
>
> - I review suggestions from writing experts for *honing the craft* of writing.

Data Represented in Three Ways: An Exemplar

In the text *The Thrice-Told Tale* (1992), Wolf, an ethnographer, publishes representations of field data in three ways, with reflections on the original field experiences and representation process. The first representation is the original field notes, the second is the traditional research report, and the third is a fictionalized tale. Wolfe's work is one of the texts I use in the course I teach on qualitative writing. Students read the book early on, so it provides a foundation for helping them consider how they might best represent their writing in three ways over a semester. (We are cautious not to overuse data in an unethical way and indicate in our representations that they are part of a larger body of work.)

For some time, I have been intrigued by this idea and found the opportunity to try multiple representations with an extensive data set provided by a research group study I was part of. The following representations were created from a year-long study of an International Doctoral Student Support Group.[1] A colleague, Heng-Yu Ku, and I formed this group as a way of exploring how best to support international doctoral students as they transition into the academy. Data collection included pre and post questionnaires, interviews, and observations of support group meetings.

Traditional Qualitative Thematic Research Article Excerpt: First Representation

While the article was published (Ku et al., 2008), the following excerpt exploring metaphors is from the conference version of this article. Portions of the article considered most creative (containing metaphors for the graduate school experience) did not make it into the published version of the article. The published article followed the thematic qualitative writing style

---

[1]Updated portions of this chapter originally appeared in Ku et al. (2008) and Lahman et al. (2009). Thanks to my coauthors for their initial work with me on these ideas.

Richardson (1994) referred to as the "practice of quoting snippets in prose" (p. 522). These snippets came from interview questions in which the students were asked to summarize their experience through a metaphor for graduate school and a saying from their culture.

In this research, metaphor was used as "understanding and experiencing one kind of thing in terms of another" (Lakoff & Johnson, 1980, p. 5). Within this wider definition, similes and images may also be seen as metaphors. Richardson (1990) has said, "Metaphor is the backbone of social science writing, and like a true spine, it bears weight, permits movement, links parts together into a functional coherent whole—and is not immediately visible" (p. 18). We extended this understanding to how the participants used metaphors to sum up their entire experience in graduate school.

Metaphors and Cultural Sayings. *A Taiwanese student shared, "Graduate school is like swimming. We . . . put our heads in the water and swim hard towards the end of the pool . . . sometimes we almost can't breathe. If we know how to push our heads out of the water to breathe, we won't die, and we can go on." Another Taiwanese student also used a water metaphor: "Graduate school is like . . . the ocean because you cannot see the inside of the graduate school from the surface." A European[2] student described graduate school as "the monster in the closet . . . like a lot of things in life. . . . it seems scary until you actually do them. . . . A monster in the closet . . . the only way to get rid of that is to open the closet to see . . . there is no monster." A different Taiwanese student emphasized the need for hard work, saying, "It's . . . like a mill. You have to grind the grains or corns into powder. That means you have to put a lot of efforts to make solid stuff into powder so that you will have good products." A Japanese student stated, "For me, it's kind of like tunnel . . . in the dark. Toward the end, there's . . . the light out there. . . . So we're still struggling in the tunnel and then trying to walk toward the end of the tunnel, where there is light." Another Taiwanese student shared that graduate school "is like a piece of dark chocolate. It tastes bittersweet just like there were good days [sweet] and bad days [bitter] in grad school."*

When asked to share a cultural saying for education, a student from Thailand shared a powerful saying her father had instilled in her: "I remember when I was young, my dad always said that study is like eating. . . . When someone gives you a big bag of rice and wants you to eat it within three months, you should eat it little by little, every day. If you don't, and you eat it on the last day, you will die because your stomach will blow out." A Western student shared, "The saying I have is actually written in Latin. . . . 'Don't let the bastards grind you down.' Don't get worn down by those who would like me to have been worn down or to quit." This quotation is compelling coming from this mild-mannered, easygoing student.

---

[2]Students represented by their home continent or global region were uniquely identifiable by their country of origin in the study.

Interview Transcription Poem in Free Form: Second Representation

Transcription or data poems[3] occur commonly in the research poetry literature (Furman, 2006; Lahman et al., 2010) and perhaps they are accepted since drawing on the data directly feels more "objective" to some. Much of the methodological dialogue in the literature is about how to create these poems from interview transcripts (Lahman et al., 2010) or from archives and documents (Lahman, 2011). Drawing on the work of Richardson (1994), Glesne (1997) defined poetic transcriptions as "the creation of poem like compositions from the words of interviewees" (p. 202). These types of research poems, in general, follow a freestyle format. I created a transcription poem from the international graduate student data.

The Monster in the Closet: International Graduate Students' Experiences

Graduate school is swimming.
We have to put our heads in the water and
swim hard towards the
end of the pool.
We work so hard that sometimes
we almost can't breathe.
If we know how to
push our heads
out of the water
to breathe,
we won't die,
and we can go on.

Learning is rowing a boat
up the source of the river.
If you don't row,
you will go backwards and
never get to the source.

---

[3]See Chapter 8, "Poemish Research Representations," for extensive information on the creation of research poetry.

Graduate school is the sea.
You cannot see
the inside of
the graduate school
from the surface.

Education changes
the life of a single person,
the life of a family,
the life of the country.

The monster in the closet or the
monster under the bed
seems scary until you actually
open the closet to see
there is no monster.

If you wish to be the best man,
you have to be prepared to suffer
the bitterest of the bitter.

Graduate school is a mill to
grind the grains or corns into powder.
You have to put a lot of efforts
to make solid stuff into powder
so that you will have good products.

There is teaching among three people.

Graduate school is [a]
tunnel in the dark,
but toward the end, there's light.
We're struggling in the tunnel and
trying to walk toward light.

When I was young,
my dad said that study is like eating.
When someone gives you a big bag of rice
and wants you to eat it within three months,
you should eat it little by little, every day.

If you don't,
and you eat it on the last day,
you will die because your stomach will
blow out.

Graduate school is like
a piece of
dark chocolate.
There are sweet days and
bitter days.
Don't let the bastards grind you down.

Senryu Poem: Third Representation

Inspired by Furman (2006) and his use of the poetic form of the Japanese *tanka* to create research poetry, I followed the haiku poetic form. The haiku may be described as an unrhymed, syllabic poem adapted from the Japanese, consisting of three lines of five, seven, and five syllables per line respectively. The haiku, "a clear picture designed to arouse a distinct emotion and suggest a specific spiritual insight . . . is deeply serious, drawing on the commonly held associations of seasons, birds, elements, etc. that the haiku exploits" (Harmon & Holmon, 1996, p. 241). The traditional Japanese haiku requires some reference to nature or the season; thus this poem is termed a *senryu*. The *senryu* is a related form distinguished from haiku as being concerned with "human nature" or social and personal relationships (http://poetry.about.com/od/poeticforms/g/haiku.htm). I composed a *senryu* based on the data:

Graduate school is
A monster in the closet . . .
There is no monster?

For another example of representing research in multiple ways, see Appendix B for Erin Pachett's research representations created during a doctoral course. Erin represented the research as a case study, a poster, and a poem. Aesthetic representations may be created out of any type of research methodology, including mixed methods and quantitative. See Onwuegbuzie (2012) for a mixed-method example of research poetry. Onwuegbuzie's poem is placed at the end of a thought-provoking article—the only change I would make, if I dare offer a suggestion to a distinguished researcher, is to place the poem first to grab and hold the readers' attention!

Representing Qualitative Research: A Reflection

Traditional qualitative representations, such as the thematic piece I presented in the first representation, are the primary form that novices, untenured professors, and professors who have begun to explore qualitative research and writing must learn how to write and publish. (See Chapter 5 for an in-depth discussion of the traditional qualitative research article form.) However, some of us are in a position to consider how we can build on or even break the traditional qualitative form. We take up this endeavor because we are drawn to art forms and believe different types of representation allow knowledge to be understood and transmitted in new and powerful ways. We desire to create a safe space for exploration of aesthetic representations in research where novices may also create and learn.

I have also found that if novices are allowed safe spaces to explore new aesthetic forms during courses and encouraged to present these forms on campus it increases their confidence and ability to integrate some of what they are learning into their dissertation. If their larger field infrequently represents data in an aesthetic form, interested students should advocate for themselves with faculty and see if they may add some of these creative elements to a traditional dissertation. Ideally, the faculty who work with students become intrigued and attend sessions where they can develop an understanding of what is occurring in the larger qualitative field in the area of representing data. One of my former provosts, a quantitative researcher, always enjoyed popping by my students' presentation area on campus research day or research evening to "see what Lahman's students have been up to."

Consider the representations I reviewed about international graduate students' experiences and Appendix B for examples of a doctoral student's qualitative research representations.

- What has been lost or gained in each representation form?

- What resonated for you?

- What did not work for you?

- What might be allowable in your field?

- What might not work in your field?

Identify a data set or a qualitative manuscript or article of yours that you can work with as you read through the remainder of this text. Look over the chapter headings in this book, and create a plan for three representations of the data. If you are uncertain about this writing challenge and need to concentrate on traditional publications, do so. If you find yourself responding to the alternative forms, see how you might push yourself or your field.

Qualitative representation has room for all—we want to be cautious not to cut off any form, traditional or novel. What we might lose and have already lost is incalculable.

Honing the Craft of Writing

cultivate, develop, hone, improve, perfect, polish, refine, sharpen, smooth

I challenge the assumption that academic science writing, in general, is quality writing and suggest that it is instead more properly understood as a dominant form in higher education. A reason this form continues to dominate is that in the high-pressure world of academia we do not have the time to hone our craft. Peer review—while vital for many reasons—means that an essential part of the review process is about the research content and not the representation quality. Peer review also means that amateur editors are part of the process. This is why style guides are leaned on heavily and stultifying article or manuscript templates detailing exactly how qualitative research representations should proceed exist. Busy academics are able to rely on these rules as measures of quality, instead of understanding that they are simplistic, reductionist guides. This is why I include a section on honing the craft of writing in a book that is already full of information. I also choose to draw on the advice of nonfiction writing experts since they dwell in the world of writing every day and not just when it is time to prepare research for publication.

What does the word "hone" mean? Combining various definitions, to hone is the act of using a whetstone to sharpen or smooth a tool such as a knife. It has also come to mean, metaphorically, the refining of a skill to make it more acute, effective, and improved (Merriam-Webster, n.d.-b). Honing the craft of writing for writers such as myself can be an effort to strengthen our writing or for skilled writers a way to polish the final draft into a glossy sheen. This is not a bid toward perfectionism. "Perfectionism," Anne Lamott (1994) writes, "is the voice of the oppressor. The enemy of the people. It will keep you cramped and insane your whole life, and it is the main obstacle between you and a shitty first draft" (p. 28). Honing, instead, is an ongoing process of becoming a skilled writer through multiple writing representations over a career. Toward this end, I review ideas for honing the craft of writing in the sections that follow.

"It Was a Dark and Stormy Night": First Sentences

In the world of literature, much has been written around the importance of the first sentence, paragraph, hook, or opening. In academia, it would almost seem that writers avoid an interesting opening in favor of dry entries (e.g., "In this article, the authors . . . "), perhaps due to notions of objective writing. This does not do much to create interest for readers. "The most important sentence in any article [writing] is the first one. If it doesn't induce the reader to proceed to the second sentence, your article is dead" (Zinsser, 2006, p. 54). This importance is underscored by the existence of first-sentence competitions (e.g., http://www.bulwer-lytton.com/). A recent winner wrote,

> The elven city of Losstii faced towering sea cliffs and abutted rolling hills that in the summer were covered with blankets of flowers and in the winter covered with blankets, because the elves wanted to keep the flowers warm and didn't know much at all about gardening. (Kate Russon, Loveland, CO)

"It was a dark and stormy night"—perhaps the most infamous first sentence in the English language—was written by Edward George Bulwer-Lytton in 1830. The opening sentence, which has been made fun of in literature, movies, and speeches, is a staple of the *Peanuts* comic: Snoopy, a beagle, is depicted, in multiple comic strips, seated on top of his doghouse pounding out the sentence on a manual typewriter, tapping into the universal experience of writer's block. But Madeleine L'Engle (1962) demonstrates that a talented writer can take a tired hack and twist it into the opening of a novel that captivates and endures:

> It was a dark and stormy night.
>
> In her attic bedroom Margaret Murry, wrapped in an old patchwork quilt, sat on the foot of her bed and watched the trees tossing in the frenzied lashing of the wind. Behind the trees clouds scudded frantically across the sky. Every few moments the moon ripped through them, creating wraithlike shadows that raced along the ground. (p. 3)

As qualitative research writers, how might we open our work? A traditional thematic article will likely have the obligatory yet helpful orienting paragraph that reads just as an abstract; however, consider situating a concisely written, attention-capturing opening before this paragraph. Caulley (2008), calls this "open[ing] with text that is vivid and vital" (p. 424), pointing out that skilled writers understand how conversation captures readers' attention. As qualitative researchers, this conversation can be an effective opening if you are using the words of the research participants. What quotes seemed salient, conveying the overall idea of the problem of interest or the findings clearly? What vignette or micro portrait might situate readers in the context of the study at hand? Opening sentences may also be a quote that is ripped from news headlines, from a famous public figure, or a notable research scholar; a piece of fiction or poetry; or a statistic or research finding that is compelling and orients the reader into the heart of the problem. See Text Box 3.1 for examples of hooks qualitative researchers have employed.

3.1 THE HOOK: EXAMPLES OF FIRST SENTENCES IN QUALITATIVE WRITING

MARIA LAHMAN

Dissertations

"How would you describe yourself as a writer?" I asked a colleague, a young woman whose skill at teaching writing set her apart from her grade level team. "I'm a horrible writer," she said, "just horrible." In the same conversation, she said: "I learned how to write by teaching writing. And now I use the same strategies my students use, so I can write. But I'm a horrible writer." (Hamilton, 2011. p. 1)

In 1989, I walked into room 105, Candelaria Hall, at the University of Northern Colorado, not knowing what to expect. Little did I fathom I would be sitting in a classroom with 25 other students, all White. This situation was the first time I had been surrounded by so many White students. . . . One of the first questions the professor asked everyone was to provide an introduction. The first student volunteered (I was not about to volunteer). He started by saying "I was born in Greeley my parents were born in Greeley. I have lived in West Greeley the majority of my life. I want to major in English just like my mom." As I listened to what other students were saying, I thought about how I got to this country. (Gonzales, 2013, p. 3)

Articles

With several audiotapes and piles of printed transcripts in front of me, I sat back and sighed, "Wow, that was a learning experience." (Bird, 2005, p. 226)

In 1994, Doug Healy, whom I would marry the following year, graduated from pharmacy school and moved to Tampa, Florida. His trainer at work, David Holland, would alter the course of our lives. (Tillmann-Healy, 2003, p. 729)

I could not fall asleep. I tossed and turned in my bed, trying to ignore the anxiety churning through my stomach. (Bochner, 1997, p. 418)

Mea culpa. (Denzin, 2010, p. 269)

"At least half of those who start the doctoral process, don't finish it," stated my professor matter-of-factly. (Eisenbach, 2013, p. 1)

Books

"I never hauled trash with a professor before" declares Mone. (Magolda, 2016)

All adults—including anthropologists—were once children. (Allerton, 2016, p. 1)

"A professor who encourages the use of Wikipedia is the intellectual equivalent of a dietician who recommends a steady diet of Big Macs with everything." I am such a professor. (Jemielniak, 2014, p. 1)

Style or Voice

Few people realize how badly they write.

—Zinsser (2006, p. 17)

In Chapter 2, I discussed the need to revise a piece multiple times and to draw on professional advice in this area. An essential part of the revision process, a challenge for me, is cutting out unnecessary words, phrases, sentences, and even paragraphs. See Text Box 3.2 for a list of words to consider cutting. Zinsser (2006) says that if you were to give him an eight-page paper he could show you how to edit it to four and while you might "howl and say it can't be done . . . you'll go home and do it, and it will be much better. After that comes the hard part: cutting it to three" (p. 17). This type of editing uses journalistic writing strengths but fits well with the space constraints academics face outside of the dissertation writing form. For qualitative researchers, word constraints can be challenging because of their use of quintessential data quotes, vivid, vigorous vignettes, and fulsome, flowery language.

Style is how a text is written and is the voice of the writer (Literary Devices, n.d.). While writing style can be sorted into major types, including expository, descriptive, persuasive, and narrative, it is how the writer works within the type that creates their voice—at times called *signature* or *persona* (Ely, 2007). Zinsser (2006) points out that considerations of style may be a reason why writers are reluctant to pare back their words—wondering, "If I strip everything to its barest bone will there be anything left of me?" (p. 15). Comparing writing to carpentry, Zinsser challenges writers to strip their work down to a sturdy frame and then with care and thought build the components of the structure—writing—on that frame. These components, then, are your writing style.

The style I labor to have in a textbook, research poetry, or autoethnography is a sense that I am speaking with the reader as we might if they had dropped by my office for a research methods consultation or a chat. I seek this style because I want what I am saying to be accessible and have room for you to disagree with, augment, or build on what I am writing. I never feel I have adequate time to rewrite any of my work other than research poetry (which I hold on to for years before publication and have no pressure ever to publish). So, you can imagine the distinct tingle of pleasure I had when a student said to me, "What I like about this text is that it seems like you are speaking to me, as though we were in class." I was so pleased with this reflection that I became befuddled and doubt I even replied coherently. Other feedback in this area equally tickled me irreverently. A textbook reviewer wrote, "You have a clear voice that many will appreciate, others will not." How could they know how succinctly that sentence sums up my career as a qualitative researcher in a quantitative world?

3.2 WORDS TO DIE BY
MARIA LAHMAN

Substitute "damn" every time you're inclined to write "very." Your editor will delete it, and the writing will be just as it should be.

—Mark Twain

Mark Twain makes a ~~damn~~ good point. Ross Larson (1999) delicately calls these words superfluous and indelicately, "fat."

> Just as your speech is filled with many words that add nothing to what you say, your writing is often larded with words that obscure your meaning rather than clarify it. Trim this fat to direct your reader's attention to important words and ideas. (p. 3)

I conducted a review of words writers should edit out of their writing and compiled the following list. I find "very" a provoking, weak word that adds little. I overuse "that" to such an extent that I run a find function and check for the word "that" to consider if each instance of "that" could be dropped.

that	most times
very	in order to
like	often
one of	absolutely
some	just
thing	only
so	really
mostly	perhaps

iStock.com/Big_Ryan

maybe	a lot
simply	sort of
somehow	kind of
basically	as
almost	adverbs (words that end with "ly")
slightly	
seemed	phrases that start with "the" and end with "of"

To read more about words to eliminate from writing, see Joe Bunting's (n.d.) article "Want to Be a Better Writer? Cut These 7 Words" and Zinsser (2006).

Lights, Camera, Action: Verbs

I recall admonishments from writing teachers to show and not tell both in my writing and in my research notes. A simple example, "Bob is bad," rather than "Bob stepped on the puppy's tail and laughed," makes immediate sense to writers. When it comes to showing, "verbs are the most important part of all your tools. They push the sentence forward and give it momentum" (Zinsser, 2006, p. 68). Describe research in a vivid but not overdone manner, with active verbs that highlight important aspects of the writing.

Passive Voice. *Avoiding the use of passive voice is related to using active verbs. In passive writing, "a research participant was sad," "was bad," "was reluctant," whereas in active writing "a research participant cried," "deflected," "avoided," "beamed." Finding the linking "being" verbs in your writing, the "killer be's," helps you identify the use of passive voice (see Text Box 3.3). Note that the proceeding examples of passive voice all used the linking being verb "was." If you write in Word, there is a readability check available that I recommend turning on. It will report on the "grade level" you are writing at as well as your use of passive voice. There are other sources, involving payment, such as Grammarly, that will also highlight passive voice. Avoiding passive voice will add strength and clarity to your writing (Zinsser, 2006). See the blog post by Jerry Jenkins (n.d.), "294 Strong Verbs That Will Spice up Your Writing," for a list of powerful active verbs.*

3.3 KILLER BE'S

MARIA LAHMAN

The killer be's include: *am, is, are, was, were, be, being, been, has, have, had, had been, shall, will, should, may, might, can, could, to be,* and so on. In fourth grade, I learned this group of verbs under the name linking being verbs but was never taught to avoid them in my writing. While I cannot always recall where I last parked my car, this list will pop into my head out of nowhere—reminiscent of a playground jump rope chant. What a relief to put the list into a good-riddance framework. When possible, substitute killer be's with active verbs. Watch for verbs ending in "ing" since killer be's often hover before them: he *was* walk*ing*, she *is* jump*ing*, they *are* cry*ing*.

Rewrite the sentence "Bob *is* the manager of a fast-food restaurant" as "Bob manages a fast-food restaurant"—creating a descriptive, concise sentence. Combine short sentences by removing the killer be verb. The sentences "My dad went to school at UVA" and "He is now a professor at EMU" are rewritten as "My dad, a professor at EMU, graduated from UVA."

Read more on this topic in *How to Swat the Killer Bes Out of Your Writing* by Nancy Owens Barnes (2009).

First Person Whenever Possible

Traditionally, style guides for researchers indicated that the third person should be used. However, in several editions of the APA style guide, first person has been recommended. APA has reviewed the reasons why first person is preferable. First, the phrase "the authors" or "the researchers" to indicate in third person the authors of the current article can be confused with the authors and/or researchers of the literature that is being referenced. Second, anthropomorphism, while an important part of creative literature, becomes a deadly prop for the third-person and "objective" voice in third-person research writing—such as "studies demonstrate" and "research finds," instead of "we demonstrated" or "I found" (McAdoo, 2009)

I would add that researchers have been taught to write in the third person in order to seem objective. This is the primary reason why qualitative researchers should write in the first person. Qualitative research is based on a rejection of false notions of objectivity. Qualitative researchers actively attempt to engage with our bias, understanding that people cannot be objective. For us, a false sense of objectivity is not a goal. Instead, we seek deep, reflexive engagement with our biases. (See Chapter 10 for an in-depth discussion of reflexivity.) Qualitative researchers write in the first person so readers can access the research in active ways that help deepen their understanding of the contexts and phenomena of interest.

APA's recommendation of the first person does not mean that the journals you submit articles to will allow the use of first person. Check the writers' guidelines for potential journals, and locate sample copies of journal articles to use as models. But challenge yourself to write in the first person whenever possible so you begin to unlearn the third-person writing style most of us have been forced, through repetition, into feeling is natural (McAdoo, 2009).

See Text Box 3.4 for a review of a slim creative volume that is another resource to enhance readers' ability to hone their craft in clever and engaging ways.

The past, the present and the future walked into a bar.

It was tense.

(Riordan, 2019)

3.4 ONCE, TWICE, THRICE TOLD TALES: THREE MICE FULL OF WRITING ADVICE
BECKY DE OLIVEIRA

There are seemingly endless books offering writing advice. With classics such as *The Elements of Style* (Strunk & White, 1918/2007), *Bird by Bird* (Lamott, 1994), *On Writing Well* (Zinsser, 2006) and *On Writing* (King, 2000) in circulation, why would any writer need anything else? How much advice can any one person absorb? How much *should* they absorb? Why make room on your shelf for yet another advice book on writing?

Once, Twice, Thrice Told Tales: Three Mice Full of Writing Advice (Lewis, 2013) offers more than just a cute title and a black-and-white line-drawing interface (visually it looks a little like one of the *Diary of a Wimpy Kid* books), and it might be worth adding to your writing library. It provides 92 very short chapters (with one or two illustrated pages each) detailing various literary and writing devices—everything from suspension of disbelief to sentence diagramming. Some of these are more applicable to the scholarly writer than others, but virtually any of them can help spark creativity and provide a new way of looking at familiar things or insight into concepts you've perhaps never heard of before! The book also includes a helpful appendix with each term defined in a more traditional format. Some of the more mechanical segments that might be especially useful for scholarly writing are Vocabulary and Syntax, Mechanics, Transitions, Revision, Diction, Exposition, Research, and Structure.

Source: Reproduced with permission from Becky De Oliveira

iStock.com/Alek_Koltukov

Paraphernalia

In this section, I forward some important aspects of writing that are not easily grouped into a unifying section—bits and bobs, miscellany, paraphernalia—sentence structure, repetition, over qualifying and pointless self-reference, contractions, punctuation, and parallel form.

Vary Sentence Structure. As academics, we need to attend to cutting back long sentences with multiple parts. This editing allows for clarity of thought. However, use of only short sentences can create a jarring staccato effect, referred to as "choppy writing." A variety of lengths and types of sentence structure will create a pleasing experience for the reader—as perhaps illustrated in this paragraph.

Remove Pointless Repetition. At times, a writer repeats words for effect, as I did in some subheadings in this book—Read, Read, Read and Revise, Revise, Revise—making a point that reading and revision cannot occur too often for writers. Other instances of repetition are used with little effect. Avoid towering behemoths, sobbing and weeping clients, beginning preservice teachers, and childish kids in your writing. Identify unnecessary repetition of words that when removed do not alter meaning in the sentence. I see pointless repetition in my writing, what I call "the tiresome threes"—three supporting sentences to every topic sentence, three descriptive words for every point, and even a desire to have three findings highlighted. This is a holdover from being taught to write in this manner early on by teachers who, while well intentioned, were not writers themselves. Larger hidden Western cultural beliefs in groups of three are also surely a part of this tendency.

Overly Qualifying and Pointless Self-Reference. Avoid overly qualifying and pointless self-reference. This is another area I find difficult due to my training in scientific writing. Before graduate school, since my writing training was from fiction and nonfiction writers, this would not have been difficult. Academic writers tend to qualify statements—"it may be," "in some cases," "in certain ways." We are hedging our bets and hearing dissertation and thesis committee members' scathing comments still ringing in our ears—How do you know that? In all cases? What is the probability? For the same reason, even though a piece of writing, such as this book, is my opinion on qualitative writing, I find myself typing over and over "I think," "I hope," or "I believe." Editing overuse of qualification and self-referral allows your writing to sound confident.

Can't Use Contractions? Style guides (e.g., Modern Language Association, APA, Chicago) traditionally indicated that contractions should not be used. Contemporarily, these guides allow for some qualified use of contractions—thoughtful use, avoidance, limited use. For example, the APA blogged that science writing does not "need to be stuffy," just formal and allows contractions in brief editorial types of asides seen in footnotes (Lee, 2015). Qualitative research writers should continue to use contractions in participants' quotes, in quotes from literature that uses contractions, and when writing nontraditional forms (e.g., autoethnography, poetry), but they should avoid unnecessary use of contractions in formal research posters and traditional articles. As someone who lived in the South of the United States from age 3 to 32 years, I appreciate the welcoming feel of contractions wherever they pop up. I am suspicious that avoiding contractions is another form of the racism, regionalism, and classism that seems accepted without comment in academia—controlling the language of groups that are othered. On a lighter note, I fully expect to start seeing contractions more frequently in formal qualitative writing.

Punctuation. In academic writing, you will never go wrong using traditional punctuation: colons, commas, semicolons. However, I want readers to be aware that contemporary understandings of the semicolon and colon have changed in nonfiction writing, with writers' preferences often being the em dash—a long dash achieved on a Mac keyboard by holding down the shift and option key and then typing the hyphen. Zinsser (2006), who has been telling readers how to write well since the 1970s, says "there is a 19th-century mustiness that hangs over the semi-colon. . . . Therefore, it should be used sparingly by modern writers. . . . The colon has begun to look even more antique than the semicolon" but is still helpful in the case of lists. Also, regarding the em dash, he says, "Somehow this invaluable tool is widely regard as not quite proper—a bumpkin at the genteel table of good English. But it has full membership and will get you out of many tight corners" (p. 72). How then might the em dash be used contemporarily? The Punctuation Guide (n.d.) offers the following assistance:

> The em dash is perhaps the most versatile punctuation mark. Depending on the context, the em dash can take the place of commas, parentheses, or colons—in each case to slightly different effect. Notwithstanding its versatility, the em dash is best limited to two appearances per sentence. Otherwise, confusion rather than clarity is likely to result.

(See Text Box 3.5, "Eureka!: The Exclamation Point," for some more punctuation points to ponder.)

Use of Parallel Form. Checking for parallel structures in your writing can feel tedious and reminiscent of a high school writing course. However, for research writing and the long dissertation/thesis forms, this type of detail guides the reader through a logical structure. While examples of parallel form are usually given within one sentence, as in "For work, I wait tables, juggled, and am an Uber driver" being rewritten in parallel form as "For work, I wait tables, juggle, and drive for Uber," in my writing I find I need to be most attentive to parallel form in paragraphs or sections of a research paper where I am laying out points. For instance, if you write "first," then what follows should be "second" and "third," not "secondly" and "furthermore." Attention to these details along with clear use of headings and subheadings are the signposts of a research paper that will engage and guide readers. See a discussion about the way in which the title, abstract, *and research questions need to be parallel in Chapter 5, in the section Titles and Abstracts and Keywords, Oh My!*

Choosing a few of these points to start with will help us continue our writing journey. For readers who wish to read whole books on writing style and form, and for reputable places to start, I suggest Zinsser (2006) and Strunk and White (1918/2007), and *Adios, Strunk and White* (Hoffman & Hoffman, 1997) for updates on classic writing. A more extensive list along with several websites is available at the end of this chapter. Choosing to follow even a few pieces of the advice presented will tighten your writing in ways that will refine and burnish your craft.

3.5 EUREKA!: THE EXCLAMATION POINT

MARIA LAHMAN

> *Cut out all these exclamation points. An exclamation point is like laughing at your own joke.*
>
> —F. Scott Fitzgerald

If you have engaged with a style guide such as the APA's, you will be aware that exclamation points are not used in research writing and are considered unprofessional by some. For many journals and in high-stakes research writing such as a thesis or dissertation you must develop facility with the style guide that dominates in your field, such as the Modern Language Association, Chicago, and American Anthropology Association style manuals. However, I find it is essential to recall that these are merely style *guides*, not to be enacted as facts or judges of our level of scholarship. Many people can look up APA rules and muddle through, but not everyone can design, enact, analyze, write, and publish a research study.

Therefore, when someone says to me *can't* (APA also does not allow contractions) in the area of writing, I have the (un)fortunate reaction of trying to consider how I might or *can*. There has been fruitful writing on the tyranny of academic style (e.g., Bleakley, 2000; Dane, 2011; Zeller & Farmer, 1999). With all due respect to Fitzgerald, my mom laughed at her own jokes and humorous narratives in such a full-bodied fashion it was a delight to join in with her!

Endings

> *How to stop.*
>
> —William Zinsser (2006)

A quality conclusion ties up loose ends and may drive the overall point home one more time and, in Western culture, often circles back around to the beginning in a satisfying loop. The ending satisfies the reader but leaves them thinking long after the reading is over. To achieve this ending in qualitative research, consider how you began the piece. Can you end back in a setting that was studied, with a participant you introduced, with a quote that set the tone of the whole piece—finishing in the context of the data? "The perfect ending should take your readers slightly by surprise and yet seem exactly right" (Zinsser, 2006, p. 64).

A great ending is hard to write, so consider (a) writing several, (b) sharing ending drafts with others, and (c) writing the conclusion first or at least when you are not tired. All pieces of the research point to the ending, so make it count. "The positive reason for ending well is that a good last sentence—or last paragraph—is a joy in itself. It gives the reader a lift and lingers when the article [writing] is over" (Zinsser, 2006, p. 64).

The following are examples of good endings in literature:

So, they went off together. But wherever they go, and whatever happens to them on the way, in that enchanted place on the top of the Forest, a little boy and his Bear will always be playing. (*The House at Pooh Corner*, Milne, 1956).

But I don't think us feel old at all. And us so happy. Matter of fact, I think this is the youngest us ever felt. (*The Color Purple*, Walker, 1982)

He turned out the light and went into Jem's room. He would be there all night, and he would be there when Jem waked up in the morning. (*To Kill a Mockingbird*, Lee, 1960)

It is not often someone comes along who is a true friend and a good writer. Charlotte was both. (*Charlotte's Web*, White, 1952)

How wonderful the flavor, the aroma of the kitchen, her stories as she prepared the meal, her Christmas rolls! I don't know why mine never turn out like hers, or why my tears flow so freely when I prepare them—I am as sensitive to onions as Tita, my great-aunt, who will go on living as long as there is someone who cooks her recipes. (*Like Water for Chocolate*, Esquivel, 1995)

The Gist

This chapter had two central thrusts in the form of writing challenges. The first was a challenge to be taken up during the reading of this book—to write or rewrite a qualitative data set in three ways. One practical approach would be a traditional qualitative article, while others might be a research poster, research poetry, autoethnography, a medley, a visual representation, performance, and so on. The second challenge focused on ways for writers to hone their craft.

Start by choosing a few things to do—rid your work of unnecessary adverbs, attempt a circular opening/closing to a piece, reduce linking being verbs; see what you think, and then choose a few more ideas the next time you write. And when it is time to end, end.

Reflexive Questions

Representation

What research representation forms, if any, are you comfortable working within (e.g., qualitative journal article, autoethnography, research poster)?

Which of these forms could use some updating?

For example, do you know how to add QR codes to research posters?

What new forms of representation might be worth exploring?

Honing Your Craft

After reviewing the section Honing Your Craft in this chapter, which of the suggestions would you choose to implement first? Why?

If you already use the suggestions from the section Honing Your Craft in this chapter, would reading a more in-depth book on the topic be beneficial? If so, check out the list of books in the resources.

Reflexive Activities

See Appendix C for details about the following activities:

How Do We Write?

Top Tips (Have group members brainstorm, on their own or as a group, a list of their top tips for honing writing.)

Technology Share

What new technology have members been using that help with honing their writing? (For example, I use Grammarly.)

Manuscript Review

Professional Writers Panel or Guest Speaker

What's in Your Writing Space?

Speed Discussion (Possible topics follow.)

a. What are the research areas you are considering writing about?

b. What are the challenges you have to successful writing?

c. What is your top tip for successful writing?

Many Voices

Resources

Internet Resources on Writing

Tips on How to Write Well: https://www.youtube.com/watch?v=FtkSjed0Ymc

Oxford Online English: https://www.youtube.com/channel/UCNbeSPp8RY KmHUliYBUDizg

The Punctuation Guide: https://www.thepunctuationguide.com/

Guide to Grammar and Writing: http://guidetogrammar.org/grammar/index.htm

Lessons from "On Writing Well" by William Zinsser: https://www.youtube.com/watch?v=lHbqoJpymRs

Check to see if your university has writing centers both online and in person. Here is one example: Writing at the University of Toronto: https://writing.utoronto.ca/

Books on Writing

Accidental Genius by Mark Levy

Adios, Strunk and White by Gary and Glynis Hoffman

Being a Writer by Peter Elbow and Pat Belanoff

Big Magic by Elizabeth Gilbert

Bird by Bird by Ann Lamott

Edit Yourself by Bruce Ross-Larson

Effective Writing by Bruce Ross-Larson

Once, Twice, Thrice Told Tales: Three Mice Full of Writing Advice by Catherine Lewis.

One Continuous Mistake by Gail Sher

On Writing by Stephen King

On Writing Well by William Zinsser

Rhetorical Grammar by Martha Kolln

Spellbinding Sentences: A Writer's Guide to Achieving Excellence and Captivating Readers by Barbara Baig

Style: Ten Lessons in Clarity and Grace by Joseph M. Williams

The African American Writer's Handbook: How to Get in Print and Stay in Print by Robert Flemming

The Artist's Way by Julia Cameron with Mark Bryan

The Courage to Write by Ralph Keyes

The Craft of Research by Wayne C. Booth, Gregory G. Colomb, and Joseph M. Williams

The Deluxe Transitive Vampire by Karen Elizabeth Gordon

The Elements of Nonsexist Usage by Val Dumond

The Elements of Style by William Strunk, Jr. and E. B. White

The Handy English Grammar Answer Book by Christine Hult

The New Well-Tempered Sentence by Karen Elizabeth Gordon

The Writer's Journey by Christopher Vogler

The Writing Life by Annie Dillard

Wild Mind by Natalie Goldberg

Writing Down the Bones by Natalie Goldberg

Writing From the Inside Out by Dennis Palumbo

Writing the Natural Way by Gabriele Rico

Writing With Power by Peter Elbow

Zen in the Art of Writing by Ray Bradbury

Qualitative Dissertations: The Three Rules

There are three rules for writing a quality qualitative dissertation. Unfortunately, no one knows what they are.

—Maria Lahman, riffing liberally on Somerset Maugham

The qualitative dissertation currently and excitingly has developed into forms of representation outside of the "traditional" five chapters. A review of dissertation advice books reveals that existing "texts . . . offer a rigid model . . . that follow[s] a set format and style" (Kamler & Thomson, 2008, p. 507). While the innovation is laudable, it is important to note that a decade after this review was conducted there are still students who need to understand how to write the traditional qualitative dissertation and seek support from resources such as this chapter. As a methodologist, I am often asked to give a talk or write a guide for the quality qualitative dissertation. I suspect what most students want is simple linear advice on how to write the traditional model. This advice, however, may work against the organic nature of qualitative research. The proposed talk or guide would be in conjunction with that of a quantitative methodologist, who would certainly have a tried and true formula (when proofreading, I realized I had written "tired" instead of "tried").

I have always resisted joining in this sort of discussion outside of the classroom since I believe that while the qualitative proposal has a certain structure, the qualitative dissertation depends on the discipline the doctoral student is in, what the graduate school and dissertation committee are willing to allow, and what the doctoral student can conceive of as the best ways to help others make sense of the data. This means that apart from years of developing course materials, activities, and lectures, this is my first foray into formal writing on the qualitative dissertation. Even as I am writing, doctoral students are coming up with new and meaningful ways to capture and convey knowledge through the dissertation. Therefore, this chapter is framed within the spirit of Somerset Maugham's famous quote, "There are three rules for the writing of a novel. Unfortunately, no one knows what they are" (in Daigh, 1977, p. 7).

In this chapter, I

- set forth guidance and advice, assuming that readers will think with and adapt material for their unique contexts, aspirations, and assets;

- review the dissertation proposal;

- detail the traditional qualitative dissertation;

- give tips and pointers on the process and politics of writing a dissertation;

- review innovative dissertations, including

  o manuscript dissertations and

  o art-influenced qualitative dissertations, including plays, research poetry, and medleys; and

- provide text boxes containing researchers' views on dissertation writing and actual experiences written by doctoral students.

For most, writing a dissertation is a novel experience and one that will not be repeated. The closest experience may be a master's thesis or a research project, but not all doctoral students write a thesis prior to their doctoral research. Professors may go on to direct dissertations and be members of dissertation committees (I have served on 70-plus dissertation committees at the time of this writing), but they do not write a dissertation again—thankfully! The absence of the need to repeat the dissertation form is a major point in the argument for changing the form. However, in the meantime, many qualitative doctoral students will need resources on how to write a traditional qualitative dissertation. Also, the traditional dissertation writing process allows for valuable honing of writing abilities, including in areas that may feel dry or procedural but are necessary and practical, along with experience of working with deadlines, completing rewrites, and meeting committee expectations, which may be conflicting. Much of my nonresearch writing as a faculty member is in the formal tone of reviews—nothing innovative but necessary to advance the work of a university.

I wrote my dissertation long enough ago—two decades—when my degree-granting university was just transitioning to qualitative research. This meant that I did not have significant qualitative methodological support until I was finished with the proposal. Fortunately, my major committee members, while initially all quantitatively trained, were supportive of my research ideas and enjoyed the more personal writing style I tend to employ. This did mean, however, that I conducted a traditional qualitative case study that only had literary elements reflected in the use of quotes I pulled from A. A. Milne's Winnie-the-Pooh—*appropriate for research with young children—and in the vignettes and participant characterizations I was allowed to develop. Nonetheless, even this limited yet personally powerful experience meant that as a professor I sought out ways to use innovative forms in research representations and support students' innovations in dissertations.*

4.1 A DISSERTATION PROPOSAL TABLE OF CONTENTS
MARIA LAHMAN

Chapter 1
    Research Problem
        Purpose
        Research Question(s)

Chapter 2
    Review of the Literature Around Major Constructs in the Research Question(s)
    Review of the Methodological Literature

Chapter 3
    Theoretical Framework
    Researcher Stance (this is at times in Chapter 1)
    Research Questions Repeated
    Methodology
        Participants
            Demographics
            Recruitment—How Participants Will Be Asked to Be in the Study
            Justification of Sample Size Theoretically and Practically
        Setting
        Data Collection Methods
        Data Analysis
            Organization and Storage
            Analytical Choices
        Trustworthiness
            Research Ethics

The Dissertation Proposal (or Chapters 1–3)

I once asked a young dissertation writer whether her suddenly grayed hair was due to ill health or personal tragedy; she answered: "It was the footnotes."

—Joanna Russ (1983, p. 137)

In many ways, the qualitative dissertation proposal is not meaningfully different from the quantitative proposal. Also, much of what qualitative researchers have been taught about borrowing from literary conventions or using salient quotes, vignettes, and rich data does not apply at the proposal stage. Chapters 1 to 3 are best viewed as a written contract between the dissertation committee, the graduate school, and the student as to how the student proposes to conduct research for their dissertation. I have also seen the metaphors of a recipe (see Text Box 4.2), a long trip (Roberts, 2010), a traveler's guide (Foss, 2015), and a road map (Bloomberg & Volpe, 2018) used effectively to help students think through the many steps this daunting document entails.

4.2 LASAGNA RECIPE FOR A PROPOSAL
WILLIAM MERCHANT

I like to think of a research proposal as a *very* detailed recipe. Imagine you have been tasked with creating a special meal for a distinguished guest.

You chose lasagna. Your first chapter will be an introduction to what lasagna is, why it's important, how people eat it, why *your* particular lasagna is worth making, and how it will contribute to lasagna culture and knowledge.

Your second chapter will be a detailing of all things lasagna, including, but not limited to, a history of pasta, tomato sauce, cheese, sausage, and famous chefs who have made lasagna, and any other conceptual components essential to this dish.

Last, Chapter 3 will be the recipe itself. It needs to be detailed enough so that someone else can create your lasagna with descriptions of the basic cooking steps as well as technical descriptions of all cooking techniques and materials (e.g., "What does it mean to 'brown the meat'?" "Why should I salt my pasta water?" "What is the physical makeup of your baking pan?"). After all of this is collected and summarized into a nice and lengthy lasagna recipe, you will be ready to create the lasagna and share it with your guest.

Source: Reproduced with permission from William R. Merchant

Chapter 1: Introduction

A tip I heard *after* I had written my dissertation proposal was that Chapter 1 is easier to write when written last. Having now written multiple longer documents, this makes sense to me since Chapter 1 is a review of what is to come. However, two exceptions are the research questions and the purpose of the study, which should be drafted at the outset so they can be workshopped with classmates, colleagues, and committee members. See Text Box 4.3 for a student's perspective on writing a dissertation.

The Opening. The opening to a qualitative dissertation should be much like the opening to a qualitative journal article. (See more information in Chapter 3 of this book, including a discussion of first sentences in Text Box 3.1.) At the proposal stage, the opening to the introduction of Chapter 1 will most likely be a quote or some compelling research information, such as a statistic. This opening may be viewed as a hook designed to grab and keep the reader's attention. This is not a gimmick but a way to focus the attention of readers on research you have deemed to be important. When the researcher is familiar with the context of the study they are researching, I have also seen a short opening vignette used with great effect. After the data are collected and analyzed, the opening to the dissertation is often modified, and a quote or observation from the data forms the opening.

After the short and catchy opening should be placed a paragraph designed to orient the reader to what will occur in the chapter. Some writers are resistant to these organizing paragraphs, and if so, as an advisor, I would let this go. However, it is important to understand that as tedious as this type of orienting paragraph may be—usually placed at the beginning and the end of each major chapter—organizers function to keep readers on a clear track within a lengthy and at times tedious document. Very few people will read a dissertation from cover to cover aside from the advisor and the committee. The majority of readers will be using the Table of Contents (ToC), headings, and orienting paragraphs to help them get to the information they wish to read as quickly as possible.

Here is a sample orienting paragraph. Readers should use these words or modify them as needed without reference to me:

> In the introduction to the proposed study, I situate the readers within the context of the problem as illustrated in the literature and state the purpose of the study. I explain why the study is important, and finally I put forward the major research question and subquestions, that will guide this study throughout.

Boring to write and read versions of this over and over again? Yes. Helpful to the varied needs of readers? *Yes!*

The Research Problem. The bulk of Chapter 1 will be a presentation of the research problem, which Merriam and Tisdell (2016) have described as "a carefully crafted essay" (p. 79). The research problem will include brief contextual references to the most salient aspects of the literature review—designed to create a context and a compelling argument for the study, known as the significance of the study. This context will also highlight any gaps in the existing research, which, while lending themselves to an argument for the need for research, will not in and of themselves make an acceptable argument for conducting the study. This includes any gaps in methodology, such as the area having only been researched quantitatively. The reason why these gaps cannot be the sole argument for research is that just because something hasn't been researched before doesn't mean it is an issue weighty enough to justify serious inquiry. The purpose of the research study, written in a clear and concise fashion, will be followed by the research questions. (See Merriam & Tisdell, 2016, for several examples of concisely written research problem statements.) In a dissertation, there will be more room to amplify the problem than in a much shorter journal manuscript.

The Purpose of the Study. *The purpose of the study is the most concise part of the road map or recipe for developing a research proposal. Here, you try to capture in a single sentence (or at times a paragraph) what all the aspects of the study are about. The phrasing traditionally begins with "Therefore, the purpose of this study is . . . "*

Many qualitative methods writers (e.g., Creswell, 2013; Merriam, 1998) have discussed aspects of the qualitative purpose statement. One of the most important is writing in language associated with qualitative research. If you were trained initially in quantitative research, this may be one of the most difficult aspects of writing a purpose statement. This is why it is important to show the statement to researchers with qualitative expertise. Qualitative language will contain wording such as "The purpose of this study is to *describe*, or *develop*, or *discover*, or *explore*, or *understand* . . . ". Another feature of qualitative writing is avoiding words that are associated with quantitative research. While this is unfortunate because these words would be useful qualitatively, they are so overly associated with quantitative research that the naive quantitative researcher will begin to look for quantitative features in the study. Typical words to avoid include directional and causal words such as "relationship" or "comparison."

Opening the purpose statement with the type of methodology that will be employed, even if it is simply essential qualitative research, sets the reader into the context methodologically right away. See Chapter Five for information on essential qualitative research. Include the major constructs(s) or phenomenon of interest, and reference who the participants will be in general (e.g., nursing graduate students, preschool children).

John Creswell (2012) has crafted a useful purpose statement that he has stated individuals should feel free to use. He has provided a clear discussion around this purpose statement, which I have quoted below. As you gain more experience, you can work on crafting it in your own words.

The purpose of this _____ (narrative, phenomenological, grounded theory, ethnographic, case) study is (was? will be?) to _____ (understand? describe? develop? uncover/discover?) the ___ (central phenomenon of the study for/of ____ (the participants) at/in _____ (the site). At this stage in the research, the _____ (central phenomenon) will be generally defined as _____ (a general definition of the central concept). (p. 135)

The following is an example I created using Creswell's template:

> The purpose of this <u>qualitative case</u> study <u>is</u> to <u>describe</u> the <u>experiences of preschool children participating</u> in <u>a caring, "at-risk" preschool setting</u>. At this stage in the research, <u>caring</u> will be generally defined as <u>an intentional disposition on the part of the teacher to act in a loving, supporting manner to the children.</u>

Creswell's many qualitative introductory texts (e.g., Creswell, 2013) and the recent addition with Poth (Creswell & Poth, 2018) have been and continue to be valuable to many students and faculty alike who are venturing into qualitative research for the first time.

Qualitative Research Questions. *The qualitative research question is best written as one overall question that may be thought of as a guiding question or overarching central question (Creswell, 2013). This idea is supported by fiction-writing professors who taught me to state the entirety of a piece of writing in one sentence—otherwise there would be too many ideas or tangents that need reconciling. I think of C. S. Lewis's The Chronicles of Narnia books, in which some of the marketing on the back of the text states the plot of each book in one sentence. For example, in my edition of The Lion, the Witch, and the Wardrobe, the plot is summarized on the back of the cover as "How Aslan, the noble lion, freed Narnia from the spell of the White Witch" (Lewis, 1978). My first department chair referred to this as the cocktail conversation about what your dissertation topic is, and I have heard it called "the elevator answer." A well-stated research question provides enough information to gauge if there is genuine interest in further conversation or if your audience's eyes are starting to glaze over.*

Write the overall qualitative research question expansively so you do not prematurely leave some important area out. Consider how you might approach the topic in the most expansive manner. Most qualitative committees will allow judicious fine-tuning of research questions as the research process develops organically. Be careful to have only one question in the overall research question and not introduce multiple versions of constructs of interest through the use of synonyms. While synonyms are useful in keeping writing lively in most contexts, in research questions and purpose statements, they indicate additional constructs that will be explored. Consider constructs of interest carefully since each one may represent a vast body of research literature that will require expertise in and representation of in Chapter 2. For example, use of the word "attachment" is quite different in general writing from what it is in research writing (e.g., Ainsworth, 1978; Bowlby, 2008).

After the major research question has been written, there may be a few, carefully chosen subquestions. These are questions you know will be of interest given the nature of the study and your goals. For instance, if you tend to notice gendered interactions and have an interest in studying them as they relate to the research questions, gender might be the emphasis of one of the subquestions. These questions should focus the study without unduly limiting the research. While they are not written as interview questions, subquestions often denote specific areas where interview questions may be asked. An easy way to distinguish interview questions from research questions is that interview questions will be written in such a simple, concise, conversational manner that they can be asked of anyone. Research questions, while also needing to be concise and devoid of jargon, are so formal they would seem awkward if asked in conversation. (See Text Box 4.4 for examples of research questions.)

Concise Contextual Literature Review. *As referenced earlier in this section, Chapter 1 should also include a short literature review. This review allows the reader to situate themselves within the most important aspects of the study. This literature is the most relevant and may include original historical pieces and recent cutting-edge research. Again, as in the opening to the chapter, this is not to be used as an attempt to be melodramatic or highlight sensational literature but instead should include the sources that best help you convey an argument about a topic you think is important. This literature provides a brief context and sets the background as to why the research problem is significant, and the Chapter 2 that follows is dedicated to an expansion on this literature.*

4.3 WRITING THE DISSERTATION
CHRISTINA TAYLOR

My dissertation research was an ethnographic case study with a purposefully broad qualitative research question: "What is the culture of an early childhood education preschool setting that is philosophically grounded in contemplative education and traditions?" In brief, the answer was "The culture of Alaya preschool is one of care and meaningful work where everyone is presumed to be basically good and embodied presence cradles genuine relationships grounded in kindness." One of my goals was to align my research methodology and methods with my project's topic and to be mindfully present during their execution. I had no idea what a challenge that would be. I remember how one late night, after weeks of writing at every available moment, tears of weariness splashed my keyboard. As I took a break to make a cup of tea, I realized that my brain was not resting. It was busy rewriting the lumpy sentences I had hoped to abandon. With determination, I tried to push the pesky edits aside and literally could not! I suddenly became aware that the act of writing this work had consumed me. I had been writing while driving, doing chores, having conversations, and even during meditation. I could not recall the last time I had been truly present in a moment—an unsettling realization incongruent with my plan. As I stumbled back to my computer, I thought, "Fine! I surrender! This won't last forever!" Surprisingly, it was six months post-graduation before my first waking thought each day was about something other than my dissertation.

Chapter 2: Literature Review

Ideally, Chapter 2, or at least a draft of this chapter, is written first. Traditionally, Chapter 2 is a review of the literature the research study will be contextualized within and justified from. This means that a clear sense of what research has already been conducted and what research scholars are recommending should occur next is provided. Merriam and Tisdell (2016) have underscored that this may even be an iterative process where the researcher moves back and forth between the research questions and the literature while forming the literature review. While it is a grounding of the research topic in the literature, the review is also an exhaustive—and at times exhausting—demonstration that the budding scholar knows the field and the history of the field prior to its inception. This demonstration will usually not make its way into a subsequent publication other than in a highly truncated form, but it allows a dissertation committee to follow the doctoral student's academic understandings. An understanding of the literature then allows you to go back to Chapter 1 and develop a well-thought-out research problem statement (see the proceeding section on Chapter 1).

"A literature review is a narrative essay that integrates, synthesizes, and critiques" (Merriam & Tisdell, 2016, p. 95) existing research literature. However, a common error in the lengthier and novice dissertation literature reviews is a tendency to string each piece of research in a row, almost as though the writer is simply cutting and pasting abstracts or bibliographies back to back. To avoid this unacceptable review style, create an outline of the major constructs in the research question(s) and those yielded in the literature review in an arrangement that will develop support for conducting the research. Then, group the relevant literature under the outline headings. A research study may be referenced multiple times under different headings.

Since they are earning methodology degrees, my students are also required to review how their research interest area has been researched methodologically. This allows the researcher to potentially contribute methodologically to the field. Finally, I ask my students to add a research question in the area of research ethics and include literature on this topic in the literature review. Examples of areas explored have included what constitutes consent to research culturally and how people who are homeless feel they should be compensated during research.

I have started to hear advisors on committees I am a member of ask students to keep the literature review concise and straightforward. This request will help the student acquire practical experience in reviews that might be used in the much shorter research articles. As you can see, there is a lot of room to create a literature review that is relevant and not simply a womb-to-tomb document with little use outside of the dissertation. See the resources at the end of this chapter for suggestions on where to read more about writing a literature review.

4.4   HOW TO WRITE QUALITATIVE RESEARCH QUESTIONS: HONING WRITING

MARIA LAHMAN

- Create one overall question covering all of the areas you are interested in. If you find there are tangents that won't fit beneath this question, then your topic is not focused enough.
- The question should indirectly point to how data will be collected.
- Write clearly.
- Be concise.
- Avoid jargon—an educated person who is not an academic should be able to understand the research question(s).
- State the setting when applicable.
- Identify participants (be specific); instead of simply writing "teachers," state what kind of teachers (middle school, veteran, preservice).
- Avoid terms indicating quantification or those highly associated with quantitative research, such as these:
  o affect
  o influence
  o determine
  o cause
  o relate
- Pose the question with nondirectional wording.
- Describe rather than relate variables or compare groups.

Examples of Research Questions

- What are physical education preservice teachers' views of the physical environment in elementary physical education classroom settings in Taiwan?
- How do owners of service dogs feel the dogs mitigate symptoms of post-traumatic stress disorder?

Chapter 3: Methodology

Chapter 3 is where the metaphors of a contract, road map, or recipe are most appropriate. Similar to a well-written recipe, Chapter 3 should have enough detail that someone could follow the same research design without needing any extra information, yet it should not have so much detail that the reader gets lost and begins to flounder.

iStock.com/Big_Ryan

Getting Started. *Ask your chair and committee members to suggest several dissertations that they would recommend as models for you. Examine the, Table of Contents, closely and assemble one that touches on those aspects of the ToC you are reviewing that work best for your research study. Once you have a ToC ready with a detailed Chapter 3 outlined within the ToC, meet with your chair, and go over the ToC together. When you have an approved draft of the ToC, you should be ready to work for extended periods of time on your own without wandering off track and writing extensive pieces that may not be used. See Text Box 4.1 for an example of a ToC for Chapters 1 to 3.*

Methodology is the major heading in Chapter 3 under which all other sections will fall. The opening to this chapter is where it is common to overly justify the use of qualitative research with an explanation and defense of qualitative research, which may also include a review of major qualitative methodologies. Instead, I believe Chapter 3 should start with a brief overview of the major qualitative methodology that will be used (e.g., narrative inquiry, bricolage, case study) while at the same time highlighting what specific aspects of this methodology will be utilized in the proposed dissertation research. When people I am consulting with feel reluctant to cut the review of qualitative research, I ask them to consider when the last time was that they read a quantitative dissertation that explained what quantitative research was and why it was justified. This convention is clearly from a time when qualitative research was not supported or understood. If, however, a committee or chair believes that this section must be in place, it is not worth the effort to argue; save the discussion for crucial aspects of the dissertation, such as what a rigorous sample size or data set may entail.

The methodology will be the largest part of Chapter 3. This section will open with a discussion of the major methodology that will be employed. Examples of these are numerous—photovoice (Wang, 2003), bricolage (Berry, 2011), portraiture (Lawrence-Lightfoot, 2016), appreciative inquiry (Reed, 2006), connoisseurship (Eisner, 2017)—but they are often organized into case study, ethnography, narrative inquiry, grounded theory, and phenomenology (Creswell, 2013; Merriam & Tisdell, 2016). You will describe the methodology and how it will allow you to best explore the research question. This allows you to dispel any misconceptions readers may have and to provide reference citations where they can read more if they don't fully follow your intent. You may also wish to draw on several methodologies and can use phrases such as "This study is informed by photovoice" to indicate that you do not plan to follow every step of photovoice as it was originally conceived.

While the entire methodology section needs to have enough information that someone could conduct the study without speaking to the author, traditionally it is often also an overview of each area. For example, qualitative sampling might be discussed in general beyond what is actually occurring. I feel this lengthy style should be avoided since it adds distracting information that will not be used. In each area, literature should be cited related to what you are actually planning to do. It is important to include rich citations so motivated readers can look beyond the dissertation for more information about the dissertation's methodology.

I prefer to place the theoretical framework toward the opening of Chapter 3, usually right after the methodology. This is because theory will guide all aspects of the study. Some committees may also require that sections on axiology, ontology, and epistemology be included. See Crotty (1998) and Schwandt (2014) for more discussion on these philosophical concepts. See Figure 4.1 for a graphic depiction of how theory and methodology connect with methods.

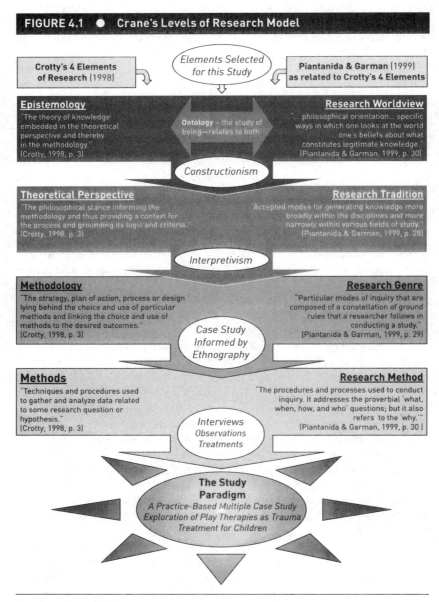

FIGURE 4.1 ● Crane's Levels of Research Model

Note. From Crane (2005).

Source: Reproduced with permission from Susan Crane.

Theoretical Framework. *Chapter 3, as previously stated, will include the theoretical framework. While the writing of the theory section is beyond the scope of a single chapter, I do have a few tips. Start thinking about theory early on, and try to engage with theories you are not familiar with. As a professional in early childhood education, I just missed having concentrated education in behaviorism. Every degree I obtained emphasized some version of constructionism; so I always joke that I am not sure if I am a constructionist or was just conditioned to be one, pun intended. As part of my doctoral and early-career work, I engaged heavily with feminism, critical race theory, and queer theory, which are a natural fit for my work in many ways. This engagement has allowed me to create a sort of theoretical patchwork cloak, which I am articulating as critical feminist whiteness See Delgado and Stefancic (1997) for foundational reading in critical white studies.*

While theory fits naturally at the start of Chapter 3 as the perspective guiding all areas of the study, I have also seen it discussed in Chapter 1 and as a standalone chapter. You will want to consider a large social science theory used in research along with a more field-specific theory used mostly within your specific area of study. See the section Theory of the Study and Figure 5.1 in Chapter 5 for more discussion about theory in research accounts.

Researcher Stance. *The researcher stance is a natural fit after theory has been discussed. It allows the researcher to link the "universal" and political to the personal. If theory is one of the most formal voices you will use as a researcher when writing, then the researcher stance may be the most intimate voice. Consider the most basic researcher stance to be similar to a brief reflexive resumé statement. What have you done and are doing in life that informs the perspectives you bring to this study? For example, I might say that I taught young children for 10 years in public schools and university laboratory schools.*

Another aspect of a researcher stance needs to be determined by the individual researcher and is not something that can be required by reviewers or editors. This is the likelihood that some intimate experience has drawn you to investigate the topic of interest: *I was drawn to explore loss through a wrenching ectopic pregnancy. I am comfortable writing about this experience now but have not always been so.* Students have written in their researcher stance section about siblings with a disability, students with unique learning needs, inadequate parents, and violence—experiences that have drawn them to their research line. These perspectives can be powerful to share with both readers and research participants and clearly help orient the study in a deeper context. But always remember that published writing lasts and is easily accessed through the internet, so be sure you are comfortable with what you are sharing. See Chapter 10 for an in-depth discussion of the researcher's stance.

Methods

The methods often constitute one of the largest sections in Chapter 3. Methods need enough details that another person could follow them and conduct the research without reference to the researcher who planned the study.

Subsections of the methods section include participants, setting, data collection methods, data analysis, and trustworthiness.

Participants. *This section should include (a) what type of people will be asked to participate in the study, (b) how you will go about recruiting them, and (c) the approximate sample size. Recruiting scripts should be in the appendices (e.g., emails, social media posts, bulletin board posters).*

At the proposal stage, you will have criteria for who you wish to recruit and a pretty good hunch as to the demographics of this group. For example, if you want to recruit preservice elementary teachers from a university, you would know that they would most likely be women and what their age and race/ethnicity would be. Then, you need to decide whether you will recruit for variability (men, older students, race/ethnicity diversity) or for similarity.

It is also acceptable to have personal research goals that guide the way you conduct sampling. As someone from the field of early childhood education, I always try to include girls and ethnic/racial diversity in a sample if possible. This is because the history of my field provided for the robust study of boys and white children, with limited and poorly conducted research on girls and non-white children. I have received pushback for this stance, but I would challenge you to consider the history of research in your field and work against any negative aspects.

In the final dissertation, include demographics for each participant. This might be in the form of a short description written in prose about each participant, or if the number of participants is more than 10, consider using a chart as a handy reference tool for readers. In Chapter 5, see Table 5.1 for an example of a participants' chart and Table 5.2 and a section titled "What's in a Name—Pseudonyms" for a rich discussion around naming participants. See Text Box 4.5 for an example of a rich vignette that describes a participant.

Many committees will ask you to justify the sample size theoretically. This is the methodological question I am consulted about most frequently. While you certainly may look for general guidelines in the field (e.g., 10 participants), adequate sample size is really a sense of what the researcher gauges when they start to see data repeated that are similar to data they have already collected. This may be termed *data saturation* or *redundancy*. If the goal of your research is not to generate themes, this guidance does not work as well. Keep in mind the interplay between the number of participants in the study and the number and length of data collection incidences (e.g., an incident could be one interview, one observation time, etc.) as a way to guide this decision. For example, if you are interviewing people for 5 minutes about product placement as they come off a ski lift, you will want to have many more interviews than most qualitative researchers would. If you are conducting multiple conversational, in-depth interviews lasting around 90 minutes about the death of a parent, the number of participants will be less. If in this sensitive research, you are also asking participants to provide mementos to be photographed and to keep a grief journal, the number of people may be even less. We can quickly see how individualized the sample size question is.

However, practically speaking, conduct a review of the journals to which you will send the manuscript you create from the dissertation. Identify what sample size the qualitative articles tend to have and what the data consist of. While this cannot be the only concern, there is no doubt you will want to publish a study beyond the dissertation so that more people can be aware of the findings and to add to your vitae for future opportunities. A review of potential journals prior to the design of the research study will be invaluable in this process.

4.5 PARTICIPANT VIGNETTE

MARIA LAHMAN

The following is an example of a rich description that could be used to introduce a participant. The purpose is to introduce some data and context but, more important, to situate each participant in the reader's imagination so they can recall them as the text progresses. I find this most effective if the number of participants is 10 or less or if each participant is quite unique. For example, if I interview 20 professional moms, it would be difficult to use this sort of description due to readers not wanting to read that many descriptions, the length the descriptions add to the manuscript, and the way the moms start to blend into one another. If, however, each participant held a different role at a university (instructor, student, academic staff, professor, coach, custodian, president, etc.), the use of participant vignettes effectively introduces each one.

Hye-Won was a five-year-old South Korean girl born in the United States shortly after her family moved from Korea for her father to go to school. Her father, Jun, and mother, Sook, were both fluent in English. Sook was also highly educated in the area of child development. Hye-Won attended a reputable local day care where she had been a student for two years. Sook and Jun were pleased with Hye-Won's day care situation. Jun said he liked the school that Hye-Won was attending. He trusted the teachers, and he believed that Hye-Won was happy at the school. He had several opportunities to observe the classroom and was pleased that creativity was encouraged. Jun also noted that "Hye-Won has friends from diverse backgrounds, including American children and Korean [at the Korean church and neighbors], so she can understand the diversity and differences and easily accepts them." Hye-Won was first observed for this study several years into her schooling. She was an active member of her class and worked busily with classmates, calling out ideas and commands, moving quickly through the room, bobbed jet-black hair swinging at her shoulders, shouting, "Christa, leave Ralph alone!" Hye-Won was reminding Christa of a class rule to let children wake up from nap at their own pace. (Lahman & Park, 2004, pp. 135–136).

iStock.com/Big_Ryan

Setting. *A description of the setting usually will occur in one of two ways. First, in an essential research design as discussed in Chapter 5, or if interviews are the only way data are collected, a basic description of the typical places where the interviews took place may be warranted. It may be that the interviews took place over Zoom, at the campus library, or in a park. Some information about the city or university where the study was situated would be helpful to readers. Second, a study that has an observational component to it, such as a holistic case study or ethnography, will have a much more detailed description that allows readers to feel they are actually picturing the research site. This may include details about the immediate setting, surrounding area, and historical setting.*

Data Collection Methods. *In this section, there will be a subheading for each way data will be collected. Each section should include citations from methodological literature and enough detail so that someone else can conduct your study without needing to consult you. Examples of subheadings might include interviews, conversational interviews, observations, participant journals, participants' photos, mementos, and so on. Holistic research designs such as case study will have multiple subheadings, whereas an interview-driven study may just have one.*

Data Analysis. *The dissertation, as both a longer form and a document where students demonstrate to faculty the breadth and depth of their understanding, has more room for expounding on methodological choices than other research accounts. I find that data analysis is one area where dissertations provide extensive information. This is in all likelihood due to the difficulty in explaining to others how analysis choices were made. There are areas of analysis that are intuitive and occur as we write the research context into being (Richardson, 1993).*

At the proposal stage, write the analysis steps out as clearly as possible, perhaps even numbering the steps. The goal is to provide as much clarity for the dissertation committee as possible (see Text Box 4.6). Then, at the final dissertation writing stage, go back and update anything that occurred in the process that was different from what you anticipated, providing examples when possible. See Text Box 5.2 in Chapter 5 for Logan's discussion of how he conducted thematic analysis.

In this section, you will need to explain (a) how the data will be organized and managed and (b) the type of analysis conducted, including the steps that occurred within the analysis.

Organization and storage as part of analysis: How the data will be organized and managed including where the data will be stored, how the data will be backed up, and what, if any, data analysis software will be used (e.g., NVIVO, Atlas ti). The software in and of itself is not the type of analysis, but do be aware that the use of software will influence analytical choices.

Choice of data analysis: There is too much information to cover on analysis, but I do want to provide several tips. Certain methodologies indicate the analysis that would follow, but not in a narrow fashion. Phenomenology, for example, should have a phenomenological analysis. However, there are many different types of phenomenological analysis that you will want to review as you narrow down your choices before making final decisions (e.g., Colazzi, 1978, cited in Shosha, 2012; Moustakas, 1994; Vagle, 2018). If the analysis choice seems highly prescribed, as one might see in original grounded theory or photovoice, while you may follow the steps laid out, you may also borrow from the analysis what is relevant for your goals and state this as follows: "The analysis was informed by photovoice" or "I constructed the analysis from several types of analyses." Then, carefully explain how this occurred.

The following are questions to consider as you decide what type of analysis is appropriate for the study:

- Does the methodology indicate certain types of analysis?

- What beliefs about research is the analysis embedded within?

- What terms are used to convey the analysis process?

- Would a chart of the analysis process be helpful to your readers?

- Can you identify examples of how the analysis occurred to share with your chair or dissertation committee as needed?

This last question will allow for clear communication.

Trustworthiness. This section includes two subareas: (1) the major literature you are drawing on to enhance trustworthiness and (2) the trustworthiness procedures you will conduct in this area. For the first area, qualitative researchers often use Lincoln and Guba's criteria (1985), which includes four areas—credibility, transferability, dependability, and confirmability. Be aware of other criteria that exist. Subsequently, Lincoln (2007) went on to develop "authenticity criteria," rejecting major trustworthiness criteria. Richardson's (1999) "creative analytic practices" (CAP) are often used in art-informed research representations. There are many more criteria. But some find much of this a distraction from a needed emphasis on the researcher's personal ethics and reflexivity.

The second area of trustworthiness—that is, procedures (triangulation, member check, reflexivity, peer check, etc.)—is well developed, so reference introductory textbooks to determine which ones would work best for your study. For example, triangulation has possibilities beyond data triangulation, which many are familiar with—convergent, complementary, divergent, theoretical, method, researcher (Janesick, 1998), and the development of the construct "crystallization," which moves away from the constraints of triangulation (e.g., Ellingson, 2011). You can easily see that these research study enhancement methods merit digging into the rich literature in this area.

There is no room in this chapter for a lengthy discussion of this important topic, so see Figure 5.4 in Chapter 5 for rich information on trustworthiness as a starting point. I will only offer a few of my original ideas here.

I developed the trustworthiness method *expert check* when as a student I was sternly reprimanded for using the standard phrase from the field, "peer check" (Merriam & Tisdell, 2016), in reference to faculty. If your faculty have the need for a firm hierarchy between students and faculty, consider using the phrase *expert check*. What both of these phrases indicate is that someone who is outside of the research process, such as a colleague who has an expertise in the area, checks in on different aspects of the study or is a person you can discuss the research with reflexively. A dissertation chair and committee are perfect for this role, and the phrase "expert check" may be suitable for them.

Openness is a trait to strive for as a researcher. I think of this as being open to *serendipity* in research—the unanticipated that allows for a new happening or insight. This may occur in something as simple as material data or an observation you did not expect to see or as profound as an insight into who you are as a researcher or a realization during analysis that upends your previous thinking. Openness allows us to experience these profound and unexpected moments, which we can then process and act on through reflexivity. In Chapter 10, I discuss reflexivity at length, which, when infused with ethics, I find to be the most vital area of trustworthiness.

A final point—the major error I see in this area is researchers indicating, after different trustworthiness procedures have occurred, that the research is trustworthy. Instead, this should be worded as "the procedures *enhanced* the trustworthiness of the study." Rigor in a study is ultimately a process, a perspective, and a judgment made by the reader, so we can never fully claim to have achieved trustworthiness.

Research Ethics. *This section of the dissertation includes a statement that either you have received permission to conduct the study from the university Research Ethics Board (e.g., Institutional Review Board [IRB]) and any other necessary ethics groups, or you are in the process of applying for permission. Accompanying documents will be in the appendices.*

Research ethics approval is a minimal procedural ethics process, so be sure to consider what areas may have potential ethical issues that are not addressed by an ethics board. Liamputtong's (2007) text about those who are vulnerable in research is an excellent resource in this area. In the area of culturally responsive research ethics, I have written, with coauthors, extensively about aspirational research ethics with children, people who are homeless, LGBTQ+ folx, and immigrants, and in visual and virtual research (Lahman, 2018).

After the Proposal Is Accepted

When your dissertation proposal has been accepted by your committee and the graduate school, take a moment to celebrate. Do some of the things you have been putting off, from self-care to cleaning to work items. Then, address any edits that the committee provided to you. This is a huge amount of work for the committee to generate and one of the few times you don't pay directly for editing services. While you are editing, change the proposal into past tense. Most qualitative dissertations are written in the past tense, as in "I did" instead of "I will"—unless the research is written in the ethnographic present to be sure the reader feels directly engaged with the action occurring.

4.6 SUSAN CRANE'S DISSERTATION FRAMEWORK

MARIA LAHMAN

Susan Crane personalized Benson and Piercy's (1997) research advising model for Chapter 3 of her dissertation (Crane, 2005; Figure 4.2). See this model in Chapter 6 of this book, on writing qualitative research manuscripts. At the dissertation proposal meeting, Susan left the chart up as a visual slide during the discussion on research methodology. Some audience members had not worked extensively with qualitative research at this point, and the model clearly showed connections between paradigmatic terms that allowed people to quickly become comfortable with Susan's proposed research.

FIGURE 4.2 ● **Susan Crane's Dissertation Framework**

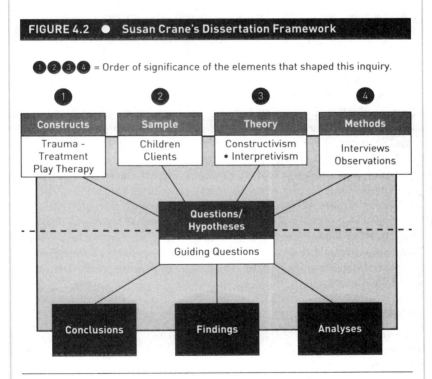

Note: Components in the top half of this figure represent the essential elements of the research proposal. The full figure represents a complete dissertation. Adapted from Benson and Piercy (1997) by Susan Crane.

Source: Reproduced with permission from Susan Crane.

The Dissertation (or Chapters 4 and 5)

Chapter 4: Findings

This chapter is the fruit of the dissertation, where all your hard work and that of the participants comes to bear. This also means that Chapter 4 is often much too long. If having consideration for your committee members is not motivation enough to edit your writing, respecting the participants and the point of the research should be. The point of Chapter 4 is not to write such a lengthy piece that no one will finish reading it or to make it thick enough to use as a footstool. Instead, after conducting careful analysis, highlight the data directly addressing the research question(s) first. Then, if warranted, a portrayal of data relevant yet unanticipated by the research questions may be highlighted.

A discussion of the findings is an important feature of a dissertation. It may be found in Chapter 4 or 5. I like to think of the discussion as the story your data is telling. The discussion creates ties back to the literature or underscores contrasts. It sets the context for the remainder of the dissertation which I discuss under Chapter Five. Choose the most salient parts to discuss.

If the number of participants is at around 10 or less, a captivating way to open Chapter 4 can be with brief descriptive introductions of each one of them. If, on the other hand, the number of participants is greater than 10, readers cannot retain the information pertaining to each person separately in their minds, so creating a reference chart with names and demographics will be more helpful. Some committees will want this chart regardless. Even if you are conducting research such as narrative, where a chart does not seem to fit well, I would add one if asked to and simply leave it out of any subsequent publication. Another style that works well is to open Chapter 4 with a longer vignette, such as a day in the life of a principal, a day on a campus, or football game day on a campus (e.g., Delich, 2004).

Before writing Chapter 4, review many qualitative dissertations. Ask your chair and committee members to recommend recent students' dissertations for you to review. If you have committee members who have written a qualitative dissertation in the recent past, it is advisable to review their work also. In all likelihood, the primary style you see, no matter what the major methodology is, will be a thematic presentation, where major findings are presented in sections with subsections of smaller themes.

Chapter 5: Conclusion

Chapter 5 is similar to Chapter 1 in that it is also a difficult chapter to write. I think this may be so for two reasons. First, students are tired when they begin to write the final chapter. They have now made it through almost all the stages of the dissertation and are beginning to prepare for one of the most nerve-wracking ones—the dissertation meeting (defense). At this stage of their doctoral career, they are most likely simultaneously interviewing for jobs or already in a high-level professional position. Second, for much of their academic career, students have been asked, and perhaps quite sharply, "How do you know that? Whom are you referencing?" In Chapter 5, they are required to say what they "know" in reference to their own research. This knowledge is in the form of inferences and recommendations, so it is not direct data. Chapter 5 is consequently often an oversell or an undersell of the findings—claims that we now know such and such will certainly occur or unclear statements that do not adequately highlight the dissertation findings. Wolcott (1994) has instructed researchers when writing up the conclusions to research to draw inferences right above the data—almost hovering above the data and not shooting so high as to burn up in the stratosphere.

The sections that are in a Chapter 5 include an introduction paragraph that reminds readers what has occurred during the dissertation research by briefly reviewing the research problem, restating the research questions, and highlighting how data were collected. Following that, a brief review of the major areas of the findings is provided. While all of this may seem redundant, recall that readers may only read Chapter 5 in an effort to get to the implications of the study. Committee members may reread Chapter 5 as a review prior to the defense.

The implications for practice section comes next and is one of the two major thrusts of the chapter. Choose areas for implications carefully. This should not be a laundry list of every implication you can think of. It might be helpful to think about who the major constituents in this research area are. For example, a pre-K–12 education dissertation may provide implications for policymakers, education faculty, teachers, preservice teachers, parents, and students. You can quickly see that by the time these sections are written, this will be a thorough chapter.

The second major thrust of Chapter 5 is what you as the researcher, the person who knows the most about this study, recommends for the next steps in this area of research. Again, this should not be a laundry list of all possibilities. Choose the next two to three research ideas indicated by the findings, and explain why they are important. Perhaps you noted that gender seemed to play an important part of the context but did not have adequate time to explore this area, or you realized that observing the phenomenon in the context would add deeper dimensions to interviews. Craft each recommendation into a concise paragraph.

Finally, create a conclusion. Qualitative writers try to be attentive to good writing practices. Endings are as important as openings. Since this is research, I always say end in the data. Highlight the participants' words and actions one more time. It is often pleasing to readers and helps with sense making to have the conclusion come back around and touch the opening. My dad taught me that this is called "tucking in the tale" (tail). I never knew if he meant tail or tale! I have also seen this idea referred to as *circularity*. As researchers, a satisfying way to tuck in the tail/tale is to end back in the data with an interview quote or observation. Do not introduce a topic you haven't discussed. The ending should be reflective of the whole and push forward the outcome of the dissertation one more time. If you are writing a dissertation that is more postmodern or contains art influences, as I will discuss in the innovations section of this chapter, it may be best that you end the dissertation with more questions than answers or in an unresolved "cliff hanger" manner. However, you will need to know your committee and your field since this can leave some people confused, disconcerted, and ultimately cause them to reject your research endeavors.

Politics and Process of the Dissertation

I love deadlines. I love the whooshing noise they make as they go by.

—Douglas Adams

Most graduate experiences until the dissertation are the type of experiences that students have been successful at, or they would not be working to attain a doctoral degree. Course work typically has deadlines, while many dissertation advisors do not give deadlines, and if proposal and dissertation draft timelines are given, they are generally not *actual* deadlines. However, there are important deadlines to consider, which include when the graduate school will close a student's degree without completion and the dates within which a graduate school allows dissertation events to occur. Finding out what these dates are and working backward from them to create a reasonable calendar of to-do dates is a first important step toward becoming an independent researcher and successful doctoral student. As part of this calendar, be sure to consider the time required for the dissertation chair to review the proposal and the dissertation multiple times before sending it to the committee for review. Then, the dissertation committee will need a certain amount of time, which may be a matter of policy, to review the dissertation. At my university, this is 10 business days, not including weekends and university holidays.

As a student gets closer to finishing, I ask them to create two timelines. The first one is what they hope will happen and the second is the backup plan. This allows me to be sure they understand graduate school deadlines and turnaround in feedback expectations. If a student is able to give their writing to me at a scheduled time, I will set aside a block of time to read their writing right away. If they tend to give me drafts without any warning, then I have a strict two-week turnaround time. Both styles of writing are productive but necessitate different feedback timelines.

Aside from a book, the dissertation is most likely the longest document a student has written and may write in their career that follows. Since the dissertation writing process is long and often isolated, I recommend that students take control of this situation by creating supportive contexts within this process. These may take the form of a dissertation writing group, scheduled meetings with the dissertation chair and/or committee members, and joining internet support groups. See Chapter 3 for general writing support ideas and the resources at the end of this chapter for dissertation-specific support.

Choose your dissertation topic carefully and with advice from those around you. For many, their dissertation will lay out the next 5 to 10 years of research they conduct, affect the type of job they take, and influence the content examples presented in the courses they instruct. Aspects of my dissertation regarding ethics were woven into an article I wrote, a research ethics course I developed, and ultimately a book I wrote on research ethics (Lahman, 2017a). It would have been impossible for me at the time of writing my dissertation to look down the road to where parts of the work have taken me. For instance, my determination to conduct a qualitative research study even with limited methodological resources meant that a door into methodology and becoming a qualitative methodologist was opened.

Tensions

Tensions are a large part of completing any big project, including a dissertation.

- How do you value family and friends and still create space for the dissertation?

- How do you grow intellectually and emotionally yet still be authentically present for those who are important to you who may not be ready for the change that will happen in you?

By the time you are proposing and writing a dissertation, you are well aware of the many difficulties related to graduate school.

A first step toward managing tensions is to evaluate how much time you have to give to the dissertation process.

- Do you have family literally dependent on you?

- Do you have a full-time career while you are also a doctoral student?

- Do you have limited resources and limited graduate assistantships?

If you answer yes to any of these questions, then try to assess how many hours a week you can commit to the dissertation process and how many years are feasible.

- If you do not work full-time, what type of support is available from the graduate school in the form of teaching or research assistantships?

- What research grants might provide income?

Depending on the answer, you may want to pare your research topic back to one that still has quality yet is doable in a reasonable amount of time. As trite as the following statements are, there are important nuggets of truth in them.

No one gets an A plus on a dissertation. The dissertation is pass or fail.

The best dissertation is a done dissertation.

The first step to getting what you want (in a dissertation) is getting rid of what you don't want.

Managing the Topic

At this point, many students will no longer be in courses. I personally advise students to continue to take or audit a course while they are writing their dissertation. I have found this experience to be invaluable both as a student and as an instructor of students who are actively writing their dissertation. As a student, the course I was enrolled in meant that I was forced to leave the basement where I otherwise felt chained to my computer writing and writing. I interacted with fellow students and professors in meaningful ways, which were often around inquiries about how the dissertation was going. The additional courses I took were all in qualitative methodology, which became an integral part of the research professor position I later secured. Students who are actively writing their dissertation bring a deep richness of experience and advice to their interactions with classmates about what is to come.

That being said, many students will not take courses, and some are no longer actively on campus or in a position to regularly see their advisor. This means that it is important to negotiate what your new relationship will be with your advisor. The Writing Center (n.d.), University of North Carolina at Chapel Hill, suggests the following questions to ask your advisor:

- How often should I be in contact with you about my progress? (Also find out what form the contact should take)

- Do you prefer to see whole drafts of chapters, relatively polished drafts, or smaller chunks of less well-formed writing?

- If I give you a draft of a chapter on Monday, what do you think the turnaround time will be?

- Do you want to see the chapters in the order I write them or in the order they'll wind up?

Politics

While the reason you are at the university is vital to you, recall that the faculty and staff may have been at the university for years and may be there for years after you are gone. Avoid engaging in any conversations, especially documented ones, such as emails or social media posts, that could be seen as gossip. Of course, everyone does need to process their experience at some point. Asking advice from other students about faculty may be helpful, but you will quickly see who is genuinely giving advice and who is escalating situations unhelpfully. Unfortunately, I have found that some of the first people who reach out to you, seemingly in deep candor, are also willing to talk about what you share to others. So take your time in sharing until you have developed trustworthy relationships, and avoid writing down negative information that can be forwarded and shared with others.

The core of the dissertation student/committee relationship is not about friendships. Even with the most engaging and appealing faculty, more than a close collegial relationship is not a wise idea. You will be around the people at your university for many years, perhaps at dinners in their homes, getting coffee, grabbing a lunch, traveling to conferences, and even staying in the same hotel rooms at times. Qualitative researchers may write about and therefore discuss deeply intimate issues such as cancer or date rape. All this can create boundary confusions, so remind yourself why you are at the university, and stay focused. It is not your job to fix all the problems around you. This, of course, is different if you are part of a situation that is an actual offense and not just offending. I do not write this lightly because we all know that there can be terrible situations involving power relationships and social justice inequities that occur during the dissertation process. However, keeping in mind that ultimately your PhD will put you in a position to create more substantial change will help you keep interactions framed within this context.

Process

Early in your program, familiarize yourself with the graduate school and your academic unit's website, handbook, and policies. If the graduate school or your academic unit uses social media to disseminate information, such as a Facebook page, Twitter, or Snapchat, sign up for these so you will be aware of any changes. Attend informational meetings that are available. Pay close attention to the graduate school calendar. For example, you may have a plan to defend a proposal at the start of a semester and the dissertation at the end of the same semester. The graduate school, however, may have a policy that requires these two important steps to not occur in the same semester. If that is the case, is the summer considered a semester? A second example—how much time are you required to give your dissertation committee to review your dissertation? Does this time exclude weekends and university holidays? These are examples of important information that you need to have as you plan timelines and work to secure assistantships or research sites that are likely time sensitive. Do not rely on other graduate students or your chair for this sort of information. While they may be valuable sources, what is written policy will always supersede other advice. Find out if your department has a graduation checklist, and if it doesn't, create one for yourself. If your chair seems amenable, share with them as you complete different tasks.

Keep a Paper Trail. *For decisions you and your chair agree on or paperwork that is important, keep a paper trail. If the agreement was made orally, follow up after the meeting by email with a simple thank you that also reviews what occurred at the meeting. This not only helps in the case of changes within your committee or a capricious advisor, but also for overwhelmed chairs like me, it is a handy reminder of what we agreed on.*

Writing a Really, Really Long Document. *For many people, this is the first time they have written such a long paper. The length of the dissertation often calls for strategies that have not been needed in the past but would be helpful for any type of writing. One of these is to set up the correct style and formatting ahead of time.*

Style and Formatting. *I ask my students to communicate with the expert at the graduate school on style and formatting at the proposal stage. This is because the dissertation is at its shortest length at this point. After this consultation, all these types of issues should be laid out correctly going forward. This prevents a lot of tedious work that might have to occur at the last moment with impending graduation deadlines and when the student is completely exhausted from the dissertation defense. I recall a student standing in my office doorway saying that they had more than 100 edits to make in their dissertation that the graduate school had noted. When they were done venting, I was pleased to be able to say, "Does it help at all that I was just emailed that you won the dissertation award?" This type of editing has little to do with research quality but can be a holdup to others accessing your work and a timely graduation. For me, it meant that I missed one more Easter celebration with my extended family while I remained on my own, sequestered, getting the edits done in time for graduation.*

Persistence. *An important part of the dissertation process and one characteristic that distinguishes those who finish from those who don't is a trait such as grit, perseverance, or persistence—the ability to keep going. I found that during the dissertation process all of my prior notions about quality writing situations were set aside. I wrote when I was tired, the house was messy, and my desktop was cluttered. I wrote when I was hungry. I wrote when my eyes were swollen from crying. I broke all the conventional rules I had received around when and how to write and just wrote. It has been said before but will always bear repeating that having something on paper that you can rewrite (e.g., a crappy draft or childish writing) is far better than nothing. Persist in writing, writing, writing.*

Knock, knock.

Who's there?

Orange.

Orange who?

Orange you supposed to be writing your dissertation?

Change Is in the Wind

It is exhausted; it is exhausting; it has run its course; it is no longer tenable in terms of student interests and prospects.

—Sidione Smith (Council of Graduate Schools, 2016, p. 3)

iStock.com/Alek_Koltukov

Changes have been increasingly made to the dissertation format for some time (e.g., Thomas et al., 1986), but they are typically seen as innovations that are possible alternatives to the long-standing dissertation form, not replacements. Change is slow because of many tensions, including faculty concerns that an innovative dissertation will hamper doctoral students' academic job attainment. Independent scholars and groups such as the Council of Graduate Schools are initiating conversations where scholars can engage with one another to think about the usefulness of the dissertation. Some questions include the following, which I quote from the Council of Graduate Schools (2016):

- What is a dissertation? What is its purpose? Who are its audiences and what are their needs?

- What skills are or might be gained as a result of writing a dissertation?

- What does completing a dissertation demonstrate?

- What formats besides the proto-monograph would support the desired purposes and results of a dissertation?

- Can nontraditional formats coexist with traditional ones?

- What is the role of the dissertation in the employment marketplace?

- What cultural and disciplinary barriers exist to rethinking the dissertation? (p. 1)

The Council of Graduate Schools (2016) underscored this concept: "The ecosystem of the dissertation is changing, as it is for scholarship in general, including the ubiquity of big data, wide and instantaneous dissemination of research, and shifting funding models" (p. 2). In the following sections, I highlight the manuscript dissertation and dissertation innovations in the social and educational sciences that draw on the arts.

Manuscript Dissertations

In the United States since the 1980s, there has been discussion and an increased acceptance of what is termed at times as a *manuscript dissertation* (Freeman, 2018). The thought behind this major change in a dissertation's content is that manuscripts in hand allow a recent doctoral graduate to convert their dissertation into a scholarly publication in a more seamless and timely fashion. The manuscript dissertation is variously termed a *manuscript dissertation* (Anderson et al., 2021) or, as compiled by Freeman (2018), a *publication-based thesis* (Sharmini et al., 2015), a *PhD by publication* (Butt, 2013), a *PhD by published work* (Badley, 2009), or a *paper-based thesis* (Pretorius, 2016). It is important to note that the major difference potentially seen within these types of dissertation is if any of the manuscripts must be *published* prior to graduation or if they more realistically must be deemed *publishable* by the dissertation committee.

Freeman (2018) defines the manuscript dissertation as "characterized as a lengthy, scholarly document that includes multiple published or publication-ready research articles" (p. 276)]. Practically speaking, this document may still be as long as the traditional dissertation, with an opening and an ending chapter and two to three manuscripts as the middle part of the document.

The manuscripts may be the result of empirical research, or one of the three manuscripts may be a literature review piece developed from the traditional Chapter 2 literature review. I want to note that while some seem not to value a literature review–type article for tenure and promotion purposes, it is obvious that we all find them invaluable when we are looking to update an area of research literature we are working on in a timely fashion. Along with the three-manuscript model, I am also familiar with a two-manuscript dissertation and a daunting model where, after writing the entire traditional dissertation, a manuscript developed from the dissertation forms an appendix or the final chapter.

I suggest that if you are writing a manuscript dissertation each manuscript be developed with a particular journal in mind. When you have determined the best journal outlet for your work, meet with your advisor to get their input. Then, find the submission guide and follow it carefully as you format. I ask my students to reference each guide or place them in the appendices so committee members who are not familiar with the journals have easy access to the journal requirements.

Innovative Dissertations

The true sign of intelligence is not knowledge but imagination.

—Albert Einstein

Summarizing two days of workshops dedicated to promoting thinking and discussion around the future of the dissertation, the Council of Graduate Schools (2016) wrote,

> The traditional American scientific dissertation was likened to the internal combustion engine. It has served us well. . . . Innovative and revolutionary . . . a powerful force for scientific research and industrialization from 1860 . . . it is being overtaken by other energy sources. (p. 2)

(See https://twitter.com/hashtag/dissfwd for the Twitter conversations from the meeting.)

Multiple recommendations for innovations to the dissertation were generated from this meeting—community projects, articles, essays, ensemble dissertations, teaching innovations, dissertations in practice, translation, visual mapping, curation, and tool building—to which I would add artistic areas such as performative scripts, videos, image compilations, music, art, visuals, poetry, and so on.

I am not personally calling for completely ridding ourselves of the traditional dissertation. It is clear to me from working in a department that includes statisticians and quantitative methodologists that the traditional form is valuable to many scholars and works well as a format to feature their research. However, this is not the case for some qualitative researchers in the humanities and the social and educational sciences.

Change can be slow, so you may wish to consider incorporating elements of innovation within the larger dissertation document. R. David Johns's dissertation (2014) is an excellent example of this. Johns's dissertation committee consisted of professors with both qualitative and quantitative research expertise, who were supportive of this combination. The resulting document included a thematic presentation of in-depth interviews and research poetry developed from the transcriptions. Johns then went on to publish an article about the research (Johns, 2017a) and a separate article about the research poetry and the process of creating research poetry in top qualitative journals (e.g., Johns, 2017b). Clearly, the final outcome of Johns's dissertation experience is ideal and may be an exception. In the following sections, I will briefly highlight just a few examples of innovative dissertations that draw from the arts. (See Four Arrows, aka Jacobs, 2008, for an entire textbook dedicated to innovative "authentic" qualitative dissertations from an Indigenous perspective, which explores dissertations as a potentially spiritual process beyond what I present here.)

Music. *Laura Beer (2012) created a dissertation where she composed music to represent the researched and the researcher's experiences, which she later described in the article she published from the dissertation:*

> [Innovative] formats have opened doors to re-inventions of traditional thick, rich descriptions and provided living, intentional metaphors through which a reader can filter data via their own emotional, cognitive, spiritual, and scholarly lenses. Music, however, is one area that has been minimally used as an approach to mining and re/presenting data. This piece explores the use of music in a qualitative research project. My intention is to initiate a conversation on how music can capture both participant and researcher experiences in a way that naturally challenges words, thoughts, reactions, and assumptions. (p. 1)

As someone who had the privilege to attend the dissertation defense, the representation of the data and the resulting conversation were powerful. Innovations in this area of representation will not be without new challenges, and one that I wondered about at the time was how a larger audience would access the music. The university did not support hyperlinks within dissertations at that time. It is of note that the journal where the findings were published *did* support hyperlinks to the music, but at the time of this writing the links seem to be broken.

A more recent example of musical representation of data may be seen in Carson's hip hop album titled *Owning My Masters: The Rhetorics of Rhymes and Revolutions* and an accompanying dissertation (Carson, 2017). When asked how he would defend a rap dissertation representation, Carson answered that the defense is the same as the reasoning used for the study of different forms of literature: "for empathy—so that we have ways into worlds that we don't fully understand" (Young & Martin, 2017). This is the powerful argument behind artistic innovations in research. Given the recent publication of his dissertation, Carson was able to make the music representation available on Sound Cloud (https://soundcloud.com/adcarson).

Art. *Lindsay Beddes (2017) conducted a dissertation in which she employed art at several levels. Participants were given time in an art studio with a professional artist to represent their experience. Beddes, also a professional artist, observed the art sessions and did some consultation. After all the data were collected and as part of the analysis, Beddes created an art portrait of the participant who accompanied the prose portrait. In Beddes's words,*

> For each participant portrait, I engaged in a creative and contemplative process of drawing or painting to discover the aesthetic meaning present for me in that subset of the data. Once I had a visual representation formed for a participant, I returned to the data and used the aesthetic information I created in the visual representations to further interpret the findings. The visual portraits that I created for each participant were included in the open gallery and are presented with the written portraits as inseparable components of the findings. (p. 71)

I appreciate Beddes allowing me to include a series of portraits so that readers can follow her process. The portrait of "Berna" (see Figure 4.3) reflects her experiences with transformative justice and in particular a case where a man under the influence of alcohol disabled a woman during a car wreck. As part of the transformative justice process, the woman asked for a bouquet of flowers from the man. The man then went on to give her flowers once a year for several years on the date of the wreck. Berna, consulting with the studio director and Beddes, created flowers out of license plates (see Figure 4.4).

Poetry. *As part of a dissertation on content area literacy, Veronica Richard (2010) created poetry that combined participants' words with images they had chosen from a black-and-white image photo bank. The images represented metaphors about their preservice teaching experiences. Richard went on to publish an article on the dissertation process that termed the poetry as graphic portraits (Richard & Lahman, 2015; see Figures 8.3 and 8.4 in Chapter 8).*

Writing about the dissertation process, Richard (2010) said, "In addition to chronicling and coding the research texts for themes, I also created at least

FIGURE 4.3 ● "Berna," a Visual Portrait

Note: 16" × 20" oil painting on canvas.

Source: Reproduced with permission from Lindsay Beddes.

FIGURE 4.4 ● "Harm Transformed," a Progression of Art Created by Berna

Note: Mixed media: wire and aluminum.

Source: Reproduced with permission from Lindsay Beddes.

one research poem for each theme" (p. 137). Describing the poetry process, Richard wrote,

> Using the language of the participant provided an "exploration of the lived experience" and enhanced the findings of the narrative interview (Furman, 2006, p. 562). Because poetry made new configurations of words, it allowed the reader to see, hear, and feel the world in a new dimension. Thus, research poetry is "a practical and powerful method for analyzing social worlds" (Richardson, 2000, p. 933). In writing the research poems for this study, I chose phrases and words that created a rhythm and flow to highlight the emotional and lived experiences of the participants. (Butler-Kisber, 2010, p. 129)

Performances. *Katrina Rodriguez (2004), in a compelling dissertation combining interview and focus group with discussions the participants had about a painting where two comadres leaned across a fence chatting, wrote,*

> Hearing the voices of those who embody multiple subjectivities is critical in making a space for research participants to be agents and co-creators of knowledge. As a method of placing Latinas at the center of the study, a performance text, in the form of a dramatic script, is created to illuminate participant's life histories and college experiences. . . .
>
> Findings relating to Latina college students' perceptions of the body politic through the lens of ethnicity, class, and gender emerge through a process of braiding, combing, and rebraiding strands of data through both researcher and participant lenses. (p. iv)

The following is an excerpt from the focus group data discussion about the painting (published in an article by Rodriguez et al., 2011):

Elizabeth:	Mario, this is the picture you call "Las Comadres," right?
Mario:	Yes.
Jo:	I read that you were happy that "Las Comadres" doesn't have an English translation.
Mario:	That's right.
Yesy [restating]:	It really doesn't have a translation [trying to explain the concept of *comadre*]. My dad has a *comadre* . . . do I say, "friend"?
Katrina:	It's not an ordinary friendship though. A *comadre* is respected as a sister, and you share the deepest secrets with her even though she isn't a true blood sister. It's a commitment to friends who are like sisters.

Angelica:	Mario, so what's their story? The women in the picture?
Elizabeth [her eyes shining brightly]:	He'll probably tell us they're spreading rumors.
Jo [agreeing with a sly smile]:	Yeah, *chismas.*
Leneise:	Okay Mario, are you going to tell us?
Mario:	Nope. I'm not going to reveal the story until tonight.
Yesy:	Maybe it's about their work; they have a basket full of towels.
Jo [pointing to the picture]:	She has a baby on her back.
Elizabeth:	They are hard workers. How do you say? They are traditional. She has her long hair in a braid, apron, and a baby on her back.
Yesy:	The colors say something; they are not bold, but they stick out. They set the scene.
Katrina:	It's like the sunflowers are . . . listening?

Graphic. *A recent innovation may be seen in the area of graphic dissertations or comic dissertations. Research topics about graphic novels have been growing, but in this case, I mean the dissertation itself is represented through graphics. Of this, Paul Kuttner and colleagues (2020) write, "In recent years, this interest has taken a methodological turn, with scholars integrating comics creation into the research process itself" (p. 195). In their work, the researchers "document this emerging, interdisciplinary field of methodological practice" and go on to "lay out key affordances that comics offer researchers across the disciplines, arguing that certain characteristics—multimodality, blending of sequential and simultaneous communication, emphasis on creator voice—afford power-ful tools for inquiry" (p. 195). I strongly recommend reading the researchers' article and handbook chapter (Kuttner et al. 2017). I feature Nick Sousanis's dissertation here.*

On the back cover of the book based on his dissertation, Sousanis (2015) wrote,

> *Unflattening* is an insurrection against the fixed viewpoint. Weaving together diverse ways of seeing drawn from science, philosophy, art, literature, and mythology, it uses the collage-like capacity of comics to show that perception is always an active process of incorporating and reevaluating different vantage points. While its vibrant, constantly morphing images occasionally serve as illustrations of text, they more often connect in nonlinear fashion to other visual references throughout the book.

In another deeply engaging example, Megan Parker (2017) created an over 200-page thesis titled *Art Teacher in Process: An Illustrated Exploration of Art, Education, and What Matters*. The research was part autoethnography and partly an inquiry into the meaning that occurred when making and studying art in a public school classroom. Parker's thesis is represented as a graphic novel. Parker reported that while the university was highly supportive there were some negative comments on social media along the lines of "Anyone including my child can do this or get a master's" and "Get your crayons out for a master's" (Goodyear, 2018). The lack of understanding of the perception, intent, and skill it takes to represent a complex experience graphically is unfortunate. For readers of this volume, Parker has graciously allowed several graphics from her thesis to be reprinted here. See Figure 4.5, which fits the process and politics of the dissertation section of this chapter well, and Figure 7.1 in Chapter 7, which captures autoethnographic reflexivity.

Qualitative researchers will in all likelihood immediately recognize the powerful ways in which graphics convey research data to readers, yet one will need to conceive of ways to defend the choice of graphics to some audiences. A review of the literature around communication through visual images (see Chapter 9 of this book) and discussion in the dissertation will go a long way to convince detractors that color and images catch and keep attention and help us recall information.

FIGURE 4.5 ● Reflection Is Hard

Note: From Parker (2017).

Medley. *Assemblage, assortment, compilation, hodge-podge, hotchpotch, min-*
gling, montage, mélange, mash-up, mosaic, mosh, pastiche, quilt, tableau

An exciting area of innovation is when varied representations are drawn
together to form a whole or what I am calling a *medley*. I frame the outset of
this section with words that are synonyms of "medley" and may provide readers with additional nuances. "Medley" is a term that readers may associate with
music, but the more general definition is "varied mixtures of people or things; a
miscellany" (Lexico, n.d.). "Medley" has a connotation that the end result will
please the creator and the audience in some manner. In this case, it seems to
me that the pleasure would be through a deeper or new sense of knowing. The
whole may have a unified and seamless appearance that the author constructs
or may be jagged and dissonant to represent the complexities and unfinished
questions of the study. The author may smooth out the final representation
or leave the edges rough to signal a postmodern sense of understanding being
ongoing, a becoming, or to allow readers to make their own personal constructions (e.g., Ely, 2007). The word "hotchpotch" (related to "hodgepodge"), for
instance, originates from a thick soup that was made from many ingredients
but today may be used in reference to any heterogeneous mixture (Merriam-
Webster, n.d.-c). Ely (2007), writing under the term "pastiche", : described this
style of representation as a battle against linearity: "Pastiche is the product
of textual experiments that seek to challenge linear simplistic descriptions of
meaning" (p. 586). Unlike how these descriptive words might seem at first
thought, this choice of representation is intentional, thoughtful, and reflexive.

Christen Garcia's (2018) recent dissertation is an excellent example of these
sorts of evocative texts set to beguile and bewilder the reader. In the words
of Garcia, the dissertation employs "pragmatic and poetic text and image to
reflect on experiences of multiplicity, intersection, and the undervisible merg-
ing spaces of the borderlands" (p. 73). Garcia goes on to write in the abstract (I
added the italics for emphasis),

For this study, I employ a methodology of *borderlands art practice,*
a practice-based research that addresses border artist practices and
undervisible borderlands spaces. *I engage in practices of making food,*
images, video/GIFs, and performative writing. Next, I use theories and
concepts that emerged from the art and performative processes as well
as the disciplines of food, public, and border pedagogies *to create an*
uncertain art pedagogy. A multiplicitous mass of doings emerged from
this study that performed the borderlands of identity, race/ethnicity,
authenticity, and hybrid and impure food practices of the in-between.
The visual and performative outcome of this study is fragmented,
ambiguous, uncertain, and ambivalent. These processes sit on the
borderlands of art education and are comfortable with liminality and
uncertainty. . . . This dissertation occupies an uncertain discipline space
in-between art, art education, Chicana/o and Latina/o studies, and food
studies. Neither fully art, art education, food nor Chicana/o/Latina/o

studies, this study is what queer Chicana writer and feminist theorist Gloria Anzaldúa describes as a borderland, "a vague and undetermined place." (p. iii)

Katherine Brown (2018) used the word "assemblage" to describe the methods she drew on for research and creating representations. In this research, the assemblage was specifically around the grief and potential healing she experienced with the death of her mother:

> I used photo-text to illustrate how the grief assemblage is becoming a healing assemblage. Just as the assemblage collapses, folds, vibrates, and performs constant movements, I found myself assembling, dismantling, and re-assembling the data into various configurations which culminated in the alternating pages of photographs and text as I conversed with my mother and all the other forces in the assemblage. I found that I am performing healing as I continue to move with the assemblage (p. vi).

These innovative researchers who have artistically informed dissertations are just a sample of the possibilities. As A. D. Carson (2017) stated, varied representations allow researchers and readers to understand the world and the people in it in new and vital ways. This area is burgeoning, and the potential is as vast as the array of people we conduct research with and as deep as our willingness to always push ourselves to be "becoming."

The Gist

Writing . . . is like driving a car at night. You can only see as far as your headlights, but you can make the whole trip that way.

—E. L. Doctorow (in Plimpton, 1986)

In this chapter, I reviewed representations, both traditional and innovative, of the destination the long journey of writing a dissertation finally arrives at. Readers will want to review the questions they need to ask themselves and the resources I have listed in the following sections since there is no doubt that the dissertation is a journey of such a particularly intense and long-term nature that it is best not to make it without rich and varied support. An important aspect of successfully finishing is understanding that the doctoral degree does not necessarily go to the most brilliant but instead is earned by the most persistent. This is not to say that exceptional ideas and research are not the hallmarks of doctoral work, but something more is needed, such as grit, resilience, or passion, in order to be *Phinishe*D!

Reflexive Questions

1. What are your primary goals in writing a dissertation?

   - Which of these goals are deal breakers (as in you *must* achieve this goal)? For example, in my case, I felt I needed to research children in a school setting using solely qualitative methods and let go of other ideas that were also important to me.

   - Which goals can you let go of if need be? This is a really tough question, but recall that achieving the PhD opens up many possibilities for future research, so ideas you have now may be acted on later.

2. What form might your dissertation take?

3. Will your department accept manuscript dissertations?

   - If so, is this a good choice for your research?

   - What types of manuscripts might you develop?

   - Which journals would be the most appropriate and reasonable outlets for your dissertation research?

4. Will your department accept innovative dissertations?

   - If so, will an innovative dissertation impede your future job success?

   - If so, what might the department consider to be innovative?

   - If not, can you add elements that are innovative within the larger document? For example, committees may allow the addition of research poetry to a larger thematic qualitative dissertation.

5. Are you familiar with the graduate school and its procedures and timelines?

6. What types of communications have you signed up to receive about the doctoral process at your institution?

7. Where are you at in the dissertation process?

   - What are the next steps that are vital in this process?

   - What timelines and policies do you need to be aware of?

8. Have you attended an oral (proposal) and the final dissertation meeting?

9. Have you had an opportunity to review the dissertations your advisor and other students recommended?

10. Is there a strength you have that you could bring to an innovative dissertation? For example, are you a graphic artist, artist, photographer, poet, musician, or dancer? Also, maybe like me

you have an interest in an area that you have not been able to fully develop. I had some minimal training in poetry, but I have a deep interest in it that I have developed to incorporate into my scholarship. Innovation is not restricted to professionals. See my discussion of good enough and "-ish" in Chapter 7, where I call for a safe space for research scholars to draw on artistic forms without being professional artists.

Resources

Literature Reviews

Pan, M. L. (2016). *Preparing literature reviews: Qualitative and quantitative approaches*. Routledge. https://doi.org/10.4324/9781315265872

Ridley, D. (2012). *The literature review: A step-by-step guide for students*. Sage.

Innovative Dissertations

Council of Graduate Schools. (n.d.). *Additional resources, the future of the dissertation*. https://cgsnet.org/additional-resources-future-dissertation

Polanco, M. (2013). Democratizing academic writing: A revision of an experience of writing an autoethnographic dissertation in color. *The Qualitative Report, 18*(17), 1–17.

Websites

Dissertation Recipes: http://www.dissertationrecipes.com/

The authors of this website also have a textbook:

Simon, M. K., & Goes, J. (2011). *Dissertation and scholarly research: Recipes for success*. Dissertation Success.

Purdue OWL: https://owl.purdue.edu/owl/purdue_owl.html

This web resource has writing support that can span the course of your career from general to specific style support, writing genres such as a dissertation or job talk, and short guides in all areas of scholarly writing.

The Writing Center: https://writingcenter.unc.edu/tips-and-tools/dissertations/

Internet Humor

The following links provide a well-needed sense of release and perspective. As you can tell from the joke bubbles I have inserted throughout the textbook representing different genres of jokes in Western culture, I think that levity needs to be a part of the dissertation- and research-writing process. However, a word of caution: As with any outlet that allows us to destress or vent about the frustrating experiences involved in the dissertation process, much of this sort of thing may become a distraction or, even worse, an excuse for not surmounting the obstacles that occur in a doctoral program.

Lego Grad Student: https://brickademics.com/; @legogradstudent

PHD COMICS: http://phdcomics.com/; @PHDcomics

The Thesis Whisperer: https://thesiswhisperer.com/about/; @thesiswhisperer

Dissertation Textbooks

Biklen, S. K., & Casella, R. (2007). *A practical guide to qualitative dissertation*. Teachers College Press.

Bloomberg, L. D., & Volpe, M. (2018). *Completing your qualitative dissertation: A road map from beginning to end*. Sage.

Jacobs, D. T. (2009). *The authentic dissertation: Alternative ways of knowing, research and representation*. Routledge. https://doi.org/10.4324/978020 3870501

Meloy, J. M. (2001). *Writing the qualitative dissertation: Understanding by doing*. Psychology Press. https://doi.org/10.4324/9781410602695

Piantanida, M., & Garman, N. B. (Eds.). (2009). *The qualitative dissertation: A guide for students and faculty*. Corwin Press.

Innovations in Dissertations

Council of Graduate Schools. (2016, September 21). *Dissertation forward: Rethinking the PhD thesis*. YouTube. https://www.youtube.com/watch?v= VElB_2kQqRc&feature=youtu.be

Jacobs, D. T. (2009). *The authentic dissertation: Alternative ways of knowing, research and representation*. Routledge. https://doi.org/10.4324/978020 3870501

Imagining the Dissertation's Many Futures: http://cgsnet.org/gradedge-march-2016

Unflattening Harvard UPress: http://spinweaveandcut.com/unflattening-harvard-upress/

Dissertation Competition and Awards

American Education Research Association Qualitative Significant Interest Group: Qualitative Research SIG 82 Outstanding Dissertation Award: http://www.aera.net/SIG082/Qualitative-Research-SIG-82

Dance Your Dissertation Contest: http://www.sciencemag.org/news/2017/11/announcing-winner-year-s-dance-your-phd-contest

International Congress of Qualitative Inquiry Dissertation Award: https://icqi.org/dissertation-awards/

Reflexive Course Activities

Set Goals and General To-Do Lists

From where you are at currently in the dissertation process, set specific goals for moving toward the next step. For example, if you have not finished comprehensive examinations yet, have you attended an oral or proposal meeting (defense)? Try to attend ones in your discipline area and with committee members who are on your committee or you hope might be on your committee. Check to see if your department has a to-do checklist. My department has a checklist, and I am familiar with other departments or even professors who use these to help guide students.

Dissertation Table of Contents

If you have not written a dissertation proposal yet, write a draft of the ToC. First, review several dissertations your chair and committee members have recommended, look at the style guide set forth by your graduate school, and use these as templates to create the ToC for your proposal. When the time is appropriate, set a meeting with your chair to review a draft of this ToC.

Library Resources

What resources are available at your institution's library? The university I work at has hard copy as well as virtual library guides, along with specialty librarians who hold PhDs and offer invaluable support to doctoral students and professors who seek out their help. The librarians organize general research information sessions on topics such as how to use reference organizer software and dissertation-specific topics.

Review of Dissertations That Utilize Innovative Representations

Choose a dissertation from the list provided or one that you have identified for review. Then, dip into the dissertation, and consider the possibilities it presents for your work.

Authoethnography

Gonzalez, M. (2013). *¡Si se puede! First-generation, Latino immigrant college success stories: A transformative autoethnographic study* (Publication No. 3588557) [Doctoral dissertation, University of Northern Colorado]. ProQuest Dissertations and Theses Global.

Composed Music

Beer, L. E. (2012). *"It was beautiful, but it wasn't supposed to be there": Spirituality in the work lives of higher education administrative leaders* (Publication No. 3523413) [Doctoral dissertation, University of Northern Colorado]. ProQuest Dissertations and Theses Global.

Graphic or Comic Novel

Parker, M. (2017). *Art teacher in process: An illustrated exploration of art, education and what matters* [Master's thesis, Simon Fraser University]. Simon Fraser University Summit. http://summit.sfu.ca/item/17806

Sousanis, W. N. (2014). *Unflattening: A visual-verbal inquiry into learning in many dimensions* (Publication No. 3622816) [Doctoral dissertation, Columbia University]. ProQuest Dissertations and Theses Global.

Multiple Artistic Elements

Heise, K. S. (2003). *Depending on the light: Writing my change in sexual orientation* (Publication No. 1417251) [Doctoral dissertation, University of Northern Colorado]. ProQuest Dissertations and Theses Global.

Performative

Rodriguez, K. L. (2004). *Las comadres: Cuentame su historia: Latina college students make meaning of the body politic* (Publication No. 3130541) [Doctoral dissertation, University of Northern Colorado]. ProQuest Dissertations and Theses Global.

Research Poetry

Johns, R. D. (2014). *Narratives of competency, creativity, and comfort: Religion and spirituality in counselor education* (Publication No. 3687922) [Doctoral dissertation, University of Northern Colorado]. ProQuest Dissertations and Theses Global.

Writing the Qualitative Journal Article: Of Rice Cakes, Tortillas, Bread, and Butter

Don't quarrel with your bread and butter.

—Dostoyevsky (1866/1950, p. 29)

Depending on what brought you to qualitative research, this chapter will either be a much-valued resource or make you impatient and consider skipping the chapter altogether. Writing is deeply personal, and norms for "scientific" writing have changed dramatically over the past few decades. "Postmodernist critiques of traditional qualitative writing practices have resulted in the emergence of incredible diversity in representation" (Merriam & Tisdell, 2016, p. 268). Traditional qualitative writing practices are exemplified in the basic thematic journal article, which reports research findings in a series of major themes identified in the data. I refer to basic thematic research as essential qualitative research. Throughout this book, I detail multiple forms of research representation, including dissertations, thematic journal articles, methodological articles, autoethnographies, research poetry, graphics, installations, music, collage, art, and photos. Yet I find both this chapter (on writing a thematic journal article) and Chapter 4 (on writing dissertations) to be the most important for novice researchers. Why? Because as Picasso said, "Learn the rules like a pro, so you can break them like an artist."

What might Picasso's advice mean to us as writers? In part, we need to be finishers. I always have research and writing ideas storming around my mind, yet I found I was not what I think of as a finisher. I was never *done*! The next idea had already appeared and taken over just when I needed the discipline to focus on the research writing at hand. I was great at *conducting* research but not at *publishing* it. Recall that Wolcott (2009) sets out a strong injunction: "There is no such thing as *unreported* research" (p. 163). My maturation as a research writer occurred when I learned how to finish rewriting and not view rewrites as tedious. Instead, I began to appreciate rewriting as a time to hone my thoughts and craft.

When I wrote my first research ethics request (to the IRB), it was boring, and the document was intimidating. I wanted to get to the fun part—research with real people and creatively writing it up. Nothing I took pleasure in—how research with children is different from that with adults or novel ways to represent research experiences—was a part of this process. I had the same tedious experience when I wrote my dissertation proposal. Now, I advise people that after they understand the rules of research, after data are analyzed, and perhaps, for some of us, after we graduate or gain tenure, we can begin to bend the rules— even break rules—as we represent the research findings. I do not mean breaking ethics, morals, field quality standards, or funding obligations. I mean reintroducing higher education to ways of knowing and representing that have been lost to us in the quest for objectivity—the senses, humor, indigenous experience, metaphysical understandings, spirituality, religion, raw reflexivity (see Chapter 10), art, and literary writers' deep understanding of how to convey an experience.

But to get there, I believe you must know how to write the qualitative thematic research article. This ability may be what helps you secure a research assistantship, a first professor position, or tenure. The thematic qualitative article, which consists of the representation of a thematic analysis of data, is the "bread and butter" of the field—rice, the dominant staple in the world; tortillas, which outsell white bread in the United States; or whatever staple is yours (e.g., corn bread, injera, naan, bagel, chapati, crepe, lavash, ugali, bean bread, or the U.S. southern biscuit). The thematic article is a scholar's initial sustenance, which helps feed their continued work. If you choose to move from the basic first recipe at some point, these guidelines will be the foundation from which you work. What does this staple need? Grain and some sort of moisture (e.g., water, butter, oil, milk)—data, analysis, and some form of representation. Choices of salt or leavening, what types and amounts will change the end result in rich ways. So let's get baking!

In this chapter, I address the following:

- Creating a plan for organization *before* the formal writing
- How to write the basic thematic qualitative research article, including the
  - title, abstract, and keywords;
  - introduction;

- o   literature review;

- o   methodology;

- o   thematic analysis;

- o   research findings; and

- o   discussion and conclusion

- Naming participants in manuscripts

- The qualitative methodological article—challenging more qualitative researchers to engage in this type of representation

- Predatory publishers

- Research poster creation (see Text Box 5.3)

- Resources, including lists of qualitative-friendly journals

- Reflexive questions

- Reflexive activities to extend readers' understanding

Before the Formal Writing

Before the formal writing begins, you can take several steps to make the writing process more organized. This will help you avoid staring at an empty Word document on your computer screen—a sure way to make any writer take a break from writing too early. Try one or more of these ideas:

- Create a manuscript file by copying and pasting anything you have already written that might be related to the study into a computer file under subheadings for your manuscript.

- Create a working title for the manuscript.

- Write the working abstract and select the keywords.

- Determine the audience(s) you are writing for.

- Conduct a journal review to create a list of three journals to send the manuscript to. Submit it to only one journal at a time.

In the following sections, I review these steps in detail.

Create a Manuscript Computer File

Staring at a blank document can make the writing process more intimidating than it should be. As a prewriting activity, collect everything you have written related to the final manuscript, and paste it all into a computer file. These sections may be from your research ethics application (e.g., to the IRB), a grant you wrote, or perhaps a proposal. Elements to look for include the research question, the initial literature review, the methodology section, and references. Create headings and subheadings for the manuscript, and paste your writing in the appropriate areas.

Titles, Abstracts, and Keywords, Oh My!

I do not recall receiving any instruction on writing titles, abstracts, or keywords during my higher education degrees. While this is never good for a budding scholar, in the digital era, not knowing how to write these small yet powerful parts of an article could make the difference between your publication languishing and it being cited and utilized. The following are guidelines to write your manuscript's title, abstract, and keywords *before* writing the manuscript. Our natural inclination is to write these items last, after the manuscript is complete. I advise you to write these organizing features *first* as a strategy to ensure the backbone of the manuscript is strong—without ideas unrelated to the theme. If you cannot write the abstract at this point, the manuscript will have a fundamental issue of coherence.

Titles

A compelling title should clearly and concisely convey the contents of your research manuscript. Consider the study's research question(s). Using the major constructs in the research question(s), write a first draft of the title summing up what the manuscript is about. The first version of the title may be laborious, but it is enough to work with for now. A great way to check the effectiveness of the title is to ask someone who is not familiar with your research to read it. Does the title make sense when it stands alone, requiring no additional explanation?

Acronyms and other abbreviations should not be used in titles, which complicates my next point—don't create a lengthy title. Qualitative titles already tend to be long since qualitative researchers endeavor to write "catchy, clever titles" (Zeller & Farmer, 1999). A lengthy title is effective if you add a phrase comprising data from a transcript or observation that either sums up the study or gets at a lingering question as a subtitle. This puts the reader immediately in the data at the outset of the manuscript while demonstrating your respect for the participants' words and experiences over your own scholarly academic prose. One way to shorten titles is to avoid unnecessary phrases—for example, "One Doctoral Student's Examination," "A Qualitative Exploration," or "A Case Study." These phrases can be included in the abstract, which will allow readers to conduct a methodological search. For example, what if someone wants to read examples of case studies in education? These words should be in the abstract to highlight methods, but there is no need for them to appear in the title.

While qualitative research writers are challenged to draw on the nonfiction arts to create lifelike accounts, avoid being "cute" at the expense of your research. We are generally researchers first, drawing on the arts second. I crafted the title of this section as "Titles and Abstracts and Keywords, Oh, My!" for the purpose of consideration. Does this title work for you? I believe it works to use titles in a book that allude to the broader culture, but sparingly. I also wanted to ensure that readers would glance at this section, even if initially out of disdain. This section contains essential information that some still see as insignificant. A potential problem with this title for a serious research article is that the allusion to *The Wizard of Oz* is overused to the extent that some would call it hackneyed or too cute. But as worded, the title conveys the contents of this section.

Academics will not agree on this topic. For example, a text box title in my book on research ethics reads, "Look Ma, No Hands!: Ethics Go Mobile." One reviewer said it was condescending; others appreciated it as lighthearted. The takeaway point is this: Don't sacrifice someone engaging with your research seriously for a "catchy," clever title that might just be cute. The only time I would completely break with this advice is if a participant is being quoted. When we speak, we do use multiple metaphors, cultural allusions, and "cute" comments. If a quote from the data sums up the research in a profound or thought-provoking way, the title might be the very place for it.

General Tips. Consider the following when developing titles:

- The title should convey the research question when read on its own.

- Keywords and phrases should occur naturally in the title.

- The title should indicate who the participants are as precisely as possible (e.g., mothers, women, Latina youth).

- Do not use acronyms or abbreviations.

Abstracts

A well-written abstract serves many purposes. It allows readers to find your research efficiently through search engines. Crafting elements of your research manuscript to respond well to an internet search is referred to as search engine optimization. SAGE Publishing reports that readers will usually not look past the first 50 articles they summon. An abstract gets to the essence of the research efficiently so busy readers do not waste their time. A well-written abstract is like the summary on the back of a book cover, an engaging elevator pitch, an enticing display for a window shopper, or the honed pitch given at a job interview.

Write the abstract before writing the manuscript. Rewrite as needed throughout the manuscript creation and during the final check before submitting it for publication. Writing the abstract first will give writers a sense of focus and may be uplifting. If you are coauthoring, each line of the abstract can serve as part of the coauthor agreement—Author 1 is writing the first draft of the literature review, Author 2 the methodology, and so on.

Parts of an Abstract. *The parts of an abstract reflect the parts of the manuscript. State the issue you explored through the research and why readers should care about it. This is answering the "so what?" question. This section may include a restatement of the major research question. Concisely explain the methodology, including the theoretical framework (which is commonly overlooked) and the corpus of the data (e.g., how many interviews/how long). Some potential readers will conduct searches to find examples of research from a specific theoretical perspective, so leaving this out is a missed opportunity to highlight theory. Finish the abstract with the findings and implications; state each finding in one word or phrase so they are searchable.*

Abstracts are generally 100 to 250 words in length. Check the requirements of the conference or journal you are submitting to. The guidelines will be clear, and sometimes failure to follow the word limit is a reason for rejecting the work. Online forms may not take abstracts with words above the limit.

Third Person and Past Tense. *The abstract is the only place where I recommend writing in the third person—using terms like the author and the researcher instead of I. Third-person prose reads as though the editor of the journal has composed the abstract, featuring and promoting the research. It is one of the few parts of any article that people can access for free. After the research is conducted, it is generally written in the past tense since the study is over. An exception—the ethnographic present—is deliberately chosen to place the reader in the middle of action that occurred during the study. Present tense causes these types of written scenes to be more lifelike.*

Abstract Template. *Feel free to modify this template for your own abstracts (there is no need to cite me):*

> Through in-depth interviews, the author explored mothering during the COVID-19 pandemic. Ten interviews were conducted with professional women, who were also mothers, who began working at home full-time due to the pandemic. While the literature is abundant in the areas of mothers who work out of the home, the unique nature of professional mothers working at home has not been deeply explored. Findings and implications in the areas of transitions, home–work boundaries, a sense of the unknown, and increased family time are highlighted.

General Tips. *The following will help you write professional abstracts:*

- Write in the third person.
- Utilize active verbs when possible.
- Avoid jargon or colloquialisms. You are writing for as broad an audience as possible.
- Repeat key constructs and phrases naturally.

- Write in complete sentences.

- Do not use citations.

Keywords

Keywords are placed below the abstract and used in a search for your article. There are generally three to seven keywords. The term "keywords" is a bit of a misnomer since they are often actually key phrases—*narrative inquiry, child development,* and so on. Carefully chosen keywords are an essential part of search engine optimization. Some journals will have a list of commonly used keywords you can choose from. However, if you are working in a cutting-edge area, you may still need to supply your own keywords. Consider how you search for articles. At times, you may choose to use a keyword search. If you are unsure which ones to choose, look at the title, abstract, areas of findings, and headings in your manuscript. What are the major words that should be placed as keywords? Some of them will be the same words or phrases you searched during the manuscript's literature review. What methodological words could be included? If you are allowed enough keywords, could the name of the theory be added? Once you have a list of keywords, run any of them you have not searched before through a search engine, and see if they summon the research literature you think fits your manuscript best. For areas that seem new or unfamiliar, your research librarian can be invaluable in suggesting keywords.

General Tips. *Use the following tips to maximize your selection of keywords:*

- Keywords can be single words or phrases (e.g., *children, Latinx youth, tennis players*).

- Include variations (e.g., *adolescents, minors, youth*)

- Place keywords naturally in the manuscript's title and abstract.

- When submitting your manuscript, some journals will suggest keywords.

- Place them below the abstract.

- Generally, three to seven keywords are used.

- They are presented in alphabetical order.

Titles, abstracts, and keywords are not solely the outcome of a creative process. The digital era has moved us firmly into needing to balance natural readability, an on-point message, and utilization of search engines. Think of how good it feels, as a researcher, to efficiently identify the literature you need. As an author, you are helping design the same experience for potential readers, while maximizing the impact of the research participants' and your own hard work.

Who Is Your Intended Audience?

Before you start writing, determine who your audience is. Do you plan to use your data to write more than one manuscript? Different manuscripts may have different audiences. Each manuscript must be a unique contribution; publishing multiple variations of the same work is considered unethical. A caveat here: Some excellent research writers do not agree with the concept of determining your audience. "One of the myths of academic writing is that it should address a specific audience. Nothing could be more wrong" (Czarniawska, 2008, p. 17). Instead, some believe you should feel an allegiance to writing how you wish to be read and for the broadest audience possible. I appreciate this perspective and have had writing published that was written this way. However, when I was a novice researcher, thinking through "the audience" was an important step in providing focus and keeping me from becoming overwhelmed. I often did not have a full sense of the different audiences that existed—for instance, the difference between publishing for a broad general qualitative audience and a field-specific audience representing all types of research methodology.

The type of manuscript you are writing—research, methodological, review of the literature, art informed, practitioner—helps determine the audience. There will, of course, be overlap between audiences. Research professors read practitioner reports, and all readers access literature review articles for various reasons. Possible audience members include researchers, instructors, government officials/policymakers, practitioners in the field (e.g., clinicians, principals), journalists, and your university community. Determining a general sense of the audience will help guide your journal choice.

Choosing a Journal

The advice I give that is the least followed is to identify the journal you will submit your manuscript to *before* writing. Heeding this advice achieves two things: (1) you will review more qualitative articles in your field and be familiar with what research is published and written and (2) you will save valuable time (including the time of the journal's staff) by not submitting to poorly matched journals.

Identifying a journal is not the same as conducting a literature review. Instead, it is a review of which journals in your academic field accept qualitative research submissions and what the editorial board of each journal believes constitutes "qualitative research." The field of qualitative research has many voices describing what it is. A great place to start the review is the journal's website. There you can read sections like *About This Journal* and *Aims and Scope* and browse the abstracts of current issues, online-first publications, and past issues. When you see promising articles that could serve as models, you can then locate them through your library system.

I made the mistake pretenure, when timelines are arguably most important, of taking an editor's statement that their journal published qualitative research at face value. I received a "reject and do not resubmit," with peer reviews from only two scholars because the editor regretted that they could not identify a third who knew qualitative methods. Both peer reviews were conducted from a quantitative perspective. Over the past two years, this journal had published two qualitative articles, both of which were based on funded studies that utilized large numbers of participants. The articles were not typical accounts of qualitative data that someone conducting initial research would have and didn't reflect the kind of work I had written. Wow, did I waste my time! Demoralized and perplexed, I conducted the journal review I should have in the first place and discovered a more time-efficient way to publish.

From this perspective, my review advice is as follows: Review journal articles posted on the journal's website. If these examples seem promising, then dig deeper into the past two years of issues. Journals change and evolve. (The journal I had the challenging experience with regularly publishes qualitative research now.) Does the journal have a mix of qualitative and quantitative research? If so, the next step is to examine the types of qualitative research that tend to be published in the journal. Are the articles highly theoretical? Are the articles traditional qualitative research, such as grounded theory and phenomenology? What does the number of research participants tend to be, and what is the size of the data set? Are visual and art-based qualitative research studies also represented? Rank the journals from the most preferred to the least. You will send your manuscript to one journal at a time. Simultaneous submissions are not allowed due to the large amount of time invested by the editor and reviewers in deciding to publish. If fortunate, you will not need to use the full list of potential journals, but you should be prepared to submit to the next on the list should a rejection occur. Here are a few tips to help you maximize your chances of success.

General Tips on Choosing a Journal

- What is your chance of having the manuscript accepted (Thompson, 1995)?

- What is the journal's visibility (Thompson, 1995)? For studies from a course or initial studies, this may not be a crucial consideration.

- Is the journal respected? Watch out for predatory journals that may never even publish your manuscript. See Text Box 5.1 for more information on predatory publishers.

- Cite the journal, if possible, in your article. If you are not able to do this, reconsider whether the journal is a good match.

- Choose several backup journals, but only send your manuscript to one journal at a time.

- How long does it take the manuscript to be accepted and then published (Thompson, 1995)? If a journal has an online publication first option, this helps with the lag time.

- Does the manuscript "fit" the journal? To determine this,
  - ○ read the journal's aims and scope and
  - ○ identify two articles from the journal to use as style models.
    - ❖ The methodology should be similar.
    - ❖ The sample and type and size of the dataset should be similar

To summarize this section, "Write as you like to read, imitating authors that you like. Painters, too, begin their training by imitating their masters, then rebel" (Czarniawska, 2008, p. 17). For qualitative journals, journals receptive to qualitative research, and publishers, see the following website: https://qualpage.com/journals-publishers/.

5.1 PREDATORY PUBLISHERS
BECKY DE OLIVEIRA

Predatory journals are those that charge fees for publication and offer little in the way of "quality control" (Clark & Smith, 2015). Predatory publishers, as Clark and Smith (2015) point out, should not be confused with open-access publishing. The difference between the two is stark: Open-access publishing offers studies free for everyone to access—helping to quickly disseminate information in ways that are beneficial to people all over the world—and therefore a fee is charged. Predatory publishers have only one goal—to make as much money as possible. They do not follow standard publishing practices, such as robust peer review and editorial services, and they are not even indexed in reputable search systems, making the information nearly impossible for others to find.

Jeffrey Beall, a librarian at the University of Colorado, compiled a list of predatory publishers known as Beall's List (2017). In 2015, he recorded nearly 700 offenders. There are currently about 1,300 known or suspected predatory journals on the list. The list is curated at https://beallslist.net/.

How do you identify a predatory journal? Well, you could start by checking Beall's List, but new journals appear all the time and may not be listed at the time you need the information. Look for these classic signs:

1. The journal offers an unrealistic turnaround time. Publication in reputable journals typically takes months if not years from submission to publication. Journals offering to publish within 72 hours, for instance, will not have time to put the article through a rigorous peer review process let alone editorial and proofreading safeguards.

2. The journal requires payment of an excessive fee, but the article will not be open access. While some areas of research have article-processing fees, most social science journals do not have excessive fees.

3. Frequent soliciting by email is a red flag. Most legitimate publications are inundated with submissions and rarely go out of their way to pester potential authors with requests to submit work. Always do your research on any journals that approach you by email; go so far as to read a few of the articles on their websites. Many unscrupulous publishers will publish work that is riddled with obvious errors.

Many novice researchers may be tempted to use unscrupulous publishers in an effort to "pad their CV . . . in order to obtain employment, grants and promotions" (Bartholomew, 2014, p. 384). This may appear to offer a short-term solution to the immense pressure to publish, but it is a mistake in the long run. Not only will your work be discredited by your affiliation with predatory publishers, but it will also be less likely to ever be read by those who could benefit from it. It is far better for your career to go through the rigorous process of learning to publish through legitimate means. Have faith in your work and your ability to make an important contribution to your field.

Source: Reproduced with permission from Becky De Oliveira

The Qualitative Thematic Article: Bread and Butter of Qualitative Research

In this section, I detail ideas for turning your initial qualitative research studies into journal articles. This is the type of research Merriam (2009) refers to as *basic* or *generic*. While it is a helpful category, the words "basic" or "generic" have a simplistic connotation that for me does not capture the careful planning and extensive time and resources that go into conducting qualitative research. I prefer the term "essential." *Essential* as the name of a type of qualitative research indicates research with the requisite features of qualitative research while not belonging to a specific methodology, such as grounded theory or case study. This is a helpful distinction since a common error researchers' commit is claiming one of these methodological genres when the study is in fact a basic interview or focus group design. In these instances, call the study precisely what it is—for example,

- "This qualitative research was a focus group design."

- "In this qualitative study, I conducted in-depth interviews and weekly two-hour observations over a semester."

The mislabeling of methodology I see most often is research labeled as *phenomenology* that is actually essential interview research. There is nothing wrong with interview research that is not phenomenological. Calling a study phenomenological means that it needs to have phenomenological features in the theory section, methodology, and analysis. Also, the writer needs to hold one of the many phenomenological belief systems. Not all qualitative researchers adhere to phenomenological beliefs and research goals.

Manuscript Length Estimations

Before I move into detailing each section of a manuscript, let's consider how the contents might be broken down into each section lengthwise. For a 30-page, double-spaced document running at about 7,500 words, a general breakdown might be as follows. (A double-spaced page contains approximately 250 words.)

- *Abstract:* 100 to 250 words

- *Introduction:* 250 to 500 words

- *Literature review:* 500 to 1,000 words

- *Methodology:* 500 to 1,000 words

- *Findings:* 2,000 to 3,500 words

- *Discussion and conclusion:* 500 to 1,500 words

Be sure to check if the journal includes references in the page number limit. (One of the major journals I publish in does.) I have wondered if this is an attempt to discourage "string" citations. We have a tendency to defend our work by citing every piece of literature we can identify, causing multiple citations for one statement when one, well-chosen citation would suffice. This probably comes from the dissertation literature review model, which requires students to cover the literature from "womb to tomb." I have indicated in Chapter 4 that I prefer a concise, lean literature review. If references are included in the page count, reducing string citations will allow more room to highlight data in the findings section.

The most crucial point is that *the findings are always the bulk* of the manuscript. Descriptions of context, direct quotes, images or descriptions of material data, and reconstructions of observations and the interactions between participants and researchers within the observations should make up the bulk of the manuscript. A standard novice error is to use up a large amount of the space on the literature review and methodology and spend little time representing the data. The reader must have as much access to the data as possible to get a full sense of the data and see if they agree with the manuscript's findings, implications, and conclusions.

Next, I review ideas for representing the introduction, literature review, methodology, findings, and ending of the manuscript.

Introduction

The first sentence and paragraph of the introduction should capture the readers' interest; that is, "open with text that is vivid and vital" (Caulley, 2008,

p. 424). My recommendation is to start with the data by featuring a participant quote, an observation, a short vignette, or an image or description of material data. This places the reader immediately in the research context. A participant's quote could be offset as an epigraph, as I have offset Dostoyevsky's quote at the beginning of this chapter.

Other opening hooks include quotes from famous people in society, recent compelling statistics, notable research, or "ripped from the headlines" references, such as the one referring to Matthew Shepherd's horrific murder given below. If the journal is open to art-influenced research, allusions to the larger world of art and history may grab attention.

Examples of First Sentences From Student Papers

- "The blood was red and hot and coming uncontrollably from the stab wound in the young student's side."

- "A gay college student was brutally beaten by two men, tied to a fence, and left to die."

- "Latinos. Chicanos. Mexicanos. Ticos. Cholos. Guatamatecans. Cubanos. Hispanics."

The first sentence given as an example was from a research exploration of reasons why professionals seek a postbaccalaureate teaching certificate. The sentence moved into a short vignette depicting a research participant running past a high school and intervening in a fight. Incredibly, this encounter inspired the participant to become a teacher. The second example was about LGBTQ+ campus members' fear on campus. It is of note that a peer reviewer stated the opening was "sensational." I strongly disagree since we know this is factual, and indeed, the details were downplayed in the opening sentence. In response, I had the student author add a reference for further reading. The final example became the opening to Krista Malott's (2005) dissertation. The study, an exploration of how Latinas choose identity labels, grabbed my attention. I have borrowed the idea of placing words to help us think about a topic at the beginning of sections of my work in books and articles—as you have seen in this book.

The Second Paragraph of the Introduction

While I teach students the above information, I find that for those who are advanced in research training it is hard to write this way again. Increasingly, students report that during their education they have never been taught writing in a literary sense. Instead, what I get is the traditional research introduction, which is necessary but filled with information I believe should be placed in the second paragraph of the introduction.

The traditional introduction has important features that are placed at the beginning of the article as a courtesy to the reader, so they do not have to wade through a lengthy document trying to determine if it contains what they are looking for. It includes a statement of the problem, the research question(s), its rationale, the significance of the study, and brief references to the literature. (See Chapter 4 for details on how to write a traditional introduction.) The literature referenced in the introduction should be the most compelling, allowing you to make the case that the research is needed. It may include both recent literature and original historical literature.

Literature Review

There is not a discovery in science, however revolutionary, however sparkling with insight, that does not arise out of what went before. "If I have seen further than other men," said Isaac Newton, "it is because I have stood on the shoulders of giants."

—Isaac Asimov (1964, pp. 7–8)

The literature review is both an opportunity to situate your work within the research of others, as reflected in the quote from Asimov above, and an opportunity to make a case for the contribution your research is making to your field. Kamler and Thomson (2014) detail the primary reasons why a review is conducted. I quote them in the bullet points below.

- Sketch out the nature of the field or fields relevant to the inquiry indicating something of their historical development.

- Identify major debates and define contentious terms.

- Establish which studies, ideas and/or methods are most pertinent to the study.

- Locate gaps in the field.

- Create the warrant for the study in question.

- Identify the contribution the study will make. (p. 28)

A qualitative literature review's function is the same as that of a quantitative or mixed-methods literature review. The major difference is some qualitative authors integrate literature throughout the manuscript and remove the stand-alone literature review. While this may seem surprising at first, consider the last good nonfiction book you read. The author does not separate the other sources they cite from their own commentary and analysis. Instead, the ideas of others are woven throughout the text according to the topics under discussion.

All reviews should cover all kinds of research literature—qualitative, quantitative, mixed methodology, and evaluation. It is disheartening to see researchers ignore research paradigms—at our peril. I also call for qualitative researchers to cite artistic research representations in literature reviews—making it a truly comprehensive literature review (Teman & Lahman, 2019). In these days of bean counting, citations and impact factors can matter, but more important, weaving artistic expressions into our literature reviews shows that we value the knowledge they generate and allows a broader readership to experience artistic publications. If you look at the poetry in Chapter 8, poems on suicide, death, a transgender person's murder, the graduate school experience, and more could be referenced and excerpted into appropriate literature reviews. See Chapter 6 Text Boxes 6.3 and 6.4 for more information on journals' impact factor and authors' H index.

Literature Review Styles to Avoid

There are styles novices tend to use that should be avoided—the "crowded review" and the "he said/she said" (Kamler & Thomson, 2014) review, which should be updated as the "they said" review and is related to what I call the *bibliography review.*

Avoid the bibliography review style. This reads as a list ("They said this, and they said that"). This style is probably used because compiling an annotated bibliography for a course is something that one is familiar with from high school through graduate work. Students are used to this preresearch activity. It is also easier to write this way if you are unsure about your writing. The ease of a cut-and-paste bibliography style allows writers to paraphrase abstracts cut from articles. However, while an annotated bibliography is the compilation and examination of literature related to the topic, a literature review is an evaluation of the research conducted and the inferences the authors make. Ultimately, it is a synthesis of the existing literature that allows the writer to present points of agreement and disagreement. The same sources could be referenced multiple times under differing subtopics in the literature review. This literature review will read as though woven together and not as discreet index cards laid out in a row.

The *crowded literature review* has many sources, long block quotes, and so little paraphrasing that readers cannot get to the points being made. Crowded literature reviews often occur when students are given little guidance. I recall being told to "cover the material." I did so in a much too long, historical, womb-to-tomb, dissertation literature review that did not help me learn how to write a succinct review for an article. A crowded literature review can be pared down through the use of subheadings, which ensure that the reader can follow where all the points are headed and that points are directly related to the research questions. Block quotes should be used sparingly. Instead, paraphrase and cite information while using a few short, direct quotes chosen for their powerful and precise wording.

The literature review is often thought of as being composed in a discrete time before the research begins, but in all research—and in qualitative particularly—reviewing the literature again at least before writing the manuscript draft and submitting the manuscript to a journal is recommended. As Kamler and Thomson (2014) point out, "Commentators (e.g., Dunleavy, 2003; Hart, 1998, 2001) stress that literature work is an evolving and ongoing task that must be updated and revised throughout the process of writing" (p. 35).

It is also important to know when to stop updating the literature. I have worked with people who do so repeatedly, fearing they will miss something. I think it is wise to see what your advisor, faculty, and dissertation committee members have published. While I don't advocate citing people for political reasons, it would be an oversight not to know you are working with someone who has expertise in your interest area. As you move toward submission, the inclusion of literature from the year in which you are writing is helpful due to the lag time some journals have in reviewing and publishing.

I dread typing all the references for a literature review, but

do I mind when someone references my publications?

Not et al.

(See upjoke.com/research-paper-jokes *for versions of this joke.)*

Throughout the following sections, I will give examples from the study idea I referenced earlier—moms who have transitioned to working from home due to the COVID-19 pandemic. These examples will be offset in italics. Readers should feel free to draw on the basic wording without citing me.

Methodology

Methodology is the research beliefs and approaches that support a research design. This may also be referred to as *research methods*. As a methodologist, I prefer the word "methodology" as an expansive umbrella term overarching all of the research processes. *Research methods* or *data collection methods* are a sub-section within the major heading "methodology" that detail the actual steps taken. The methodology includes research beliefs such as an ethnographer's need to participate to observe; a traditional phenomenologist's assumption that researchers can "bracket" (i.e., put aside our own biases and experiences), or a case study methodologist's belief that the close examination of a single unit sheds light on the whole.

The description of the methodology is placed at the beginning of the methodology section, allowing for writing to start expansively, focusing on theory first and then moving into specific, finer-grain details. The metaphor of a funnel or a camera's zoom lens may be helpful, as broad moves to narrow and far away to close up. The methodology also proceeds somewhat chronologically, with research ethics approval being discussed near the beginning and data analysis toward the end of the section. The methodology section needs to include citations since there are crucial differences between particular methodologists' interpretations and descriptions of their methodology. For instance, take the differences between Stake (1995) and Yin (2017) in case study methodology, Husserl (1999) and Vagle (2018) in phenomenology, and Glaser and Strauss (1999) and Charmaz (2014) in grounded theory. However, since this is a basic thematic manuscript, in all likelihood you may cite introductory qualitative authors—Merriam and Tisdell (2016), Creswell and Poth (2018), Rossman and Rallis (2016), or Flick (2018), among many others. If, however, you are doing basic work in a specific area such as focus groups, be sure to read, utilize, and cite focus group methodologists (e.g., Morgan, 2018). If your discipline is fortunate enough to have an introductory qualitative text, that will be what you will want to heavily draw on. For example, Sparkes and Smith (2013) is an excellent introductory text in the area of sport.

This description should be a crisp paragraph or so, not a treatise of the methodology's development and breadth. An example follows:

> For this study, I employed in-depth interviews. Merriam (1998) points out that interviews are needed for behavior we cannot observe. I chose this methodology so I could explore the moms' thoughts and feelings about their experiences. I used semi-structured interviews (Merriam, 1998), so topics and wording of questions were thought out ahead of time, but I still maintained the flexibility to change course during the interview because of the context of interviewing busy professional moms who were also schooling their children at home.

Theory of the Study

As part of your graduate experience, you should be reading deeply about theory and exploring different theories to see if they coincide with your worldview. Some fields are so dominated by specific theories that it can be hard for a novice to know what they personally believe. For example, in my field of early childhood education, versions of constructivism have been dominant throughout all of my degrees. While I adhere to this theory, I know I was influenced by my education. I wish I had been explicitly introduced to social justice theories (e.g., critical theory, feminism, queer theory, critical race feminism, critical whiteness) earlier in my graduate work since they fit deeply with my worldview. As a female from a conservative religious community, even the subgroups considered "socially liberal" when I was growing up were more conservative regarding feminist issues than I was. It was common for me to feel out of step, but I was fortunate to have a family that tried to support my journey of discovery. An introduction to critical theory would have allowed me to think more deeply about my experiences.

The type of theory I am referring to are broad theories, or "Big T" theories—spanning vast areas of social science. Such theories include *interpretivism, constructionism*, and *critical theory*. Broad social science theories are recognized across disciplines as macro explanations of the complex dynamics that make

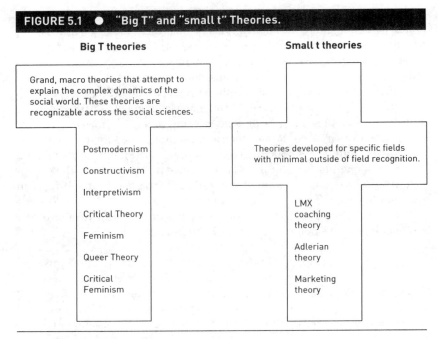

Note: LMX = leader–member exchange.

up the human world. See Figure 5.1 for a graphic of "Big T" and "small t" theories. Good places to start reading about these at an introductory level are Schwandt's *Qualitative Dictionary* (2014) and Crotty's (1998) *The Foundations of Social Research: Meaning and Perspective in the Research Process.* As certain theories resonate with you, dig in deeper by exploring a qualitative research handbook or by reading the original theorist's works. Referencing these theories allow readers across the sciences to speak clearly to one another about beliefs, biases, and intents.

After you have written a concise paragraph about this theory and how it connects to the study at hand, you may want to write about a "small t," field-specific theory. These theories are well developed in your area, but educated individuals outside your field may not be familiar with them. Examples from myriad possibilities include *LMX (leader–member exchange) coaching theory* (e.g., Chieu, 2005; Sue-Chan et al., 2011), *Adlerian theory* (Mosak & Maniacci, 2013), and *marketing theory* (Baker & Saren, 2016). Along with an explanation of the field-specific, "small t" theory, links between it, the "Big T" social science theory, and the study at hand should be established.

Examples of a Theory Section in an Article. *The first example is a straightforward theory section that may be placed in most manuscripts sent to journals that are not highly theoretical.*

I framed this study in social constructivism—the belief that people construct knowledge in an attempt to make sense of their experiences. There is no preexisting reality or truth. "Reality" or "truth" occurs in the interactions, interpretations, and representations people form through lived experiences (Crotty, 1998). Social constructivism can be seen in the study through the semistructured interview format I employed, which allowed room for interviews to be flexible and organic; the researcher journal I kept reflections in; and the multiple attempts I made for member checks at the point of transcription, initial themes, and the draft of the manuscript. I sought participants' opinions about the interpretation I was creating of their constructions.

Coauthor Theory Statement Example. *The following example is from a published article (Lahman et al., 2011). It shows how theory could be addressed by multiple coauthors. This section is more extensive than some journals would have space for, but the article's topic was about culturally responsive research.*

For this article, our shared perspectives on constructivism, feminism, and critical race theory frameworks, as well as our understandings of culturally responsive practices, informed our research. Janesick (2000) advocated using multiple theories in research as a primary way for researchers to broaden their understandings.

Constructivists assume reality is socially constructed (Denzin & Lincoln, 2000; Schwandt, 1994). People's ways of knowing come from their thoughts about experiences and contexts. Acknowledging multiple realities is essential in the interaction between the researcher and participants (Baxter Magolda, 2001). By design, constructivist focus groups allow participants and researchers to co-create knowledge together rather than uncover the one singular Truth about a research question.

Feminists do not hold a single epistemology. Olsen (2005) characterized feminist work as "highly diversified, enormously dynamic, and thoroughly challenging" (p. 235). However, there are essentials feminist researchers share:

A focus on gender and power

A goal to conduct empowering research.

Emphasis on alternative ways to conduct research (Olsen, 2005)

Feminist researchers have been central to deconstructing the power dynamic between those researched and the researcher. Further, feminists place at the center of research the voices of those who have typically been marginalized, most often women's voices (for example, Minister, 1991) and have extended their advocacy to the understanding of groups such as children, persons with disabilities, and those who identify as LGBTQ+ (Olsen, 2005).

Some of the research portrayed in this article is informed by a Chicana feminist epistemology, which creates methodological strategies and techniques that create a space for the construction of knowledge through the experiences, lives, and voices of Latinas (Bernal Delgado, 1998; Elenes, 2001; Gonzalez, 2001). This epistemology relocates Latinas' lived experience to a central position in the research and views their experiences at the intersection of the social identities of race/ ethnicity, class, gender, and sexual identity (Anzaldua, 1987; Delgado Bernal, 1998; Gonzalez, 2001). The Chicana feminist framework distinguishes Latina participants as coresearchers in the meaning-making of the emerging data.

Considering focus groups from a culturally responsive perspective is also grounded in critical theories (Freire, 1970; Kamberelis & Dimitriadis, 2005) and, in particular, critical race theory (CRT). A critical frame emphasizes researchers' work "with people and not on them" (Kamberelis & Dimitriadis, 2005, p. 889). CRT researchers' specific goal is to "trouble" conventional ways of conducting research by addressing intrinsic racism, which is enmeshed with society and frequently invisible to dominant powers (Ladson-Billings, 2000). CRT researchers attempt to "speak explicitly back to the webbed relations of history, political economy, and everyday lives of women and men of color" (Fine & Weis, 2005, p. 66) and challenge conventions for viewing and conducting research (Rossman & Rallis, 1998). At the heart of this challenge is the need to acknowledge research involves power, is conducted by "raced, gendered, classed, and politically oriented individuals" (Rossman & Rallis, 1998, p. 66), is interpreted at an intersection of one's race, class, age, sexual orientation, and gender, and has historically pathologized marginalized groups (Liamputtong, 2007). (pp. 401–403)

Researcher Personal Stance

In this section, the author's personal connection to the research is featured, so readers can access the multiple lenses the author views research through—both personal and professional. This section is a natural fit after theory, moving from a formal, more distant-sounding discussion of theory to one of personal, close experiences. This section is often written as what I term a *researcher resume stance*—summarizing the kind of work you have done and how many years you have been attached to the topic. Ideally, this also offers a personal glimpse into you as an individual, perhaps by sharing the story of a sibling who experienced the issue being studied and how this connection moved you to do the research. This second type of stance is one I call an *intimate researcher stance*. Choosing to create a more intimate stance depends largely on how your field and associated journals might respond, but it is important to know that personal revelations by researchers are accepted and considered "standard" in qualitative research.

If you are comfortable, I think it is important to always be nudging field-specific areas to a broader way of thinking about and representing research.

See Chapter 10 for a lengthy discussion and multiple examples of how to represent yourself as a researcher in writing.

Participants

In this section, you will include information on how you purposefully (Merriam, 2009) recruited participants and how many participants were in the study, and as detailed as possible a description of the participants given space restrictions. Recruitment is generally simple to write about since you will already have a recruitment strategy approved by the Research Ethics Board (e.g., IRB) and by anyone who is supervising your work.

The description of the participants is more varied and is a place in the methodology where you can really begin to place the readers in the context of the study. If you have 10 participants or fewer, a brief description of each participant works well. However, if you include more than 10 people, readers will struggle to hold these descriptions in their minds, and they can become tedious reading—unless they are written as characters in an active ethnographic account. For studies with more than 10 participants, a demographic chart works well. This allows readers to reference it as they move through the manuscript. (See Table 5.1 for an example.) Such a chart includes the person's name, or pseudonym,[1] and demographic characteristics you are reporting. If the chart gets longer than a page, it is best presented in aggregated categories, similar to the way quantitative researchers report. In qualitative research, avoid the use of percentages when reporting. Percentages have the unfortunate effect of causing naive readers to apply them to an entire population. Since purposeful sampling and not statistical sampling is the goal of qualitative research, applying findings statistically is inappropriate. Shortened examples from Tyler Kincaid's (2019) dissertation follow. My thanks to Tyler for allowing the use of his work.

Tyler also described the participants by using their own words when possible. Tyler used the pronoun "they" as another way to protect the participants' privacy. These descriptions, while providing for confidentiality, also allow readers to hold images of the participants' contexts in their heads as they interact with the data in the findings. I have excerpted a few examples below.

Examples of Participant Descriptions. *The following examples show how participants can be described in compelling ways.*

> *Texas: "I hate this more than anything (crying). . . . I've been on the housing list for like six years or more, and I mean it's hard, you know. I hate this life. I hate living out of a bag. I mean, I've had places to stay, but I haven't had a home in like . . . it's been almost nine years now . . . and it sucks."*

---

[1] See a section of this chapter titled What's in a Name for a discussion of issues around naming participants.

TABLE 5.1 ● Participant Demographics (excerpt)

ID	Participant	In role	Location
P1	Texas	Homeless	Rural city
P2	Jeffro Gets	Homeless	Rural city
P3	Tree	Homeless	Rural city
P4	Poison Ivy	Homeless	Rural city
P6	Grandma	Homeless	Rural city
P7	Shopping Cart	Homeless	Rural city
P8	Mountain Man	Homeless	Rural city
P9	Professor	Research expert	Urban university
P10	Leader	Program director	Rural city
P11	Songbird	Program director	Rural city
P12	Programmer	Data manager	Urban city

Note: Gender, age, and race/ethnicity, while usually detailed, are not shown here to protect the identities of the participants, who in this case are mostly homeless. Each participant chose the name they wanted to use for the study. Adapted from Kincaid (2019).

Source: Kincaid, T. W. (2019). Methodological considerations for researching hidden populations with an emphasis on homeless research sampling methods. [Doctoral dissertation, University of Northern Colorado]. Reproduced with permission from Tyler Kincaid.

Texas was open to talking about their past experiences with homelessness and drug addiction and the link between the two. They discussed at length their past as the victim of domestic abuse and how this led to drug addiction and homelessness. Texas was kind and funny and continually apologized for showing strong emotions, like crying at one point.

> *Jeffro Gets: "I'm here because love fucked me up (laughs). . . . My girlfriend left. . . well, drugs are involved too. But it was the fact that she left and went to prison and that leaves without, you know, her income and my income. . . . it only took two months for all that to happen, to get to the way I am right now"* [homeless].

Jeffro Gets spoke briefly about previous experiences with episodic homelessness. Jeffro had a strong demeanor and a solid handshake and was soft-spoken and caring throughout the interview. Their hands were stained with charcoal-colored grease, like you would see on a car mechanic.

> *Poison Ivy: "I don't have to be homeless. I can get a place for free because of the baby, over at the church, but I don't want to be away from him"* [Matt-Man, their partner].

Poison Ivy (and Matt-Man) had been homeless for more than six months after leaving their hometown in the Midwest to relocate to Colorado. They spoke about not having plans to find permanent housing when they arrived in Colorado, but Poison Ivy was now pregnant and expecting to deliver within the next couple of months. They had both left a self-described "bad situation" and had no intention of returning to it. They talked about wanting to stay hidden and not be perceived as "homeless." They had the unique dilemma of whether to stay together by sleeping outdoors in the woods or separating so that Poison Ivy could access the social care networks available for pregnant women.

Setting

The setting of a study can be stated in a general geographic sense and through a description of the close context. For more sophisticated studies, see multiple types of settings, such as temporal and historical (Lawrence-Lightfoot & Davis, 1997). In general, though, essential thematic research articles do not have room for complex discussions.

The geographic setting might be described as, say, the Midwest or East Coast—be careful not to use colloquialisms. For example, I work in the state of Colorado in the United States. When I ask students to give a general location for Colorado, they may say "West" or "Midwest," depending on which part of the United States they are from. These areas of the United States are really different from each other. For Colorado, it is probably more accurate to say a Rocky Mountain state, although these states also have variance in terms of culture and demographics.

The close context will be where the interviews and observations occur—chemistry class laboratory, middle school literature classroom, nursing station, and so on. If there are no observations, a description of the specific setting may not be as essential but could read as follows:

- "Interviews were conducted in a study room at the local library."

- "Participants were given the choice of being interviewed at their home, a local park, or the campus library."

- "I stood at the bottom of a ski lift and conducted five-minute interviews with people as they exited."

- "Virtual interviews were conducted via Zoom."

- "Walking interviews occurred through a part of the university campus the student chose."

Data Collection Method(s)

Data collection methods may be written up in a single straightforward paragraph or, when several methods are used, in more detailed paragraphs.

If interviews, observations, and material data are part of the research, each of these data collection methods merits a paragraph and citations of its own. There are many other ways data may be collected, but most of them may generally be sorted into one of these three areas: (1) *observations*, (2) *interviews*, and (3) *material data*.

Observations. *What was your goal as a researcher, for example, participant observation or observation where interactions were only initiated by the participants? How long were the observations? How often did they occur and over what period of time? What role did you tend to play as a result of either your own choice or participants' assignment? How did you take notes? An example of how the observation methods section may be written up follows. I continue to use the example of possible research with professional moms staying at home to work during COVID-19.*

> Observations yielded rich data. While I sought to be in the role Gold (1958) described as "observer as participant," each woman interacted with me in her own way—from pseudo friend to colleague, to confidant. Each mom welcomed me into her home three times for an approximately one-hour visit over three months. There was social distancing and the use of face masks. Interviews were only scheduled at times when the area was on a low level of COVID-19 restrictions. Given that these women were professionals, I wondered if the data would yield much that wasn't part of a professional veneer. As time passed, I found the women dressed in a more relaxed fashion, and their homes, like mine, were comfortably cluttered. Children passed in and out of the spaces I occupied and either greeted or ignored me. During the first observation, I was given tours of the moms' working space and, if children were school age, their school space. I asked detailed questions about any transitions in the space that may have occurred as the mom moved to work full-time from home. With permission, I took photos of the work and school spaces. I recorded notes in my phone memo app to be as unobtrusive as possible. As soon as I left the observation, I moved these notes into expanded field notes on a laptop. At the final interview, I asked each mom how it felt for me to be observing them in their home and how the masks and social distancing may have affected the research experience.

Interviews. *What is your goal for the type of interview you conducted? Was it semi-structured or conversational? Was it in person, on the phone, or computer mediated? Was it one-on-one, a dyad, a triad, or a focus group? Researchers who interview in counseling or with families often have more than one* *person at the interview. Points to address when writing include the length of the interview, how it was recorded and backed up and whether anything happened during the interview that readers should know about (e.g., the recorder stopped working; the interview was interrupted multiple times by people dropping by the home office). Here is an example of how the interview methods section could be written:*

> In-depth interviews were held with 10 participants. Each participant was interviewed twice. Interviews varied in length from 45 minutes to one hour. I set up the interviews to be semi-structured and organic in nature because of the bustling homes I assumed I would encounter. However, in some cases, the mom asked older siblings or the spouse to supervise the younger children. So while no interview remained uninterrupted, they were much more focused than I had anticipated. Most of the interviews occurred in the "office" space the women had carved out for their work in a busy home.
>
> The interviews were recorded on my smartphone with a backup recorder from a music device. As soon as I left the homes, I backed the interviews up on a laptop and ultimately the university server.

Material Data. *Material data may include documents, records (Merriam, 2009), and physical items such as chairs, photos, signs, and layout of spaces. While many introductory texts refer to material data as documents and records, I prefer the term "material data" because it encourages us to examine all the physical traces (Hodder, 2000) of human lives, including physical items beyond those used for written communication and the layout of settings. Questions to address as you write include the following: Did you ask for certain material data or just try to be aware of serendipitous ones? How did you record the material data (with field notes or perhaps by taking a photo)? Were material data discussed during the interview process? Here is an example of how material data may be written about:*

> Each mom enthusiastically agreed to allow me to photograph their home office. Some moms grimaced or made self-deprecating comments at their perception that the space was untidy. For example, Joan said laughing, "Cluttered desk, organized mind." I photographed their offices with my smartphone camera on the highest resolution setting available. Each mom looked at the photo both on my camera and later in large print and agreed to its use.
>
> Figures 5.2 and 5.3 are parts of a photo of a mom's Zoom space, allowing her to look out of a window when possible. Figure 5.2 shows how Zoom looks, and Figure 5.3 shows the whole room.

FIGURE 5.2 ● Angle 1 of a Mom's Zoom Space.

FIGURE 5.3 ● Angle 2 of a Mom's Full Zoom Room, Including Space That Does Not Show Up on Zoom.

Procedures

Not all qualitative research accounts have a procedures section, but writers who have been trained traditionally often use up valuable space writing this section. A helpful way to decide if you need a procedure section is to ask yourself, "Is it redundant?" If the procedures have been laid out in previous sections and this section does not provide new information or a greater level of detail, it is not needed.

Procedure sections are helpful in studies that have multiple steps that need to proceed in a particular order. For example, if math educators are studying how students respond to a specific type of instruction and have a pre- and a post-interview, followed by a series of computations students think out loud about while being video recorded, these procedures would need to be laid out so readers clearly understand what occurred and in what order, so another researcher is able to follow the steps.

Trustworthiness

The trustworthiness section of a manuscript is where you establish, through qualitative actions using qualitative terminology, how the study's validity and reliability were enhanced. There isn't room in a manuscript-length product for a long discussion about qualitative perspectives in this area. Instead, state the type of trustworthiness you are working within, citing a particular researcher who has published about this (e.g., Lincoln, 2007), and detail the methods employed, such as a member check or triangulation. See Figure 5.4 for some major areas of trustworthiness and ways to enhance it. Be sure to cite these methods so novice readers can investigate them more thoroughly. This is not a place to discuss methods you did not use. For example, other than those using ethnographic methods, it is rare for a qualitative researcher to have long-term engagement in the field; so if this is not something you did, it should not be addressed in your manuscript. If the manuscript length allows, briefly explain how each method was enacted. It is really frustrating as a reader to simply read coded phrases such as "data were triangulated," "member checks occurred," or "I attempted to be reflexive throughout the study" without knowing what *happened* and *how*. We may suspect that behind the scenes no one responded when the researcher attempted member checks, participants simply replied to the researcher that the transcripts or data looked okay. Explaining more about strategies like member checks will give a more complete picture of the participants and the measures you took, increasing confidence in the results.

Questions to address in this section include the following: Who are you citing? What methods did you use to enhance the study's trustworthiness? How did these methods play out? Clearly an important part of your journal review will be to determine how this important topic is communicated. Here is an example of how to write a short trustworthiness section:

> I followed Merriam's (1998) instructions on how to enhance trustworthiness. Triangulation, member checks, and a peer check were employed. Data were triangulated within each participant's specific

data—interviews, observation, and material data—and then across all participants. This process was established so I could speak to overall themes and individual notes within the data. While the research was member checked through a transcript review, not much of note occurred. However, at the final interview, questions about how the process of the research was experienced by each mom and her family yielded rich reflections on the research process, which will make up one area of the findings. Finally, throughout the study, I deliberately performed peer checks as I spoke with the many professional moms in my life (colleagues, relatives, neighbors, friends) about what I was learning, and in turn they gave me more to think about as we discussed this transition all of us have been going though one way or the other together.

FIGURE 5.4 ● Trustworthiness and Rigor in Qualitative Research

Trustworthiness and Rigor in Qualitative Research

Maria Lahman and Becky De Oliveira

Trustworthiness Criteria

1 Credibility. Confidence in the "truth" of the findings. Achieved through prolonged engagement, persistent observation, triangulation, peer debriefing, negative case analysis, referential adequacy, and member-checking

2 Transferability. Findings are applicable in other contexts. Research produces "thick description" providing a strong foundation to make judgements.

3 Dependability. Findings are consistent and could be repeated. An audit trail, including all notes and reflective diary entries, helps explain influences, demonstrating that conclusions are justified.

4 Confirmability. Findings are shaped by the respondents and not by researcher bias. Achieved through use of an audit trail, triangulation, and reflexivity.

Authenticity Criteria

1 Fairness. Uses a wide variety of viewpoints to collect data and to shape the study.

2 Catalytic authenticity. Causes action to take place with the view to creating change.

3 Ontological authenticity. Helps members of the public to arrive at a better understanding of the world.

4 Educative authenticity. Helps expand knowledge about the issues experienced by the people affected.

5 Tactical authenticity. Empowers stakeholders to take action.

Qualitative Term	Methods
Trustworthiness	▌ triangulation ▌ member check ▌ peer/colleague examination ▌ expert examination ▌ research stance ▌ prolonged engagement in the field
Dependability Whether the results are consistent with the data.	▌ triangulation ▌ peer examination ▌ audit trail
Reader Generalization or Naturalistic Generalization	▌ thick description ▌ multi-site designs

Eisenhart's 5 Standards for Validity in Educational Research

1. Fit between research question, data collection methods, and analysis
2. Effectiveness of data collection and analysis
3. Alertness to and coherence of prior knowledge
4. Value constraints
   —research is valuable (so what?)
   —ethical
5. Comprehensiveness

Richardson's Standards for Creative Analytic Practices

1. Substantive contribution
2. Aesthetic merit
3. Reflexivity
4. Impact
5. Expression of reality
(Richardson, 2000)

References
Eisenhart, M., & Howe, K. (1992). Validity in educational research. In LeCompte, M., Millroy, W. & Preissle, J. (Eds.), *The handbook of qualitative research in education.* (pp. 643-680). Academic Press.

Lincoln, Y.S. & Guba, EG. (1985). *Naturalistic inquiry.* Sage.

Richardson, L. (2000). Writing: A method of inquiry. In N. K. Denzin & Y. S. Lincoln (Eds.), *Handbook of qualitative research,* (2nd ed., pp. 923-948). Sage.

Note: From Lahman and De Oliveira (2018).

Source: Reproduced with permission from Becky De Oliveira

Analysis of Data

Reporting about analysis should always include (a) how the data were organized and managed and (b) the type of analysis conducted, including the steps that occurred within the analysis. A third area sometimes included is an example of how the analysis occurred. The choice to include an example depends on the complexity of the analysis, space in the journal, the style and preference of the journal, and, at times, requests by the editor or reviewers.

Qualitative Analysis. *The following questions should be considered when you write about qualitative analysis in general. What type of analysis are you using? What terms are used to convey the analysis process? Would a chart of the analysis process be helpful to your readers?*

Template for Thematic or Categorical Analysis. *Here is a thematic template you may rewrite as necessary to fit your research and voice without referencing me. (See Logan Schuetz's discussion of thematic analysis in Text Box 5.2.)*

> I transcribed all the interviews in full. The transcripts yielded 48 pages of single-space data. After transcribing the interviews and organizing the observational notes and supporting material data, formal analysis was initiated. The data were read, read, and reread to identify major themes and salient quotes. For the purpose of this article, five of the major themes are presented.

Alternative words that could be used follow:

a. Instead of "read, read, and reread": distilled, sifted through, combed, reduced, broken apart, analyzed

b. Instead of "themes": categories, areas, topics

c. Instead of "salient": supporting, exemplifying

Examples of other possible analysis phrases are as follows:

- "The recorded interviews were fully transcribed after the completion of the interview process."

- "The transcriptions and observation data were read thoroughly."

- "Keywords were marked, and notes were written during the process of reading the transcriptions. Based on the keywords and notes, meaning units were identified. Comparing and relating all the emerged meaning units, categories were developed—for example, 'Not sure when work office reopens,' 'Will kids be online or face-to-face for school this month,' and 'If school resumes, we aren't sure if we want to send our children back' had similar meaning units regarding uncertainty. Therefore, the category 'Uncertainty' was developed based on each participant's meaning unit."

- "According to the categories, interpretations and conclusions were drawn."

5.2   THEMATIC ANALYSIS
LOGAN SCHUETZ

In an introduction to qualitative research course, I conducted research with a group of women who are a part of the fan base for the University of Notre Dame women's basketball team. I chose to study these individuals due to my past experience there as an employee. They are unique and possess a strong desire to not only be a fan but also be a part of something more. Thus, I started conducting my own research on their motivations for being season ticket holders as well as being connected to a women's volunteer group that largely views players as their daughters. When I needed to write about how I went about analyzing data in my Introduction course, I definitely felt challenged at first. I began to explore which of the methods fit my style and the data best. I was instantly connected to thematic analysis. Once I assessed it, I felt as though I had a strong backing to execute it on this study.

The first draft I submitted for class was reviewed by several peers. I then had some time to rewrite the final paper, and the following is my final proposal draft:

> To analyze the findings in the data for this study, I will be using thematic analysis, a foundational method for qualitative analysis (Braun & Clarke, 2006). Braun and Clarke (2006) describe thematic analysis as "a method for identifying, analyzing and reporting patterns (themes) within data. It minimally organizes and describes your data set in (rich) detail. However, frequently it goes further than this, and interprets various aspects of the research topic" (p. 79). Thematic analysis has been popularized and defined notably by Braun and Clarke; however, previous scholars have utilized thematic analysis in studies (Boyatzis, 1998; Guest et al., 2012; Holloway & Todres, 2003; Roulston, 2001). Thematic analysis requires a step-by-step guide that follows a set of six general phases (Braun & Clarke, 2006). Additionally, it is critical to understand that thematic analysis is not a linear progression, where the researcher goes from one step to the next and so on; it is much more a recursive process, where the researcher is required to move back and forth as needed, throughout the phases, to correctly interpret the data. The six phases of thematic analysis are (1) familiarizing yourself with your data, (2) generating initial codes, (3) searching for themes, (4) reviewing themes, (5) defining and naming themes, and (6) producing the report. Braun and Clarke (2006) do state on the thematic analysis process that "there are no hard and fast rules in relation to this [thematic analysis], and different combinations are possible" (p. 86).

What this meant is that I applied this method to my interview transcripts. I closely examined the data to identify different common themes, topics, ideas, and patterns that came up repeatedly. Where thematic analysis excels is in its flexibility. Thematic analysis is a looping process, and by bouncing back and forth, you are able to familiarize yourself with data and generate themes in a notable way.

Source: Reproduced with permission from Logan Schuetz

Research Findings

The findings of the study are the bulk of the manuscript. The findings section is made up of a presentation of *themes* identified through thematic data analysis. It may be that you are familiar with the phrase "categorical analysis" also. These terms for analysis are used interchangeably. I prefer "themes" because "categories" sounds more discrete to me. Qualitative research themes can and will overlap—the choices we make as researchers determine which data are primarily included in particular themes.

The findings ultimately need to "tell a story." I use quote marks because in narrative research the data will *literally* tell a story. In thematic research, data are placed in smaller chunks under different themes. However, as someone who sees the world as storied, I still see these thematic chunks as small stories—experiences, explanations about what went on in a person's life, or their opinions on the research question being explored. So it may help some writers to consider if their supporting data tell the story of the themes being illustrated and if all themes tell the story presented in the research question.

At the point of writing, the primary themes have been identified through analysis. Carefully choose which themes to present. Each theme must be reflected in the research question. While the themes presented are usually those participants addressed most often, don't forget that an idea mentioned even once could represent a new thought the field should be exploring. If this is the case, the final theme could be a note of dissonance in which someone said something new or disagreed with the other participants.

Use a combination of short quotes with some longer quotes to support the themes you are advancing. If you have observational and material data, be sure to draw on them adequately. A common critique of findings is that material data are collected but then not represented. Another common error is simply using large blocks of quotes without any context or commentary by the researcher. If possible, feature quotes from each participant. Avoid using quotes primarily from just one or two participants. If you find yourself tending to do this, ask yourself if there is something about those participants that might warrant a small case study to place within the larger findings.

In thematic articles, research is usually reported in one of two ways (Burnard et al., 2008). Either (1) each theme is presented with supporting quotes, observation notes, or material data, or (2) when each theme is presented, it is also discussed by the author and related back to the relevant literature.

The discussion is where you create connections between the themes and the literature. Data are referred to directly to increase the credibility of findings. You will then need to interpret the data. Even if it is in an opening epigraph or vignette, at some point mention why you chose these data. There are some who suggest writing a paragraph in this order: Highlight a theme by giving the context, show supporting data, and then comment (e.g., Weaver-Hightower, 2014). These models will be helpful for writers who are feeling unsure, but ultimately you should work toward achieving some paragraph variation. Overly predictable writing becomes deadly.

Graphics

Many readers respond well to seeing portions of the data or themes presented graphically. A judicious use of figures, tables, and/or charts can help the reader understand the data and easily share them with others. As you develop these graphics, show them to other people, and make sure they can understand them apart from the research manuscript. A graphic should be able to stand on its own with only the heading that accompanies it. When your manuscript is published, these graphics can easily be used in educational media and during presentations to relay your research.

Subheadings

In the findings section, consider using short phrases from participant quotes as headings to capture readers' attention and direct it to the data. Avoid headings that include numbers, such as "Theme One," unless the numerical order has some sort of chronological meaning. See the following examples:

- "It Happened So Fast!": Transitions

- "Kind of Like a House of Cards": Uncertainty

- "We Eat Together Three Times a Day": Quality Family Time

Example of a Findings Paragraph

Colleen directly supported the theme "Uncertainty" as she reflected on her changing mind-set during her transition to working at home. "At first I thought, 'Well, it is the kids' spring break; we were all going to have time together anyway, so let's just do some fun stuff in our home and figure out all the COVID-19 stuff later.'" Colleen seemed wistful as she thought back over this family time before the reality of COVID-19 began to sink in. After spring break, Colleen was swamped at work, as professionals often are after a break. She then began to ask herself how long this was going to last and how seriously she had to plan for school and work at home. Colleen laughed and said, "Wow, were we naive! I am pretty sure we still don't know how long this is going to last."

This could also be written in the reverse order for variation.

"Wow, were we naive! I am pretty sure we still don't know how long this is going to last," Colleen exclaimed while laughing. "At first I thought, 'Well, it is the kids' spring break; we were all going to have time together anyway, so let's just do some fun stuff in our home and figure out all the COVID-19 stuff later.'" Colleen seemed wistful as she thought back over this family time before the reality of COVID-19 began to sink in. After spring break, Colleen was swamped at work, as professionals often are after a break. She began to ask herself how long this disruption was going to last and how seriously she had to plan for school and work at home. Colleen's ruminations directly support the theme "Uncertainty" as she reflected on her changing mind-set during her transition.

Discussion

This section will only be included if you did not have a discussion in the findings section. In the discussion and the conclusion sections, avoid introducing new points that were not stated in the findings. As mentioned earlier, the discussion section is your opportunity to make direct links from the findings to the literature. Try not to infer too much from the study; but a good discussion is warranted. Solving the problems of the world should be avoided, but don't let the data stand by themselves uninterpreted. Instead hover right above the data, pointing out what you, as the expert who has conducted this particular study, have determined are the inferences of note.

Conclusion

In the conclusion, you will summarize the answers to the research question(s) and provide the implications that seem most notable, along with considerations about the research and areas for future study. Implications can be stated for practice, policy, theory, and scholarship. A shorter thematic manuscript will often have implications for practice alone. Suppose the study is about education—implications may be stated for school districts, principals, teachers, and college education programs.

Considerations *Not* Limitations

Qualitative research manuscripts do not address limitations in the same sense as quantitative research accounts do. Quantitative research limitations may focus on population representation, sampling, or control issues, which are handled differently in qualitative research. Quantitative research accounts will not address limitations to the research paradigm. A common error made by many qualitative researchers when required to write limitations is addressing limitations to the paradigm itself. I have seen researchers state limitations to their study noting that it was qualitative in nature, had a small N, or contained bias. Grappling with bias, instead of trying to control bias, is actually a hallmark and strength of qualitative research. Since a quantitative researcher would not state that the limitations of the study included that it lacked context and depth, collected surface data on a large sample, or isolated the researcher's voice and context in an objective fashion, a qualitative researcher should not state the essence of the qualitative paradigm as a limitation to the research. Unless you are writing for a journal that also publishes quantitative research and mixed methods, this section should not be titled "Limitations" at all. I suggest titling this section "Considerations" and writing about areas that readers should know about in a reflexive sense—*considerations, notes of dissonance, shortcomings, unexpected contextual happenings, serendipitous discoveries*, and *reflections*.

Future Research

During the study, ideas for building on your research will have occurred to you; in this section, put forward one or two of these ideas. This is not intended to be an extensive laundry list of every idea that occurred to you. It is also not intended to be a place to undermine qualitative methods. Avoid merely saying this should now be studied quantitively. Choose the ideas that make the best sense to address areas the study didn't cover or new questions that emerged from the research.

Ending

In the same manner that you started the manuscript in the data, end it in the data. The data are the most essential part of the study, so bring the reader back one more time to the data with a well-chosen quote or short vignette that highlights the major findings and implications—a synthesis of sorts. A good ending is like a last note in a song, the thump of a good book being shut, and a satisfied sigh at the end of a good meal. See the section Endings in Chapter 3 for more discussion.

Example of a Conclusion

Encouragingly, this research revealed there were many positive aspects to working at home while children were also being educated there. However, questions remain on these moms' minds—from the quality of their children's education to concerns about health and safety, to wondering when the pandemic will end. A question I will continue to reflect on long after completing this study is, "How does a researcher conduct authentic research during a time of heightened health concerns?" While there are many related areas for future research, two areas I will highlight that should be explored are (1) single moms who are essential workers and have children in school at home and (2) moms' professional transition after COVID-19—are they back in the office, at home, or in some sort of hybrid state? Colleen's pithy comment, "I guess the settlers who first came out West would laugh at what I am finding hard to cope with," is a fitting end.

In the following section, I take a moment to discuss issues around how to name the participants in the manuscript.

What's in a Name? Pseudonyms[2]

Pseudonyms, pervasive in human research, are a primary way to enhance the confidentiality of research participants. Their ubiquitous nature may be a cause for minimal instruction to novice researchers (for notable exceptions, see Behar, 1993; Guenther, 2009; Nespor, 2000). In 2015, I reviewed 78 qualitative research articles and found a sparse reference to pseudonyms. My experience echoed Hurst (2008), who said,

> I have searched diligently in many methodological sections . . . for reflections on this issue but have failed to find any satisfactory answers. . . . I am concerned about the power of the researcher to rename . . . respondents. But there are no good guidelines that I have seen, of how to go about doing the renaming. (p. 345)

Encouragingly, since then, the scholarly discussion has increased (e.g., Deller, 2018; Jerolmack, & Murphy, 2019; Mukungu, 2017; Vannier, 2018). Yet, in practice, researchers may apply pseudonyms with little thought. (For an example of an exception, read Hoonaard, 2003.)

Researchers may assume that their discipline or the federal government (e.g., IRB) requires the use of a pseudonym. The U.S. federal government does not require a pseudonym and provides avenues for those participants who wish to use legal names (e.g., Giordano et al., 2007; Grinyer, 2002). Given the potential vulnerability of a participant, I believe there are research studies where pseudonyms are needed to increase confidentiality. Participants may be involved in illegal behavior, actions society stigmatizes (e.g., Peres, 2016), or whistle-blowing (Elliston, 1982; Jensen, 1987).

Hurst (2008) writes of her concerns about the power in naming, saying, "Personal names do matter" (p. 345). An example of power is when researchers change participants names to Western, English-language names. "Anglicizing a person's ethnically identifiable name, say renaming a German named Jurgen 'John,' can become a serious misrepresentation. Even more so, if a German named John is renamed by the researcher as 'Jurgen'" (p. 346). Power may be seen in many facets of the traditional pseudonym process (Guenther, 2009; Lucock & Yeo, 2006). Researchers have the power to strip a name to a number (Subject 1), an acronym (Subject AC12), a label indicating a seemingly disloyal person (Informant 1), or a joke (Curly Locks).

However, for participants or researchers who would like to use real names, the addition of language to the consent form clearly stating the participants' desire to use their own name and their understanding of the contexts in which

---

[2]Parts of this section are updated and excerpted from Lahman et al. (2015).

their name will be used allows researchers to proceed with honoring this request (Kaiser, 2009). When discussing with a participant whether to use real names, there are three major considerations among many possible pros and cons: (1) *relational*, (2) *developmental*, and (3) *economical*.

Relationally, when real names are used, the people directly associated with the participant are also known. This concern has also been termed *third-party issues* by Hadjistavropoulos and Smythe (2001), who stated, "The main ethical problem stems from the fact that these individuals did not give consent to have stories about them circulated in this way" (p. 169). *Developmentally*, as time passes, will participants still be happy they used their real name? This raises the question "Should another person be allowed to consent for the use of a given name" (e.g., a parent or guardian)? *Economically*, could there be an unanticipated impact on current or future work? When using real names, clearly documenting and conducting discussions with the participant throughout the research is necessary.

Here are a few general tips for choosing pseudonyms and an example of the kind of brief statement that could be included in articles regarding the naming process (see Table 5.2). In a longer reflective article or book, a page or so dedicated to this topic may be warranted.

General Tips

- When possible, allow participants to choose their own pseudonym.

- Avoid changing the ethnic and cultural associations of the names you reassign.

- Use names as pseudonyms; do not use numbers or letters for names.

- Honor participants' requests to use their real name.
  - o   Review the pros and cons of real-name use.
  - o   Gain signed consent for the use of real names.

- Consider keeping the sense of a name, assuming it would still be confidential (e.g., Melody/Lyric, Rose/Lily). See Peres (2016) for an interesting counterpoint to this.

Research Posters

Research posters are often developed in tandem with first drafts of manuscripts depending on what type of presentations you are accepted to give at a conference. The research poster can be thought of as one of the most visual and succinct research accounts a researcher will use when presenting research data. See Erin Patchett's research poster example in Text Box 5.3 and Figure 5.5, and for her full paper and research poetry derived from transcripts from the same study, see Appendix B. See Appendix D for more tips for creating research posters. I appreciate Erin allowing readers to have access to all of these forms of her work.

TABLE 5.2 ● Possible Participant Naming Statements	
Type of qualitative study	**Possible statements in the article**
A large-*N* or sensitive study	Participants were given randomly generated names to increase confidentiality.
A relational or qualitative study	Participants chose their own pseudonyms.
	Participants were given the option to use part of their legal name or a nickname.
A study where monikers are part of a subculture of study (Internet or gaming).	Participants were given the option to use their moniker from the subculture they are a member of, reflecting the culture being studied.
	Participants were aware that monikers are potentially identifiable.
Sensitive research	Participants chose their own pseudonyms. Pseudonyms were utilized to increase confidentiality.

5.3 RESEARCH POSTERS

ERIN PATCHETT

Not everyone who encounters a research poster will look at it with as much excitement or enthusiasm as a doctoral student at a research event. In fact, both on the giving and on the receiving end, some people may not feel compelled to look at a research poster at all when it features heavy blocks of text. As a practitioner-scholar, my research must be accessible, practical, and helpful to other administrators in my field. In knowing that not everyone may be drawn to a three- by four-foot poster with a wall of text, I sought to utilize basic graphic design elements to enhance how my research was displayed, including color, shape, space, typography, and balance. This process allowed me to learn more about design and challenged me to find succinct yet informative ways to articulate data, with the end goal of engaging more people through the research poster design and pragmatically sharing my research.

Additional considerations when preparing for a successful research poster include

- looking off campus for surprisingly affordable places to print, such as a party store;

- saving space by using a QR code to link readers to your references and other supplemental information; and

- practicing an "elevator pitch" summary of your research to help entice passersby to stay and dialogue with you further.

Source: Reproduced with permission from Erin Patchett.

FIGURE 5.5 ● Methodology

METHODOLOGY
- **Paradigm:** constructivism (Creswell, 2013)
- **Design:** instrumental case study (Stake, 1995)
- **Sampling:** purposeful
- **Interviews:** four (one before and one after training observation with each participant), semi-structured

Participants: Sarah (returner) and Jay (new)
- **Observations:** one (staff in-service)
- **Artifacts:** various (staff onboarding documentation, staff training documentation, department website)
- **Analysis:** transcription, open and axial coding, triangulation, member check

RQ1: What are the experiences of CR student employees who attend inclusivity trainings?
- **RQ2:** How do student employees understand the role of inclusivity within CR departments?
- **RQ3:** What aspects of diversity and inclusion trainings are influential?

RESEARCHER

My interest in this topic is grounded in my decade of experience with supervising and training campus recreation student employees. It is my hope to contribute scholarly work on this topic and inform the profession of best practices for stimulating oppression in the variety of forms it shows up in collegiate recreation

EXPLORING THE EXPERIENCES OF CAMPUS RECREATION STUDENT STAFF IN INCLUSIVITY TRAININGS

ERIN M. PATCHETT
UNIVERSITY OF NORTHERN
COLORADO GREELEY, CO

(RQ 2&3)

ADDITIONAL FINDINGS
Role of CR
- Creating Safe/Welcoming Environment
- Meeting Differing Needs
- Training
- Use of Activities
- Personal Stories
- Conversations

DISCUSSION
- Articulation of the department's values, programs, and services related to inclusion
  Less depth around their personal knowledge, skills, and awareness of diversity, inclusion, and social justice.
- New vs. returning employee: differing views on value of the observed training.
  More intentionality in the structure of training for new versus experienced staff?
- Personal stories were valued but can supervisors incorporate them into inclusivity trainings without the burden falling to marginalized students?
- Peer group discussions outside of formal training were impactful.
  Are supervisors/departments creating opportunities for conversations to continue outside of formal trainings spaces?

(RQ1)

EMPATHY
- Discussed increases in insight of how "othering" exists for patrons of CR

S: "If you are the one different colored M&M then you're like one out of many. And you kind of stand out a little bit more."

J: "A lot of people at the Rec Center, they're surrounded by a bunch of people that are different from them and that might be hard."

LITERATURE

Programs, facilities, policies, and staff training have all been explored as methods to create safe and inclusive campus environments for students with marginalized identities (Burdick et al. 2012; King, 2012; Patchett & Foster, 2015). The purpose of this study was to further explore the staff training component of creating inclusive recreation environments.

INCREASED AWARENESS
- Discussed increases in general awareness as well as self-awareness

S: "I feel it's really helped me understand that not everybody is the same."

J: "Most people's plates had generally the blue M&Ms representing [that] most people in their lives are white."

BEYOND "THE REC"
- Discussed how knowledge from CR trainings impacted them in academic and personal environments

S: "Now teachers say things that aren't appropriate and I'm just like, 'Oh stop, that's not okay.'"

J: "Even outside of the Rec Center, I'm like more keen to notice anti-inclusive language, behavior – it stands out a little bit more now and I'm more actively aware of it. So I can do something about it now."

UNC
UNIVERSITY OF
NORTHERN
COLORADO

Note: From Erin Patchett.

Reproduced with permission from Erin Patchett.

The Methodological Article

If you want to understand what a science is, you should look in the first instance not at its theories or its findings, and certainly not at what its apologists say about it; you should look at what the practitioners of it do.

—Clifford Geertz (1973, p. 5)

Qualitative methodological articles can be some of the most fascinating and valuable reading and writing a researcher can engage in. While this is the primary type of scholarship a methodologist should engage in, I actively encourage all researchers to pursue methodological work even though it may be a secondary line of inquiry. Here are some examples of areas current and past doctoral students I work with have explored methodologically:

- How might a methodology developed for research with children work with adults? (e.g., Beddes, 2017; Lenzy, 2019a)

- What are the ethical considerations for research with the sample under study? (e.g., DeRoche & Lahman, 2008; Kincaid, 2019; Landram, 2018)

- How do the choices of technology in data generation affect the research process? (e.g., Landram, 2018)

A more detailed example such as shoulder-to-shoulder research with children (Griffin et al., 2014) could easily be adapted with adults. This interview method is built on our understanding that when we are interviewing a person, rather than looking them in the eye, looking together at an activity (building with blocks, creating a collage) makes the process more comfortable, relaxed, and culturally respectful, especially to groups that do not make eye contact with semi-strangers or authority figures for long periods of time. The following abstract gives a sense of the methodological study:

The authors present a methodological study with children where two different interview methods were utilized: the *walk-around* (a form of a mobile interview) and the *shoulder-to-shoulder*. The authors review the methodological aspects of the study and provide a brief review of the history of methods employed in research with children. Finally, the authors consider issues around conducting research *with* children in data generation, interview environment, power, and participant engagement. Throughout the article, narrative interludes and the authors' personal reflections as parents and researchers are provided space for thought and narrative glimpses into the research experience. (Griffin et al., 2014, p. 18)

Another example, from "Methodological Considerations for Conducting Qualitative Interviews With Youth Receiving Mental Health Services" (DeRoche & Lahman, 2008), follows:

Use of qualitative interviews with individuals currently receiving mental health services has increased over the last decade in the United States due to calls for system change that emphasizes individuals' perceptions of their own progress. However, interviews with youth receiving mental health services are rarely encountered. In this article, an overview of methodological considerations when conducting an interview inquiry with youth currently receiving mental health services will be discussed, incorporating suggestions from the published literature and our experiences with previous interview studies. Major areas of concern: appropriate interview questions, youth development of cognitive ability, ethical issues, power relationships, cultural competency, and interview inquiry methods.

Methodological research should accompany the study the researcher is conducting. This is particularly relevant when a topic is not covered by methodological sources or it seems to be dated or used only with specific groups of people, such as white men, and has not been explored with other groups. Examples of methodological areas for research follow:

- Should participants be compensated for research, and if so, how much should they receive and how? What amount could be considered coercive? Does the idea of coercion through compensation become heightened depending on the participant's perceived power due to age, class, or income?

- Focus group literature traditionally indicated that sensitive topics were not appropriate for focus groups. This does not seem to have held up over the passage of time. Why is this? We might speculate that social media has brought sensitive topics to the forefront, or since support groups around sensitive topics such as death or addiction have existed historically, perhaps thinking certain topics were not appropriate was the result of oversensitivity on the researcher's part.

If these ideas are intriguing to you, I believe you should consider conducting methodological explorations. Methodological literature is vital to the development of each of our respective fields of research.

The Gist

In this chapter, I sought to provide concise information on how to go about writing a thematic qualitative research manuscript. I advocated for this manuscript being the outcome of research courses and assistantships during graduate work, believing that novices should begin to learn the craft as students and not while trying to achieve tenure. All recent doctoral graduates have a dissertation in hand. Research articles demonstrate their ability to publish beyond the requisite dissertation. I presented areas to consider when naming participants, ideas for constructing research posters, and a review of how to identify a predatory publisher. Additionally, I introduced the methodological manuscript as a vital, scholarly contribution readers should consider creating. In the resources section, I provide examples of articles published from my introductory qualitative research course. Were they perfect? No. But the articles demonstrated the students were finishers, budding scholars who persevered in an arena where not being able to finish publication is deadly—*publish and persevere!*

Reflexive Questions

Before Writing

1. What type of manuscripts might be ethically developed from this research (e.g., practitioner, literature review, research, methodological)?

2. Which journals would be a good fit for this research study? (Compile a short list.) Have you conducted a journal review to be sure of this list?

3. Have you identified several articles to serve as loose models from the journal to which you are planning to submit?

   a. Check to see if the journal publishes research studies with similar research designs and sample sizes. The journal may seem like a good fit topically. Still, if there is no evidence of qualitative studies or qualitative studies with the sample size you have, it will, in all likelihood, be a waste of time to submit a manuscript to the journal.

   b. If you identify journals in your discipline and qualitative multiple-discipline journals (e.g., *The Qualitative Report*), consider which journal would be a better fit.

      i. Have you published before? If so, in what type of journals have you published?

      ii. Is it preferable to demonstrate your ability to publish in your field?

Resources

Journal Articles From an Introductory Qualitative Research Course

The following articles were initially developed by students in the introductory course I teach. The first assignment in the course is to read these so students can build confidence in their course research work potential and see an array of research designs. Many more students present introductory research at conferences.

Andrew, L. (2007). Comparison of teacher educators' instructional methods with the constructivist ideal. *The Teacher Educator*, *42*(3), 157–184. https://doi.org/10.1080/08878730709555401

Casper, J. (2006). You can't be serious, that ball was in: An investigation of junior tennis cheating behavior. *The Qualitative Report*, *11*(1), 20–36.

Choi, A. J., Stotlar, D. K., & S. R. Park (2006). Visual ethnography of on-site sport sponsorship activation: L.G. Action Sports Championship. *Sports Marketing Quarterly*, *15*, 71–79. https://repository.usfca.edu/cgi/viewcontent.cgi?article=1021&context=ess

Correa-Torres, S. M., & Howell, J. J. (2004). Facing the challenges of itinerant teaching: Perspectives and suggestions from the field. *Journal of Visual Impairment & Blindness*, *98*(7), 420–433. https://doi.org/10.1177/0145482X0409800704

Farnsworth, C. R., & Luckner, J. L. (2008). The impact of assistive technology on curriculum accommodation for a Braille-reading student. *Rehabilitation Education for Blindness and Visual Impairment*, *39*(4), 171–187. https://doi.org/10.3200/REVU.39.4.171-187

Peterson-Beeton, R. (2007). Minority students' perspectives on chemistry in an alternative high school. *The Qualitative Report*, *12*(4), 705–728.

Traugutt, A., Augustin, J. D., & Hazzaa, R. H. (2018). Perceptions of athletic identity: A case study of a niche club sport. *The Qualitative Report*, *23*(4), 875–888. https://doi.org/10.46743/2160-3715/2018.3083

Other Articles

Caulley, D. N. (2008). Making qualitative research reports less boring: The techniques of writing creative nonfiction. *Qualitative Inquiry*, *14*(3), 424–449. https://doi.org/10.1177/1077800407311961

Thompson, B. (1995). Publishing your research results: Some suggestions and counsel. *Journal of Counseling & Development*, *73*(3), 342–345. http://doi.org/10.1002/j.1556-6676.1995.tb01761.x

Thompson, B. (2016). On the various aspects of publishing journal articles and academic books. *Research in the Schools*, *23*(1), 1–7.

Books

Fox, N. (2013). *The structure of a qualitative paper*. University of Sheffield.

Kamler, B., & Thomson, P. (2014). *Helping doctoral students write: Pedagogies for supervision*. Routledge. https://doi.org/10.4324/9781315813639

Merriam, S. B., & Grenier, R. S. (Eds.). (2019). *Qualitative research in practice: Examples for discussion and analysis*. Wiley.

A Partial List of Qualitative Journals

Action Research

Ethnographic Encounters

Ethnography

Ethnography and Education

Field Methods

Forum: Qualitative Social Research

Global Qualitative Nursing Research

The Grounded Theory Review

International Journal of Qualitative Methods

International Review of Qualitative Research

Journal of Autoethnography

Journal of Contemporary Ethnography

Journal of Ethnographic & Qualitative Research

Narrative Inquiry

Qualitative Inquiry

The Qualitative Report

Qualitative Research

Qualitative Researcher

Visual Ethnography

Reflexive Activities

1. Complete a qualitative journal review.

    a. This activity will help in three major areas. First, you can identify which journals will be an appropriate outlet for your research. (See the list of qualitative journals at the end of this chapter under Resources, but consider journals in your own discipline first since these will reach scholars directly in your area.) Second, identifying several articles that are similar to yours sample wise and methodologically serves not only to provide you an excellent model to use as you write but also as a guide to whether the journal is a good match. For example, an editor once told me that their journal published qualitative research. But a review of more than five years of the journal's issues allowed me to see that they had published just two qualitative pieces, both of which had samples of more than 50 and were grant funded. This support of qualitative research is obviously only for certain types of manuscripts. Without a thorough understanding of the journal to which you are submitting, you can waste valuable time during an already lengthy publication process. Third, you will be able to identify appropriate literature to reference from the journal you submit to. For many, at first thought, this may seem like an ingratiating act. However, editors have pointed out that if you cannot find any literature to cite from the journal, it is obviously a mismatch, which seems sensible to me. You should not overly cite the journal or rewrite your whole literature review but instead thoughtfully choose some articles to integrate into your work from the target journal.

2. Become a journal manuscript reviewer.

   a. Sign up to be a reviewer for a research conference or journal. Some will allow graduate students to conduct reviews. If they do not, check with a professor you work with regarding the journals they review for. When they receive a manuscript, the professor can ask the editor if you can conduct the review simultaneously. This is a common joint activity I do with both my advisees and my students in my writing course. This experience allows you to see both the process and the rating scales that editors use from behind the scenes. It provides valuable experience to review the work of others in ways that are constructive, not needlessly cruel, and the work bolsters your vita.

Publish and Persevere: The Publication Process

The unread story is not a story; it is little black marks
on wood pulp. The reader, reading it, makes
it live: a live thing, a story.

—Ursula K. Le Guin (2017, p. 198)

Harry F. Wolcott (1994) wrote that research has not occurred unless it is published. One way to make sense of this statement is to consider that research should be disseminated in a form that continues to be accessible to others. For example, if research is disseminated through an oral conference presentation, how can anyone other than the attendees access it? The need for engagement between the writing and readers is also reflected in the literary world, as expressed in the quote I opened the chapter with from Le Guin (2017), where she describes the need for readers to engage with writing in order to make writing "live" (p. 198). As researchers, we would see this as an opportunity for others to extend our research. Having said this, I remain convinced that there is impactful qualitative research that languishes for many reasons—some reasons can be attended to more easily than others.

Pratt (2008) referencing Karen Golden-Biddle and Karen Locke's (1997) statement that qualitative researchers are in essence professional text writers, adds, "We are known, as a profession and as individual scholars, by what we write and what we publish. However, as a profession, we tend to be more forthcoming about how to conduct studies than we are about publishing them" (p. 482). I wholeheartedly agree, and therefore, the primary purpose of this chapter is to bring transparency to the publication process. The phrase "publish or perish" is an ominous adage that can still quicken one's heart years after becoming well published. I advocate for turning the phrase on its head and helping others *publish and persevere.*

Early in my career, I was contacted by a special-issue journal editor and asked to write an article on research ethics in higher education. Due to the short time-line, I flew my mom to my home to care for my young son during the extra time I needed to write. I worked unceasingly in the basement to get the piece out. After I submitted the manuscript, I was told they could not use it since it was too long. I had not been given length guidelines but had kept to the standard length of articles. Shocked, I replied I would edit it to a shorter length and asked for specific guidance. I also asked for the reviewers' comments. After all, I had been contacted and asked to produce the manuscript, and I assumed I would at least receive feedback on how to revise it. The special-issue editor then told me that the regular editor of the journal did not think the article was a good match for their journal. She comfortingly, and I felt condescendingly (my interpretation was perhaps due to feeling bitter), went on to say she was sure I could get a book contract to write about the topic—as though it is a simple thing to get a book contract, let alone turn a journal manuscript into a book-length project. To this day, I remain confused about what actually happened and am suspicious that the rejection was due to the critical, feminist, and culturally responsive foundation the article rested on and the first-person, direct writing voice I strive to adopt.

This story has a good ending. Several years later, I published the article in a journal that had a better ranking than the initial journal. Years after that, I did use the article as a foundation for my first book prospectus, which I went on to publish with SAGE under the title Ethics in Social Science Research: Becoming Culturally Responsive. *Not all such stories have a good ending. The culmination of this writing took so long that the hard work I had invested did not help any of my first promotions and it occurred after I was a full professor. I can clearly imagine a different ending to this story.*

In this chapter, I fill a gap that may occur after a research course is over, an oral conference talk or poster presentation is given, or the dissertation is completed. Novice researchers are often guided through the research and writing process of a course paper and thesis/dissertation, but the publication process may remain a mystery. This is at times due to their mentors and professors also encountering behind-the-scenes struggles with publication. It is difficult to balance being a productive researcher, instructor, and service provider throughout one's career. Researchers who have had success with publishing may have periods of inactivity and publication areas where they have little experience, publication tales that are still befuddling—worse yet, defeating—or a need to stay abreast with changes in the field of publication. Struggling writers have expressed to me a sense of feeling like an imposter (see Text Box 6.1 for a courageous discussion of this from a student perspective). Making the publication process permeable can reduce some of the uncertainty.

Towards this goal, in this chapter, I

- walk the readers through the publication process for an article step-by-step;
- address controversial and high-stakes issues including
  - ○ authorship,
  - ○ length of time for reviews, and
  - ○ promotion of publications; and
- feature text boxes with examples of student researchers' experiences with publication.

More than 20 years ago, when I initially developed the course materials that this chapter emerged from, I had not published yet. Rereading the chapter, I can see how even though I use my own experiences as the primary material, the core organization draws directly on Bruce Thompson's (1995) work and a conference presentation I attended that he gave as a journal editor where he discussed the publication process. I appreciate his clear and concise direction. I also see Harry Wolcott's (1994) and, more recently, Mitchell Allen's (2016) presence throughout this chapter. I want to acknowledge the help I received through their clear explanations, writings on publication, and clarifying the hidden nature of publishing for a novice.

6.1 IMPOSTER: PRESENTING RESEARCH IN A BOOK CHAPTER

CHERJANÉT LENZY

I developed a book chapter from a study I conducted during my doctoral coursework (Lenzy, 2019b). My biggest challenge in putting the research together for the chapter was navigating my constant imposter syndrome. I explored the experiences of Black women activists and their intersectional identities in race-based activism.

Toward the end of the class, I was asked to consider writing a book chapter for an upcoming book. I was elated! I couldn't believe that a friend and colleague felt that my work was worthy enough to be included in the upcoming work!

(Continued)

(Continued)

Of course, I thought this was a mistake. As I read the list of people who were asked to submit a proposal, names of well-known scholars and activists popped out at me. I couldn't believe that my name, let alone my writing, could potentially be among the same pages. Though I knew it was the imposter syndrome talking, I felt that anything I could come up with wouldn't be good enough. Still, I really wanted to do it. I hadn't told many people, but it was a long-held dream to write a book chapter (and eventually a full book).

After talking to the professor teaching the qualitative research class about his thoughts on my research fitting the chapter proposal criteria, I took a stab at cleaning things up to submit. The whole process was overwhelming, but I persisted. Though I thought what I wrote was good for class, I didn't know if it was good enough for a book chapter. But I figured I wouldn't know if it was good enough until I submitted it.

Sometime after the final edits of the book happened, the authors were notified that there would be a digital book launch. This would be a time for the authors of each chapter to spend 10 minutes discussing their respective chapters in a webinar format. Though it was voluntary, I felt that it was a great opportunity and I should do it. Again, I immediately felt uncomfortable and kept trying to talk myself out of participating. I mean, I wrote the book chapter; my name was in the book. Why did I need to show my face and talk about it? What brought me over the hump was realizing that this is what I had been asking the universe for. And now that it had been delivered, I was basically being disrespectful and not honoring the gift that was given to me.

I watched the recording of the launch a few days later and was impressed with myself. I should have been. I know what I'm talking about. I worked hard for this, and I'm an expert in this research. I still struggle with being comfortable and confident about my work. I know I work hard. I know I'm a good writer, but I still fall back on humility. In some ways, I battle with the balance of confidence and arrogance.

Even in writing this short text, I am obsessing about each word I type. Unfortunately, I don't think this will ever end, no matter how much research writing I do. I think, at least for me, part of feeling like an imposter is also about my perfectionism and my desire to do good work. So maybe the real thing to work on is believing in the value of my own words and that the words will land the way I want them to and speak to who is supposed to hear them.

(See Cherjanét Lenzy (2019a) for an extension of her research in her dissertation.)

Source: Reproduced with permission from Cherjanét Lenzy,

Getting Organized

I assume, for the purpose of this chapter, that readers have research written up in an unpublished manuscript form. This may be a research course paper, a conference paper, or a completed thesis/dissertation. I suggest finding that manuscript and working through this chapter using the manuscript as your writing project. If this cannot happen, try to picture a specific manuscript and make notes to yourself on what the next steps toward publication should be.

Incorporate Any Appropriate Existing Feedback

A first step in getting organized is to consider how best to incorporate input you received from people such as instructors, professors, conference paper reviewers, discussants, conference attendees, or committee members. At this point, until you receive the review of your manuscript from the journal, it is your choice which edits to accept or ignore. You may have received extensive helpful feedback that enhances the research manuscript, or the input may be from people who do not fully understand qualitative research or only understand one portion of such a vast field. It is also typical to receive feedback from a quantitative perspective, which should not be incorporated into a manuscript going forward.

Authorship

Whether the research was conducted as a solo endeavor or with co-researchers will guide the authorship. At times an additional author may be invited to work on the submission of the manuscript for the expertise they bring. In the area of authorship order, consider who had the idea for the research and what the contribution levels were of the various coauthors, along with your discipline-specific guidelines. No one has the automatic right to authorship, including course professors, committee members, and advisors. The issue of authorship may be contentious due to changing ways of thinking, cultural norms, and discipline expectations, so I want to be clear that in a contemporary Western setting, qualitative research authorship includes people who have worked on a manuscript after a course or defense is over. Before that these important people are merely doing their job—what the student has paid them to do. (See Sections 8.12 a, b, and c of the American Psychological Association Ethics Code and Section 15 of the American Education Research Association's Code of Ethics for more guidance on ethical authorship: http://www.apa.org/ethics/code/index.aspx and http://www.aera.net/Portals/38/docs/About_AERA/CodeOfEthics(1).pdf, respectively.)

At this point, if you have not already done so, send an email to all the authors outlining the contribution expectations of the manuscript (who will do what) and author order. Be sure to note that the authorship order will change if the workload changes, since this is often an organic process that cannot be fully anticipated. Keep a file of the initial email and the replies from the authors. Be sure the coauthors know that they need to alert you to communicate changes since the publication process can take a long time. You will also need the coauthors' names as they wish them to be written, along with their degree level and current affiliation. Throughout the journal submission process, send all authors copies of the final submissions and letters to and from the editor. Ask them to save the copies and save your own copies in multiple places.

6.2 EXAMPLE AGREEMENT FOR CONTRIBUTION TO A PUBLICATION

MARIA LAHMAN

Self-Portrait Reflexivity Article

Hi All,

I also put this information in the discussion description on Canvas.

If you would like to be part of this article, please note the following:

1. Upload a reflection on the process to the discussion on Canvas.

2. Upload any photos you took of the process.

3. Comment on some of the other reflections.

4. Look at all of the portraits in Dannon's link, and make a comment or reflection about them.

5. You will have an opportunity to agree/disagree to the use of the photos you are in that you submitted along with the article.

6. Be sure I have your new email as you graduate and leave the university.

7. Let me know of any other ideas you have.

We will revisit this plan as a class in several weeks and again in January.

Article Agreement

Author order: Maria, Becky, Dannon, (alpha by family name hereafter), Morgan, Kimberley, Michelle, Amber, Margaret, Kritika, Rowen, and Jennifer. Order is subject to change given your contributions.

Working title: Own Your Walls: Researcher Reflexive Self-Portraits

Working abstract: As part of an advanced doctoral research course, members participated in an in-depth exploration of the methodology portraiture. In this article, the authors, course instructor, and 10 students represent themselves as researchers through collage portraits and written reflexive responses. A brief review of portraiture, collage in research, and researcher reflexivity, along with relevant course experiences, is presented. Images of the collage process and resulting portraits are highlighted. A collage of a class emerges as issues of transparency in research, the role of the researcher, and representation are explored.

Predators

A word about predatory academics—the push to publish can be so strong that colleagues may actually steal your ideas or try to force you to allow them to join your

work. *In my case, I witnessed an example of this early in my graduate work, which along with being the child of an author prepared me to avoid these types of situations. As sad as this advice is, it is best not to talk about your research ideas in groups that might utilize them. Also, discuss research projects after the grant is secured or the manuscript is in press. My father, a fiction author, did not talk a lot about writing during the writing process. He felt the more you talked, the less your writing progressed. I have found some people talk about their research a lot, but it hasn't ever been published. I do talk to my students about my writing and publication. I think it is incumbent on me to do so as part of helping them peek into the publication process. Whatever I am writing and publishing during the semester I am teaching, I share with the class at appropriate times. I do not mean that I force a captive audience to listen to my ego, but instead I use my ups and downs as possible lessons we can all learn from. Before I had tenure, I found it also helped to have a well-thought-out deflection that gave me time to see if the person offering to work with me was productive, a quality collaborator, and sincere. I would say, "My department chair says I am overcommitted, so I will have to get back to you." Then, I would check the person's vita and discreetly ask around to see if they were an active scholar and a well-thought-of collaborator. In hindsight, I am still struck by how many well-thought-of researchers still were not able to deliver. I can also see this in my own interactions. I work hard not to overpromise and overload myself, but still I know I have let potential co-authors down at times.*

Journal Review

If you have not already conducted a review of the journals in your field and qualitative journals in general, do so now. Unlike a literature review, a journal review focuses on which journals would be the best match for your manuscript. I suggest developing a list of three journals in the order of which one you will submit to first. That way if you do receive a rejection, and most published authors have, knowing where the manuscript will be sent next shortens the amount of time you yearn to curl up in a ball and never look at the manuscript again. When reviewing potential journals, read the journal's description of what they publish and the author's guide. If the journal seems like a good fit, go a step further and find a few articles that match your methodology and sample size. The research area does not need to be the same. This will give you a sense of whether your work is a good fit. As a novice, a publication shows you have an understanding of the process, and, importantly, that you are a *finisher*, who knows how to move research through the entire process. This is more important than the rank of the journal. Sending a manuscript to a highly ranked journal may not be the best choice due to the amount of time it takes for peer review to occur and the probability of rejection. See Text Box 6.3 for James Hodges's discussion about how he considers the impact factor and what an h index is.

For qualitative journals and journals receptive to qualitative research, see the following website: https://tqr.nova.edu/journals/. For an in-depth discussion about how to choose journals to submit to, see Chapter 5 under the section Choosing a Journal.

6.3   JAMES SPILLS THE TEA ON THE IMPACT FACTOR

JAMES HODGES

Okay, so think of journal impact factor (JIF) like this: It's a number that tells us which journals are doing big things in a certain field. The higher the impact factor, the more impactful your journal is. Obviously, because you want to be on the winning team, you may want your articles to be published in journals that have high impact factors. Some members of the scientific community use the impact factor to choose which journals they want to submit their articles to.

Some people aren't really feeling the impact factor though, because a high-impact factor number on a journal can mean absolutely nothing for the majority of the articles in that journal. Just because an article is in a high-impact journal doesn't mean that it's a high-impact article or that the journal has a lot of high-impact articles. Mind you, impact factor is an average measure. So if a journal published 10 articles in the past two years and 9 of them got 0 citations and 1 got 3,000 citations, that means that those 9 authors with 0-citation articles can boast that they are in a high-impact-factor journal though they contributed nothing to the cause. Some sources say that as many as 75% of articles used in a JIF calculation can actually have fewer than the reported average number of citations (Bohannon, 2016). Also, are all citations created equally? Should you get to brag about being in a high-impact journal if you aren't a principal author?

Calculating the impact factor is easy. Basically, you take the total number of all the citations a journal received for the past two years and divide that number by the total number of articles published by that journal in the past two years. The result is your JIF:

$$JIF = \frac{\text{Total citations Year 1} + \text{Total citations Year 2}}{\text{Total articles published Year 1} + \text{Total articles published Year 2}}$$

Overall, I suggest that you don't take the impact factor to heart. It's a good number to ballpark the *presence* of an impact and not necessarily the *magnitude* of an impact. Don't trip if you want to publish an article in a low-impact-factor journal; because of the inadequacies of JIF, most members of the qualitative research community won't put you on blast if your article is published in a journal with a low impact factor.

(For further reading, see Bohannon, 2016.)

Source: Reproduced with permission from James Hodges.

Tools to Support Writing Collaboration

Deciding as a group how you will work on drafts of the manuscript is a crucial step. The ability to track changes and comment in a document has dramatically enhanced writing communication. Some edit functions also allow reviewers to attach voice clips. No longer do we have to work to decipher cramped, spidery handwriting or scrawls on our written work. At times, after hours of grading by hand, I would look back to review my notes for final comments and not be sure what I had written. However, when a document is printed and edited on paper, I believe more errors are generally identified and a fuller sense of how the entire draft is functioning can be ascertained.

Initially, it may be best to have some face-to-face meetings, phone calls, or internet meetings. However, in this case, we are discussing a draft of a completed manuscript, so the most efficient way to finalize the draft may well be through computer-mediated communication. Some writing groups still prefer to email the manuscript to a group member who updates it, passes it on to the next person, and so on. However, there are many ways to collaborate in writing that allow multiple authors to work on a document simultaneously, such as Google Docs.

Computer-mediated collaboration tools should be carefully considered. Some of the benefits include the ability to work with groups that are geographically dispersed—even to the extent that when one member is finishing writing, others may be starting their workday and are able to continue advancing aspects of the document. The COVID-19 pandemic clearly underscored safety as a reason to use computer tools. Points to attend to include (a) the security claims of the site, (b) retaining ownership of the work you upload to the site, (c) coauthors' ability to use the site, and (d) associated costs.

Regarding security, for example, some universities do not allow raw data to be put into sites such as Dropbox because of security concerns. If a manuscript is in full draft form, it should no longer contain any data in it that would be potentially problematic. Getting coauthors up to speed with new technology is not usually difficult. When I have had co-authors who are not familiar with the technology we are proposing to use, or I am the one who needs updating, it has always been a simple matter to find an instructional video on the internet or have one of the knowledgeable members go over the process smoothly and quickly. Finally, when working with student coauthors and unfunded research, it is always best to look for collaboration tools that are free or cheap.

6.4 JAMES SPILLS THE TEA ON THE *H* INDEX
JAMES HODGES

Hey—it's me again.

Though calculated differently, think of the *h* index as an impact factor but for individual authors. The *h* index is a single number that measures the influence and impact of an author's entire body of work (Spicer, 2015). So *all* of their articles are considered in the creation of the *h* index (contrasting to JIF, in which recency is a latent contributor since only articles from the past

(Continued)

(Continued)

two years are used in the calculation). The *h* index is the point at which the number of articles an author has published and the number of times each article has been published are the same. So if I have three articles (A, B, and C) and they've been cited 4, 9, and 275 times, respectively, then I have an *h* index of 3 because I have three articles that have *all* been cited at least three times.

I'm guessing you can see the issue already with my example, huh? That single number does not tell me the entire story. So you're going to tell me that I'm going to be punished with a low *h* index of 3 for doing non-influential articles early in my career even though I've vindicated myself with a groundbreaking article that has been cited thousands of times and changed the course of my field? Well, basically yes. That single number is so easily influenced that it doesn't make sense. It's kind of like the impact factor when I asked, "Are all citations the same?" Did they include citations from all types of your work? Should your contribution to the cited work be considered? What if I boost my citations by allowing myself and frequent coauthors to cite the work we've done together previously? How do you reconcile the differences in *h* indices when one field demands 20 articles per year versus another field requiring only 5 articles a year?

When considering *h* indices, keep in mind (a) how long you've been in the field, (b) the normal number of articles your field expects you to publish, and (c) the stories being told that the single number cannot tell you (quality of your paper, etc.).

(For further information, see André Spicer [2015] and Becker Guides at https://beckerguides.wustl.edu/authors/hindex#_edn1.)

Source: Reproduced with permission from James Hodges.

Keeping Track of Multiple Projects

I am usually involved in many writing projects that are at different stages. At this point, it bears reminding all of us to back up our work as part of the process of staying organized. (See Text Box 6.5 for reasons to back up work) I find it helpful to keep a simple chart of my writing projects and what stage each is at (see Table 6.1). On my computer, I also have items color coded—a green font would mean I am actively working on the writing, and red would mean I really need to consider what the next step is. I only update the chart three times a year at the end of each semester and the summer term, so I can have what I will be writing in the next few months in focus. I have found that a hidden delay tactic of mine, and of many students I teach, is organizing at the expense of actually writing, so keep the chart and your interaction with it simple and efficient.

TABLE 6.1 ● Writing Projects Chart Excerpt (2016–2017)			
Author order	**Topic**	**What stage/ where submitted**	**To do**
Lahman, R.	How to write research poetry	Sent very rough draft to Vee. 2.16	Submit by Dec. 1
Lahman	Mothering poem	Submitted to QI 10.29.16	
Lahman	Hannah: Infertility auto	Unfinished draft	
Maria, C. L. Rest of class	Collage article		Need to send to Lindsay
Lahman	Ethics book prospectus	Submitted to Sage 2.26.15, under contract	Submit all 1.1.17 List of contributors, rewrite, R. permission
Teman, Lahman, and Richard	LGBT IRB Paternalization	Submitted to AERA	

6.5 BACK UP!

MARIA LAHMAN

I have been collecting stories over my career of times when documents, data, and manuscripts were not backed up. I go over these stories in the introduction to the qualitative research course I teach and ask for more examples, so the list has become long.

Here is a sample of the most awful:

- A squirrel was electrocuted on a power line, which then fried the computer inside the house.

- An apartment complex burned down, and a student's data and computer were lost.

- A couple separated during the dissertation process, and when one of them tried to pick up their data the other one said, "What data?"

- Audio recordings on cassettes were erased in airport security.

- A box of data was stolen from an unlocked car.

Back up!

Preparing the Manuscript for Publication

Good writing is like a windowpane.

—George Orwell

At this stage, I feel people tend to get rushed and not attend to details or hold on to their writing much too long, pouring over it in excruciating detail. Neither of these practices lends itself to publication. In this section, I will go over some of the final aspects that should be taken care of before submission, including writing quality and attention to detail.

Writing Quality

Of this, Thompson (1995) wrote, "Present your work in the best shape it can be, because you may not get a real second chance" (p. 342). Identify the style guide that the journal requires, and then attend to its requirements closely. This is one of the few areas where you can be guaranteed that what you are doing is "right." However, do not confuse a style guide with your actual writing style or with good writing. As I have already stated in this book, style guides may be said to be an important part of why academic style is at times boring, or inaccessible to nonacademics. (See Text Box 6.6, written by a student researcher, on the vulnerability that sharing drafts of our writing for editing involves.).

The journal style guide will provide essential information such as abstract length, manuscript length, whether this length includes references, and so on. Neglecting to follow these requirements can result in the outright rejection of a manuscript without any review.

Getting professional feedback, editing services, and informal feedback prior to submitting a manuscript can all be an essential part of the process. I work with colleagues who are professional editors, and they say they would not hire an editor themselves; however, two of my family members are professional editors and writers and strongly feel that *everyone* benefits from the services of an editor. The editor provides a fresh outsider's perspective—new eyes. If you can afford it, use a professional editor whenever possible. Other ways to obtain editing include trading services with another writer, where you edit for each other, which is also a benefit of being in a writers group. Paid supports such as Grammarly (https://www.grammarly.com/) can also provide help but are not in tune with details such as APA style guidelines. SAGE offers editing services (http://languageservices.sagepub.com/en/services/editing/), which I employed for one chapter of this book, prior to submitting it for review, to see if I would recommend them. The service was excellent and quick but costly. Other similar services do exist, but be careful to determine if they understand academic writing. Graduate schools may suggest editors, but in my personal experience, these can be hit or miss, so it is best to try out a short paper with a new editor before committing to something larger. A benefit of this type of editor is that they often know the style the graduate school requires for dissertations.

6.6   VULNERABILITY IN SHARING UNFINISHED/FIRST DRAFTS

AUSTIN HAMILTON

Many times, sharing my first draft of any written work can feel a bit vulnerable. I suppose this makes sense given that these first few stabs at writing are often raw and less filtered—you know, before I have the chance to edit away anything that could be confusing to the reader. Often, the first few drafts have my readers chasing obscure, superfluous facts that I found interesting at the time of writing. Think Alice chasing the White Rabbit toward who-knows-where but with the Queen of Hearts nipping at her heels.

So when the time came to share, my natural reaction was always to shy away. To ease myself into a greater sense of vulnerability, I often reframed the interaction with classmate-editors. For me, it was helpful to think of classmate-editors as *test readers*. I figure, if they can't follow what I'm writing about, future readers won't stand a chance. Of course, it also helps if you find yourself with helpful and supportive fellow writers who are trying to make your writing the best that it can be. Most of the time, I volunteer to help edit my colleagues' work as well. In this way, writers are also editors and subject to vulnerability. So go ahead and stretch yourself to your most creative limits, knowing that you will ultimately have a cowriter/coeditor to reel you back in if you stretch too far.

Source: Reproduced with permission from Austin Hamilton.

The Details

Pay attention to details such as the identity of the current editor of the journal and whether your name should be removed from the document (for some journals, this means even in a third-person literature review), and consider running a self-plagiarism check. Check the reference style and whether all references are cited and citations referenced. Thompson (1995) says that around 40% of the manuscripts he has worked with as an editor had errors in this area. These steps all help tighten the manuscript submission process. Putting the article into single-space format and proofreading it in that form can highlight issues that are not easily seen in double-space format. Once, when proofreading in single space, I noticed I had started several paragraphs, in a row, using the same phrase. I could not see this in the double-spaced format. Conduct a find-and-replace search for "lazy" writing words—overused words (e.g., "very," "good," "use," "that," "notion," "various," "ly" adverbs). Identify these words in your writing and weed them out. While not printing on paper is an important part of being environmentally conscious, I do find that if I review a printed draft prior to submitting, I see errors I cannot see on the computer screen.

A researcher's journal manuscript was stolen.

She vowed to find the thief, saying—"You have my words"!

Submission

Submission to a journal may occur by email attachment, via postal mail, or, increasingly, through a computer program where you upload the manuscript. You will need a letter to the editor (include all your contact details) and at least one copy (three to four for postal mail) of the manuscript without your name or any identifying information. Replace your name with "the author" (first author, second author, etc.). Put your name back in the manuscript at the acceptance stage. You may need an author's biography. Keep this short and sweet. The following is an example:

Author Biography

Maria K. E. Lahman, Ph.D. is a professor in the Department of Applied Statistics and Research Methods at the University of Northern Colorado, USA, where she teaches qualitative research. Her specialty areas are the advancement of ethical qualitative research with an emphasis on diversity, research with young children, and aesthetic representations of research.

Some journals permit you to make specialized requests at the time of submission (e.g., *Qualitative Inquiry* allows requests for an alternative format). This will enable words and images to be laid out in a specific fashion. For example, I had a poem shaped like a heart, which could not be printed in a two-column format (Lahman, 2018). I requested a one-column format and was granted this particular layout.

At times, you will need to pay a fee when you submit to a journal. The amount of money varies, but most journals I work with do not ask for any money. None of the journals I submit manuscripts to ask for money from students. Be cautious; if a large amount of money is requested, you may be working with a predatory publisher. I have found my university librarian to be invaluable in helping sort out questions I have about a journal's legitimacy. (See Chapter 5 Text Box 5.1 for a discussion on predatory publishers.) The journal may ask you to provide the names of potential reviewers. These reviewers typically should not be people you know well or who work at your university.

Ready to Submit?

If you can't explain something simply, you don't understand it.

—Albert Einstein

The following should not be a delaying tactic. Conduct these steps efficiently, with purpose. As you move into submitting, reread the abstract to ensure that it aligns with the title, keywords, and findings. Rewrite as needed. If the manuscript has languished for a while, update the literature review for the months or years that have gone by. If there are appropriate articles from the journal you are submitting to, add them. Some say this is pandering, but I heard a respected editor say that if in the history of the journal there is not one article you can reference, how could the journal be a good match? The argument makes sense to me. As you run through these last few details, continue to ask yourself if you have expressed everything as clearly and as simply as possible. Edit for overly pompous academic speak and cumbersome sentence structures.

Submit!

The Editor

Now that you have submitted your article, let's take a look at the process of what is most likely happening. You should receive an email of receipt. This may be an automatic receipt of your uploaded manuscript and therefore almost instantaneous. If you do not receive this email within a few days, check the submission system, or if you submitted outside of a system, email the editor. Lack of a letter of receipt generally means there has been some error in submission. This can waste precious time.

After receiving your manuscript, one of the editors or their assistants will review the manuscript to determine whether it fits the mission of the journal and to see if you have followed the journal's major writing requirements, including removing your name from the manuscript. Be aware that there are a few qualitative journals that do not use a "blind" review process, preferring instead a more transparent and collaborative mode of peer review. If the manuscript is determined to not meet the journal's mission or standards, you will get a "desk rejection" from the editor without the manuscript receiving a peer review. Some editors will suggest alternative journals.

Another essential role of the editor can be to guide you if there is disagreement among the reviewers. In the area of academic humor, which is a type of grisly, laughing-through-tears humor, the contrarian, impossible-to-please reviewer is called "reviewer number two." See the Facebook site Reviewer 2 Must Be Stopped (https://www.facebook.com/groups/reviewer2/?fref=ts), the Tumblr account Shit My Reviewers Say (https://shitmyreviewerssay .tumblr.com/), or the Twitter account Shit Academics Say (https://twitter .com/academicssay) to obtain a fuller sense of how frustrating this type of review may be.

If the reviewers are contradicting one another, look to the editor's letter for guidance. Thompson (1995) says, "We should believe everything an editor says except about turn-around times" (p. 343) for reviews. While I have never had an editor tell me to ignore a reviewer, they have emphasized one reviewer's points and obviously made no mention of another reviewer's points. (See Text Box 6.7 for the major areas a qualitative journal editor should consider when reviewing qualitative manuscripts and Text Box 6.8 for thoughts from a student editorial assistant.)

Three reviewers walk into a bar.

Reviewer 1 orders a drink.

Reviewer 2 says, "This is not the bar I would have gone to."

Reviewer 3 says, "We are in a joke."

Reviewer 2 says, "Well, I am not a joke."

(Inspired by Shit Academics Say, 2018)

6.7 DATA AS STAR: THREE POINTS TO CONSIDER (CHENAIL, 1995)

Maria Lahman (with appreciation, paraphrasing Ron Chenail, creator and longtime editor of *The Qualitative Report*)

Chenail created the first online, open-access English-language qualitative research journal, *The Qualitative Report*, more than 20 years ago. As a longtime journal editor and leader in the field, Chenail (1995) makes three points about creating publishable qualitative research:

1. *Methodological "openness":* "In addition to seeing the results of the [research] labor, the reader should have ample opportunities to examine the particulars of the inquiry: What choices were made by the researcher in the construction of the study, what were the steps in the process of forming the research questions, selecting a site, generating and collecting the data, processing and analyzing the data, and selecting the data exemplars for the paper or presentation" (pp. 1–2).

2. *Data as star, or data rich:* The focus is on data, not on the methods, author, interpretation, or discussion. The main focus in qualitative

research is on the data themselves, in all their richness, breadth, and depth.

3. *Juxtaposing data:* "Juxtapose data excerpts with . . . talk about the data. Be it in the presentation of categories, themes . . . pictures, or drawings, the essence of presenting qualitative research comes down to how well you are able to juxtapose the data with . . . descriptions, explanations, analysis, or commentaries" (p. 5)—that is, discuss the data.

Anticipating the Reviews

Manuscript: Something submitted in haste and returned at leisure.

—Oliver Herford (Fine Dictionary, n.d.)

Time passes slowly when waiting for manuscript reviews so while you are waiting, consider if there are other articles you can ethically write from the research experience. Be careful not to send the same data representations and findings to two different journals. This is considered unprofessional and, in some cases, unethical. Examples of articles that are of different genres include (a) a review of the literature, (b) a practitioner article, (c) a methodological article, and (d) an alternative or aesthetic representation. See Chapter 5 for a more extensive discussion of these types of articles.

The Review

The review process should take around 12 weeks, but it often takes much longer. One article of mine took two years to be reviewed. I emailed the journal multiple times, to no avail, indicating that my coauthors had now all become professors and needed the publication. On the other end of the spectrum, *The Journal of Qualitative Inquiry* has a prompt turnaround time. At the 12-week point, query the editor by email as to the status of the manuscript. Some discipline ethics guidelines cite an overly long review process as a violation of ethics. For example, the "Code of Ethics: American Education Research Association" (2011) says, "Publication Process: *16.03 Responsibility of Editors* (f) When serving as journal editors, education researchers take steps to provide for the timely review of all manuscripts and respond promptly to inquiries about the status of the review" (p. 154).

The reason a delayed review may be seen as unprofessional and perhaps even unethical is that delays (a) impede the dissemination of knowledge, (b) cause research to become more dated, and (c) have repercussions for annual reviews, tenure, and promotion.

Usually, there are three reviewers for an article, but I have often had just two. My understanding is that this occurs when (a) there are not enough volunteers, (b) one of the reviewers does not conduct a timely review, or (c) the reviewers for the journal are not familiar with qualitative research. I am glad to say that I have not encountered the latter for some time. (See Text Box 6.8 for detailed information on the peer review process, still referred to as a "blind review" by many, including those who Margaret cites, which always feels like it should be anachronistic and seems awkwardly ableist to me.)

The reason for a peer review is to increase the likelihood that the research is appropriately conducted and reported through the review of peers who do not know who the author is. However, this adds to the difficulty in breaking through entrenched beliefs in research areas and around ways reports should "look."

After the review process, you will receive a letter from the editor indicating if the journal *accepts*, *accepts with revisions*, would like you to *revise and resubmit*, or *rejects* the manuscript. Along with this letter, you will receive the reviewers' comments. Try to prepare yourself for how acidic some reviewers' comments can be. I saved these comments to share in my courses with students and to use in my writing and in the titles of articles.

6.8 PEER REVIEW PROCESS

MARGARET SEBASTIAN

Early in my graduate work, I decided to write a paper on the journal manuscript peer review process so I could clearly understand it. What I learned follows.

The peer review process has been a formal part of scientific communication since the first scientific journals appeared more than 300 years ago. The *Philosophical Transactions of the Royal Society* is thought to be the first journal to formalize the peer review process under the editorship of Henry Oldenburg (1618–1677; Elsevier, 2018). Despite many criticisms about the integrity of the anonymous (e.g., "blind") peer review process, the majority of the research community still believes peer review is the best form of scientific evaluation. The process occurs when a research manuscript or conference proposal is reviewed by an anonymous peer.

There are multiple types of reviews, including highly edited reviews, peer reviews, single-blind reviews, double-blind reviews, and triple-blind reviews. Highly edited reviews are professionally edited, usually by paid staff, with primary emphasis on exposition, graphic presentation, and editorial style, rather than on content and substance. Peer review employs predetermined reviewers, in the case of program committees, or ad hoc reviewers, in the case of most journals, who individually read the submitted manuscript and prepare a written review. Usually, the reviewer is in a similar educational field and on a similar track professionally (Greve et al., 2013). Single-blind reviewing is used in the vast majority of reviewer database conferences and journals; the identity of the reviewer(s) is not revealed to the author(s), ostensibly to ensure more objective reviewing. Double-blind reviewing is used when the identity of both the authors and their institutions is kept from the reviewers. And triple-blind reviewing occurs when not only the reviewers are not told the authors names and the authors are not told the reviewers' names but also the editors are not told the authors' names (Cox & Mongomerie, 2019). Additionally, "blinding" the manuscript occurs when the identity of the author is removed from the submitted manuscript, by taking the name of the author, any personal information, and any information that connects the author to a particular institution off the manuscript. The three major concerns of blind reviews are (1) fairness, (2) review quality, and (3) efficacy of blinding (Armstrong, 1997).

Source: Reproduced with permission from Margaret L. Sebastian.

Revise and Resubmit

Respond to every point the editor and reviewers make, indicating where changes occur in the manuscript. Traditionally, authors responded to reviewers' comments with a letter noting where changes were added. See an example letter below. However, consider using a chart for this process since the chart makes changes clear and concise. See Table 6.2 as a possible example. You do not need to make all the changes reviewers request, but you should make many of them. Justify all instances where you do not make changes. You will notice in the authors' response that my co-author and I did not always make every change a reviewer requested, but we did address every request. I am not suggesting we push back on all statements we don't agree with, but there are times when you are not going to be able to make a change and be faithful to the article and the methodology you are representing. You will need to weigh the need to get research findings out to the public with the importance of what you are being asked to alter.

A revise and resubmit letter to the editor:

Dear Dr. _____

Thanks for your time and effort in reviewing our work. We are highly pleased to have our work invited for revision and resubmit for [journal name]. We have made the following revisions to the article.

Sincerely,

Maria Lahman, PhD

1. Discuss how journalists handle the issue surrounding named and unnamed sources and pseudonyms.

   Please see the following addition at the bottom of page 10 of the manuscript.

   Further, within the journalistic community, naming presents an issue concerning anonymous sources. The Society of Professional Journalists ethics code may be argued to be almost the opposite of human researcher ethics stating,

   > Identify sources clearly. The public is entitled to as much information as possible to judge the reliability and motivations of sources. Consider sources' motives before promising anonymity. Reserve anonymity for sources who may face danger, retribution, or other harm, and have information that cannot be obtained elsewhere. Explain why anonymity was granted. (SPJ Code of Ethics, 2014)

   Sources of whistleblowing or controversial information are reluctant to have their identities exposed for fear of retaliation or unwanted media spotlight. However, news consumers may judge the credibility of a story based on whether the source is named (Farell). The identity of the source may indicate to the public what information is credible, fabricated, or severely skewed (Farell). Like narrative research, how a story merits credibility can lie squarely in the way sources are interpreted by the reader depending on the writer's representation of participant naming.

2. Show how your discussion would affect the issues surrounding anonymity and the protection of subjects as outlined in IRB regulations.

   See top of page 3 for the following addition:

   > Human subject protection codes and discussions in this area of the federal guidelines revolve around privacy and confidentiality. One can see how the solution to these crucial issues is interpreted in part as a need for pseudonyms. However, for those participants who desire to use their own name, an addition to the consent form that clearly states the participants' desire to use their own name and understand the contexts their name will be used in allows relational researchers to proceed with honoring this request. Forcing biomedical standards on research participants risks paternalizing participants and taking away their autonomy, which is a fundamental reason human research ethical codes were created. See Bradley (2007) for an in-depth example of how some university IRBs have a limited understanding of this type of relational research and requests for the use of their name from participants.

TABLE 6.2 ● Authors' Response to a Revise and Resubmit Review

Reviewer's comments	Action taken
1. If the writer is working within a psychological paradigm, this needs to be stated in the abstract, and that is the research that needs to be cited in the abstract. It also needs to be built into the framework more fully. However, when field notes are brought in, then some of the work in ethnography needs to be accounted for (or psychologists need to come up with their own terminology).	We added the phrase "critical race feminism". While we feel ethnographers are aware that other methodologists have borrowed the term "field notes" and it is indicative of the impact of ethnography, we have changed the word "field notes" to "notes" throughout.
2. *Abstract:* Rework the second sentence as it rambles and is unclear.	We changed the wording.
3. Missing facts on enforcement of "modest" dress for women throughout the Saudi state; a fear of standing against authority can be manifest in a society in which women can suffer corporal punishment for wearing "immodest" garb.	On page 3, we included a statement on different views on whether wearing the hijab is required by religion and culture or not. We also provided more references.
4. In reality, the first full paragraph on page 4 could be dumped and also much of the romanticizing of Saudi Arabia.	The words "dumped" and "romanticizing" do little to enhance our collegial dialogue. We are working in a very tricky area here where much of what is currently portrayed in the media is demonizing of Saudi Arabia. We agree much of it was not directly relevant and has therefore been deleted.
5. On page 5, cite the study that built the constructs you bring up in the first sentence of the literature review.	We added that the study is under review.
6. The pronouns relating to research are confusing: sometimes "we," sometimes "me." Try to eliminate these or stay consistent.	We addressed this concern. We believe it is imperative to be clear who did what work and used footnotes to make it clearer for the readers.

If you are asked to do something unethical, communicate with the editor, and if there is no resolution, withdraw your work. For example, a student I consulted with was told by an editor that the manuscript needed to be changed to a feminist theoretical orientation from a constructivist perspective. As a feminist, I could certainly see how the research might have been framed differently to make a powerful contribution. However, as disappointing as it might be to the editor and to me, the student was not a feminist, had not thought about the study through a feminist lens, and therefore should not have been asked to adopt a theory that was not one she actually believed in.

Something that was not known to me is the revise and review process may occur several times, and while this is infrequent, your work may still be rejected after the revision process has happened. That is painful and something I learned firsthand.

Reject

Rejection itself has no meaning except the closing of a particular door at a particular time.

—Michael Alvear (2017, p. 12)

Rejection is one of the most challenging aspects of publication—and indeed of life in general. Regarding the opening quote, Alvear (2017) goes on to write, "The meaning of the event [rejection] is strictly up to interpretation. . . . While you have no power to reverse a rejection, you do have the power to reinterpret its meaning so it doesn't leave you gutted" (p. 12). You will want to think through a plan for handling rejection, so it does not become debilitating publication-wise. Early on, I found it useful to ask a colleague to read over my rejection letters. One such letter was written in such a belittling fashion I thought it was a rejection, and then my colleague said, "Don't you see it says revise and resubmit at the bottom of the letter?" I could not even see these important words on the first read due to the condescending tone—I would have assumed anything so awful could never be revised.

If the letter is an outright rejection, I have found a suggestion from a colleague to be helpful—have a preestablished list of where to send the manuscript next. After taking some justified time to feel let down, move forward by rereading the rejection in case the editor has provided reviewer comments or editorial comments. Only make the revisions indicated in these comments that seem warranted or that refer to actual errors. It is possible that the next journal review may not yield the same comments. Then, send the manuscript straight back out. I had a well-published colleague who said they send manuscripts back out within one week of receiving a rejection. I have never been able to pull off that time frame, but it is an excellent goal.

Accept, and Accept With Revisions

That's very nice if they want to publish you, but don't pay too much attention to it. It will toss you away. Just continue to write.

—Natalie Goldberg (1985, p. 214)

When you receive an acceptance letter, do what is indicated as the next step right away, and then truly take some time to celebrate. At first, the publication may seem unreal. Sir James M. Barrie, the author of *Peter Pan*, said it well: "For several days after my first book was published, I carried it about in my pocket and took surreptitious peeps at it to make sure the ink had not faded" (cited in Vanderbuilt, 1999, p. 42). Relish that feeling since other obligations will creep in to overwhelm it soon enough. In the opening of this section, I feature a quote from Goldberg (1985) where she references advice she received—a reminder to ground ourselves in the writing project we are currently in even as we take a moment to savor our success.

An "accept with revisions" letter is what I have often received. This letter means there are just a few slight revisions that need to be made and in all likelihood the revisions are something the researcher would agree with. It also means the revised draft will not go back out to peer reviewers for feedback again.

At the point of acceptance, you will be sent a contract to sign. Currently, signing is typically conducted virtually. In the United States, usually only the first author signs, while certifying that all the authors are aware of the journal submission. For articles, the work becomes the journal's property. While I knew this, it was still startling the first time I saw an article of mine republished in a handbook. While these additional publications help promote your work, not knowing about them can be disconcerting.

You may now be asked to resubmit the manuscript with the names of all authors and any acknowledgments included. In qualitative research, it is standard to refer to the authors by their first name if there is more than one author and in the first person. This is not merely convention but a clear statement that the author matters, is not an objective researcher, and instead of striving for unachievable objectivity wishes to actively engage with their biases throughout the process of the research. There will be exceptions to the use of author names and of the first person when submitting to some journals in content areas that are not highly qualitative. See the section titled First Person Whenever Possible in Chapter 3 for a more extensive discussion of first person.

Production

After the article is copyedited and then typeset, it will be sent to you with minor queries. At this time, you may not do significant rewriting. The turnaround time for your answers is usually three days to a week. Be sure to respond promptly to any requests from the editors. Recheck this version carefully. Do not rely on the copy editor. This is a team effort. I have found columns that are out of order, along with errors I had made. After you send back the article with your answers, the time until the hard copy of the journal comes out may be months or years. Increasingly, journals publish online quickly and then later in hard copy. This is an excellent practice that allows research to be released quickly to the public.

Common Issues

In publication in general, there are some common issues that you can avoid. Avoid dual submission; that is, do not send manuscripts out to more than one editor at a time. If editors realize you are someone who does this, it has the potential to mean that no one will look at your work. The reason for this is that you are wasting the time of the reviewers (who are doing the review as a service) as well as the editor and the staff.

While most researchers understand the need to avoid plagiarism, self-plagiarism can be more difficult. *Self-plagiarism* is the repeating of ideas, text, tables, or figures from your own published work without citing the source. This can be problematic, for example, when you are writing a section on theory in a manuscript that you have written many times and doesn't seem to warrant a citation to yourself; and there is also a need to avoid overciting yourself. With the advent of internet tools where you can check your work for plagiarism, this is an easy fix. You can see where you need to reword or maybe merely take the time to do some more reading and see what current authors are saying. Free plagiarism detection tools, which can be found by searching the internet under the phrase "check for plagiarism," are often included with a subscription to editing sites such as Grammarly or come as part of university subscriptions to virtual learning environments (e.g., Canvas, Blackboard).

When writing research, it is important to realize that your readers may be—and you hope they will be—from all over the world, so avoid *localism*. Writing only in a local context is a problem for authors, in particular for those of us from the United States. This is a type of nationalism we must rigorously edit out of our work since it signals a myopic perspective to global readership groups. For example, when writing about early childhood education, as a U.S. citizen, I would most likely say that children were in the "first grade." In other countries, this phrase does not always have the same meaning. Therefore, I should state the age of the children as 6 to 7 years old and that they are in their first year of full-day school, commonly referred to as first grade in the United States. Another example is referring to a study as occurring in a state—without a country reference. It is appropriate to say the study took place in Colorado, USA.

6.9 TIPS FROM A JOURNAL ASSISTANT EDITOR

CHRISTINA TAYLOR

During the major part of my doctoral program, I was the graduate assistant for *The Journal of Educational Research and Innovation*, a peer-reviewed educational journal at the university where I studied. My role was to assist the editors as needed, which included working with authors and reviewers; editing accepted manuscripts for grammar, spelling, and clarity; as well as style formatting and copy setting for publication. The journal frequently received work from novice authors, and our editorial staff was committed to providing ample support to those new to publication (fair warning—this commitment is not universal). As a novice author myself, I was ignorant of what might complicate and delay the review and publication process. Once I was on the receiving end of manuscripts from authors all over the world, I quickly learned. For anyone new to the publication process, consider the following common issues I observed:

- Submissions not suited to our journal

- Missing information about authors and manuscripts

- Submissions that failed to meet the journal's guidelines regarding length and formatting

- Plagiarized material

- Inefficient communication between journal staff and contributors

I recommend the following:

Choose an appropriate journal for your content, otherwise your time and effort to submit are wasted, as is the energy of a journal's staff when they consider your submission and respond to you. If you are unsure whether your work might be a good fit, perhaps an exploratory email to the editors would be informative. When you first submit your work, include all of the information requested about you and your manuscript, and keep your contact information current. Only necessary information is requested, and if you do not complete your submission entirely, journal staff may not be able to move your submission forward in the process, especially if they need to reach you but cannot. Also, follow a journal's manuscript requirements to the letter. Particularly, use the requested style manual to make it easier for volunteer reviewers to help you improve your work and editors to proof your formatting. Submit only original work, enough said. And last, respond as quickly as you can to communications you receive about your submission. Depending on the journal, the publication process from start to finish can take more than a year, so it helps if everyone keeps the ball rolling.

Source: Reproduced with permission from Christina Taylor.

Done, Done, Done! (Not Really): Promoting Publication

advance, advertise, advocate, aid, assist, bolster, boost, champion, circulate, contribute, develop, disperse, disseminate, endorse, engage, enhance, forward, further, foster, market, nurture, nourish, promote, publicize, sponsor, stimulate

Why should you promote your research? If you want to create change, enhance transformative possibilities, and/or work for social justice, people need to have opportunities to engage with your research. While the numbers are debated, it seems safe to say that more than 1.8 million research articles are published each year, and this number is rising (Allen, 2016). It is increasingly important for you to find ways to make your work stand out in your field. In the following sections, I will briefly highlight multiple ways to promote your work.

If you are uncomfortable with promoting your own work, consider why this is. Perhaps you have heard people make negative comments about self-promoters, perhaps you tend to be modest, or you aren't involved with any type of social media. If this is the case, consider some of the synonyms for the word "promote" I placed at the opening of this section. Reframe promotion to be about the research you have conducted and not about you: "We do feel our research is important and want to create change for the good"—so this is not a time to be reserved. Choose a word that works better for you, such as "advocate" or "forward," as you start to create a plan for the best first steps to let others know about your work.

Search engine optimization increases the chance your publications appear higher in the results returned by search engines. Effective optimization means you can gain more readers, achieve higher visibility, and increase citations. To enhance search engine optimization, carefully choose keywords that occur in the title, abstract, and body of the article. (See Chapter 5 for more information on this topic.) Captions with keywords should also be added to all figures and images. Headings and subheadings should have keywords.

Announce your publications to your university through college and university communications. Add the publication to any bulletin boards or display cases that house local work. Announce it on your personal university website and add hyperlinks to content as appropriate. Utilize university social media and other educative outlets such as a podcast. My university is always looking for faculty they can develop a podcast with. My podcast (https://www.unco.edu/bear-in-mind/29-research-ethics.aspx) took a minimal amount of effort on my part due to being asked questions in an area of expertise and working with a highly talented podcaster, who edited my words to create a helpful podcast. Use all of the library resources available to you. Utilize your campus depository. This resource is free and can be added as a link to your websites. See Digital UNCO (https://www.unco .edu/library/digital-unc/) as an example from my campus of what a campus depository is.

Use all of the publisher resources available to you. Share your free e-prints with colleagues. Currently, e-prints are a link to your article, which you are allowed to share a certain number of times—usually 50. These resources are changing quickly, so keep current by following your publishers' social media outlets. Graphic, comic, and video abstracts are a newer form that is increasingly available. See the resources section in this chapter for links to how-tos. For an example of a video abstract, which I had created for my first book, see https://www.youtube.com/watch?v=82Tiv97SGg0.

6.10 SAGE: WAYS TO INCREASE USAGE AND CITATION OF PUBLICATIONS USING SOCIAL MEDIA

As readers' expectations change, it is important that your article is visible when the user starts their search.

- *Wikipedia* is an online, free, open-content encyclopedia created and recreated by a collaborative community of users. If there are pages that relate to themes, subjects, or research that your article covers, add your article as a reference, with a link to it on SAGE Journals Online. If there isn't an existing page, consider creating one.
  - o I would add though that there is a deep bias against Wikipedia among educators. I personally see Wikipedia, from a critical perspective, as an emancipatory resource that allows many voices, often excluded, to join in knowledge creation and curation. I often use Wikipedia as a first place to go to when I am thinking over a new idea. Does that mean I would cite it without looking at the original citations? Absolutely not. Does it mean I would cite Wikipedia judiciously? Absolutely.

- *Twitter* is a microblogging service that enables its users to send and read messages, known as *tweets.* Authors are increasingly promoting their content via Twitter, which is then picked up by other researchers and practitioners. Twitter allows you to set up search terms to enable you to monitor what is being discussed in your areas of interest; you can then comment on the relevant conversations. The more you engage, the more people will follow you to listen to your comments and recommendations. As followers come to you, instead of you approaching them, Twitter is an ideal way to reach new audiences.

- *YouTube:* SAGE is seeing an increasing amount of traffic to their journal sites via YouTube as students use video as an initial way of exploring a topic.

- *Blog:* Consider taking up blogging about your area of research and articles that you have published—and/or other related documents in your field of research. Don't forget to link to them from your blog.

- *Academic Social Networking* is increasingly using social communities as a way of meeting and conversing with people who share the same research interests. These sites offer an immediate way to monitor what other people are looking at in your field of research and a way to commission papers around online conversations you think are interesting. If there aren't any groups talking about your research interests, set one up. Take a look at MyNetReseach, Academia, and ResearchGate, for example. There are others too—perhaps you can

(Continued)

ask your colleagues which groups they are a part of to decide what suits you best.

- *Website:* Do you have your own website? If not, create one. You can create a clean and straightforward site using Google Sites.

- *Methodspace:* Sponsored by SAGE, Methodspace is a new online community for research methods. On the site, you can connect with other researchers, discuss methodology issues and controversies, discover and review new resources, find relevant conferences and events, and share and solve methodology problems.

- *LinkedIn* is an interconnected network of experienced professionals from around the world, with more than 55 million members. It is not just for career opportunities. When you are creating a profile summary of your professional expertise and accomplishments, why not include a mention of your articles too?

- *Facebook* lets users add and message friends and update their personal profiles to notify friends about themselves. Additionally, users can join networks organized by city, workplace, and school or college. You can also join and create groups according to your interests or areas of expertise.

- *Instagram* (owned by Facebook) is a photo- and video-sharing site that currently has great appeal to a large and diverse audience. See https://www.instagram.com/p/Bi9unPEAnnj/ as an example of the thousands of posts regarding qualitative research.

- *Snapchat* is a personal messaging system based on visual messages that disappear after a while. Universities are utilizing Snapchat with great success, making it easy for scholars to join in the conversations.

While social media is increasing in importance, there are other options to draw attention to your latest work: Email your networks or post on list-servs and websites about your recent publication, and add your article to your course reading list when appropriate.

The contents of this text box, except for the addition of Instagram and Snapchat, are adapted from a tip article on SAGE that seems to be no longer available on the internet. See this link for an updated version: https://us.sagepub.com/en-us/nam/promote-your-article.

Fair Use

"If you are in any doubt as to whether or not you can use the material as 'fair use,' you should clear permission, or leave the material out" (SAGE Publishing, n.d.-a). "Fair use" means that "portions of copyrighted materials may be used without permission of the copyright owner provided the use is fair and reasonable, does not substantially impair the value of the materials, and does not curtail the profits reasonably expected" (Merriam-Webster, n.d.-a). This is an essential concept for writers to understand in general and with regard to how they may utilize their own work after publication. According to SAGE Publishing (n.d.-a), fair use involves four factors:

1. The purpose and nature of the use

2. The nature of the original material

3. The amount of the original material being used in relation to the original work as a whole

4. The effect the use will have on the market of the original work

While aspects of a research or scholarly publication are subject to *fair use*— that is, the text, photographs, illustrations, and/or figures—the more creative the (nature of the) original work, the weaker the basis for a fair use argument. If the new work is "transformative—the purpose of the use is different than the purpose of the original creation" (SAGE Publishing, n.d.-a)—the evidence for fair use may be met. For example, I have written a poem that is entirely re-created from other authors' research articles. I then reference each article in a footnote.

Promoting a Book

Some of your book promotion will be done by the publisher. However, you can help the publisher by letting the *book marketing division* know well in advance of any conference you might attend. This is so they can set up book signings and author chats. The publisher may also have brochures that high-light your book and can provide discounts to conference attendees.

Draw on your *university resources*. Develop an article or book talk with the campus library. My librarian helped me hold a book signing with a panel of authors from the book, refreshments, book sales, and a book giveaway. They were able to draw on more resources than I have, and in this specific case, their space is much more attractive than the ones available in my college.

The publisher of a book will most likely sell it on Amazon in addition to their own publishing site. If they do, set up an Amazon author page that is personalized to you. The page allows you to upload your image, bio, the book's bio, videos, podcasts, and so on. At the following link, you can see John Creswell's author page: https://smile.amazon.com/John-W.-Creswell/e/B001H6M9V4?ref=sr_ntt_srch_lnk_1&qid=1551725304&sr=1-1.

Amazon also allows you to create interest in your book by having a *free book giveaway*. When you give a conference talk or course lecture—anywhere you speak about the book—have a giveaway. I have made this a simple and fun process by taping a picture of the cover of the book under someone's chair. Whoever sits in that chair gets the prize.

Email each significant *contributing author* in the book a thank-you note that makes it clear you could not have done this work without their prior work. Ask each of them to promote the book on their social media websites and to buy it for their university libraries. Email all of your connections at a university library and ask them to consider ordering the book for their library. Advertise the book through your university press release, to your past degree-granting universities, and to institutions you have worked at since you obtained your degree.

Place a hyperlink to the book as part of your email signature. I saw a colleague did this, and it simply said, "Check out my new book!" I did check out their book and bought it right away since the book idea was of interest to me. I now do the same in my signature when a new book is coming out.

If appropriate, use the book as a course text. This is often a good fit since many textbook authors are pulling together materials from a course they have taught and developing the ideal textbook they have longed for. Along with your book, use other rich and varied materials so both you and your students continue to develop your thinking and stay current.

Get Started Promoting Your Publication

So enough of reading about promotion—start promoting. Create a to-do list of what can be done quickly and cheaply and what might be a more long-term project that needs some funds. Be aware of the fine line between promotion ideas being helpful and becoming a way to delay the hard work of writing. Consider making some sort of rule where you will only spend a certain amount of time on sites such as ResearchGate and limit the number of times the sites can contact you. You should be the one to choose when you go to a media site. Also, only take time to promote existing publications after you have worked for a while on a new project.

The following are some first steps I suggest. As soon as you publish, make sure you have a Google Scholar profile. If you are gearing up for a job search, LinkedIn, which is a professional networking platform, is a good option. In the literature on social media and promotion of research, some suggest Research-Gate, which is specifically for researchers with university affiliations and allows scientists to post updates and questions about research projects. Twitter recently increased its character limit, making it easier to discuss research, and the platform includes many researchers and academics. While I am new to professional Twitter, I have learned a lot through the platform. My professional Twitter handle is @lahman_maria, and I follow professional journals and editors in Twitter, such as @HelenSSalmon.

ORCID: Register for an ORCID (Open Researcher and Contributor ID), which "provides a persistent digital identifier that distinguishes you from every other researcher and, through integration in key research workflows such as manuscript and grant submission, supports automated linkages between you and your professional activities ensuring that your work is recognized" (https://orcid.org/). ORCID is more than a DOI (digital object identifier) since it links you with your publications and will continue to do so even if you have a name change or use different versions of your name.

Be bold yet humble when it comes to promoting your work. If this feels awkward, think of all the reasons that caused you to want to research this topic, recall all the problematic hurdles, and the time research participants gave you. Then, with humility, recall that you and your research are more than the sum of your impact factors, and always give credit to everyone who helped your work come to fruition.

The Gist

Writing is an extreme privilege, but it's also a gift. It's a gift to yourself, and it's a gift of giving a story to someone.

—Amy Tan

In a speech for the Academy of Achievement, Amy Tan spoke of the multiple ways in which writing may be a gift (https://achievement.org/video/amy-tan-20/). Publishing our writing allows the gift to be received by more people. In this chapter, I worked to make the publication process transparent in an effort to move readers toward an ability to *publish and persevere*. Reflexive questions and activities follow to support readers into moving deeper into this topic. Importantly, speak to people in your direct contexts about the publication and promotion process since they will have specifics and nuances that are beyond this book chapter. My best wishes as you persevere.

Reflexive Questions

Authorship and Credit for Contributions

What types of experiences have you had with authorship?

If these experiences have been negative, how can you work to avoid negative experiences?

What guidelines, if any, does your discipline ethics code have about authorship?

Journal Publication

What are the major journals in your area that accept qualitative research?

After a review of these journals . . .

What is the description or mission of each journal?

What is the size of the data set the articles represent?

What types of qualitative methodology are used (e.g., case study, photovoice)?

What does the writers' guide specify about submission?

Which qualitative journals would be a good match for your research (e.g., *The Qualitative Report, International Journal of Qualitative Methods, Qualitative Inquiry*)?

Promoting Publications

How do you feel about the idea of promoting your research?

If the idea of promotion is a natural fit for you, which ways suggested in this chapter will be easier for you, and which may be more difficult? Challenge yourself to try promotion ideas you have not tried before. As part of writing this book, I joined Twitter professionally and created a website for the first time.

If you are reluctant to promote your research, try to identify why. How can you most effectively work to reframe the idea of promotion to one that feels comfortable to you? Maybe thinking of the time participants spent with you as something you should honor by trying to get many people to read their words will help, or just telling yourself you believe in your work and want to cause change might be the key.

Reflexive Activities

For more details and activities, see Appendix C. These activities can occur virtually, in person during a class, or as part of a writers' group.

Journal Review.

Considering the section in this chapter on reviewing journals for an excellent qualitative match, conduct a review and create a list of journals that might work for you and the type of manuscript you are preparing.

Technology Share.

What new technology have members been using that helps with their writing process?

Manuscript Review for a Journal.

Students need to identify a professor who is willing to conduct a review of a qualitative manuscript with the student.

Personal Writing: A Reflexivity Experience.

Choose one of the following writing topics. If you are in a course, after these are completed, meet in a small group to discuss what you wrote about.

a. What are your short-term writing goals for the next three months?

b. What are your long-term goals for the year?

c. How does writing about these make you feel, and why?

Professional Journal Editor Panel or Guest Speaker.

Assemble a panel of experts on the topic you are considering; be sure to include as many members with different identities and professional backgrounds as possible.

Speed Discussion.

I created this activity from the idea of speed dating. Form two circles, one within the other. Course members, in the inner circle, each share their perspective on a topic, and then the outer circle rotates one person clockwise, and they repeat the process. In a virtual meeting, the speed discussions occur in breakout rooms. Use a timer, and keep the time short—one to three minutes. Possible topics about publishing follow.

a. What are areas in the publication process that seem intimidating or confusing?

b. What are some challenges you have to successful publishing?

c. What are the next three steps you need to take toward publishing?

Interview an Editor.

Choose an editor from your discipline or one who teaches research writing to interview.

a. Decide together if you will record the interview. I suggest doing so for a review and in case the two of you want to teach a session or give a conference talk on writing someday.

b. What is the editor's editing process?

c. What editing and publishing stories do researchers share? Beginning stories, good stories, negative stories, and so on.

d. Consider presenting a poster or writing an informational article, perhaps with the editor, on the information gained.

Resources

Internet

Cartoon Abstracts: https://authorservices.taylorandfrancis.com/cartoon-abstracts/

Elsevier: https://www.elsevier.com/authors/journal-authors/graphical-abstract

MedComms. (2016, July 18). *Editing: Things they don't tell you about what journal editors want.* YouTube. https://www.youtube.com/watch?v=vLojaTRoBuc

Taylor & Francis. (2015, July 27). *What to think about before you start writing.* YouTube. https://www.youtube.com/watch?v=fxYVyL_s3P0&app=desktopResearcher Academy: https://researeracademy.elsevier.com/

Video Abstracts: http://authorservices.taylorandfrancis.com/video-abstracts/

Books

Allen, M. (2016). *Essentials of publishing qualitative research* (Vol. 12). Left Coast Press. https://doi.org/10.4324/9781315429298

Wa-Mbaleka, S. (2014). *Publish or perish: Fear no more.* CentralBooks.

Wolcott, H. F. (2009). *Writing up qualitative research* (3rd ed.). Sage. https://doi.org/10.4135/9781452234878

Articles

Bowen, G. A. (2010). From qualitative dissertation to quality articles: Seven lessons learned. *The Qualitative Report, 15*(4), 864–879.

Thompson, B. (1995). Publishing your research results: Some suggestions and counsel. *Journal of Counseling & Development, 73*(3), 342–345. https://doi.org/10.1002/j.1556-6676.1995.tb01761.x

Aesthetic Representations of Qualitative Research

In Part 2, I write first for researchers who wish to begin exploring or find a way back to subjectivity, rich experiences, science imbued with emotion and art, and research that "breaks your heart" (Behar, 1996)—which may be full of joy, pain, and happiness. Many of these scholars are researchers first and foremost, but some of us started in the arts and lost our way as we stumbled through higher education degrees and tenure attainments—traps of neutrality, third person, barren language—crippled with self-doubt and gagged by the dominant majority, beginning to believe there is but one way to be a good researcher. Second, I write for those of us who have embraced what Sandra Faulkner (2017) calls "being a bad (BAD!) social scientist" (p. 148). Even if this is a position you will never embrace, it is helpful to understand what other colleagues are attempting to do. All of us could improve the accessibility of our research for broader audiences by drawing on just some of the ideas within Part 2 of this book. Third, I write for novices who may be, as I was, unsure how to obtain solid mentoring, isolated, and adrift. I want these students to know they have a community of scholars eager to welcome them in the academy and ready and willing to think and grow with them.

Part 2 of this book consists of four chapters on aesthetic representations. In Chapter 7, "Auto-ethnography: A Kaleidoscope of Knowing," I review the history of autoethnography, highlight experiences of mine in writing and reading autoethnography, and feature text boxes with excerpts from autoethnographies and reflections on the process. The many ways autoethnography may be positioned, including *heartfelt*, *critical*, and *multivoiced*, are detailed with examples provided. The process I followed to write an autoethnography on loss is described in an effort to make this form transparent to more writers. I present possible first steps for writing an autoethnography and ideas for how to lay out the final piece. The intent behind these steps and ideas is not prescriptive. It is for readers to become comfortable with the genre and inform or break from what is presented to create new possibilities of representation and understanding.

Research poetry, the representation area I have worked with the most, is presented in Chapter 8, "Poemish Research Poetry." I first conceived of extending the idea of "ish" from children's literature to research poetry and now through this book am opening *ish* up as a research stance in general. I review *ish* and goodness as safe spaces for researchers and highlight many forms of research poetry—including transcription, concrete, formed, autoethnographic, and critical—and more recent ideas such as typewriter poetry and Twitter poems. This review is intended to give readers a wealth of ideas to build on. Throughout, poetic interludes will occur, where readers can engage first hand with published and unpublished poems by literary poets and research poets. Ideas to enhance our poetic "sensibilities" and research possibilities are shared.

Chapter 9, "Visuals in Qualitative Research Representation: In the Blink of an Eye," is where I explore research representations that use visual data within a traditional qualitative article and representations that rely on visuals. Representations discussed include collage, art installations, galleries, and participant art creation. Areas for close consideration when publishing visuals are suggested. Throughout the chapter, student-researcher-created visuals from qualitative research are featured.

Reflexivity is a concept undergirding all qualitative research but is often enacted in private and represented in perfunctory ways. In Chapter 10, "Reflecting Reflexivity in Research Representations," I review reflexivity and the primary ways in which it is represented in research, including what I term the *researcher resume stance* and *vulnerable researcher stance*. Throughout the chapter, I feature examples of reflexivity representations. I challenge readers to look for ways to deepen reflexivity and advocate for a stance I call *raw reflexivity*.

Most of us love research—the enactment of a detailed plan, exploring the world through others' eyes, the sudden pop of discovery. More of us could love writing—the re-creation of thoughts that propel, detailing others' worlds, the crisp crackle of a well-turned phrase. In the words of Kamand Kojouri, "Oh, how scary and wonderful it is that words can change our lives simply by being next to each other" (QuoteFancy, n.d.). In this section of the text, all of us should take up the challenge to place participants' words and experiences "next to each other" in innovative and invigorating ways.

Autoethnography:
A Kaleidoscope of Knowing

Writing is a socially acceptable form of getting naked in public.

—Paulo Coelho (2011)

We are in the public hall of a lab with Doctor. I have just finished a proce-dure that allows the doctor to assess the state of my remaining fallopian tube. Doctor tells us the tube is blocked and that in this condition I am infertile. We stare at the carpet illuminated by fluorescent lights. This is a public setting, so we try to be numb.

I am infertile.

I found out in a public hallway, under a fluorescent light, by a dusty plastic plant.

The plant is infertile, as am I.

Now I will gather dust.

—Lahman (2021, p. 127)

Shedding light on a matter of interest in ways that are new or unexpected—turning perspectives inside out, upside down, creating a *kaleidoscope* of knowing—is one goal or outcome of qualitative research. The kaleidoscope, perhaps seen as a child's toy, has a fascination for many. I pass a collection of kaleidoscopes around in class when we are considering autoethnography and reflexivity. Based on aspects of its definition—reflecting an endless variety of variegated, changing scenes and patterns; a diverse collection, using light and reflection (Merriam-Webster, n.d.-d)—a kaleidoscope is a fitting metaphor for autoethnography.

The methodological writing around autoethnography can be highly theo-retical, but in this chapter,[1] I try to present autoethnography in an accessible manner while providing resources for those who wish to dig in further.

In this chapter, I share

- a brief history of the methodology and
- the primary forms—described with examples provided:
  - o he*art*felt
  - o critical
  - o multivoiced
  - o emerging
- The process I followed to write autoethnographies is described.
- Excerpts from my autoethnographic writing are included.
- I ruminate on the sacredness of stories and the impact working with so many personal autoethnographies may have on a methodologist.
- I briefly review the existing tensions in the following areas:
  - o Subjectivity
  - o Anonymity
  - o Research ethics compliance
  - o Vulnerability
  - o Finality of the written word
- A summary of the chapter is provided in the section titled The Gist.
- I end with
  - o reflexive questions designed for continued growth,
  - o reflexive activities designed to support researchers working with autoethnography for the first time, and
  - o resources aimed to enhance further exploration, including lists of welcoming journals and conferences.

Background of Autoethnography

Much academic writing sounds the same—stilted, distant, and overly qualified.

—Dane (2011, p. 332)

---

[1]Parts of this chapter were excerpted and partially revised from the following auto-ethnographies: Lahman (2009, 2020, 2021).

personal narratives, narratives of the self, personal experience narratives, self-stories, first-person accounts, personal essays, ethnographic short stories, writing stories, complete-member research, personal ethnography, literary tales, lived experiences, critical autobiography, self-ethnography, socio-autobiography, narrative, personal writing, reflexive ethnography, confessional tales, ethnographic memoirs, ethno-biography, auto-biology, collaborative autobiography, ethnographic autobiography, experiential texts, narrative ethnography, autobiographical ethnography, ethnographic poetics[2]

Carolyn Ellis, the modern mother of autoethnography, and Arthur Bochner provided this helpful list of similar terms to autoethnography, which allows readers to see where this methodology's underpinnings are derived from (Ellis & Bochner, 2000). Autoethnography literally means "self-culture-writing." Along with the other words referenced, it is worth noting that "auto" may also mean automatic or spontaneous—much of my personal writing was not intended for autoethnographic publishing in the first outpouring.

auto	**ethno**	**graphy**
self	**culture**	**writing**
personal	**people**	**representing**

Autoethnography has grown in prominence in higher education over approximately 30 years (Adams & Herrmann, 2020), as evidenced by journals and conferences that feature autoethnography and the 2020 inaugural edition of the *Journal of Autoethnography*. Academics have added rich dimensions to this methodology,

> including . . . education, anthropology, music, gender studies, cultural studies, media studies, communication, Asian studies, sport, sociology, accounting, performance, Latinx studies, and African American studies. . . . A Google search for "autoethnography" yields nearly a million results; a Google Scholar search for "autoethnography" yields more than forty thousand sources, many of which have hundreds—even thousands—of citations. (Adams & Herrmann, 2020, p. 1)

Autoethnography has also been described by Holman Jones (2005) as follows:

- Setting a scene, telling a story, weaving intricate connections among life and art, experience and theory, evocation and explanation . . . and then letting go, hoping for readers who will bring the same careful attention to your words in context of their own lives.

---

[2]This list of terms comes from Carolyn Ellis and Arthur Bochner's (2000) handbook chapter on autoethnography. The overlap of these many genres is instructive.

- Making a text present. Demanding attention and participation. Implicating all involved. Refusing closure or categorization.

- Witnessing experience and testifying about power without foreclosure-of pleasure, of difference, of efficacy.

- Believing that words matter and writing towards the moment when the point of creating autoethnographic texts *is* to change the world. (p. 765)

To understand autoethnography, it is helpful to think of this methodology as a combination of autobiography, narrative inquiry, and ethnography. It is an examination of personal culture as related to the larger culture (e.g., Ellis & Bochner, 2000).

Autoethnography differs from other types of self-writing, such as autobiography. It reveals the researcher in vulnerable and personal ways—and may explicitly provide cultural connections, thus raising social awareness. Autoethnography adds to research findings by providing deeply personal accounts that are difficult to obtain otherwise. Readers experience fresh understandings or revisit their old understandings, seeing them in a new light (Holman Jones et al., 2013). Autoethnography

can make what seems mysterious . . . comprehensible . . . make tacit knowledge explicit . . . teach us about ourselves, our friends, . . . families, . . . workplaces, . . . world . . . offer us the ability to empathize with others, make strategic . . . positive personal and cultural change, and become better and just researchers and people. (Adams & Herrmann, 2020, p. 6)

Autoethnographies offer a kaleidoscope of knowing through stories we thought were clear or had simply left—either knowingly or unknowingly—untold.

Major Genres of Autoethnography

I just think that good stories are stories that reflect ourselves back at us and each other.

—Elisabeth Moss (in Mulkerrins, 2017)

He*art*ful Autoethnography

The original autoethnography, sometimes termed as he*art*ful (Ellis, 1999), written to emphasize the *art* in the word "heart," has been described as emotive and evocative, where the researcher seems to simply—deceptively simply—write from personal experience. These writings are profoundly personal in nature and may be crafted without direct references to outside sources (e.g., Ellis's now classic *With Mother With Child*, 2001). At other times, personal sources are referenced and either interwoven with text in a seemingly effortless fashion or offset by italics, footnotes, text boxes, or some other literary device. Personal sources that augment the narrative, bringing a fuller sense to the story, may include, for example, diaries, journals, quoted conversations, cards, emails, composites of characters or conversations, tweets, letters, and family heirlooms in the form of images inserted in the autoethnography. In the case of one of my autoethnographies, I drew on emails, a poem my niece wrote, commercial greeting cards, journal reviewer comments, my researcher journal, and reconstructed conversations (Lahman, 2009). In another autoethnography, I utilized reconstructed conversations with my mom about family recipes, a reference from a popular book about my Mennonite culture, notes from a conference experience, lyrics, and cookbooks from my cultural group (Lahman, 2020).

As researchers, we use emotive recall to reflexively consider an experience and begin to write about it. These initial writings may be outpourings, notes, or jottings but will eventually lend themselves to careful revisions as we work to hone the writing into its final form. Ultimately, we are seeking to co-construct along with our readers as they engage with our work. This means writings will leave room for more questions by both the author and readers—ideas to continue pondering—with few solutions offered.

Reflexivity, a hallmark of qualitative research (see Chapter 10), will be your close companion in this journey. Depending on the topic, the reflexive experience can be a difficult one as we travel back into painful times. Of this, Ellis (1999) has noted, "I agree with Ruth Behar . . . who wrote that social science 'that doesn't break your heart just isn't worth doing'" (p. 675). Authentic portrayal of intimate events allows the experience to resonate with readers and brings new or deeper insight to all (Adams et al., 2015).

Beneath the Lemon Tree: An Interrupted Family Story (An Exemplar)

(An excerpt from Lahman, 2020, p. 86)

My mother grew up in Africa at the foot of the Ngong Hills.[3] Over seventy years ago she was born in Tanzania, then Tanganyika. Mom, a child of Mennonite missionaries, lived in East Africa until she was sent back to the United States to stay with relatives for her high school education.

At an international conference for Mennonite fiction writers, a speaker discussed incorporating recipes into a piece of fiction—I wish I could recall who the speaker was. Familiar with this idea from mysteries and some female-oriented fiction, including works featuring conservative Amish and Mennonite women (e.g., Miller, 2017), I became intrigued with extending the consideration of family recipes to conveying family story through autoethnography.

Source: Lahman, M. K. E. (2020).

---

[3]Here I allude to Isak Dinesen's opening line to the novel *Out of Africa*, which was also the opening line to the movie based on the book.

Family and Food

potluck, spread, Jacob's join, Jacob's supper, faith supper, covered-dish-supper, dish party, bring-and-share, shared lunch, pitch-in, bring-a-plate, dish-to-pass, fuddle, fellowship meal, carry-in

The family table and the process of food preparation have been a central place for families to enact their narratives. This form of family narration may be eroding with the increased consumption of fast food, the use of microwave ovens, the ease of accessing media and social media while eating, as well as the increased inability for many people to prepare food from "scratch." Capturing family narratives centered on food has powerful implications both for the narrator and for those reading. As a Mennonite, sharing food, family, and story constitutes a foundational part of my narrative, with the extensive amount of group eating within the larger Mennonite community termed "potluck theology" by some.

After the conference, when I next saw Mom, I asked her what family recipes she would consider to be "handed down" from her family through the generations. Between the two of us, we could identify none. I shouldn't have been surprised. I know my family history is an interrupted one, but given the amount of cooking all the females and some of the males in the family are able to produce, I was caught off guard and felt an odd sense of being unmoored.

Mom suggested recipe after recipe as I pointed out with increasing irritation, "Isn't that food from Dad's side of the family?" Dad had taught Mom much of her beginning cooking and how to work with modern kitchen equipment since, being five years older, he had experience in the kitchen. Mom had come straight from rural East Africa, where her mother often cooked with an outdoor stove, to dormitories in the United States, where she learned little in the way of practical domestic arts. What I had pictured through a biased lens as a special time discussing food and family was not emerging. Mom and I both left this conversation feeling slightly baffled and frustrated.

My sister is the type of cook[4] I saw described on the back of THE *Mennonite Community Cookbook*[5] (I added the emphasis), who could organize food for a barn raising.

Food for a Barn Raising

Emma Showalter (1709/1950) made the following observation about the list of food shown below: "Homemakers of our day will no doubt be astounded at all the food consumed in one day. What is more difficult to believe is that it was all made in Great-grandmother's kitchen" (p. 455).

---

[4]I use the word "cook" throughout—as opposed to "chef"—to emphasize the practical and informally trained (at a mother's hip) nature of this sort of food preparation.

[5]While there are many Mennonite cookbooks, the one my family and many people I know refer to as THE *Mennonite Community Cookbook* is authored by Emma Showalter (1950), who was also the first Mennonite female to earn a PhD.

Recipe: Barn Raising

Ingredients:

115 lemon pies
500 fat cakes (doughnuts)
15 large cakes
3 gallons apple sauce
3 gallons rice pudding
3 gallons cornstarch pudding
16 chickens
3 hams
50 pounds roast beef
300 light rolls
16 loaves of bread
Red beet pickle and pickled eggs
Cucumber pickle
6 pounds dried prunes, stewed
1 large crock stewed raisins
5 gallon stone jar white potatoes
and the same amount of sweet potatoes

Enough food for 175 men

This type of cook is anonymous since a good Mennonite cook is humble and may choose not to sit at the table with the recipients of her food—hovering around the table or sitting to the side on a stool to serve as a waitstaff, "bus boy," and cook in one. This cook is represented solely through the list of ingredients needed for a barn raising, a family reunion, or a homeless shelter meal.

My sister is a contemporary Mennonite version of a barn raising cook. A thoroughly modern Mennonite living in Manhattan, she does not need to buy and prepare all the food for a barn raising, but she can cook pasta for more than 100 people at a homeless shelter and dozens of Christmas cookies for a fundraiser, including difficult cookies such as rolled out, cut out, decorated sugar cookies, and sand tarts (thin and short[6]).

"Lemon meringue pie!" Mom pronounced with a flourish when I answered the phone.

"Great, but what are you talking about?" I lived a four-hour flight away from Mom and knew this could not be a dessert invitation, as appealing as it sounded.

---

[6]A *short* cookie means the end product is crisp and buttery, with a large ratio of butter to flour. This is hard to achieve for a cook like my sister, who does not use lard and has two vegetarian daughters as sous chefs (see Durand, 2019).

"Maria, that is a family recipe of mine!"

"What? Come on, Mom. That pie is from Better Homes and Gardens.

"But first it was made by my mom in Tanzania from lemons from her own lemon tree."

I felt stunned. Much of what I gleaned from family folklore was about thrifty missionary Mennonites with little money to spare. The black-and-white images did not conjure up a decadent pie with many eggs, lemons, and granulated sugar.

"Yes, lemons were to us as apples are to you." I suddenly saw my plainly clothed mother and grandmother beneath a lemon tree—the heady scent and (to me) exotic contrast of deeply green glossy leaves to bright pops of yellow, which I have only seen in California. A piece of my fractured food story seemed to fall into place, and I started to see this autoethnography in an exciting new way, not perceiving what was yet to come.

 ## Mom's Recipe for Lemon Meringue Pie

Ingredients:

- 1 cup sugar
- 6 tablespoons cornstarch
- 1 ½ cups water
- 3 slightly beaten egg yolks
- 2 tablespoons butter, cut up
- 2 teaspoons finely shredded lemon peel
- 2/3 cup lemon juice
- 3 egg whites
- 1 teaspoon lemon juice
- 6 tablespoons sugar

Directions

Bake a pastry crust and allow to cool. In a pan, stir together the 1 cup sugar, cornstarch, and gradually stir in water. Bring to boiling, stirring constantly. Reduce heat; cook and stir over medium low heat for 2 minutes. Remove from heat. Gradually stir about 1 cup of the hot mixture into beaten egg yolks; pour yolk mixture into remaining hot mixture in saucepan. (This is to avoid cooking the eggs in a scrambled egg fashion at this point.) Bring to a gentle boil; cook for 2 minutes more in order to thicken, stirring constantly. Remove from heat; stir in butter and shredded lemon peel. Slowly stir in 2/3 cup lemon juice. Keep filling warm while preparing the meringue. (Mom covered the filling with plastic wrap at this point. The wrap touches the filling to avoid a "skin" forming.)

Prepare meringue—in a large mixing bowl beat egg whites and 1 teaspoon lemon juice with an electric

```
mixer on medium speed about 1 minute or until soft
peaks form. (Modern cooks may wish to use meringue
powder since this meringue may not be heated to
safety standards. I doubt most people would be able
to taste a difference.) Gradually add 6 tablespoons
sugar, beating on high speed about 4 minutes or
until stiff peaks form and sugar dissolves. Pour warm
filling into cooled crust and spread smooth. Spread
meringue over filling, sealing to edge of crust to
prevent shrinkage. Bake in a 350 degrees F. oven for
15 minutes or until peaks of the meringue begin to
brown. Keep a close eye on the pie while cooking.
Cool for 1 hour and chill for 3 hours before serving.
```

Mom died, both unexpectedly, during the writing of this autoethnography, and expectedly, over 10 days, dying with grace as she struggled against intense pain due to an unsuccessful heart surgery. Having conceived of the autoethnography and discussed it at length with her several times during the initial writing yet having her dead during the final writing, editing, and submission process means this story represents even more clearly the bittersweet aspects of a lemon.

Exhausted after all the death rituals and hunkered down at home, my young children and I, at my spouse's suggestion, have baked a memorial lemon meringue pie. I take a first bite from my slice—the yellow layer a stunning burst of color against the white meringue—and hold back tears, not wanting to weep as the meringue does on my fork.[7] I give my leg a quick, sharp pinch under the table, as Mom did when I was young and not behaving during mealtime. This is a time for celebration—tears will have plenty of time later. The tart tang of lemon and the sweet meringue recall my relationship with Mom as I savor the history of my interrupted family narratives on my tongue.

Critical Autoethnography

Autobiography is awfully seductive; it's wonderful. Once I got into it, I realized I was following a tradition established by Frederick Douglass—the slave narrative—speaking in the first-person singular, talking about the first-person plural, always saying "I," meaning "we."

—Maya Angelou (in Plimpton, 1990)

Even as critical researchers seek to understand the intersections of identities as related to power and dismantle oppressive forces, critical autoethnographers seek to deepen understandings of these global purposes through the personal, for, as illustrated in Maya Angelou's quote above, *the personal is political. Critical autoethnography* (CA) allows researchers to explore the personal and explicitly

---

[7]Meringue is said "to weep" when it forms drops of condensation on top.

connect it to the larger political culture in ways that shed light on issues of oppression, intersectionality, and power situated within a theory. "The "critical" in "critical autoethnography" reminds us that theory is not a body of knowledge—a given, static and autonomous set of ideas, objects, or practices. Instead, theorizing is an ongoing, movement-driven process that links the concrete and abstract" (Holman Jones, 2016, p. 229).

Critical autoethnographers share goals—identifying stories that society does not allow to be narrated or has marginalized, highlighting connections between the personal and the political, unearthing the deep relationships between power and privilege, and pointing to social justice issues (Adams, 2017). Fundamentally, "critical autoethnographies identify personal/cultural offenses and potential remedies for these offenses" (Adams, 2017, p. 79).

Holman Jones (2016) suggests that critical autoethnographers consider attending to the following ideas:

- theory and story work together in a dance of collaborative engagement

- critical autoethnography involves both a material and ethical praxis

- doing critical autoethnography engages us in processes of becoming and because of this, shows us ways of embodying change. (p. 229)

Of CA representation, Homan Jones (2016) has written, "For qualitative researchers who use narrative techniques—autobiography, personal narrative, oral histories, and my chosen method—critical autoethnography—theory and story share a reciprocal, inter-animating relationship" (p. 229). While critical research does not have to be performative or represented artistically per se, there is no doubt that critical researchers have pulled the field into these creative areas in deep and meaningful ways. This is likely due to researchers' ability to express themselves more creatively through the arts, along with a felt need to access modes of inquiry and representation long denied to researchers by the patriarchal, white, oppressive voice of objectivism.

Infertility . . . A Loss of Innocence (An Exemplar)

When today's woman first attempts to conceive in her mid-30s, she has probably not considered infertility as part of the envisioned experience.[8] That was true for me. After a stunning, world-altering ectopic pregnancy that resulted in the loss of a much-loved fetus and a fallopian tube (Lahman, 2008), I entered the category "at risk for infertility." Eighty-five percent of women (see The Ectopic Pregnancy Trust, n.d.) have a successful pregnancy after an ectopic pregnancy. I have no idea how the loss of the fallopian tube altered that percentage of possibility for me. After the ectopic pregnancy, I did not conceive and began the stumbling downward slide into a daymare of infertility counseling.

---

[8]ReproductiveFacts.org (n.d.).

It is still dark—a snowy morning—and I am driving 40 miles to the neighboring town to deliver the sperm specimen my spouse provided that morning. We are sure the infertility lies with me, but it is cheap and easy to get the possibility of the father's infertility out of the way first. Consider for a moment the experiences veiled behind the words "specimen" and "provided"— embarrassment, shared laughter, privacy, ecstasy, cringing hope. The specimen is in a sterile plastic receptacle tucked inside my cleavage as I tensely navigate snow-covered roads across the backside of a town I am unfamiliar with. I was instructed by Doctor to put the receptacle in my cleavage to keep it warm. This was done with some laughter on Doctor's part, which I did not share. I laugh now harshly, without pleasure, as I picture telling some police officer why I need to hurry. I only have a set amount of time to deliver the sperm before the results are skewed. Perhaps I will be provided a police escort. Later that day, a call comes telling us the sample is excellent. We know now the fertility problem will be mine, all mine. We make light of this burden as we joke about the sperm's modality and viscosity. Now I will be "infertile Hannah." It is a lot to bear. I tell myself I will be fine. I lie. (Lahman, 2020, p. 87).

Source: Lahman MKE. A Loss of Innocence—Infertility. *Qualitative Inquiry.* 2021; *27*(1):125–128. doi:10.1177/1077800419883305

Multivoiced Autoethnography

Multivocal, multivoiced, poly-vocal, or duo (Sawyer & Norris, 2009)—also called *co-constructed* (Cann & DeMeulenaere, 2012)—are autoethnographies characterized by more than one author writing together in a reflexively shared fashion to explore and unravel the tangled yarn of relationships. Multiple authorship allows researchers to evocatively explore an experience from many perspectives, and CA researchers to take a critical intersectional approach toward the web of positionalities the researchers hold. Working with a diverse group of autoethnographers allows us to explore varying experiences of orientation, class, gender, race/ethnicity, disability, and so on, always situated within larger systems of culture, power, oppression, and social privilege. Here, the kaleidoscope is viewed through a plural gaze rather than a singular one.

Cann and DeMeulenaere (2012) have this to say about a critical co-constructed autoethnography:

We have spent the past few years exploring narrative in autoethnography [and] . . . in critical race theory, critical theory, and feminist theory. . . . We contend that a critical co-constructed autoethnographic methodology aligns with activist research by capturing the process of praxis (Freire, 1970/1993), rooted in critical theory and pedagogy. Also, as a methodology, it allows collaborating researchers and writers to more accurately represent the tempo (Bourdieu, 1977), intimacy (Tillmann-Healy, 2003), uncertainty, and complexity of relationships—creating a space for colleagues engaged in critical work to reflect together. Further, critical co-constructed autoethnography generates opportunities for solidarity among marginalized groups as well as across difference, inspiring those in spaces of privilege to be allies in social justice work. (p. 147)

I find multivoice to be an ideal way for novices in autoethnography to venture into writing in this form. There is a sense of camaraderie in writing as a group that can offset the deep and public vulnerability autoethnographers experience. See Cann and DeMeulenaere (2012) for an excellent example of multivoiced ethnography.

Emerging Areas in Autoethnography

New areas in autoethnography parallel developments in qualitative research in general—poetry, performances, visuals, images, videos, graphics, comic, art informed, collage, and so on. The two poems that follow are examples of auto-poetry I wrote about pregnancy loss (Lahman, 2021).

Remembering an Ectopic Pregnancy

Researchers expressed surprise
when women shared
that they still thought
of their ectopic pregnancy
OFTEN 18 years later.[9]

There is not room enough
in a poem to demonstrate how
often I have thought of you
or a way to explain how
I carry you everywhere
like one carries their own
breath,
soul,
marrow.

August—Back to School

I open course files
to start putting together
a class.
I begin
to tremble all over.

---

[9]Lasker and Toedter (2003).

My notes from
the first day of the semester
a year ago read—

You were losing your pregnancy . . .
Let class out after going over the syllabus.
State you are not feeling well.

Figure 7.1. is taken from a graphic thesis by Meghan Parker (2017). This captivating thesis is autoethnographic in nature. I'm appreciative that Meghan

FIGURE 7.1 ● Graphic Autoethnography by Meghan Parker (2017)

Source: Reproduced with permission from Meghan Parker.

allowed me to include several of the graphic pages in this text. Please see Chapter 4 for Figure 4.6.

If trying a new form of autoethnography seems intimidating, consider adding a few creative, personal elements to your larger, traditional research representation. For example, the poems I presented here are part of a larger prose autoethnography I developed around the experience of infertility. Meghan is clearly a professional artist with art education degrees and experience. However, many of us are lapsed artists. Consider adding a piece of art you have created as one part of a larger autoethnography, or (for the rest of us) use an image of a craft, doodling, or a collage type of medium.

One Way to Create Autoethnography

My goal is the same as Dorothy Allison's (1994)—"to take the reader by the throat, break her heart, and heal it again."

—Ellis (1999, p. 675)

In the next part of this chapter, I move from describing different forms of autoethnography to considering how to go about writing one. I start with an excerpt from an autoethnography I wrote that provides a glimpse at the behind-the-scenes stress in publishing the intimate. Then I walk readers through the different steps in my writing process and ideas from experts. I end with an autoethnographic excerpt of how difficult yet rewarding it has been to consult with multiple researchers, over the years, while they write their first autoethnographies.

Behind the Curtain of an Autoethnography: An Excerpt From *Dreams of My Daughter*[10]

I log on to my e-mail account and see the editor of Qualitative Health Research (QHR) has responded with a decision concerning publication of the autoethnography I wrote about my pregnancy loss.

I cannot open the e-mail. I just sit there.

"Do it, like ripping off a Band-Aid," I cajole myself.

"Do it."

"Do it."

I continue to sit there.

Through the window I see my spouse and son biking up the driveway, returning from the farmers' market. I open the e-mail, anticipating as soon as my son, a toddler, enters the house, time for work will be over.

"The reviewers have recommended acceptance, but some minor revisions are needed."

---

[10]Lahman (2009, p. 276).

I am stunned. I cannot breathe. I choke as tears rush down my face, breathing restricted, throat tight—stumbling, I tell Brent. "QHR has accepted Festy's story."
"Isn't that a good thing?" He is puzzled and concerned.
"Yes . . . no."
Do I publish to not perish over Festy's death?
I falsely yet lovingly interact with my son and then escape to the bedroom to mull over my response and again cry. I can easily tell myself Festy's story is important for others to know. The reviewers agree, saying, "It is worthwhile for health professionals to hear about the patient's perspective," and the article "can illuminate the experience of ectopic pregnancy and contribute to what is known about this health event." This is true, yet I find as I consider the dilemma of publishing about death I must keep the tension between the possibility of disrespect and gaining a vita line from writing of tragedy with the respect of honoring life through story. It is a nebulous, hazy, gray type of space, as tenuous as Festy's life was, yet I am comfortable occupying it.

The reviewers have suggested I add methodological and theoretical aspects to the article and the editor has required this. The teacher/social scientist in me is eager to do so.

I want to warn the reader that I, like many other qualitative researchers, are drawn to autoethnography like a moth to a flame. It is a source of great joy to convey experience in a way Ellis (1999) has termed "heartfelt" and to embrace the role of emotion in research, as is demonstrated in Behar's (1996) book, The Vulnerable Observer: Anthropology That Breaks Your Heart.

A note of caution: although prior to achieving tenure I would have written Festy's story, I am not sure I would have sought publication. For almost two decades I have been contentedly housed in a department with colleagues who are all statisticians or quantitative methodologists. Although they respect me as a hardworking contributor to the department, it is difficult for many of them to view Festy's story as scholarly research. Debate about whether autoethnography constitutes rigorous research might be heated, even in qualitative circles (Anderson, 2006; Atkinson, 2006). The flame might warm or burn.

I want to ask, "What is your definition of research?" and suggest considering Zora Neale Hurston's (1991) famous quote, "Research is formalized curiosity, poking and prying with a purpose" (p. 143).

Indeed, I want to lecture—proselytize.

One of the reviewers of the Festy piece echoes my concern about sharing personal details in a professional format, saying, "At what point are we saying too much? . . . I think all autoethnographers should hold on to that question. It is a question about research ethics as it relates to disclosure about ourselves."

I agree and am willing to work within this place of tension—a complete picture inside my head at the time of Festy's death would be so incoherently full of bile, and swirling neurosis evocative of Frieda Kahlo painting as to be unreadable, unknowable. Some things do not occur in order to be shared.

The writer/mother in me says to the teacher and researcher, "Stop! How can I interpret what I don't understand? How can I tell a reader what to know? Why waste space to say all writing is inextricably linked to themes of death, and thus life?

What does any of this have to do with Festy?" Therefore, I will only say, to method-
ologically and theoretically begin to engage with autoethnography, one must read it,
write it, and live it.

Source: Lahman MKE. Dreams of My Daughter: An Ectopic Pregnancy. *Qualitative Health Research.*
2009; *19*(2):272–278. doi:10.1177/1049732308329484

Autoethnography is profoundly personal, so I imagine there are many different avenues to take when creating one. Threads of personal narratives may be
traced far back, prior to a conscious sense that one might write about the experiences as a fully formed narrative at some future point. One of the few times I
planned to write an autoethnography, about my family recipes, nothing went the
way I anticipated (see the excerpt "Lemon Tree" in this chapter). This messy muddle when first encountered in printed form, even when written in a fractured,
postmodern manner, still has the power that comes with publishing. It causes the
reader to experience the writing as fully formed and can obscure the process that
occurs *prior* to publication. In an effort to help others embarking on autoethnography have a sense of how to start, I share ideas that have worked for me.

Fumbling or Fomenting: First Steps When Writing

This part of the process includes a prewriting stage. You could focus on a
moment that may be termed an *epiphany*—an experience that has affected your
life (Ellis et al., 2011) described as "effects that linger—recollections, memories,
images, feelings—long after a crucial incident is supposedly finished" (p. 275).
You might also explore a story or collection of stories that represents something important you have been mulling over and want to write about. Most of
my autoethnographic writing begins as an outpouring of written words I create
to process a difficult event, and then I set it aside. I may or may not use this
writing in some future work, but by creating the early rough draft, I have given
myself the option to pick it up again.

If you journal, you could read through your journals to find relevant entries
or create new entries as you reflect on the experience you plan to write about.
People who are more vocal will find it helps to speak about the experience to
others who were involved or who are thoughtful listeners. At this stage, I also
identify all the material data that exist around the story—emails, letters, cards,
websites, texts, photos—and assemble them for repeated review. These items
may or may not be featured in the final product, but they assist in recall.

When writing about a recent experience that has painful elements, I find
that a free write works best. I write when I know I will not be interrupted
and do not have to look presentable, sometime soon after the experience.
Then I pour out all my feelings and memories through writing. Part of the
writing will include lists where I identify key vignettes I may later develop into
stories. Ellis (1999) has said of this process, "I start with my personal life. I pay
attention to my physical feelings, thoughts, and emotions. I use what I call
systematic sociological introspection and emotional recall to try to understand
an experience. . . . Then I write my experience as a story" (p. 671).

When writing about loss, this may mean I cry for a while or feel down, so it is important to practice reasonable self-care. I believe, however, that the writing process helps me with grief. I see this when I interact with others who shared my experience but can almost not speak about it. Writing about grief, while difficult, seems to allow me to integrate the experience into who I am so I don't need to hold it at bay.

Mulling: Middle Steps

The next important step is to set your initial writings aside. At a later point, go back to them and choose a few vignettes to begin developing. This will include

- rich description that allows the reader to feel they are in the story;

- reconstructed conversations that move the story forward;

- addition of allusions (make sure they don't overshadow the story);

- choices regarding whether the autoethnography will be he*art*ful or critical, written alone or with others;

- decisions around the use of images and their careful placement in the text; and

- continued mulling over the sound, look, and feel of the text (see the reflexive questions at the end of the chapter to assist with this).

One of the main ways I mull over my developing writing is to consider the meaning of the major words I draw on. For example, see the opening of this chapter, where I present different words related to autoethnography (Ellis & Bochner, 2002). Also, in the "Lemon Tree" excerpt, I consider the meaning and background of the word "potluck" as related to theology.

Since I tend to be a storied person, I write the stories first and then go back and weave in visuals and outside references as warranted. I imagine someone who is highly visual might start the other way—placing a visual in the piece and then writing about it.

Liberating: Last Steps

Share the autoethnography with as many people as you are comfortable with—more is better—and ask for feedback. It is usually best to start with close others and work outward to local campus workshops and conference presentations. Ask yourself the following questions:

- What type of feedback are you receiving?

- Does the feedback warrant amplifying pieces of the story or reducing others?

- It may be the feedback is not useful—if so, set it aside.

Set the autoethnography aside one last time. When you revisit it again, take a final close examination, and consider the following questions:

- Are you protecting others to the greatest extent possible?

- Are you certain you want what you have written to be permanent?

See the section Tensions in Autoethnography later in the chapter for more discussion of these points. I do not ask people to consider these questions as a way of foreclosing on the autoethnography. I want you to engage with this genre of research but not to be naive or get hurt in the process, as some autoethnographers have.

Finally, be intrepid and hit the submit button!

Never Done

Don't be surprised if long after an autoethnography is finished and published it continues to dwell with you and reveal itself at seemingly unwarranted times. While I have never been contacted years after publication about the impact of a research article, I have had multiple people contact me about autoethnographies. One person in particular told me they had to step into the stacks at their library to quiet their response to my writing. This is the power of the personal. If I have a reason to reexamine my written autoethnographic work, I see possibilities where threads could be extended. When you reexamine yours, if you find enough of these threads, consider the possibility a Part 2 is beckoning.

I close this section with a brief reflection on the impact of consulting with researchers who are creating autoethnographies—writing the personal.

Secondary Effect: Professor of Autoethnography

I am in the world of autoethnography. I have a terrible head cold in my eyes—eyes seeping, weeping. I give feedback all online now. There are pros and cons, but one con is reading on a bright computer screen with a cold. I am reading drafts to see how these adept writers have responded to my comments in their rewrites, aiming to gain ultimate impact and connection with the reader. They have pushed these stories to another level, ready to publish. I am compelled, repelled, under a spell.

Has anyone ever considered the impact of autoethnography on the professor of autoethnography? Ellis,[11] did you think of me as you led me down the scholarly path of personal torment and tragedy into the souls of my students, now reflected in their eyes when I teach? What have you done to protect yourself? Did you forget to teach the teacher?

Bochner,[12] what keeps you sane? Recently, I read a gifted writer, moving into auto the first time, recount the torture of war. I've started to tell my spouse, many times,

---

[11]Ellis (1997).

[12]Ellis and Bochner (2000).

the last visceral punch of the story—a young soldier, in a distant land, listening to a comrade's jocular recounting of the deliberate hurting of children—turning away, disillusioned by his country, himself. Each time, no words come out of my mouth, but the image burns in my memory.

Have you ever read eight autos in a row? Drifting in a world of bulimia, death, impending deafness, aborted adoption, systemic racism, war, torture, oppression, drug use, I cannot rest. How do you find rest, Adams?[13]

Do you know, Holman Jones,[14] *the first auto I read? Back then, I didn't even call it "auto." It was a researcher's stance. A student with vivid writing abilities took me by the hand and heart while we ran down the pier, exulting in our youthful bodies, diving into cool water, and the impact with the object that caused his quadriplegia. I pulled back, torn—wanting to be there for my student yet needing to surface in order to, trembling, gulp lungfuls of air. How could I edit and give feedback to this experience—something sacred and scarred, awful, and awe-ful?*

Tensions in Autoethnography

Autoethnography should produce an ethical connection to the other's suffering, a desire to transform the material conditions of the other's heartbreaking circumstances, increasing the possibility of happiness and a good life.

—Bochner (2012, p. 209)

As is the case with all types of research, autoethnography has its share of detractors and areas of tension. I believe these discussions keep a field stimulated and allow practitioners to grow instead of just continuing to do what we always have, but I have noticed the negative perspectives are often from those who have not engaged deeply with autoethnography. The issues I review are subjectivity, anonymity and research ethics compliance, vulnerability, and finality of the written word.

Subjectivity

Do not tell fish stories where the people know you; but particularly, don't tell them where they know the fish.

—Mark Twain

In the larger research community, the deification of objectivity remains an issue for autoethnographers. Insults aimed at autoethnographers are usually the result of criticisms regarding lack of objectivity, such as "navel gazer"—a sort of narcissist (e.g., Ali-Khan, 2015). My ready reply is "If more academics were to gaze at their navel with some introspection, I can only imagine the

---

[13]Adams (2006).

[14]Holman Jones (2005).

positive impact that would ensue." If the personal nature of autoethnography, however, is an issue for those who sit in judgment over the validity of your research, you may have to create autoethnography as a subgenre of your work. While the joke that follows. is a light-hearted take on this issue, it is important to consider our personal stories with a critical eye and within the immediate and larger contexts we are embedded in to avoid unchecked introspection.

How many narcissists does it take to change a lightbulb?

Just one.

They hold it in place while the world revolves around them.

(See https://upjoke.com/narcissist-jokes for this joke and others about narcissists.)

Within most of the field of qualitative research there is a deep understanding that humans learn through subjective experience; an adherence to objectivity as a standard for research has cut off important ways of knowing. I do not mean to sound flippant when I say that if you realize you will not be able to convince others who are important to your career it is best to engage with those who understand what you are saying until you are in a position where you can write and publish as you wish. A personal example: My colleagues prior to tenure were all quantitative researchers or statisticians. I chose to publish an autoethnography after tenure so we would not have to engage in discussions about the validity of my work. Interestingly, many of them said they felt it should be up to me to explain to them the standards of my field since they were not the experts. In hindsight, perhaps I should have had more trust. This is easy to write as a tenured, full professor!

If we are not seeking to be objective and instead are working in the subjective realm, what standards can we use for guidance when creating autoethnographies? I discuss credible subjectivity and verisimilitude (Ellis et al., 2011) as two ways to enhance our work. A *credible* story is what we seek in order to be thought reliable and for our representations to generalize outside the specific story. Unlike statistical generalization, readers choose what affects or generalizes to them. As researchers who work within our personal subjectivities, we know others experiencing the same event may have a different interpretation of the same story.

> Memory is fallible . . . it is impossible to recall or report on events in language that exactly represents how those events were lived and felt; and we recognize that people who have experienced the "same" event often tell different stories about what happened. (Ellis et al., 2011, p. 282)

iStock.com/Alek_Koltukov

"Accurate" recall is not the goal of autoethnographers, but instead we aim to explore and represent the import the experienced event has left with us—feelings of hurt and joy, change, understanding, questions, confusion, and more. The representation is credible in that it convinces the reader through its likelihood and connection to and extension of their known world.

Verisimilitude, or authenticity, is one way to consider validity as it relates to autoethnography. The story told "evokes in readers a feeling that the experience described is lifelike, believable, and possible, a feeling that what has been represented could be true. The story is coherent. It connects readers to writers and provides continuity in their lives" (Ellis et al., 2011, p. 282).

Anonymity and Research Ethics Compliance

When you write about yourself, the people who enter your story by way of a specific relationship to you—your mom, your doctor, the dean, the department chair, your neighbor—are identifiable. In general, I have found that no one tries to identify these people, yet their confidentiality remains an issue. Although others do not have the right to tell us that we cannot write about personal experience, it does not mean we shouldn't make an effort to enhance confidentiality. If I am writing a negative characterization, I do not use demographic clues such as race, gender, or age. I wrote about my doctor by referring to them as "Doctor" (Lahman, 2008) and about relatives by giving them a relational title without a specific name (e.g., cousin, uncle).

This issue is one reason there is often confusion around whether an autoethnography in the United States needs Research Ethics Board/IRB approval. It is clear in the IRB guidelines, referred to as the Common Rule, that it does not. Even areas that are clearly research, such as oral history, or that include narrative, for instance, journalism, are not required to have IRB approval. The Common Rule (IRB code) reads,

> Research means a systematic investigation, including research development, testing, and evaluation, designed to develop or contribute to generalizable knowledge. . . . For purposes of this part, the following activities are deemed *not to be* research:
> (1) Scholarly and journalistic activities (e.g., oral history, journalism, biography, literary criticism, legal research, and historical scholarship), including the collection and use of information, that focus directly on the specific individuals about whom the information is collected. (ECFR, 2018)

At my university where I was a board member and cochair for years, we did not require IRB review of autoethnographies. However, if the researcher uses the conventions of mainstream qualitative research, such as audio recording of conversations, then I believe IRB approval should be sought. I have not worked with a university IRB that understands autoethnography, but it is possible your institution would have some specific policies beyond those of the federal government.

Vulnerability

I do not write this section to discourage would-be autoethnographers but instead to advocate for an assessment of the safety of your publishing environment. Is it supportive? Do you have tenure, and are you in a position to be a trail blazer in your department or college? Some autoethnographers have written under nom de plumes when first embarking on autoethnography (Morse, 2002). I have colleagues who have received unprofessional, severe, uninformed repercussions from working in the personal. It is stunning and speaks to the power of autoethnography that academia, which values academic freedom—freedom from undue intrusion by law, the institution, or the public—can intrude heavily into autoethnographic work.

An autoethnographer cannot fully prepare for being vulnerable to a public audience, and social media adds a level of vulnerability that is unprecedented in academic circles (Campbell, 2017). This is due to the hidden identity of those commenting. While this is similar to the anonymity of peer reviewers in academic journals, it differs in the level of moderation or protection afforded the author. A journal editor can prevent unprofessional feedback from reaching the author. Elaine Campbell (2017) details social media comments targeted at autoethnographers who were called vile, misogynistic names and whose mental stability was called into question by anonymous commenters.

Finality of the Written Word

The idea that the written published word "wins" has been discussed extensively (e.g., Borland, 1991). For instance, if there is an oral narrative as well as a written record of an event or experience, people tend to be biased toward the written word since it is seen as a recorded "fact." It is beyond the scope of this section to do more than point out that writing is rarely a "fact." Autoethnographers will need to be aware of the permanence of their writing. I have shared earlier in this text about having my writing referenced in startling contexts. Do not publish anything you would be unwilling to encounter in unexpected settings.

The Gist

Autoethnographers are drawn to the personal story as a moth to a flame—the fire may warm or burn. Autoethnography, while new to some disciplines, has a history spanning decades and is accepted in most areas of qualitative research. Autoethnographers dwell in the subjective, crafting the personal into a form that allows readers and viewers to experience the unfamiliar or the familiar in new and proactive ways. These experiences provide opportunities for increased learning and human connection. People creating and consuming autoethnographies are vulnerable. Documenting the autoethnographic process from many perspectives may bolster resiliency among the community of autoethnographers. Autoethnographic power comes through viewing and representing the kaleidoscope of story that is personal experience

Reflexive Questions

1. What are some key experiences and/or positionalities of yours that you wish to explore in depth that others might benefit from? Areas to consider include major life-turning points, epiphanies, revelations, loss, intersection of identities, and identities that may be unknown, underrepresented, or misunderstood by majority groups. These, of course, are just some of the many possibilities to consider.

2. How best can you begin to flesh out these experiences into short vignettes or a story line that others will be able to engage with?

3. Are you in a safe space to deeply consider your new writing project? If you come to realize that you misjudged your own safety, what can you do to augment your mental and emotional safety?

4. To what extent do you want to incorporate outside information, such as literature?

5. If you choose to incorporate outside information, what is the best way for you to do so? Consider the following:

   a. Footnotes or endnotes

   b. A separate literature review section. This should occur after the autoethnography so the reader can experience the personal before considering the broader political information. This mirrors the way narrative hooks a reader and draws them in.

   c. Interspersing information throughout in bubbles, text boxes, or a different font. In this case, be sure the journal you plan to submit to allows alternative formats to traditional typesetting.

6. Have you considered including opposing viewpoints? This can occur through a literature review, readings of the history of the experience or background of your topic, asking others to read and comment on your writing, and reviewing news and social media posts.

7. Researchers sometimes seem to get caught up in how to identify an autoethnography. I suggest this is not the most critical question. However, if you need, for some specific reason, to determine if a piece of research is an autoethnography, the following are some areas to consider:

   • How is a piece classified by the researcher and the journal in the keywords and abstract? Ellis (2004) noted, "Whether a work is fiction or fact, autoethnography, or memoir, is connected to writing practices and the claims of those who are writing the work" (p. 39).

   • For example, are words such as "ethnography," "autoethnography," or "memoir" used?

- Is the piece written in first person?
- Social science autoethnographies may contain citations and disciplinary vocabulary.
- Ellis (cited in Given, 2008) has suggested the following questions to ask when considering if a piece is an autoethnography:
  a. Who published the piece?
  b. How is it promoted and labeled?
  c. Who is the target audience?
  d. What are the reviewer practices?

Reflexive Activities

1. Autoethnographic Writing Practice

Topic: Your college or graduate school experience (Other ideas are the neighborhood you grew up in, your commute to campus/work, what you did this summer, your siblings or experience of not having siblings, and a time you regret you did not stand up for something.)

1. For two minutes, list every type of activity or experience you can think of in this area of your school experience (e.g., studying, class time, commute, funding, research).

2. Take a moment to concentrate on your experiences. You may need to shut your eyes.

3. For two minutes, write down all the *emotion* words that the school experience elicits.

4. Take a five-minute break. If you are in a class during the break, feel free to share what you wrote or just chat about school or your writing experience thus far with classmates.

5. Look back at what you have written. What event or emotion stands out that you could write about more? Choose one and write for five minutes.

6. Take a five-minute break. During the break, feel free to share what you wrote or just chat about graduate school or your writing experience thus far with classmates.

7. Look back over what you wrote, and edit it as needed. You have two minutes.

8. While making sure you save your original writing, is there anything you would like to do to format the writing to make it more impactful?

For example, you might want to put words of emphasis in all capitals, use different fonts, or change the format from paragraph form. You may also wish to consider the literature you could incorporate and if there are material data or images that could be used in this work. Take five minutes for this editing.

9. If you are working within a group setting, have anyone who is willing share their work with the whole group on a document projector or virtually with screen share. The student or instructor can read the writing aloud. If the class is large, separate into smaller breakout groups. Class members should offer areas that resonated with them and new questions they have. This is not a time for critique.

2. Autoethnographic Cabinet of Curiosities

This activity is from the article "Listening to Self: An Appeal for Autoethnography in Art Museum Education" (Evans & Blair, 2016). I have retained almost all of the authors' original language here.

A cabinet of curiosities, or *kunstkammer*, was originally a personal collection of small objects of wonder that were displayed in a room or a custom wooden cabinet. These cabinets were most popular in the 17th century but have been reimagined by libraries and museums over the past century. Originally the personal collections of wealthy individuals that contained both human-made material data and objects from nature, cabinets of curiosities have reemerged to reflect the material and visual culture of our day.

Inspired by the cabinet of curiosities, this activity encourages course members to create their own literal or metaphorical cabinet filled with material data of self and culture in your office, home, or classroom. This collection can then be used as inspiration for autoethnographic writing and researcher reflexivity. Choosing or creating objects that connect, reflect, or embody elements of your personal self and history can be a gateway into arts-based autoethnographic practices. Start this exercise by asking yourself a series of autoethnographic questions to inspire material data that connect self and other, such as the following:

• What objects tell a story about my life?

• What meanings or memories do I inject into objects that surround me?

• With what objects in my museum's collection do I most connect, and why?

• What objects still invoke wonder or surprise in me when I see them?

• With what materials do I interact on a daily basis?

- Have I collected any meaningful objects during my travels or wanderings through life?

- In what ways do these life material data help define my culture of self?

You are encouraged to create this cabinet of curiosities, whether on paper as a list or collage, digitally, or even an actual cabinet in your office or classroom space. I can even picture it as the backdrop to your "Zoom Room." Do this activity with others to gain a better understanding of them and yourself. This activity is similar to "A Box of Me," which is described at the end of Chapter 10.

3. Professional Autoethnography

This activity has been modified from the one by Evans and Blair (2016). While the activity refers to educators, it can be changed to suit other professionals, such as counselors or psychologists. The goal of this activity is to use writing as a tool to explore who you are as an educator currently or who you want to be as an educator. Write about how you came to be attracted to education and why. Address the following in your exploration:

- How does learning occur?

- How does your teaching facilitate learning?

- Why do you teach the way you do (or how you would like to teach)?

- What goals do you have for yourself and your students?

- How does your teaching embody your beliefs and goals? Think especially about how audiences have responded to your teaching.

- How do you create an inclusive learning environment?

Write informally and with passion. Examine your life and the decisions you have made, the paths you have crossed, the serendipitous moments that have occurred. How you write this reflection and its contents should represent you.

Objects and Autoethnography

1. Assemble a group of objects around a certain topic you have been thinking of writing about. Unlike the cabinet of curiosities, these are narrowed specifically to that topic.

2. If these items are no longer with you or unreachable at the moment, make a list, or clip pictures and create a collage of items.

3. Think creatively—notes, social media, items in your book bag or purse, things you carry around in your car, or objects you have shoved into a crawl space. Place the items in a large empty space where you can view them while you think, and arrange and rearrange them. Consider taking photos of the different arrangements to view at a later point.

4. Begin to create notes around three of the objects that stand out to you the most.

5. Choose the set of notes that seems to resonate with you the most and develop them into a short story.

6. This activity can easily be modified to fit a virtual or an in-person class.

Resources

Books

Adams, T. E., Jones, S. L. H., & Ellis, C. (2015). *Autoethnography. Understanding qualitative research.* Oxford University Press. (Chapter 6 of this book has a list of resources)

Borland, K. (1991). "That's not what I said": Interpretative conflict in oral narrative research. In R. Perks & A. Thompson (Eds.), *The oral history reader* (2nd ed., pp. 198–225). Routledge.

Boylorn, R. M., & Orbe, M. P. (Eds.). (2016). *Critical autoethnography: Intersecting cultural identities in everyday life* (Vol. 13). Routledge. https://doi.org/10.4324/9781315431253

Denzin, N. K., & Salvo, J. (Eds.). (2020). *New directions in theorizing qualitative research: Performance as resistance* (Vol. 4). Stylus.

Ellis, C. (2004). *The ethnographic I: A methodological novel about autoethnography.* Rowman Altamira.

Holman Jones, S., Adams, T. E., & Ellis, C. (Eds.). (2016). *Handbook of autoethnography.* Routledge.

Salvo, J. M. (2019). *Reading autoethnography: Reflections on justice and love.* Routledge. https://doi.org/10.4324/9781315181042

Short, N. P., Turner, L., & Grant, A. (Eds.). (2013). *Contemporary British autoethnography.* Springer Science & Business Media. https://doi.org/10.1007/978-94-6209-410-9

Journals

The *Journal of Autoethnography* is a new journal that was launched in January 2020 (see https://www.ucpress.edu/blog/39532/new-journal-coming-in-2020-journal-of-autoethnography/). The website for the journal (https://online.ucpress.edu/joae) says,

> The *Journal of Autoethnography (JoAE)* is a refereed, international, and interdisciplinary journal devoted to the purposes, practices, and principles of autoethnography. *JoAE* publishes scholarship that foregrounds autoethnography as a method of inquiry; highlights themes and issues of past and contemporary autoethnographic research; discusses theoretical, ethical, and pedagogical issues in autoethnography; identifies future directions for autoethnography; and highlights innovative applications of autoethnography.

International Journal of Multicultural Education—Special Issue Vol. 19, No. 1 (2017): Critical Autoethnography in Pursuit of Educational Equity

Journal of Organizational Ethnography—Special Issue Vol. 7, Issue 3 (2018): Organisational Autoethnography: Possibilities, Politics, and Pitfalls

As reported in the *Journal of Autoethnography*, journals that feature autoethnography include the following:

Art/Research International

Cultural Studies ↔ Critical Methodologies

Departures in Critical Qualitative Research

The Ethnographic Edge

Health Communication

International Journal of Multicultural Education

International Journal of Qualitative Methods

International Review of Qualitative Research

Journal of Contemporary Ethnography

Journal of Loss and Trauma

Journal of Organizational Ethnography

Liminalities

Qualitative Inquiry

The Qualitative Report

Self

Society

Storytelling

Text and Performance Quarterly

Conferences

Autoethnography Conferences

Critical Autoethnography: https://qualpage.com/2020/01/30/call-for-proposals-critical-autoethnography-2020/

Doing Autoethnography: https://iaani.org/doing-autoethnography/

The International Conference of Autoethnography: http://boomerang-project.org.uk/events/23-july-2018-british-auto-ethnography-conference/

International Congress of Qualitative Inquiry: https://icqi.org

Qualitative Conferences Featuring Autoethnography

Contemporary Ethnography Across the Disciplines: https://www.facebook.com/groups/iCEAD/

European Congress of Qualitative Inquiry: https://10times.com/ecqi-troms
https://kuleuvencongres.be/ecqi2021

Organization for the Study of Communication, Language & Gender: https://osclg.org

The Qualitative Report Conference: https://nsuworks.nova.edu/tqrc/

Videos

ATLAS.Ti: Qualitative Data Analysis. (2014, July 25). *Wall, Sarah—autoethnography: Possibility and controversy*. YouTube. https://www.youtube.com/watch?v=pEWF0SV9F_s

The Audiopedia. (2017, December 28). *What is autoethnography? What does autoethnography mean? Autoethnography meaning and explanation.* YouTube. https://www.youtube.com/watch?v=uIvC0IohRVc

ICQM BGU. (n.d.). *Autoethnography in qualitative inquiry—Professor Carolyn Ellis and Professor Arthur Bochner.* YouTube. https://www.youtube.com/watch?v=FKZ-wuJ_vnQ

Examples

Ellis, C., Bochner, A. P., Rambo, C., Berry, K., Shakespeare, H., Gingrich-Philbrook, C., Adams, T. E., Rinehart, R. E., & Bolen, D. M. (2018). Coming unhinged: A twice-told multivoiced autoethnography. *Qualitative Inquiry,* *24*(2), 119–133. https://doi.org/10.1177/1077800416684874

Norwood, C. R. (2018). Decolonizing my hair, unshackling my curls: An autoethnography on what makes my natural hair journey a black feminist statement. *International Feminist Journal of Politics, 20*(1), 69–84. https://doi.org/10.1080/14616742.2017.1369890

In-Depth Reading

Sotirin, P. (2010). Autoethnographic mother-writing: Advocating radical specificity. *Journal of Research Practice, 6*(1), 9.

Poemish Research
Representations

He wasn't sure if he was writing poems,
but he knew they were poem-ish.

—Peter Reynolds (2004)

Why Poetry?

Why would a researcher ever want to engage with poetry within their research?[1]
Sometimes my students become disgruntled when asked to engage in research
poetry. During one poetry activity, a student sat along the wall engrossed
in their phone. (Ever the optimist when teaching, I hoped they were using
the phone as a writing device.) When asked to share their writing with the
class, the student smiled and said, "I didn't do the activity." Would a response
like this ever occur in a statistics class? Not likely. Another student anxiously
cornered me by the workroom microwave and said they had heard we write
poetry in the introductory qualitative course. If so, I was assured, they would
drop the course.

Have some of us had such lousy exposure to poetry that it can cause as
much anxiety as statistics does for others? If so, what can we as qualitative
researchers and professors do to make poetry accessible and meaningful to

---

[1]Early versions of this chapter and my thought process and work with coauthors
may be found in Lahman et al. (2010), Lahman and Richard (2014), Lahman,
Richard, et al. (2019), Lahman et al. (2011), and Lahman et al. (2017).

our students? Even as I write this reflection, I immediately start to see how these negative experiences could be formed into a poem. I am aware I see and hear poetry in places where others may not, but I also know my poetry would not be considered strong in literary circles. I reside somewhere in the space between a poet and a researcher—perhaps not an expert at either but an expert at guiding others on how to proceed methodologically in qualitative research and in advocating for room for researchers to explore, stumble, mess about, and then perhaps soar in the arts. The following is a homage poem I created to reflect my ongoing learning and experiences as a research poetry teacher to U.S. poet laureate Billy Collins's poem "Introduction to Poetry" (1988). In Collins's poem, he illustrates the overemphasis on critiques of poetry at the possible expense of the pleasure and knowledge obtained through poetic readings—the stress of critique might be part of the fear and distaste some people have for poetry. My poem reflects and reacts to Collins's poem throughout.

Research Poetry 101

I want to help them "to take a poem
and hold it up to the light
like a color slide
or press an ear against its hive,"
but I am unsure I know how.

I'd say "drop a mouse into a poem"
but I'm uncertain if I can show it how to
probe its way out,
"or walk inside the poem's room"
but what if we fumble for the light switch?

"I want them to . . . ski" the Colorado Rockies
"across the surface" of data poems
"waving at the" research participants on the lift
without crashing.

I think maybe
then their
poems will
refract,
reflect,

hum,
buzz,
prod,
explore,

illuminate,
burn,
slalom,
shhhs.

But all we do
"is tie the [research] poem
to a chair with rope
and torture a confession out of it."
"I am not poetry!"

We "begin beating it with a hose
to find out what it really means."
I am research poetry?

—Maria Lahman (revised from Lahman, Richard, & Teman, 2019)

The phrases within quotes are from Collins's (1988) poem.

Discussion has occurred around what constitutes quality research poetry, with some direction on how a researcher who is a novice poet might go about writing *good enough* research poetry (Lahman & Richard, 2014). To expand the existing conversation, in this chapter, I

- frame the conversation with the concepts of *ish* and *poemish* (e.g., Lahman, Richard, & Teman, 2019), drawn directly from Reynolds's (2004) powerful picture book for children titled *ish*;

- review research poetry literature, transcription poetry, and archival poetry;

- present forms of poetry and ideas from literary poets on how to read, write, and revise poetry, intended to move readers into safe attempts at creating poetry as an extension of their current research work;

- suggest activities for increasing poetic sensibilities; and

- end with reflexive questions, activities, and extensive poetry resources.

A Poemish Perspective

Poetry is thoughts that breathe and words that burn.

—Thomas Gray

In support of the goals I have for this chapter, I frame the discussion with Reynolds's (2004) idea of *ish*, or a safe space in the arts, along with the concept of *good enough* (Lahman & Richard, 2014; Lawrence-Lightfoot & Hoffman Davis, 1997). *Ish* reminds the audience of the art form the artist is working within but in some new way. In the children's book titled *ish* (Reynolds, 2004), the young protagonist, Ramon, becomes frustrated by his inability to draw a realistic vase of flowers. Each time Ramon tries to draw an image, he crumples up his attempt. Ramon's older brother is part of the problem, mocking Ramon's artistic ability and causing him to eventually stop drawing altogether. Behind the scenes, Ramon's younger sister has collected each crumpled attempt, smoothed it out, and displayed the whole collection in a stunning array on her wall. Ramon's discovery of the dramatic display of his multiple attempts to depict a vase of flowers causes him to feel free, renewed, and eager to create with the sensibility of *ish*. Ramon even creates poem*ish* poetry. "His ish art inspired ish writing. He wasn't sure if he was writing poems, but he knew they were poem-ish" (Reynolds, 2004). I have also written in a similar vein, drawing on Sara Lawrence-Lightfoot's (1985) work in the area of good enough schools, where I attempt to create a safe space for research poets and art researchers to develop *good enough* research poetry, and arts research in general (Lahman & Richard, 2014). Poemish representations of research are characterized by exhibiting features of poetry and making an effort to blend the aesthetics of poetry and scientific research into something that is poemlike, or poemish. It is within this safe space that new poets may work aesthetically in research.

Research Poetry Background

Writing a poem is discovering.

—Robert Frost

Poetry "makes the invisible world visible" (Parini, 2008, p. 181). It has the unique ability to "clarify and magnify our human existence" (Faulkner, 2016, p. 16). A distinguishing characteristic of research poetry in comparison with literary poetry is that research poetry is "both a method and product of research activity" (Faulkner, 2016, p. 20). Research poetry can be an avenue to express the seemingly inexpressible (Teman & Lahman, 2012). Doing so requires the researcher-as-poet to be "dramatic versus didactic, using [everyday] human language as opposed to scholarly language" (Faulkner, 2017, p. 226). Research poets have certain goals in mind when they set out to express their research findings in poetic form; these goals range from eliciting emotional responses from the reader (e.g., Carr, 2003) to furthering social justice (e.g., Hartnett, 2003) with critical representations, to honoring and preserving participants' words, voices, and perspectives (Nichols et al., 2015).

The field of research poetry has a well-developed body of work, including textbooks (e.g., Faulkner, 2016; Prendergast et al., 2009), conference presentations, methodological development (e.g., Faulkner, 2016; Furman, 2006; Glesne, 1997; Lahman et al., 2011; Prendergast, 2006; Richardson, 1993)—including mixed methods (e.g., Archibald & Onwuegbuzie, 2020), and supportive journals, of which *The Journal of Qualitative Inquiry* continues to be a leading force. Growing support for poetic methods and representation is also seen in field-specific journals. For examples, see *The International Journal of Qualitative Studies in Education* (e.g., Finley, 2003). *The International Quarterly of Community Health Education* (e.g., Nichols et al., 2015), *Interdisciplinary Science Reviews* (e.g., Taylor, 2014), *Journal of Consumer Research* (e.g., Sherry & Schouten, 2002), *Family Systems & Health* (e.g., Shapiro, 2004), *Consumption Markets & Culture* (Tonner, 2019), and *Management Decision* (e.g., Darmer, 2006).

Forms of Research Poetry

Writing up interviews as poems honors the speakers' pauses, repetitions, alliterations, narrative strategies, rhythms, and so on. Poetry may actually better represent the speaker than the practices of quoting snippets in prose.

—Laurel Richardson (1994, p. 522)

Transcription Poetry

The main form of poetry researchers create is *data poems* or *transcription poems* (e.g., Glesne, 1997), which are drawn directly from interview transcripts, observations, and other data sources. Much of the discussion about data poetry is methodological—examining how researchers made choices during the process of distilling raw data to compressed poetic forms and why the poems have merit (e.g., Butler-Kisber, 2010; Cahnmann, 2003; Richardson, 1993).

Laurel Richardson (1993) sought for research poetry to be aesthetic and have emotional value while remaining true to her "sociological understanding" of the participant's story (p. 696). Lynn Butler-Kisber (2002) describes the process as a nonlinear one in which she begins to "'nugget words and phrases from the chained prose [transcript]" (p. 233)—a technique she since learned is used by poets. Butler-Kisber's use of the word "nugget" has value in underscoring the identification of the most salient, valuable words and phrases—extracting these nuggets as though we were miners—panning and sifting through words for small pieces of gold.

What might a researcher identify as a nugget of gold from a set of empirical materials? Richardson (1993) advises listening for repetitions, rhythms, pauses, breath points, and emphasis. The work of a researcher then is to listen carefully to where participants take breaks in an interview and interpret these breaks as punctuation marks, new lines, and line spaces. By paying attention to the rhythms contained in a participant's speech, researchers can capture the rhythms through visual poetic representation of that speech. Researcher poets will wish to use punctuation—or a lack of punctuation—along with white space and line length to slow down or speed up the reading processes and to convey meaning and context.

> Different visual layouts of poems . . . [offer] researchers new ways to represent interview data that respect the tone and movement of the original conversation in ways that may not yet have been imagined in . . . research. (Cahnmann, 2003, p. 31)

Researchers' discussions around constructing research poems have increased transparency regarding the nature of interview transcripts. Interview transcripts are often treated as verbatim fact, with the process of human interpretation not problematized. Poland (2002) noted that there is no such thing as a verbatim transcript because of human error, fatigue, and deliberate alteration. Further problematizing transcriptions, I wish to draw attention to the extensive, but often instantaneous and hidden, decisions a transcriber—and, increasingly, a computer program—makes when transcribing an interview, choosing where to add punctuation marks, pauses, and emphasis to convey meaning for the reader.

Transcription issues aside, data research poems are accepted in qualitative research as valid representations of research participants' experiences (e.g., Gilligan as cited in Glesne, 1997; Richardson, 1994, 2000; Sorsoli & Tolman, 2008). This wide acceptance might be due in part to the poem being created directly from data or "objective" words, which one can locate in the recorded data. (See Text Box 8.1 for an example of an interview transcription research poem and Text Box 8.2 for a data poem.)

8.1 TRANSCRIPTION POETRY EXEMPLAR: EXPLORING MUSLIM COLLEGE STUDENT IDENTITY

ROWEN THOMAS, JEREMY DAVIS, SHARMARKE AHMED, JAMES KOHLES, ADRINA PAWLAK, AND MATTHEW L. P. RICKE

(Please note, the data reflected in this poetry is extremely racist and hateful.)

This poetry was developed from a course-based narrative inquiry, situated in a constructivist paradigm, on the topic "Exploring Muslim College Student Identity" through story and image, which explored the research question "How do Muslim college students make meaning of their identity?" The research team interviewed Muslim-identifying college students at a midsize public university in the Rocky Mountain region of the United States. Additionally, the research team used thematic poetic reduction to transform the transcripts into powerful poetry to complement the analyzed data.

"Y_o_ _A_r_a_b_ _S_h_i_t_" _
"G_e_t_ _t_h_e_ _f_u_c_k_ _o_u_t_ _o_f_ _h_e_r_e_._" _
The cop took ME
Threw ME out
In front of everybody
This must be a prank
This is not real
"T_h_i_s_ _i_s_ _r_a_c_i_s_t_"
The cops started laughing
I need to defend myself
They're going to get you in trouble
They're going to deport you
They're going to kill you
I don't feel welcome
There is no justice served
I have a lot of friends
There is humongous hate
Against this country
Because of the way they were treated
I just have to let it go.

—Hatoo

Starbucks,

The week after Donald Trump got elected,

There was a woman who identified as a white person—older generation—and she was like,

"You know, I just want you to know that we care about you."

I've definitely seen some hatred,

"But if there wasn't such hatred then nice people would not come out."

—Layla

Source: Reproduced with permission from Rowen Thomas.

8.2   I FEEL MORE GROUNDED, THE MORE CRISES I MANAGE

MATTHEW L. P. RICKE

This is, theoretically,
me.

These are my legs:

cement blocks on my feet,
in a soft, somewhat muddy,
surface.

But it's not:
It's something you could
sink into
more—

a good place to be.

Crisis:
The more I deal
The more solidly I feel
In my shoes
The more I sink
into the ground

I feel more
grounded,
the more crises that
I manage

this is a much bigger block
that's already down
but there's more block
to go.

I don't feel
scared
I don't feel
nervous
I don't feel
alone

I feel solid in the ground
I'm standing on

Sinking in terms of
Being grounded,

Jaymie drew the image below (Figure 8.1) ahead of her second interview, using pen on paper. The adjacent poem is from her reflections on the creation and significance of this image as it pertained to who she is as a crisis leader. She was reflecting on the ways in which crisis had shaped her. Jaymie noted how "concrete," seen here as rectangles on her feet, is impenetrable. This visual—which to some may feel reminiscent of concrete blocks on the feet of Mafia targets (as it did for me)—was to her symbolic of strength. She noted that her work is "really horribly gray" but while she is managing crisis there is a compression of options that take some of the shades of gray and ambiguity away. Crisis management has led her to feel more grounded in her whole career, which she identified as the ground at the base of the picture. She described the image carefully, thoughtfully, slowly drawing her words together as she thought through her drawing's significance.

not sinking in terms of
being enveloped in it

Solidly
in something
I feel
grounded in.

—Jaymie

FIGURE 8.1 ● Jaymie's Drawing

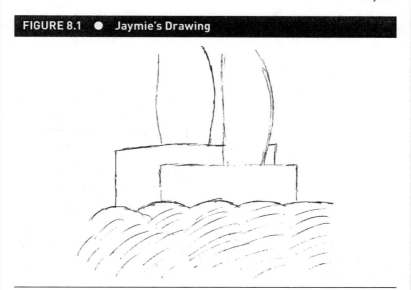

Source: Ricke, Matthew L. P. (2021). Reproduced with permission.

To create this data poem, I drew on both visual (Figure 8.1) and textual
data from my dissertation research on personal meaning making
in campus (organizational) crisis management. Engaging with a
narrative methodology, situated in a constructivist paradigm, each
of the five higher education administration participants were asked
to share their stories in two narrative interviews and participate in
a reflective art-making exercise. What came about were poignant
reflections on one of the most intense campus crises one can
manage—the death of members of the campus community. The poetry
is situated adjacent to the participant's drawing and vignette to create
a tapestry of narrative, artistic, and poetic meaning.

*(For more details, see the full dissertation at https://digscholarship.unco.edu/
dissertations/691/.)*

Source: Ricke, Matthew L. P. (2021). Reproduced with permission.

I-poems are a specific form of transcription poetry developed from Carol Gilligan's larger work (Gilligan et al., 2003). Maaly Younis reviews how to create I-poems in Text Box 8.3, while providing an example that she paired with a visual image, thus deepening the reader's understandings. (See Edwards & Weller, 2012; Koelsch, 2015, for further readings and examples of I-poems.)

8.3 THE VOICE OF THE DATA IS HEARD IN THE "I"

MAALY YOUNIS

As a qualitative researcher, I am always searching for the unique ways to explore the voices of the participants in their stories. The human experience is full of complexity and uniqueness. Demystifying the essence of these stories told by the participants requires in-depth ways of analyzing qualitative data. The I-poems as a qualitative data analysis approach offers an opportunity to explore the participants' sense of self in a unique manner. This analysis method was developed by Carol Gilligan (Gilligan & Eddy, 2017) in which she suggests that creating poems that are basically a thread of all the "I" statements produced by the participant gives the story a different dimension. These poems uncover the sense of self of these participants that is the unheard voice within the data. It is as Gilligan calls it, a "Voice-Centered" method to delve deeper in the data!

In my case study project, I explored the preservice teachers' voices by analyzing their visual teaching philosophies, using the I-poem to gain a deeper understanding of their sense of self as future teachers. I explored the experiences of the preservice teachers using Photovoice as a pedagogy to foster transformative learning. The study is action research since I was the instructor of the course (educational psychology for elementary teachers). The participants (three females and one male) were all juniors in the teacher education program.

To create these poems, I

- cut and paste all the "I" statements into a separate Word document, including the photos that matched these statements, since photos were an integral part of the data;

- read through these statements and kept only the sentences that were cohesive and presented a logical contextual flow to the poem; and

- edited the I-poems stylistically to maintain the poetic aspect within the participants' voices.

An excerpt from an I-poem follows. The poem was developed from Ruth's teaching philosophy (Figure 8.2). She was a junior in art education and planning on becoming an elementary art teacher.

Watercolors

I have chosen an unopened package of watercolors
that I just got today;
I believe this picture perfectly
sums up my teaching philosophy.

I am going to be an art teacher,
which is why the watercolors suit me well.
The package is not opened, has yet to be explored.
I am very excited to put all of these
newfound practices and methods
into my future classrooms!

—Ruth

FIGURE 8.2 ● Watercolors

Material Data Poetry

An extension of transcription poetry is a form I created, *material data* or *archival poetry*, which draws heavily on literary poetry forms such as *found poems* (Poetry Foundation, n.d.), including the *cento*. Found poetry is created from existing texts (oral or written)—poems, news, novels, speeches, social media posts, and so on. For the qualitative researcher, texts may also include transcripts, material data, and observation notes. To my knowledge, Richardson (1994) was the first to introduce found poetry to research as a way to represent qualitative literature reviews, stating, "I decided to use found poetry, which . . . takes the words of others and transforms them into poetic form to re-create lived experience and evoke emotional responses" (p. 521). Monica Prendergast (2004, 2006) has added to the idea of found poetry through extensive work. An additional definition explains that those producing found poetry

> take existing texts and refashion them, reorder them, and present them as poems. The literary equivalent of a collage found poetry is often made from newspaper articles, street signs, graffiti, speeches, letters, or even other poems. A pure found poem consists exclusively of outside texts: the words of the poem remain as they were found, with few additions or omissions. Decisions concerning form, such as where to break a line, are left to the poet. (poets.org, n.d.-c)

This form of representation is helpful when one is trying to express the inexpressible or to create a more collective or comprehensive representation of a topic. The *cento*—originally meaning a patchwork garment— typically a formed version of found poetry, borrows from various sources, creating a "literary patchwork" in a new form and/or a new order to create new meaning (Harmon & Holman, 1996, p. 86). Using "scraps" from a single author or a group of authors, poets rework the scraps to create poems related to the original topic or to create new meaning (Deutsch, 1974; Harmon & Holman, 1996).

Similarly, material data research poets identify a body of existing empirical materials from which to work. They do not necessarily personally collect empirical materials; instead, they use existing materials to create research poetry. A key difference between literary found poetry and research material or archival poetry might be that the researcher would not typically craft the words in a manner that exposes the speaker (research participant) in an unflattering or clever way, as may be seen in some literary found poetry. For instance, in Found Poem #6 by Julius Lester (2007), the poet cleverly uses former president George W. Bush's own words to create an understanding of an incompetent response to the September 11 attack on the United States.

The intent of the found poet has great merit and provides stimulation, knowledge, and pleasure to readers as they journey with the poet to a new understanding of the words. Many research poets, however, work with materials from potentially vulnerable participants as compared with an "all-powerful" president. Take, for instance, a material data poem I created (Lahman, 2011). As part of a more extensive ethnography I was supervising, I became profoundly aware of the murder of a transgender woman in my community. Angie's murder became the first crime of this nature to be tried as a hate crime in the United States. To create a poem about this experience, I located more than 100 local newspaper references and read through the texts, identifying phrases illustrating the media's portrayal of Angie's story. Attempting to retain the voice of the media and wanting to emphasize Angie's womanhood, I changed the media's reference to her as "Zapata" (her family name) to "Angie." The final material I worked with included five pages of text I rearranged to create a series of poems depicting Angie's murder and the community's reaction. An excerpt follows:

Angie Zapata was a woman.
The way she walked, talked, dressed.
The way her apartment was decorated
and the way it smelled all said, woman.
A transgender woman
who played with "girl stuff"

and felt female since the
time she was a toddler.
"Angie believed she was female.
The way she dressed,
the way she carried herself,
the way she went out in public.
She carried herself as a woman.
She was beautiful."

Man Arrested for
Transgendered Murder
Met on the internet.
Found by her sister,
severely beaten.
Second-degree murder charge.

Source: Lahman (2011)

See the chart provided in Table 8.1 to compare excerpts from poems I wrote about my ectopic pregnancy with a material/archival poem I created appropriating words from a defunct internet chat room revolving around ectopic pregnancies (Lahman, 2013). I wrote these poems at two different times and was struck as I delved into the other women's stories by how their loss of trust in the medical community resonated with my own experience (Lasker & Toedter, 1994, 2003). I sought to highlight this aspect of the women's stories through a collective voice in the material data poem. Currently, I use this chart as a

TABLE 8.1 ● Comparison Between an Autoethnographic Research Poem and an Archival/Material Data Research Poem Written by Maria Lahman	
Autoethnographic research poem	Archival or material data research poem developed from a defunct open-access website "chat" forum for supporting women who have experienced ectopic pregnancy
Doctor	Our (My/Your) Ectopic Pregnancy
I did not choose you.	this month
	my baby
You were in the office	lost
the day my body told me	life
my fetus was dead,	
the day the receptionist	later
finally let me past the gate	I nearly
to receive the help	lost
the body needed,	mine
not even a band-aide	
for the soul . . . ,	this is the story
	your stories
You joke	my story
pathologically,	
pathetically.	doctor
I can merely	cautioned
nod along	chances
weakly,	ectopic pg
. . . wondering	higher
what masks this	
need to joke?	what's up with this stuff
	brown discharge
I will be operated on	nothing too heavy
by You, Doctor,	no blood
who when introduced	dutifully consulted book
greets me in falsetto	decided to take myself to ER

Autoethnographic research poem	Archival or material data research poem developed from a defunct open-access website "chat" forum for supporting women who have experienced ectopic pregnancy
and my husband	pelvic exam haunt[s]
in a deep fake voice . . .	screamed from pain
	palpitated
Low humor . . .	whimpering
by the one charged to recall	right fallopian tube ruptured
"there is art to medicine	belly full of blood
as well as science, . . .	
warmth, sympathy,	Why?
and understanding	
may outweigh	FURIOUS
the surgeon's knife . . . "	hospital tests
	confirmed baby was ectopic
I	never anything in uterus
hate	doc missed it
you,	nearly killed me
Doctor . . .	
	trust was broken
	I feel betrayed.

reflexive pedagogical experience for doctoral research students who are considering forming poetry to represent their research findings. Several researchers have called for such experiences for novice researchers (e.g., Butler-Kisber, 2002; Cahnmann, 2003). The questions I ask students to consider include the following:

- Are we willing to tell our stories along with the participants'?
- What does it mean to write poetry about the experiences of people who might never see the poetry?
- Is poetry an appropriate medium for conveying this research topic?

In general, these questions are not strikingly different from those social scientists of any type should ask themselves when representing participants.

Personal Poetry: Researcher and Autoethnographic Poetry

"Therefore" is a word the poet must not know.

—Andre Gide

Researcher poetry might better be termed "autoethnographic poetry"; however, the word "researcher" places emphasis on poetry about the research experience. I am emphasizing two types of personal poetry. First, researcher poetry that is personal in nature and exploratory, revealing experiences in research that are usually left behind the scenes. This type of reflexive poetry allows readers to experience the research process vicariously. In the following example, Roland Schendel wrote a research poem that we placed in the methodology section of an article (Lahman et al., 2010) describing the atmosphere of each research poetry meeting our team conducted. (See Lahman et al., 2010, for all of the methodological poems.)

Setting: Restaurant

Nestled in autumn trees,
An inviting nook.
Lured by delicious scents.
Clamor, murmurs.

Friendly conversations
Poured over Belgian waffles.
A welcoming table
For breakfast
Enwreathed in researchers.
Poetry,
Eggs Benedict,
Cup of coffee.

—Roland Schendel

Context: First Meeting

Poetry
And research, Beautiful Fit.
Like a favorite hat. Modeling it for,
Others. Defining me, Who I am.
Would you wear it? Does it fit?
Go ahead, try it on. So tell me,
What do you think . . . of my favorite hat?

—Roland Schendel

The second type of research poetry is not directly about a research study but is still written by a researcher—highly reminiscent of autoethnography.

(See Chapter 7 of this book for a discussion of autoethnography.) Other than data poetry, most research poetry resides in the area of autoethnography. The following is an autoethnographic poem I wrote from a place of anguish, and it is a bookend to the autoethnography I wrote about my ectopic pregnancy (Lahman, 2009). (See an excerpt from the autoethnography, titled "Dreams of My Daughter," in Chapter 7.)

The Blue Period

I am rocking you in an
indigo recliner bought to
match your room.
I have planned
every detail of this nursery
for months.
    Am I
    crushing you or
    embracing you as we
    rock in this chair?
I am the mother in so many portraits:
Maternité; Sleepy Baby; The Cradle.
Now I know her secret.
    Does it seem I know
    what I am doing,
    because mothering,
    after all,
    is natural?
I cannot
comfort you as your face
tinges blue from
inconsolable crying.
    You are who
    I love the most?
I want to
extinguish
your cries to
cover my
secret.
    Have we been
    rocking for
    hours as I
    hold you and
    hold my
    breath?

Your baby wisps of hair
are coated in sweat
that also trickles
down my back.
 Was it just a moment ago
 I first sat here
 helpless,
 and alone
 with my week-old baby?
Within a suffocating cocoon
of lullabies your crying crescendos
and unbidden I picture
hurling you away.
Yet I cannot imagine
what happens next.
 Who protects you,
 from me—
 the perfect mother?
The visitor says,
"What is all this talk about postpartum?
Women have been pushing babies out in fields forever."
(They've also been killing babies forever)
Softly I say,
"I am not fine."
 You are who
 I wanted the most?
In the blue-black
of the darkened room
soft specters of
Yates' and Smith's
children circle.
Cringing, I think,
this can't be me.
 Do you know that I have a
 degree in child development,
 a fucking Ph.D., and have
 loved countless strangers' children?
Medea's hand beckons
in the glooming.
The c section wound
pulses with each wail.
I want to silence the screaming.
 When I take my bath each night,
 fantasizing about slipping

below the water,
    have you heard my crying?
You are quiet, and I jerk in
unspeakable fear that you are gone.
Your chest rises up and down
against mine in the
pale blue shadow of the nightlight.
    Did the doctor say this was
    normal for around
    twelve weeks?
So we rock
and I pray
you won't remember
these blue moments,
deep in your tiny bones,
delicate as night moths.

Source: Lahman, M. K. (2008). The blue period. *Qualitative Inquiry, 14*(8), 1540–1542 https://journals
.sagepub.com/doi/pdf/10.1177/1077800408318303

Visual Images and Poetry

All poetry has a visual aspect, whether on the written page, read aloud, or per-formed, but in this section, I specifically focus on the use of visual images com-bined with poetic words. A photograph or image can either enhance a poem or be used to generate a poem. To enhance or generate a poem, words are elicited using a visual such as a photo, adding concrete and metaphorical comparisons of abstract ideas. In this way, the researcher can refine the language or build on the essence of the desired message through the visual. *Collage poetry* and *blackout poetry* are two areas of visual poetry with room for rich contributions from research poets.

Collage Poetry

Collage poetry is a powerful form of visual poetry. While the collage may be made entirely of words pulled from different sources, it often includes images as well. I created a collage poem (Lahman et al., 2017) with images of my daughter, cut-out language from different IRBs (Research Ethics Boards) about children in research, and an indelible black marker (see Figure 8.3).

Richard's (2010) dissertation is an excellent example of using visuals. She combined black-and-white images that participants chose from a photo bank with the words they used to describe the images as metaphors and transcripts from interviews, creating "graphic poetry" (see Figures 8.4 and 8.5). Since that study, Richard has been placing professional photos with both participants' words and her own words of reflection to create visual or graphic poems, high-lighting participants' voices, the metaphorical processes of photo-elicitation, and reflexivity (Richard & Lahman, 2015).

FIGURE 8.3 ● A Collage Poem: Children and Research Ethics Boards

Source: Lahman, Teman, & Richard, 2017

Blackout Poetry

Blackout poetry seems to have recently been revived by Austin Kleon (2014) and has been described, at its most basic level, as crossing out the words you do not want from an existing text. Whatever is left over is the poem. While initially poets created blackout poetry from newspaper articles, any piece of writing may be

FIGURE 8.4 ● Man's Face With Shadow of a Cross

Note: # 1986 Peter Solness (www.solness.com.au).

FIGURE 8.5 ● Poetic Depiction of Meanings Conveyed Through Photographs

Robotic.

Going through the motions—
We started.
We stopped.
So much that we could have
worked on—

The human aspect?
Their minds are out of the
GAME.

Just turning a knob up and
down—

Without learning anything.

Physical Education?
Cutting it out.

CSAP scores—

Motor learning.
Moving,
Makes you a better learner.

Proven scientifically—
Perform better,

Proven—we need this.

Physical Education?
Cutting it out.

Source: Richard, V. M., & Lahman, M. K. E. (2014)

used as the creative base for a poem. The poet has only the words, letters, punctuation marks, and white spaces in the chosen piece to work with (Ladenheim, 2014). The term "blackout" refers to the use of an indelible black pen to completely mark out a word so it cannot be seen. Blackout is a current trend so ubiquitous as to be seen anywhere from Pinterest to curriculum ideas, to clothing, to people partially blacking out unwanted tattoos (see Figure 8.6).

Critical researchers should consider the word "black" more deeply when applying it to this type of poetry. I have considered calling it *mark-out poetry*

FIGURE 8.6 ● Example of a Blackout Poem

32 Balloons

The shooter ▮ identified ▮

within ▮ minutes ▮ emergency ▮ Police arrived

▮ dead

▮ police

heard ▮ final shot ▮ body ▮

▮ aftermath ▮ emergency medical

services ▮ evacuation ▮ injured ▮ Victims injured ▮ shooting

▮ Hokies ▮ 32 balloons

▮ memory

Norris Hall ▮ where the shootings

now ▮ Center for Peace Studies and

Violence Prevention

Note: From Lahman (2019b).

instead and also see some similarities to another type of art poetry called "erasure poetry" (poets.org, n.d.-b). You may also allow a portion of a marked-out text or image to be partially visible, as I did in a collage poem where I used some blackout techniques (Children and Research Ethics Boards, Figure 8.3). The partially marked out section can provoke increased interest and focus the audience's attention on an aspect of the author's work that is critical. A concept related to the term "blackout" is everything that has been "blacked out" of history in relation to persons of Othered identities (Lahman, 2008). The word "blackout" can also mean to lose consciousness. There is clearly much potential for fruitful discussion regarding this poetry form. To read more about blackout poetry in the arts, see the following website: https://www.thehistoryofblackoutpoetry.org/.

Formed Poetry

Poetry is nearer to vital truth than history.

—Plato

Rich Furman (2006) was the first to challenge qualitative researchers to attempt to create research poetry that was *formed*. Formed poetry may be partially understood as poetry with constraints. A constraint is any "rule" a poet imposes on their writing, such as a line structure (ABAB), meter, rhyme, or rhythm pattern. When a particular set of constraints is followed over a period of time, the set of rules may become a specific form of poetry, such as a sonnet, haiku, limerick, or cinquain (Lehrer, 2011). Most qualitative research poetry, until Furman's (2006) stimulating formed poetry challenge, was free verse. Furman drew on Japanese poetic forms, including the tanka and the pantoum, to illustrate his ideas. A few examples of formed poetry with brief explanations follow.

Haiku and Senryu

A haiku is a structured form of Japanese poetry consisting of three nonrhyming lines of five syllables, seven syllables, and five syllables; it always focuses on nature topics and is popular in the West. The senryu is structured exactly like a haiku, but it may be about any topic. This short form has particular appeal for research poets since it requires paring down the data to their essence—a goal of many qualitative researchers. This grabs readers' attention and may challenge them and stimulate thoughts. Below is a senryu I created from 50 interviews with doctoral students about graduate school experiences. (See Chapter 3 for a discussion of the larger piece.) I made the poem end on a question since the students had not completed their degrees and many were deeply concerned about issues that did not ultimately impede their degree progression, such as passing comprehensive examinations, while others encountered unforeseen "monsters."

Graduate School

Graduate school is
a monster in the closet . . .
There is no monster?

Acrostics

Poets using this form play with words such that the first letters typically read in a vertical fashion forming a word that is the focus of the poem. An example from a literary poet, Edgar Allen Poe (1969), is well worth looking up. Titled "Elizabeth [Rebecca]," the first letters of each line reveal the name of someone Poe deeply admired. Familiarity with this form makes poetry potentially more accessible. As researchers, we could (a) ask participants to develop an acrostic around a concept of interest, such as success or respect; (b) form an acrostic from research data; or (c) create an acrostic that reflects our research experience. Figure 8.7 is an example of an acrostic created from dissertation data on spirituality in counseling (Johns, 2017a).

R. David Johns (2017a) discusses the technique as follows:

> The theme Risk and Taboo is explored in the acrostic poem. This untitled research poem is a visual representation of the intersections of accountability, authenticity, and the vulnerability required for counselor educators to teach and supervise through example. While the words included in this poem are powerful, another aspect of the power of example, are the words unspoken and unnamed. This acrostic poem reflects the words of five of the participants. (p. 637)

FIGURE 8.7 ● Spirituality Acrostics

M

ACCOUNTABLE

D

E

VISCERAL

U

T

H

VULNERABLE

N

TRANSPARENT

I

C

Note: From R. David Johns (2017a).

Source: Reproduced with permission from R. David Johns.

Abecedarian

Note the first letters of this form of poetry—A B e C. This ancient form of poetry was most likely used by early societies to help recall poems that were vital inclusions at religious ceremonies. The acrostics previously discussed were formed from this type of poetry. Using the alphabet of the poet's language, the first letter of each line or stanza occurs in alphabetical order (Academy of Poets, n.d.).

Look back to the poem I opened the book with—"An Essential Worker" (see the Preface); if you had not noticed yet, it is an abecedarian—the first letter of each line is ordered as letters occur in the English alphabet. I had been mulling over how much the students I worked with during the COVID-19 pandemic moved me due to the research they conducted while completely isolated, caring for extended family or teaching their own children, who popped in and out of the Zoom frame. While I did not intend the poem to be an abecedarian at first, I suddenly noted I had a word beginning with a "z" in the poem. I said out loud to the empty room, "There is a z word in this poem!" I had attended an excellent conference about the post-pandemic university, and one of the speakers said we are all "Zoom zombies." Even as he spoke, I realized the phrase should be condensed into "Zoombies." This word rolled around on my tongue and resonated in my head as I repeated it to different groups through Zoom over the next few weeks—with everyone understanding the word "Zoombies" immediately. The *z* word pushed me to create an abecedarian poem, and I appreciated the deeper allusion to education and school since the poem was about research writers.

Concrete Poetry

A poem created in the "concrete" method calls for equal consideration of the words the poet employs and the shape and spacing they choose. Concrete poems—originally called *pattern* or *shape* poetry—challenge readers' engagement. Words may be written right to left, bottom to top—image and word vie for attention. If the poem is rotated, a different perspective may reveal new meaning. Both e. e. cummings and Ezra Pound are notable concrete poets. For an example of literary concrete poems, see George Herbert's "Easter Wings" (n.d.), and for powerful examples of research concrete poems, see Marcy Meyer (2017). In concrete poetry (also known as "visual poetry," a term that has taken on a distinct meaning of its own), the visual elements of the poem may even be said to take precedence over the words. (I do not fully agree with this since both seem to inform each other.) These visual elements include the use of empty or blank space. Meyer (2017) writes,

> I argue that concrete poetry may be more easily digested than other forms of poetry because it enlists visual images to help shape the reader's interpretation. Both scholars and laypersons who do not consider themselves poetry aficionados can understand concrete research poems without undue . . . burden. . . . For those of us who have been socialized not to think of ourselves as artists or poets, the creative experience of writing a concrete poem may reawaken a passion for drawing or writing that has been long dormant. When I mention this project to friends and colleagues, they often recall an experience that they had with concrete poetry in grade school. (p. 50)

It may seem at first sight that concrete poetry relates more to the visual than to the verbal arts. Within concrete poetry created in the research context, the emphasis needs to be equally on the verbal and the visual. In research, Meyer (2017) provides an excellent example of the power of concrete poetry by creating poems from transcripts of interviews with parents of children with mental illness. One of the poems is shaped in the image of a casserole dish and expresses the anguish of parents who never received the social comfort and nurture that parents of a child who is physically injured or has a socially acceptable problem might get. Meyer's poem underscores the deadly silence that occurs around mental illness, which often remains a taboo subject.

See Figure 8.8 for a concrete poem I created about the IRB (Lahman et al., 2017). "Big, Beautiful Heart" (Lahman, 2019a; see Figure 8.9) is a concrete poem I created from emails sent and received shortly before and after my mom's death. I appreciate *The Journal of Qualitative Inquiry* for allowing me to republish it here.

FIGURE 8.8 ● Concrete Poem: Institutional Review Board

```
I want to believe      I am part of the        solution, but I
get so frustrated      I feel I am on          ly fooling myself.
    I told             a new professor         the other day that
    I used             to          be          so          angry
    at the             w           ay          I           was
    used,              bl          ame         the messenger, no
    thanks             for the hard work.      Then it occurred to me
    to use             all of my knowledge     to publish. A platform
    from               which  to               h           elp
    create             chan   ge.              T           he
    vulner             able   are              a           lso
    power              ful.   Ethics           are culturally situated.
    Research           ers    should           be culturally responsive.
    Beware             eth    ical             colonistic imperialism.
BENEFICENCE            RES         PECT         JUSTICE
```

Note: By Maria Lahman.

FIGURE 8.9 ● Concrete Poem: Big Beautiful Heart

You emailed   all of us:
They really expect   this to be a straight
forward case without   surprises. They say I am
a very good candidate. They   will line up dates for surgery.
Later we emailed: Dear family and   friends of Anna Kathryn, We are
sorry to share that this afternoon, Anna Kathryn's big, beautiful heart stopped
beating. The complications from her heart surgery were too much to overcome.
Our hearts are broken along with hers. I emailed: Dr. Good, Excuse the blunt nature
of email. I flew home in March to VA to be with my mom during open heart surgery
from which, after a nine-day fight, she subsequently died. I realize her funeral was the
due date of this important commitment. My mind was scattered and I felt the review
was due in a week. Please apologize to the professor and others, I know I am holding up. I return to work at UNCO full-time tomorrow. It is my plan to have a
formal review to you by Friday of this week. Please let me know if this
plan is workable. Sincerely, Maria. I also emailed: Dear Sage
Editor, My mother died unexpectedly yesterday. Given the
deadlines on your end, would it be possible to reply
to you on Tuesday, April 5, the day after the
funeral? If not, I will attempt to meet this
deadline. Sincerely, Maria. Dad invoked,
"All will be well, and all will be
well, and all manner
of things will be
well."[1]
!?

Source: Lahman MKE. Big Beautiful Heart. *Qualitative Inquiry.* 2019; *25*(9–10):834–834. doi:10.1177/1077800418808538

An Ode

The ode is a poem many will be familiar with (e.g., "Ode on a Grecian Urn," Keats, 1820). Traditionally, odes had three sections and tended to follow a specified form with the content focused around the glorified praise of a person, object, or event. Odes may be quite dramatic and course with emotion. The contemporary ode does not need to follow a form and has added a twist that aligns with critical research, where the ode is written to a person, object, or event that would be seen as quite humble or inferior. James Hodges's ode to his desk chair during the pandemic is something academics and others Zooming from their desks for hours on end will endorse. Joseph Millar's (n.d.) poem "Red Wing" is an ode to a brand of work boot laborers wear. As the poem unfolds, we are led to see the noble quality in the worker who puts on the boot and enables the cushy lives we lead. Clint Smith's "Ode to the Only Black Kid in Class" has an animated version narrated by the author, which is well worth watching and rewatching (TED-Ed, 2019).

See the reflexivity activities at the end of the chapter for ideas on how to write an ode.

An Irregular Ode to the Chair

A silky gray, blending with the velvety darkness yet standing strong against the golden blaze of the daytime.

Freckles of the metals you are mixed with dancing in the trickles of light shine through the blinds of the window—the blinds blocking the light to steal some of the joy of your embrace with the sun in a fit of jealousy.

Long, strong rods, adorned by sweat, gentle enough not to pierce soft, medium-Brown flesh, weakened by sedentary days but strong enough to endure the 300-plus pounds it weathers every day.

300-plus pounds of anxiety—the scribbles and tiny utterances of to-dos, what-ifs, hows, and whys. The mighty rods wrap in an embrace, a hug, a holding.

300-plus pounds of frustration. The staff says more cuts. More planning for the hypothetical.

Dry replies and check-ins in which nothing is said, but everything is said.

The chair is rocked back, but the solid foundation swings back with the rock.

The chair swings back but pushes forward. A fresh breath—to say, always keep going.

Reminding that forward is the only option.

300-plus pounds of laughter. Friends share sweet wine and memories.

Reminiscences turn to shared chuckles and bellows.

The laughter vibrates along the strong metal rods.

Laughing back.

When the bed folded under pressure and couldn't handle the sleepless night, the chair with its 24-hour sign was there.

It loved the blue haze of the laptop screen against the crisp dark room.

When the sofa couldn't handle the rattles of restlessness,
the chair welcomed the hum of jittering legs and feet.

Oh, to be a chair in a global pandemic. The forgotten essential worker.

—James Hodges (in Lahman, De Oliveira, Fan et al., 2020)

Source: Lahman et al. (2020)

Three-Dimensional Poetry[2]

I hide myself within a flower.

—Emily Dickinson

Dimensional poetry has been said to "add meaning as well as beauty" to poetry (Davis, n.d.). Concrete poems, previously discussed, are the oldest form of dimensional poetry; however, they still remain on the printed page. The dimensionality occurs through techniques that bring breadth and depth to the two-dimensional space. In this section, I discuss creating research poetry with students that was structured beyond the flat surface of a page into three-dimensional spheres and flowers (see Figures 8.10 and 8.11; Lahman & De Oliveira, 2020). Similar examples from the literary poetry world include poetry written on burnt wooden matchsticks in a matchbox or lines of poetry cut out and formed into a bird or written on a birdhouse structure (California Poets, 2019).

Flower Power Poetry

my heart with pleasure fills, And dances with the daffodils.

—William Wordsworth

Flower are referenced abundantly in poetry, becoming tangible images for emotions as varying as love, sorrow, hope, and joy. The beauty of the flower itself may be celebrated, as in Wordsworth's (n.d.) writing about daffodils

When all at once I saw a crowd
A host of dancing Daffodils

---

[2]This section is drawn from Lahman and De Oliveira (2020).

FIGURE 8.10 ● Poetry Sphere

FIGURE 8.11 ● Flower Poems

Or it may be seen as a visual attack when the poet desires nothing but emptiness ("the tulips filled it up like a loud noise," Plath, n.d.). While lovely flower images may seem to dominate, an intriguing genre of poetry resists the surface beauty that the flower poems created—*resistance* flower poetry. Speaking of his move from romantic poetry to resistance poetry, a line from Pablo Neruda's (n.d.) work reads,

You will ask: And where are the lilacs?
And the metaphysics laced with poppies?

Throughout the history of poetry, flowers have also been used to illustrate resistance against poverty, class, war, race and so on. The Chinese poet Po Chu-i (n.d.; 772–846) described different social classes attending a flower market to buy precious peonies and failing to notice the lower-class people running the market and barely earning a living. An old farmer closes the poem with a deep sigh.

But this sigh nobody understood.
He was thinking, "A cluster of deep-red flowers
Would pay the taxes of ten poor houses."

Malcom London, a contemporary black activist poet, points out that odes to beautiful flowers may be the work of the privileged:

> No artist that I know in my communities has the luxury of making art for art's sake. We don't have the luxury of writing poems about flowers just for the sake of writing poems about flowers. I do not have that privilege. The way art functions in my life is directly connected to very real, lived experiences, and to this specific time in history. (cited in Parr, 2017, para. 15)

A final example of flower poetry that resists and is dimensional can be seen in "A Poppy" by Howard (2014). In this poem, Howard graphically, by forcing beauty and horror into inseparable images, depicts the atrocity of war, using Flash software to cause the words to move and shift.

Course Poetry Creation. The course time was approximately two-and-a-half hours. Course members were instructed to bring wide-line-spaced printed interview transcripts to class and cut these into thin strips, with each strip representing a transcript line. Alternatively, numerous blank strips of paper were available for those who preferred to write their lines by hand. Participants worked on creating the dimensional poetry forms while course content was shared. They finished by discussing and reflecting on the experience as a group.

Materials needed

1. Brads

2. Blank narrow strips of paper

3. Strips of paper with a line of a poem printed on each strip

4. Fine-tip markers for writing

5. Lollipop sticks

6. Pipe cleaners (often called "chenille sticks")

Prior to class, Becky, the course teaching assistant and photographer, printed lines from a poem by Maria, "The Dead Chick" (Lahman, 2019c) and cut the lines into narrow strips. Together we created a sample sphere/orb poem sphere/orb and flower poem, both to be certain we understood how the steps worked and to provide a model for the class.

Poetry Sphere/Orb Directions

1. Choose phrases from a research transcript or a reflection on the research process.

2. Write or type the phrases out in single lines.

3. Neatly cut the lines out so they are on strips of the same width and length.

4. Punch holes on each end of each line at the exact same space.

5. Stack the slips of paper in the order you wish them to be, keeping in mind that the end result will be an orb or sphere.

6. Secure the stack by securing a brad in each end.

7. Gently pull the slips apart until they are spaced out in the shape of an orb (Figure 8.10).

Poetry Flower Directions

8. If you wish to move the sphere into a flower, pinch both the brads together, and secure them in the middle.

9. You can then secure the brad to a stick such as a lollipop stick or pipe cleaner. In this case, we put the brad around a lollipop stick and wrapped a green pipe cleaner around it in a stemlike fashion. The flower poems were then placed in a vase (Figure 8.11).

Reflections

Becky's Reflection. *I like doing crafts or anything with my hands—stuffing envelopes, folding, cutting, peeling. When I can participate in an activity that takes very little cognitive effort, I find my mind wandering in all kinds of directions, and I often* *come up with interesting thoughts or good ideas. I can rarely check out and think about whatever I like during the course of an average day. So I was delighted to have this activity take up a portion of class! As Dr. Lahman's teaching assistant and a member of the class, I was involved at two different levels, as both a semifacilitator and a full participant. My prior knowledge about the activity likely gave me an advantage over the other students in terms of my ability to make meaning of the task; I knew what was happening. As a participant, I alternated between creating my own poetry flower—based on family narrative research on my father's participation as a human guinea pig for the U.S. Army during the Vietnam War—and photographing the other students' work for this article. It wasn't until I sat down and looked at my flower that I realized how jarring the cheerful daisy form was with the words printed on the strips—"biological warfare," "Eastern equine encephalitis," and "quarantine." Dawn Mannay (2010) argues for using visual methods to make the familiar strange, one of the key goals of qualitative research. I had heard my father's stories all my life, and my knowledge of his participation in Project Whitecoat was as familiar to me as my own name, but in that moment, staring at a paper daisy with a pipe cleaner stem, I found it profoundly strange and filled with possibility.*

Maria's Reflection. *I am not someone who creates crafts; however, I am well aware of the field as a former early-childhood teacher and a mother of a young three-dimensional artist and crafter. When I prepare for each semester, I always try to find new ways to push the course members' and my understandings beyond the latest literature. As a research poet who works mostly in the written form, I've recently been pushing myself to try new ways to incorporate art and poetry. To be successful in the traditional classroom spaces I am assigned to work within, the materials need to be easy to bring into the room and should take little time cleaning up. Also, some learners have not worked with art forms for many years, so the experience needs to feel as inviting as possible and not intimidating.*

When I initially found the sphere idea online (Kristin, 2011), I was drawn to its powerful simplicity and the need for the reader to hold the poem in their hands and move it in order to experience all the writing. The spheres I found were designed for a devotional exercise, making them easy enough to transition to a poetry exercise.

The same blogger also had a similar craft resulting in a flower. I was initially uncertain about the flower since I felt it was too heavily "crafty" for poetry, but then I began to consider the vast number of poems written about flowers. I gathered lines from poems about flowers and shared them throughout the class period time. Some of these are also featured throughout this article.

I chose a poem I wrote, "The Dead Chick" (Lahman, 2019c), to become the petals of the flower poem Becky and I had created prior to class. I chose this poem since flowers are often used as an expression of sympathy at a time of death. In the poem, I recount a moment when I am looking at a sweet chick that has just died and the sight rips at my memory of my mother's death—how I was unable to see her body after she died. Like Becky, I found the contrast between the contents of the poem and the form of the flower profound.

As we moved to discussion of the course, I realized that we can create experiences for students but cannot anticipate how they will react to or process the opportunity.

I am used to getting some pushback during the poetry parts of a course. This time, someone reflected on how the flower and sphere experience felt "forced" on them. I always try to remain in a listening posture in relation to these experiences and reflections. However, I must confess I'm always struck by the thought that students in a statistics class will generally do whatever they are asked to do by the professor, and even if they detested the experience, they would never express that it was forced on them or refuse to participate. What then does art inherently bring—freedom, choice, expression, power? Perhaps this resistance to research poetry is the deepest compliment of all.

Collaborative Poetry

Collaborative poetry may be written with participants or between a group of researchers. For example, Burdick (2011), working in the area of *found poetry*, has created the idea of *tandem found poetry*, where the researcher and the participant separately yet simultaneously create data poems and then meet to discuss their creations. This idea could easily be extended to a larger group of poets.

The *renga*,[3] a classic form of collaborative poetry, has also been employed by a group of researchers to reflect deeply on a shared experience. The renga, literally meaning "linked poem," emerged in Japan 700 years ago. Poets working in groups of two or more alternate writing stanzas. A renga could be hundreds of verses long. The first stanza is three lines with 17 syllables all told. The second stanza is two lines, of which both have 7 syllables. Readers may recognize within the renga the more familiar haiku. Years after the emergence of the renga, the opening lines of this poetic form birthed the haiku (poets.org, n.d.-d). Poets alternate repeating the first and second stanza form until the poem is completed. Traditionally, the renga's imagery was of nature and love, with each stanza linked only to the previous stanza (poets .org, n.d.-d).

In a graduate course I taught dedicated to writing and representing qualitative research in varied ways, the students and I challenged ourselves to create a renga around the topic of doctoral students' graduate school experiences, employing imagery from natural elements. Each poet wrote a reflection as a way of engaging reflexively with the process. Areas of note included thinking in a new way, finding the way back to a way of thinking that had been lost, the challenge in creating a poem, and power in both the process and the ensuing results.

Contemporary poets often alter the renga to their purposes, which seems to allow for even more creative possibilities (poets.org, n.d.-d). An example of a contemporary renga is "Crossing State Lines" (Holman & Muske-Dukes, 2011), in which 54 poets wrote one renga about the United States. In the case of the poem I present here, we determined that all poets would write about

---

[3]This section is drawn from Lahman, Hancock, et al. (2019). Thanks to my coauthors for such an excellent collaborative poetic experience.

the same topic since we wanted to engage reflexively in the areas of learning about research poetry and considering graduate school experiences. Our poem follows.

Seeing Through the Fog

A new day begins.
The light of dawn shows the path.

Broadened horizons.
Now it is our time to shine.

Vibrant flowers surround us.
Clear skies tell half the story.

Night's rain was fierce and cold.
Fresh perspectives.

Can you see through the fog now
blowing in from that dark place?

The wind and water redirect
for each new obstacle.

Lessons learned.
In a savage storm do you
leave or weather out the gale?

This too shall pass,
the storm calms as day breaks to reveal
a landscape changed.

For now, morning has broken,
my path illuminated.

Counter or Critical Poetry

In Lail and Lahman (2019) we drew on *counter stories*, which present alternate views of typical narratives (Solórzano & Yosso, 2002a, 2002b), to demonstrate the idea that research poets attempting to highlight alternatives to dominant stories may be thought of as *counter poets*. These critical research poets may wish to employ imagery but will invert or subvert these images to make critical points (Ziehl & Jerz, 2020). The following poem is an example of a critical or counter poem (Majmudar, 2017). I created the critical poem from found words on the internet, which was subsequently published in a series of poems (Lail & Lahman, 2017). The words documented an experience on my campus I was privileged to follow due to one of the principal activists being a student of mine at the time. Rich areas in literary poetry that are ready for methodological development by counter research poets include poetry for social justice, antiracist poetry, critical whiteness poetry, queer poetry, and trans poetry.

The Fighting Whites

The Fighting Whites,
[media said Whities]
intramural basketball team,
a response to the Native American
mascot controversy.

The college team attracted a
storm of national attention.
Satirical protest about stereotypes
of Native Americans being used
as sports mascots.

Team, included players of
Native American,
white, and
Latino ancestry,
"Fightin' Reds" high school team
not far from the university.

The Reds' mascot has been described as
a caricature Indian with a misshapen nose,
loincloth and eagle feather.
Jerseys said
"Every thang's going to be all white."

The team chose a white man
as its mascot to
raise awareness
and understanding of stereotypes
some cultures endure,
with an accompanying logo
of a stereotypical
"white man" in a suit,
styled after
advertising of the 50s.

"Let's do something
that will let people
see the other side
of what it's like to be a mascot,"
"It's not meant to be vicious,
it is meant to be humorous,"
"It puts people in our shoes."

In response to customer demand
the team began selling shirts
Sold enough shirts
to endow a sizeable scholarship fund
for Native American students.

Fightin'
Whites
Minority
Scholarship.

(You can read more about the campus basketball protest at the following link: https:// en.wikipedia.org/wiki/Fighting_Whites.)

Epistolary Poetry

An *epistolary poem* (the word "epistolary" originates from the Latin *epistula*) means literally "a poem that should be read as a letter." These types of poems, which are historical in nature, may exhibit the conventions of letters, including dates, salutations, and valedictions (closures), or may simply be directed in the first person as though to a specific reader who is not concretely referenced. Letter poems may be written in free verse or in a form the poet chooses to impose (poets.org., n.d.-a). For examples of epistolary poems from ancient to contemporary times, see "Heroides" by Ovid, "Letter" by Langston Hughes (1966), and "Dear Mr. Fanelli" by Charles Bernstein (n.d.). Subsets of epistolary poetry are typewriter poetry, email poetry, and social media poetry.

Typewriter Poetry

Typewriter poetry is a form born out of the 1960s' concrete poetry movement (discussed earlier). Typewriter poets draw on a technology that, while seemingly historical in many societies, can still be accessed but is not heavily utilized. Poets explore the use of varying paper mediums, letter case, the strike-out key, and faded-ink styles (Typewriter Poetry, n.d.). The poems seem to be written instantaneously, with little forethought and no editing. However, as research poets begin to utilize this style, I recommend rewrites and edits. The look of typewriter poetry may also be simulated through the use of computer software fonts. Research poets may wish to experiment with these ways to capture and convey data and experiences.

Email Poetry[4]

Considering typewriter poetry—which has caught on with the general public in a manner that reminds me of the "strokes and sips" type of painting and wine experiences—led me to a related concept, *email poetry*, which clearly fits the genre of epistolary poetry. I had the chance to experiment with the form personally when my mother, who is dead, emailed me out of the blue. While I knew the email fundamentally was the result of a cyber world error, I also couldn't help but see the unearthly epistle at another level—as a much-needed message, in real-time communication with my dead loved one.

I began to mull over the possibilities email poetry might afford a poet. The visual look of an email seems particularly ugly when compared with a typewriter-style font, but certainly people writing by hand in the era of the manual typewriter had felt the same way. So perhaps it is being removed from the mode of writing that causes it to look antique, romantic, and appealing. My close, daily relationship with never-ending emails contributes to my biased view. To me, email looks stark, ugly, demanding, and devoid of love and tenderness at first glance.

However, Mom's email wasn't any of these things, so as I continued to consider the form of email, the possibility of whittling down experience to its core emerged. The stark nature of the email message could be used to discuss and represent what we avoid as a society—the unrepresentable. Isn't that what poets are trying to do—present life in its essence in ways that allow people to connect and experience something for the first time or reexperience it in a new way? The poem I created from Mom's email follows:

Email With the Dead

Sun 12/27/2017, 5:44 AM
Lahman, Maria

Hi Mom,

i was surprised when you emailed
the surprise wasn't your use of email
or the contents

the surprise was due to you being dead

love,
maria

From: Anna Kathryn Eby [annaeby@myvmrc.net]
Sent: Monday, January 18, 2016 3:59 PM

---

[4]The section on typewriter poetry and the poem were first published in Lahman (2019d).

To: Lahman, Maria
Subject: Great Mom

Maria,

You are such a great mom.
Your father and I are so proud of you
and your amazing children and husband.

Love, Mom

Lahman, Maria

Reply

Today, 10:22 AM
Anna Kathryn Eby annaeby@myvmrc.net

Mom, what happens when I reply to your email?
can you receive email?

do you hear the message in my head,
through my fingers on the keys,
my deep pain for you
pushed away
so I can push on?

love (a declaration not a valediction),
maria

Source: Lahman M.K.E. Email With the Dead. *Qualitative Inquiry.* 2019; *25*(9–10):831–832. doi:10.1177/1077800418784324

Email poetry has overlap with concrete poetry as it contains aspects that will be missed if only heard and not viewed. Examples include the date; the layout of the writers' names, at times with family name first; and the email structures (Subject, Reply all, and @). Given email's abundant use in research studies and daily communication, email poetry will have much to offer poets and researcher poets alike.

Social Media Letter Poetry: Pweets and Ptexts

Another form of highly abbreviated "letters" research poets may wish to consider are tweets and texts, and of course, poets have been there before researchers, including former U.S. poet laureate Collins's (2011) #poetweet.

Examples of these poems, variously called *twihaiku, twosh,* and *micro poetry,* may be found in Cripps (2013). Short, compressed poems have been a hallmark of poetry throughout its history, with the following poem usually serving as the most concise example of poetry—often quoted by my dad to his children—whose authorship is variously attributed to Ogden Nash, Shel Silverstein, and Strickland Gillilan.

Fleas

Adam

Had 'em.

What is new here is the speed with which the poem may be shared and the mode of delivery potentially reaching an audience of 696,750,000 readers in the Twittersphere. Collins, quoted in Cripps (2013), reminds us that "restrictions, like the rules of the sonnet, can be liberating in the right hands. . . . So there's nothing wrong with poets finding a new box to play in."

Ideas for Forging Research Poetry[5]

One thing I share with poets and researchers is a love of words and the sound of words. I love syllables, rhythm, rhyme, meanings, double meanings, alliteration, interpretations, playing with words, the visual look of words, and even the silly, lowbrow writing jokes I have included in this book. I had a minor in English in college and the opportunity to take a course by a poet in residence, Jean Janzen, a premier Mennonite poet (see Janzen, 1995, 2008, for examples of her poetry). When a decade later I became immersed in qualitative methods, I thought back to these poetic experiences, making connections to the world of social science research and the burgeoning literature on how to draw on literary aesthetics and be a researcher at the same time (e.g., Lawrence-Lightfoot & Hoffman Davis, 1997). I had many examples of research poetry (and research scholars pointing out how mediocre research poetry was) to share with my students. But I had few examples that showed me how to teach them to write quality research poetry. I determined to work with like-minded colleagues toward creating spaces and highlighting ideas from literary poetry with which novices could begin to create research poetry.

Ideally, write a poem down as it comes to you, without stopping or getting interrupted. In my family, several members have an overpowering need to write in this way; so when the ideas come, others dash around supportively looking for writing tools, and then no one interrupts. I have felt powerful urges to write highly specific words in awkward places or situations, such as while taking a shower, nursing one of my children, or teaching a class. While these episodes make for humorous enactments of would-be authors writing on napkins, on scraps of paper, and in smartphone memo applications, the search to find a way to capture ideas is an earnest one.

---

[5]In this vein, research poets give some advice on how to go about writing poetry, with most of it being centered on the creation of transcription poems. (See Glesne, 1997, for an early outline of this process and Butler-Kisber, 2010, for a later overview.)

After months of wanting
to write,
and not being
able, a poem
slips through the dark
into my bed,
pulsing with each
suck of
my infant daughter's
warm, moist mouth.

"Don't go," I cry at a whisper!
"Don't leave me."
I ease my child,
back into her crib,
the title blazing in my mind . . .
then one long baby wail.
Oh, my heart clenches.

My baby
must come first—
tattered word remnants
to be gathered later.

Maybe
that
is
the
poem?

Ideas on how to develop a poem are essential to consider after the main purpose of the poem is written. Poetry may come to poets in a seemingly out-of-the-blue fashion. However, the work of the poet comes in the revisions. The discussion presented next would occur after the initial outpouring. In the following sections, I explore reading poetry, writing poetry, and revising poetry.

Read, Read, Read

Poetry is to prose as dancing is to walking.

—John Wain

To write poemish research poetry, one must first read poetry extensively and regularly (Lahman et al., 2010). Unfortunately, for some researchers I have worked with, the idea of reading poetry brings up past negative experiences.

These experiences include a feeling of intimidation, a sense of the unknown or indecipherable, or an experience of alienation. So how to start? A blogger from a seemingly defunct blog, "readingwhilefemale," had some practical tips on reading poetry that I appreciated: "Just enjoy it. Paraphrase the poem into simple explanations that will create a 'road map of the poem'—of where it begins, travels, and ends."

Yes, research poets should read research poetry, but more important, they should read literary poetry. One enriching strategy I have found to help overcome a reluctance to engage with poetry is to join a "poem of the day" virtual list (e.g., http://www.loc.gov/poetry/180/) or read a "poem of the day" book (Academy of American Poets, 2015; McCosker & Albery, 1998). These practices are rich but require a reasonable time commitment from people with already overly busy lives. When one of the poems you read inspires you, do some reflexive work around it.

1. Who is the author?

2. What era and contexts were they writing from?

3. What other poetry have they written that you may wish to read?

4. What about the poem appeals to you?

5. Was the poem formed? If so, how?

6. What poetic devices did the poet employ?

7. How might your poetry be affected by this poem?

The reading of poetry sparks the writing of poetry. For example, I had a deep desire to represent the painful and unexpected death of my mother and was floundering in too much emotion to write when I first read "End of April" by Phillis Levin (1996), a poem that expresses the inexpressible. Many of the poets and poems I reference in this chapter cannot be reprinted here due to copyright law, which leads to some unfortunate paraphrasing on my part. I am loath to paraphrase this poem as I have other poems throughout this chapter. I will simply say that Levin's poem was a reminder of how powerfully nature conveys human experience; so I went back into my own garden poetically, where I can never spend enough time, to consider death.

Hail

We made it through the first hail storm unscathed.
Just blocks up the street leaves were torn to shreds, blossoms
battered down.

In my yard, red matador tulips waved their capes jauntily,
daring any bull to charge.

You stood a day after the surgery, squeezed the therapist's hand until
wincing she cried, "Stop."

The second storm was not so merciful, all signs of spring
stamped-out in her path,

hail so thick it seemed as snow upon the ground, the flowers and you
cut down.

Crouched beneath the catalpa tree, digging dirt, deadheading
spent beauty at her feet, I

glance skyward time-to-time at the bud-less,
ravaged limbs.

How you loved a tree with scented flowers, bean pods, and a
brilliant choir of leaves.

The flowerless boughs mourn even as I rub a
dirt crusted hand across my eyes.

—Maria Lahman (2019e)

Source: Lahman (2019)

Write, Write, Write

*Poetry surrounds us everywhere, but putting it on paper is, alas, not so easy as
looking at it.*

—Vincent van Gogh

Along with reading literary and research poetry, research poets also need
to create room in their lives for experiencing and playing with words in different
ways while writing poetry. These experiences extend what one is reading
and allow research poems to move from an "abominable" to an impactful
form, so others may experience the world in new and meaningful ways as
they engage with your poetry. While considering what to emphasize from
the vast array of options in the area of how to write poetry, I reviewed textbooks
and websites on writing poetry. Since the field of how to write poetry
is so vast, I will only briefly address what seem to be primary areas: impactful
topics, imagery, clichés, sentimentality, rhythm and rhyme, sound devices,
and allusions.

Limerick of Lousy Verse
Lousy verse masquerades poetical.
Poetaster's doggerel is comical.
The good poems I have read

don't come from my head.
Research poems may be quite abominable.

—Maria Lahman

Impact

Poetry is when an emotion has found its thought, and the thought has found words.

—Robert Frost

impacting, impression, poignant, stunning, effective, moving, rousing, sympathetic, affecting, cogent, dynamic, effectual, emotional, forceful, gripping, inspirational, motivating, potent, provoking, staggering, stirring, touching

The creation of poetry with impact is a foundational area for would-be research poets to consider. One aspect of becoming an impactful poet includes considering goals for your research poetry. Poetry is not only writing about our own experiences but also trying to write primarily for the reader, so the reader can experience new feelings and understandings or reexperience them in a novel way. Here, research poets have an advantage because the science-related portion of our goals is always about others, even when we are motivated by deeply personal experiences. Qualitative researchers and research poets alike are trying to understand and represent the world for the reader. This has been deemed a move away from writing poetry to capture your own feelings—where you, the poet, are the center of the poem's universe—toward writing poetry to generate emotions in the reader. The poem exists for the reader (Ziehl & Jerz, 2020).

Imagery

Painting is poetry that is seen rather than felt, and poetry is painting that is felt rather than seen.

—Leonardo da Vinci

Poets attempt to create images in the readers' minds that will evoke emotion. Determining how to create compelling imagery is, therefore, one of the most critical areas to consider in poetic representations. To do this, poets draw on all the resources they have, such as attending carefully to the visual details of life, vocabulary, metaphors, and similes, to attempt to make the images new and perhaps unexpected (Ziehl & Jerz, 2020). An excellent example of the new and unexpected may be seen in Collins's poem, to which I wrote a homage at the start of this chapter. The idea of torturing a confession out of a poem anthropomorphizes the poem in an unanticipated fashion. An understanding of concrete versus abstract images is essential here. Concrete words allow readers to directly connect with experience through their senses, whereas abstract words are intangible and perhaps even ephemeral. A literary reflexive activity follows in Text Box 8.4 to help with understanding the role of concrete words in poetry.

8.4 CONCRETE WORDS
MARIA LAHMAN

Challenge: Chose an abstract idea such as *happiness, joy, hope*, or *sorrow.*

Concrete words: Brainstorm a list of all the concrete words you can think of that illustrate the abstraction you have chosen.

Senses: Consider the senses. Reread your list of concrete words. Are all the senses represented? Add more words as needed.

Poemish: Form the beginnings of a poem from this list.

To illustrate, I use a poem written by my then eight-year-old daughter, Kate. Kate's school assignment was to take an abstract feeling and use the human senses to make the emotion apparent to the reader through concrete imagery.

Hope

Hope is orange like a sunset.
Hope tastes like minty candy.
It is smoke from the first fireplace lit this year.
Laughter that is jolly is hope.
Hope is soft as a baby chick.

—Kate Lahman

Kate's poem evokes Emily Dickinson's famous poem on the same emotion, which uses concrete imagery throughout. An excerpt follows.

"Hope" is the thing with feathers—
That perches in the soul—
And sings the tune without the words—
And never stops—at all—
And sweetest—in the Gale—is heard—

—(Dickinson, 1861, in Johnson, 1961)

Here, Dickinson employs the image of perhaps a soft bird perched and singing in dire conditions to evoke hope. By asking Kate and her classmates to create concrete imagery with the senses, it is clear Kate's teacher knows her stuff. Imagery should draw on the five senses, with the number six sense *kinesthesis* (movement) also being employed (Ziehl & Jerz, 2020). Kate says that if she had been asked about movement she would have added "Hope is a gentle breeze blowing." Note her natural use of alliteration. The use of similes and metaphors is an intuitive way people attempt to describe abstract events to others. Poets should deliberately use these devices to help convey meaning. A simile uses the words "like" or "as" to compare two things, whereas a metaphor states that the two different things are the same. For example, Kate employed a simile when she wrote "hope is like a sunrise" and a metaphor when she said "hope is smoke."

Source: iStock.com/Big_Ryan

Avoid Clichés and Sentimentality. *air your dirty laundry, babe in the woods, calm before the storm, divide and conquer, eagle eye, fan the flames, go with the flow, hold your head up high, in a nutshell, ivory tower, justice is blind, kiss of death, lap of luxury, moment of truth, no stone unturned, out on a limb, playing with fire, quick as lightning, running in circles, sweating bullets, two peas in a pod, ugly as sin, upper crust, vanquish the enemy, weather the storm, worst nightmare, young and foolish* (Luke, 2017)

While this list of words seems hackneyed, Denise Duhamel's poem "I've Been Known" (2004) cleverly illustrates that clichés and triteness in a skilled poet's hands takes worn-out words and breathes vigor back into them. A *cliché* is defined as "a trite, stereotyped expression; a sentence or phrase, usually expressing a popular or common thought or idea that has lost originality, ingenuity, and impact by long overuse" (Dictionary.com, n.d.). Ziehl and Jerz (2020), considering concrete images in terms of cliché, write, "A work full of clichés is like a plate of old food: unappetizing" (p. 9). Research poets will want to avoid clichés unless they are composing data poems and the participant has used a cliché to convey meaning. Clichés, in this sense, bring an easy understanding of experiences to readers. Duhamel's poem challenged me to write a poem about academia—an environment full of clichés.

Ivory Tower: A Clutch of Clichés

Do you meet in an ivory tower,
with an exclusive club,
a coded knock on the
ivy covered door allowing entrée,

confirmed with a secret handshake?
No research poets allowed—
only poets.

—Maria Lahman (2018)

Sentimentality involves a blatant attempt to evoke emotion that may seem almost vulgar or crass because of the effort made. Overused examples could include baby animals such as kittens, rainbows, and roses littered with raindrops. This type of writing is not without appeal to many and may be observed in cards, advertisements, and some music lyrics. A word of caution: Research poets should represent data as sentimental if that is how the participant speaks, but in their own poetry, they should continue to challenge themselves to find new ways to portray sentiment. A literary reflexive activity follows in Text Box 8.4 to help sharpen imagery.

8.4 SENTIMENTAL IMAGERY
MARIA LAHMAN

Challenge: Choose a sentimental image—such as a puppy wandering in the rain—that conveys a sense of loss.

Brainstorm: Write down all the images you can think of that convey a sentiment similar to the one you have chosen. Here are a few to fit the experience of loss as a puppy in the rain—a stub of a candle, a sock with a hole, one mitten, unfinished knitting, Mom's items that need to be organized after her death, a puzzle missing a piece, dead flowers in a vase, and an empty place at the dinner table.

Free write one image in prose: Miriam was teaching my young daughter, Kate, to knit. At age 82, Miriam shared a knitting project laid aside more than 10 years ago because she could not find any matching yarn. I was surprised when Miriam commented that she plans to finish the knitting someday. Wondering about this, an image of Kate at some future estate sale buying Ms. Miriam's unfinished knitting and yarn pushed its way into my head.

Poemish: Rewrite the prose description of the image as a poem or as part of a poem.

Hold Death at Bay
She seems to hold death away,
with her gnarled hands
by ever working—

iStock.com/Big_Ryan

canning, collecting,
sorting through a life,
offhandedly showing
a decade old knitting project
stored away unfinished—
with plans to finish it someday.

How can death come
when the knitting remains undone?
Knitting needles hold death at bay.

—Maria Lahman

Source: iStock.com/Big_Ryan

Rhyme and Rhythm

Poetry is the music of the soul, and, above all, of great and feeling souls.

—Voltaire

Humans naturally take pleasure in rhythm and rhyme (Naylor & Wood, 2012). Poetry is an extension of this pleasure, Ziehl and Jerz (2020) remind us, as poetry is for the ear. They write,

Whatever poetry you write or read, learn to listen with the ears of your audience. Poetry is meant for the ear; pay attention to the sounds the words make. Writing in "free verse" does not excuse the poet's obligation to please the ear.

The advice about rhyme from professional poets tends to be to use rhyme with caution and/or sparingly. However, poet novices seem drawn to rhyme. Elsewhere, I have maintained that the power of the poem's topic can cause poor rhyme, along with overused or ill-used rhyme, to be palatable. (See a discussion of September 11 and rhyme in Lahman & Richard, 2014.) It is possible that novice poets are drawn to rhyme as many of the classics we are taught in school are rhyming poems created by notable poets; consider here Robert Frost's (1922) "Stopping by Woods on a Snowy Evening," Walt Whitman's (1865) "Oh, Captain! My, Captain," and Paul Lawrence Dunbar's (1899) "Sympathy."

Children's poet laureate Kenn Nesbitt (2014) has a helpful blog entry where he examines what it means when a rhyme is considered inferior or forced. Nesbitt reviews the major types of *forced rhyme*. If a line of poetry is rearranged in an unnatural way to put the rhyme at the end, it is considered forced. Nesbitt uses the following example:

Whenever we go out and walk,
with you, I like to talk.

At times, novice poets also add words that are not related to the topic of the poem to force the rhyme. A silly example of this would be

I'm in a writing slump.
My heart needs to jump
and go bump, bump.

A poet might also extend a line of verse in an ungainly manner so a rhyme may be added at the end. Readers may have heard of the term "wrenched rhyme" as it has a cacophonic sound that stays in the memory. In a wrenched rhyme, the end sounds of the words are the same, but the accents are not on the same syllables. For example,

I like to dance. I like to sing.
I like smiling and laughing.

—Nesbitt (2014)

Near rhymes are words that almost rhyme, yet this should be avoided if possible. Nesbitt (2014) suggests that one way to prevent some of these rhyming problems is to choose words that have many options for rhyming. Rhyme Zone (https://www.rhymezone.com/) is an internet site where you can type in a word and read through its rhyming words. Instructional entries such as the one I reviewed here on forced rhyme are also available.

Sound Devices

Rhyme, rhythm, and meter are major *sound devices*. Sound devices are resources used by poets to convey and reinforce the meaning or experience of poetry through the skillful use of sound. Poets try to use a concentrated blend of sound and imagery to create an emotional response. The words and word order should evoke images, and the words themselves have sounds, which can reinforce or otherwise clarify those images. The poet is attempting to allow the reader to sense a particular thing, and sound devices are among the poet's tools (Meeks, 2017). The following are just a few sound devices that poets may employ to increase the effectiveness of their work—*alliteration, cacophony, onomatopoeia.*

When employing *alliteration*, the poet deliberately places words close to each other that have the same initial sound. The sound is generally from consonants. Unless the poet is being humorous or making a critiquing point about poetry, alliteration should not be overused. As the poet edits, they will listen for alliteration that is pleasing and points to critical words but is not overdone. In the following excerpt from a poem I wrote, the underlined initial consonants denote where alliteration was employed.

Covering (an excerpt)

I wanted to wear it
Gauzy white net,
fine lace trim,
the only
dainty,
delicate,
wholly
feminine article
on my
plain,
prim,
pristine,
mother.

—Lahman (2015, p. 407)

The word "wholly" is also a play on words since a religious garment may be considered holy and the Mennonite covering often has tiny holes in the net fabric—the holey nature being a source of vulgar, colloquial jokes as in she is wearing a "sin sifter."

In opposition to alliteration, *cacophony* is formed to displease the ear. Here, the poet seeks a jarring effect that offends the ear and highlights poetic contexts that may be ugly, need a light shone on them as in critical poetry, or are naturally busy and discordant, like an orchestra tuning up or a busy city street. Christopher Meeks (2017) points out that in English the sounds /b/, /k/, /c/, and /p/ are harsher than the pleasing sounds /f/ and /v/ or the lulling /l/, /m/, and /n/. The following verse, which I had been composing while reflecting on the potentially devastating nature of the tenure process, is an example of cacophony employed to highlight conflict:

College careers careen,
collapse, crumple
in a cacophony, as

colleagues collide,
and career
in crescendo.

A word that is an *onomatopoeia* in the most conservative sense is an imitation of a sound, such as *buzz* or *chug*. Using poetic license, poets have pushed this sound device to include words that *suggest* sounds, such as *sled* or *fiddle*.

Allusions

An allusion is a subtle reference to some other historical or contemporary literary piece, happening, person, or place of a significant enough nature that a reader could be presumed to have a shared meaning. The reference is not direct, as when a writer references an event. Instead, the allusion indirectly sets the tone of the imagery the poet is creating by bringing the sense of what the larger audience is assumed to feel about the event to bear on the feelings the poet is working to evoke. In the poem that follows, titled "Mother Hood," I used the word "owl" as a concrete description with deep allusions. Many readers will recognize the idea that owls are wise, but then I invoke Minerva, the Roman goddess of wisdom—who some readers will recall was represented as carrying a small owl, which is one of the reasons why owls are symbolic of wisdom today—as a historical allusion. It is possible that more readers would have recognized Minerva's Greek counterpart, Athena, but the choice of Minerva provides an alliteration opportunity, as in Minerva mysteries.

Mother Hood (an excerpt)

"I want one," the child says,
a determined
owl glint in their eye.
"Then you can work
to get one," I reply
sweeping out of the room
to Minerva mysteries
of hooding
my chair,
her chair,
her chair's chair,
sweep behind me,
a wake of history,
tradition,

knowledge,

regalia,

motherhood.

—Maria Lahman (2017b)

Source: Lahman (2017)

Revise, Revise, Revise

Poetry is a deal of joy and pain and wonder, with a dash of the dictionary.

—Kahlil Gibran

One way to tell if someone is a poet is by their overriding need to continually revise a poem. In my experience, it is common at poetry readings for poets to stop midreading and edit their poem out loud. As I place published poems of my own in this chapter, I continue to tweak them. Poetry is a compressed form where every word, punctuation mark, and blank space matter. Some poets, such as Collins, have stated that they do little revision. However, as research poets, we are often in the position of learning art while needing to have a heavy focus on research. For this reason, I strongly recommend close attention to revision.

Revision usually occurs after the initial outpouring of poetry has been saved in a form where it can be backed up and edited. I find it helps to put the poem away for a while. When you revisit the poem, your emotions will not be so intense, and then you can use a more critical editorial eye. Due to both my demands at work and the need to be prepared mentally to work with highly sensitive topics such as death or loss, I may come back to the same poem or series of poems time after time over several years.

As you revisit poems, save former drafts and print them out or position them on your computer screen or on paper side-by-side, so that aspects of poetry such as the shape of the words, the white space on the page, and the sound and look of the words may be deeply considered. Change the poem to single space so you can see how it may look when published. If you are submitting to a journal that is printed in two columns, consider how the poem works in that form. In actual experience, research poets who publish in journals do not have control over whether a poem is in a two-column or a single-column format, but journals such as SAGE's *Qualitative Inquiry* make a great effort to allow authors to ask for an alternative layout and attend to creative requests as much as possible.

Part of revision includes reading the poem out loud both to yourself and, when you are ready, to others. Some have described poetry as an oral form that must be read out loud. While I agree, there are certain forms of poetry that are also meant to be viewed, such as concrete poetry and may make little sense if only read to someone. Even poetry that is primarily for reading out loud relies heavily on visual aspects such as white space, line breaks, and punctuation choices, all of which influence the interpretations of the poem.

Creating a research poetry writing group is also valuable. The group members should primarily read and review one another's poetry, but they could also read poetry collections and pieces on how to write poetry and then meet to discuss these. My first few articles on research poetry and several of my poems emerged from a research poetry group collaboration. Clearly, there are many aspects of creating a poemish space, but I was able to consider only some of them here.

Why did the poet cross the road?

To get to the road less traveled by.

Poetic Tensions

Poetry lies its way to the truth.

—John Ciardi

Areas of tension in research poetry exist among research poets and qualitative researchers in general. I use the word "tension" as a metaphor, referencing a rope pulled tautly. When a rope—or a thought for that matter—is pulled taut, we are engaged with it and actively considering it, unlike when a rope or thought is slack. Areas of scholarly tension in research poetry are rich with potential and ripe for poetic contributions. Some of these areas are articulated as qualifications to write research poetry and illustrate the differences between the poet and the research poet. At one end of the rope are the literary poets, who may have training in their craft and usually do not provide an explanation or interpretation to accompany their poetry. At the other end of the rope are the research poets, who may not have training in writing poetry but do have training in qualitative analysis. Research poets may want to explain or may be required to explain their poetic processes and intended meaning.

In my experience, novice research poets may be closely questioned and need to defend their use of poetry in high-stakes research situations such as a thesis or a dissertation. See Johns (2014) for an example of how this issue is addressed through a diplomatic and thorough introduction of research poetry as a component of a dissertation.

An argument could be made that historically poets had little or no training, while contemporary poets may need to have extensive training, practice, oral readings, and publications of poetry considered to be "good." Because of the expertise and implied status that comes with a literary education, there may be tension between expert literary poets and research poets. This tension leads to a discussion of what "good" research poetry should encompass.

According to research poet Sandra Faulkner (2016), there are general core themes of what constitutes "good" poetry. Faulkner's list is extensive, including ideas such as authenticity, courage, emblematic, ineffability, and engagement of the human condition. Perhaps the most powerful way to work toward research poetry that is art or at least poemish art is to hone our artfulness. For example, Piirto (2002) suggests that researchers be aware of traditions and techniques within the poetic world. "Good" research poets value the expressive power of poetry in research by creating poetry with "metaphoric generalizability" to "penetrate the essence of human experience" (Furman et al., 2006, p. 25). This may occur through applying the creative arts to your study, which facilitates the researcher's ability to express the "richness and fullness of the phenomenon being explored" (Furman et al., 2006, p. 26).

Qualitative researchers use poetry to express meaning in profound ways, not solely for literary value. Researchers create research poems for "generating or presenting data" (Furman et al., 2006, p. 3). Furthermore, as Furman et al. (2006) note,

> As a researcher, I wish to remain faithful to the participants and the stories they share. In this way, I draw on methods from literary poets to "remain faithful to the essence of the text, experience, or phenomena being represented," resulting in research poetry. (p. 3)

The Gist

The voice of the poet is needed in our prose-flattened world.

—Walter Brueggemann

Research poetry has the potential to powerfully convey experiences in their essence that capture and stimulate the senses, providing new understandings. When we commit to crafting research poems, we must also commit to reading poetry and to the close revision of our poetry. Research poets are creating welcoming poemish spaces for researchers to contribute within. Will you join in?

Reflexive Questions

1. When you think of poetry, how does it make you feel? Can you identify experiences that cause you to feel this way?

2. What were your experiences with poetry growing up?

3. Some people have had limited experiences with poetry. If this is the case, consider music lyrics you are drawn to.

    a. What type of lyrics feel powerful to you?

    b. How might lyrics be like or different from poetry?

    c. How might music lyrics affect the research poetry you will potentially create?

4. When a set of music lyrics inspires you, do some reflexive work around them.

    a. Who is the author?

    b. What era and contexts were they writing from?

    c. What else have they written that you may wish to engage with?

    d. What about the lyrics appeals to you?

    e. How might your poetry be affected by the lyrics?

5. Consider a qualitative data set you can access.

    a. How might this be best represented as poetry?

    b. Is there a type of formed poetry you could create with the data?

    c. Would the poetry function as a stand-alone piece or within a larger qualitative research account?

6. Is research poetry represented in your field of employment?

    a. If not, is there an area or resource you see as a safe space to represent poetry?

    b. If so, what are these areas, and how can you enhance or contribute to them?

7. Read over the poetry resources presented in this chapter. Which one would be a good choice for you to start to interact with?

8. A good way to increase the presence of research poetry and other aesthetic forms is to cite and use excerpts from these writings as appropriate. Consider how to cite these representations in literature reviews, in research findings, in theses/dissertations, on websites, and in educational (social) media.

Reflexive Activities

See Appendix C for details about the following activities.

Research poetry group

Poem a day

Personal writing: A reflexivity experience

Professional writers panel or guest speaker

What's in your writing space? How to infuse it with items that may inspire poetry

Flip-flop debate and speed discussion—possible topics include the following:

a. Is research poetry research? How would you justify this?

b. What is the value of research poetry?

c. Does your field accept research poetry? If not, why and how should people be encouraged to begin to accept it?

Write an Ode

Use the following as a loose guide when writing an ode. Be sure to read some odes before you write one.

1. Choose an ordinary type of person, place, or event.

2. Brainstorm a list of all the ideas this person, place, or event makes you think of.

3. How would you describe this person, place, or event? What inspires you about this person, place, or event?

4. Give the person, place, or event praise or thanks, for example, as follows:

    Here's to the one who _____.

    Oh, _____.

5. Speak directly to the reader or person, place, or event.

6. Use adjectives to describe and verbs to bring action and life.

7. Repeat lines when appropriate.

Thumb Print Poetry

No two fingerprints or two people are alike. Thumb print poetry allows the research poet to explore their unique positionalities through an autoethnographic visual poem. I adapted this research poetry experience from a poetry lesson you can easily find many versions of online. For researchers, this is a reflexivity experience where you are considering what makes you unique, what bias you hold, your positionalities, and personal narratives that are as much a part of you as your thumb print.

Some guidelines:

1. Look closely at the fine lines on your thumb that make up your thumb print.
2. Consider the topic you want to focus on.
3. Jot down or type words, phrases, and events you wish to focus on.
4. With a pencil, lightly sketch your fingerprint whorls.
5. With a fine-tip marker, start to write in the words of your poem.

You will need

1. A magnifying glass
2. A tool you are comfortable handwriting in fine print with, such as ultrathin markers, a thin sharpie, a pen, or a colored pencil
3. A sheet of paper and a pencil

Check the following website for images of the three kinds of fingerprints, arch, whorl, and loop: https://attorneyatlawmagazine.com/various-types-fingerprints.

1. With a pencil, draw very light marks in the shape of your thumb print on art paper.
2. Keep the marks spaced far enough apart that you can write on them legibly with ultrafine markers.
3. Also, keep the lines spaced closely so they resemble a fingerprint.
4. While you are drawing your fingerprint, consider what you will write about.
5. Following the path of the whorls, write your self-reflexivity poem.

Resources

1. Poetry Foundation: https://www.poetryfoundation.org/

    From the website:

    The Poetry Foundation, publisher of *Poetry* magazine, is an independent literary organization committed to a vigorous presence for poetry in our culture. It exists to discover and celebrate the best poetry and to place it before the largest possible audience.

The Poetry Foundation works to raise poetry to a more visible and influential position in our culture. The Foundation seeks to be a leader in shaping a receptive climate for poetry by developing new audiences, creating new avenues for delivery, and encouraging new kinds of poetry.

This site has a vast number of poems representing poets, articles on forms of poetry and poets, a glossary of poetic terms, and poetic topics. Audio clips of poets reading their poetry are archived. You can sign up at this site for a daily poem to be sent to you: https://www.poetryfoundation.org/poems/poem-of-the-day

2. poets.org: https://poets.org/poems?gclid=CjwKCAjwr7X4BRA4EiwAUXj bt2l9fTArRCbFN4lImdWIfjFb9DJnm6BFPux0FGODBaKlMK6Fw4lwTRo CMJgQAvD_BwE

   This is the site of The Academy of American Poets. The academy publishes a journal titled *American Poets Magazine*. There are resources for National Poetry Month, which is in April. You can sign up for poem of the day.

3. *There Is a Poem for That*: https://www.youtube.com/playlist?list=PLJicm E8fK0Egxi0hgy5Tw-NFyLcpJ4bzJ

   This is an amazing series created by Ted Ed that pairs a poet/poem with a graphic artist to create a virtual video of the poem. I have used this both for personal inspiration and in course activities.

4. *Poetry Defined*: https://www.youtube.com/results?search_query=%23 PoetryDefined

   This is an attention-grabbing video series that brings interesting content to topics such as what a poem is, how to write a haiku, and poem versus prose. The only downside is that this series seems to be over. I use this series to help me think, in teaching, and in my written work.

5. Button Poetry: https://www.youtube.com/user/ButtonPoetry

   An online source for performance poets.

6. Poets & Writers: https://www.pw.org/

   This is a nonprofit organization. On its website, it publishes poetry, nonfiction, and fiction writers' prompt once a week. It also publishes a magazine and provides a site of rich resources for writers. The magazine's archive—https://www.pw.org/archive.

Books

Faulkner, S. L. (2016). *Poetry as method: Reporting research through verse.* Routledge. https://doi.org/10.4324/9781315422411

Galvin, K. T., & Prendergast, M. (Eds.). (2015). *Poetic inquiry II: Seeing, caring, understanding: Using poetry as and for inquiry.* Springer. https://doi.org/10.1007/978-94-6300-316-2

Prendergast, M., Leggo, C., & Sameshima, P. (2009). *Poetic inquiry: Vibrant voices in the social sciences.* Sense. https://doi.org/10.1163/9789087909512

Book Chapters

Faulkner, S. L. (2017). Poetic inquiry. In P. Leavy (Ed.), *Handbook of arts-based research* (pp. 208–230). Guilford Press.

Prendergast, M., & Leggo, C. (2007). Interlude: Astonishing wonder: Spirituality and poetry in educational research. In L. Bresler (Ed.), *International handbook of research in arts education* (pp. 1459–1477). Springer. https://doi.org/10.1007/978-1-4020-3052-9_100

Articles

Furman, R., Langer, C. L., Davis, C. S., Gallardo, H. P., & Kulkarni, S. (2007). Expressive, research and reflective poetry as qualitative inquiry: A study of adolescent identity. *Qualitative Research, 7*(3), 301–315. https://doi.org/10.1177/1468794107078511

Glesne, C. (1997). That rare feeling: Re-presenting research through poetic transcription. *Qualitative Inquiry, 3*(2), 202–221. https://doi.org/10.1177/107780049700300204

Johns, R. D. (2017). A spiritual question. *Qualitative Inquiry, 23*(8), 631–638. https://doi.org/10.1177/1077800417692362

Poindexter, C. C. (2002). Research as poetry: A couple experiences HIV. *Qualitative Inquiry, 8*(6), 707–714. https://doi.org/10.1177/1077800402238075

Richardson, L. (1993). Poetics, dramatics, and transgressive validity: The case of the skipped line. *Sociological Quarterly, 34*(4), 695–710. https://doi.org/10.1111/j.1533-8525.1993.tb00113.x

Visuals in Qualitative Research Representation: In the Blink of an Eye

In the blink of an eye—the brain can identify images seen for as little as 13 milliseconds.

—Trafton (2014)

Visual research represents vast and ever-changing arenas.[1] Yet, other than instructions in style guides such as the APA manual on how to format images and figures in prose articles, little guidance exists on how to represent visuals in research accounts. Visual research has come into prominence with the advent of the current visual digital culture, where "people produce, repro-duce, diffuse and consume visual images—a process that has now become part of everyday life" (Tsang & Besley, 2020, p. 3). There is an increased under-standing of the power of visuals. This speed and impact are summed up in the title and the opening quote of this chapter. Within our culture, the visual has come to be treated as the written word, holding the same potential and prominence (Tsang & Besley, 2020).

Examples of the visual culture may be seen in recent news publications and television shows referencing and reprinting texts and tweets with emojis and GIFs (e.g., Highfield & Leaver, 2016; Vidal et al., 2016). People who participate

---

[1]My thanks to Dannon Cox for his review of this chapter and generosity with his visual expertise. I have learned through his research and way of being in our visual world.

in digital communication often create a version of their social and professional worlds through media using images (i.e., emoticons, emojis, memes, GIFs) along with written words (Tsang & Besley, 2020). Even when we choose to disengage from visual images, in a visual culture such as ours, we are still passive recipients and are bombarded with images, and the visual culture continues to signal hidden messages (Ong, 2020).

In the history of qualitative research, it is only during the past two decades that visual research began to formalize into methodological subgenres (e.g., Harper, 1994, 2000, 2005; Hughes, 2012; Knowles & Sweetman, 2004; Phoenix, 2010; Pink, 2007; Rose, 2007). Some of these subgenres are as follows:[2] *auto-driven photo-elicitation* (Samuels, 2004), *auto-driving* (Heisley & Levy, 1991), *auto photography* (Glaw et al., 2017), *collage inquiry* (Butler-Kisber & Poldma, 2010), *comic-based research* (Kuttner et al., 2020), *contemplative art making* (Bhattacharya, 2020), *digital storytelling* (De Vecchi et al., 2017), *fotohistorias* (Gomez & Vannini, 2015), *installations* (Cole & McIntyre, 2008), *Mosaic approach* (Clark, 2004), *multitimethod research* (Ong, 2020), *multimodal research* (Leeuwen, 2020), *multisensory research* (Pink, 2020), *photobiography* (Liamputtong, 2007), *photo-ethnography* (Harper, 2005), *photo feedback* (Oliffe & Bottorff, 2007; Sampson-Cordle, 2001), *photo interviewing* (Hurworth, 2003; Oliffe & Bottorff, 2007), *photonovella* (Wang & Burris, 1994), *photo research*, *Photovoice* (Milne & Muir, 2020; Wang & Burris, 1994, 1997), *reflexive photography* (Douglas, 1998; Liamputtong, 2007), *visual anthropology* (Harper, 1994), *visual ethnography, visual inquiry, visual research* (Banks, 2001), and *visual sociology* (Harper, 2005).Visual research has burgeoned into a variety of areas and disciplines, such as child studies (Thomson, 2008), ethics (Lahman, 2017a; Wiles et al., 2008), psychology (Reavey, 2011), health (Drew et al., 2010), sport (Phoenix & Rich, 2016), and education (Moss & Pini, 2016). Visual research representations include inquiry where researchers

- collect visuals created by participants,

- explore researcher-prompted visuals (see Figure 9.1),

- introduce visuals to elicit data (e.g., photo-elicitation; Banks, 2001),

- consider preexisting visuals in context,

- explore serendipitously produced visuals—produced during observations (see Figures 9.2 and 9.3), and

- create visuals as a reflection of new research understandings (see Figure 9.4).

Visual research representation includes cutting-edge areas of human research where ethical issues become emphasized. This emphasis is due to the capturing of human images and dynamic advances in technology.

---

[2]Parts of this chapter drew on and were updated from the visual portion of Lahman (2017).

In this chapter, after a brief review of the background of visuals, I will present the following:

- Exemplars of visual research representations, including
  - collage,
  - participant art creation and the Mosaic approach, and
  - art installations and galleries
- Ideas for representation, including
  - electronic theses and dissertations (ETDs),
  - hypermedia, and
  - video articles and journals
- Areas for methodological and ethical consideration, including
  - quality of reproduction,
  - dissemination,
  - copyright, and
  - ethics
- Qualitative research visuals from student researchers
- Reflexive questions
- Examples of reflexive activities
- Resources

FIGURE 9.1 ● Participants' Fraction Conceptions

Task 2: Discuss how you might prepare to teach a lesson on multiplying fractions to a group of students. What visuals or manipulatives might you use and how? What misconceptions might your students have? Consider the following example during your discussion: $\frac{4}{5} * \frac{2}{3} = ?$

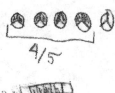

Note: Photo by Lida Bentz, Stephanie Hurtt, Wesley Martsching, and Sarah Sparks.

FIGURE 9.2 ● Little and Big

Note: A four-year-old child's name for the art they produced and gave to the researcher—a long-term classroom visitor—as a serendipitous gift. Photo by Maria Lahman.

FIGURE 9.3 ● "I'm a Trash Man"

Note: A child's cheerful song while, through his own initiative, spearing trash and organic matter on a playground with a pencil. Photo by Maria Lahman.

FIGURE 9.4 ●   Researcher Reflexivity Collage on Children's Library Experience

Note: By Christina Taylor.

Source: Lahman M. K. E., Taylor C. M., Beddes L. A., et al. Research Falling Out of Colorful Pages Onto Paper: Collage Inquiry. *Qualitative Inquiry.* 2020; *26*(3-4):262–270. doi:10.1177/1077800418810721

Visual Inquiry Background

Visual inquiry spans a historical realm of research (e.g., Collier, 1957, 1967, 2001) including areas such as art making, assemblages, collage, film, painting, mapping, installations, photography, graphic art, tattoos (Davidson, 2016), digital storytelling, sculpture, and so on. While areas such as visual ethnography and visual sociology have a long history, the past two decades have seen significant growth across many fields that employ qualitative research. This may be seen in the available textbooks, probably due to the advent of a visual social culture where members are consumers, producers, and critics. As Cassandra Phoenix (2010) puts it,

> Visual images can act as unique forms of data that have the ability to amass complexly layered meanings in a format, which is both accessible and easily retrievable to researchers, participants and audiences alike. . . .

Images are powerful in that they can do things. Images can evoke a particular kind of response. Thinking, writing, presenting and discussing with images, suggests Grady (2004), can make arguments more vivid and more lucid than alternative forms of representation. (p. 93)

Historically, there were two overarching visual research areas: (1) participants' existing visuals as data and (2) the visuals researchers produced as data (e.g., photos). As critical research expanded the field of visual research, collaborative visual research—where the researcher sets up a context for the participant to produce visual data (e.g., Photovoice) or the researcher and participants create visuals together (Banks, 2001; Beddes, 2017)—increasingly appeared. Dividing visual research into two areas is a simplified way to help readers think about a complex field. Other aspects of visual research we need to consider include decisions around how existing images will be recorded, cared for, represented, and disseminated by the researcher; when an image will be taken or produced during the research and in what context; whether the context is documented or decontextualized; whether the images are in black-and-white or color, moving or still; and what instructions are to be given to the participants taking photos or creating visuals. These are just a few questions that show how complex visual inquiry is.

Technology

The role technology plays in visual research cannot be overstated. As technology has become more ubiquitous, our understanding has moved from that of a naive consumer to active producer, or what Charmaine du Plessis (2019) terms a *prosumer*—one who both consumes and produces content. For instance, photos were first seen as a fact or a document capturing a visual piece of reality (Harper, 1994; Holm, 2008). This was most likely due to people's limited understanding of how photos were captured, edited, and produced. Soon this belief was problematized, and people began to see photos as moments representing just one of many possible perspectives or realities. "Images are not neutral and do not portray a truth but only the producers' and viewers co-constructed understanding" (Holm, 2008, p. 325). Photos can also be contrived or manipulated, and do not always allow the viewer to see the photographer, the full setting, or all aspects of the photographed. For example, we cannot see the back or the bottom half of a person in a traditional portrait. (With the current boom in internet meetings due to the COVID-19 pandemic, the broader public has a clearer understanding of the complex performativity of an image due to accidental revelations—such as a formally attired news anchor revealed to be wearing only boxer briefs under his home desk.)

As issues of perspective, interpretation, and representation continued to evolve, photo methodology developed a decidedly postmodern flare. Visual research equipment began to take on many forms—cell phones (Choi et al., 2006); disposable, single-use cameras and digital cameras (Allen, 2012); and web cameras (Holm, 2008)—and was often embedded inside other devices. As photography and video equipment became more affordable and accessible, photos and videos became ubiquitous (Gibbs et al., 2002), affecting visual research. First, visual research methodologies became more prevalent. Second, visual methodologies also took on a critical perspective—the researcher should not be the only one with the power to take photos. Now, researchers could put cameras in the hands of research participants and see through their lens. Increasingly, participants already had cameras at all times in the form of a smartphone. The cost of equipment and reproduction of images was reduced, and sharing of images became an instant possibility. Third, individuals became used to being photographed in daily life and often knew how to take photos themselves, thus increasing their comfort level with being photographed as part of research (Gibbs et al., 2002). The ever-present nature of technology comes with a need for much closer attention to ethics.

If you decide to conduct photo research, be sure to stay focused in order to see what develops.

Multisensory and Multimodal Methods: The Other Senses

How do we challenge ourselves as visual researchers to gather data with and around the other senses and then represent them? Visual researchers have had to work hard to gain acceptance of image representations since written prose is the traditional dominant form and a source of uncontested knowledge. We do honor audio but in a limited way and still ultimately through writing—interview data, quotes from interviews presented in manuscripts, and conversations noted during observations and re-created in ethnographic or case study texts—not the grunts, hums, clips, smacks, and sighs that are also part of the contexts our research words occur within. Andrew Sparkes (2009) writes, "People's knowledge of themselves, others and the world they inhabit, is inextricably linked to and shaped by their senses" (pp. 23–24). Phoenix (2010) expands on this idea, pointing out that "visual studies have . . . received criticism that sight is regularly foregrounded at the expense of other senses like smell and taste" (p. 103).

Therefore, a word about *multisensory* (Clark, 2011b; Phoenix, 2010; Pink, 2020) and *multimodal* (Clark, 2011b; Leeuwen, 2020) methods seems warranted. One of the invigorating aspects of qualitative research is the organic way in which methodologies and methods may grow and overlap, with decisions about the best ways to respectfully generate critical data with participants

iStock.com/Alek_Koltukov

taking shape throughout a given study, often within a moment. All of the visual research exemplars (e.g., the Mosaic approach) presented in the following section could be developed to be multisensory and multimodal.

Paul Stoller (1989), a veteran ethnographer, pointed out in a research reflection, *The Taste of Ethnographic Things*, that researchers have long neglected the sensual in order to be more "scientific." Reflecting on his reawakening to the senses while conducting long-term research with the Songhay people of Niger and Mali, Stoller wrote,

> Now I let the sights, sounds, smells, and tastes of Niger flow into me. This fundamental rule in epistemological humility taught me that taste, smell and hearing are often more important of the Songhay than sight, the privileged sense of the West. In Songhay, one can taste kinship, smell witches, and hear the ancestors. (p. 5)

Multisensory research represents an *understanding* of the sensual, a *recognition* that the senses—sight, smell, touch, hearing, taste, perception, and others— inform each other and cannot be separated, an *effort* to collect data in multisensory ways, as well as a *challenge* to consider how the senses are represented in our research accounts. Sarah Pink (e.g., 2007, 2013, 2020), a major voice in visual research, has noted,

> Anyone interested in using visual methods and media as part of social research needs to account for the idea that we cannot engage with the visual in theoretical or practice-based research without a theory, methodological appreciation, and practical awareness of multisensoriality. Research and scholarship have demonstrated that the senses cannot be understood in isolation from each other—as either neurological processes, in human perception, or within practical human activity. (Pink, 2020, p. 523)

From the field of early-childhood research, Allison Clark (2011a, 2011b) has developed multisensory and multimodal research for children and is extending it to adults with an "emphasis on visual and kinesthetic modes of communication alongside speech to broaden the range of modes of expression which are given status within the research—playing to the strengths of the young children involved" (Clark, 2011b, p. 313). Clearly, visual research has an essential overlap with multisensory and multimodal research methods.

Visual Literacy

Visual literacy is a complicated, cutting-edge topic that merits more space and time than I can provide. However, I think it is important to point out that visual researchers should engage in learning opportunities in this area. I provide resources to advance this goal at the end of the chapter.

Patricia Ong (2020) writes of visual researchers,

Gathering of pre-existing societal imagery . . . requires a minimum reflexive knowledge of the technical and expressive aspects of imagery and representational techniques. . . . To be able to read and utilize them in an appropriate way . . . some form of visual competence is required. (pp. 36–37)

However, higher education, in general, has been critiqued as visually illiterate, with little understanding of how to interpret and use images for communication. Joanna Kędra & Rasa Žakevičiūtė (2019) write,

Today's students were born in image-saturated environments, the era of internet, digital technologies, and touchscreens. Their communication practices are mediated visually, including photo and video creation and sharing, video chatting, and the visual language of emoticons, GIFs, and emojis. However, the moment students enter university classrooms, they are thrown into almost a completely textual world. Such a highly textual context may cause an alienation from the course material and content. In consequence, contemporary millennial and post-millennial generations, although usually technologically savvy, are often visually illiterate. (p. 1)

If this is the case in higher education pedagogy, it is most certainly so in research. The basic idea behind visual literacy applied to research is that a researcher not only can capture an image but also can set up contexts in which participants and the researcher together or separately can create images and then "read" them, thereby interpreting the possible meanings of a given image for a broader audience. "Visual literacy is about language, communication and interaction" (Harrison, n.d.). Writing in 1969, John Debes (cited in Harrison, n.d.), who coined and developed the construct "visual literacy," said of visual literacy competencies, "When developed, they enable the visually literate person to discriminate and interpret the visible actions, objects, symbols, natural or [hu]man-made, that he [they] encounters in his [their] environment" (para. 2). Clearly, increased literacy in this area will strengthen the visual researcher's work.

In the following section, I review several of the multiple visual research representations available, to place this discussion in a contemporary visual research context.

Exemplars of Visual Research Representations

The area of visual research representations is broad and burgeoning, so necessarily only some areas are addressed here—collage, participant art creation in the form of the Mosaic approach, and art installations and galleries. (See Chapter 6 for information on creating a visual abstract in the form of a graphic, cartoon, or video and for examples of graphic and cartoon dissertations and Chapter 8 for a discussion of visuals in poetry, including concrete, collage, and photo poems.)

Collage[3]

While collage as an expressive form has existed for millennia, as seen in the practice of ordinary people pulling together diverse media to create new expressions with differing elements, the formalization of collage as a movement in art is widely traced to the early 1900s. In particular, women have collected bits and pieces, leftovers, and scraps to represent their lives. Miriam Schapiro and Melissa Meyer (1977) termed this feminist practice *femmage* to encompass decoupage, collage, photomontage, and assemblage. Femmage is contemporarily reflected in refrigerator collages, Pinterest, and scrapbooking mega conglomerates such as Creative Memories.

At the outset of the modern art collage movement, the medium was seen in the creations of Pablo Picasso and Georges Braque (Vaughan, 2005; Wallach, 2012), who sought to represent and invoke feelings and to subvert the prevailing political and social norms of their day. Originally from the French, "collage" literally means "gluing," which is what these artists and others did by sticking items such as newsprint, burlap, or chair cane to canvas and then painting or drawing over the collage. However, collage has been traced as far back as the 12th century in Japan, where artists glued paper to silk. And it was first recorded in Europe in the 15th century, and later, during the Victorian era, collage caught on with the general public and became a considerable hobby, as seen in scrapbook and valentine card creation (Reilly, 2019).

Researchers, influenced by the deep connection they saw in collage to the everyday lives of their research participants and students, formally appropriated the art form for research (Davis & Butler-Kisber, 1999). As early as 1998, Janesick had published a reflexive collage experience for researchers to engage with (see Text Box 9.1, "Researcher Reflexivity Collage," for an extension of Janesick's reflexive experience). This connection and the seeming accessibility of collage for both creators and audiences seem to drive the interest of current qualitative researchers (Butler-Kisber, 2008; Butler-Kisber & Poldma, 2010; Leavy, 2008; Margolin, 2014; Vaughan, 2005). Research areas as diverse as early-childhood education (Clark, 2017), feminism (Särmä, 2016; Schapiro & Meyer, 1977), ethnography, the humanities (Kuttner et al., 2020), and methodology (Bhattacharya, 2020; Kincheloe, 2006; Lahman, De Oliveira, Cox, et al., 2020; Lahman, Taylor, et al., 2019) have employed collage as a means of inquiry and representation.

---

[3]My understanding of collage in research was expanded through experiences with multiple groups of students and is represented in Lahman, Taylor, et al. (2019) and Lahman, De Oliveira, Cox, et al. (2020). It is a privilege to learn with many researchers willing to be deeply reflexive and take risks during course experiences. This section draws heavily on these experiences and publications.

9.1 RESEARCHER REFLEXIVITY COLLAGE

IVAN BLOUNT

I was unable to attend class the night the collages were created. To participate, I created my collage at home using the same directions and collage materials provided by Maria before viewing any of my other classmates' creations (see Figure 9.4). My heart paced, and I felt anxious about what I would unravel. I did not have a process set in stone, but I went with my feelings. I allowed the pages of the magazines to speak to me through pictures, phrases, and indicators of life. Ironically, the picture in my head was not clear, and the words I envisioned as the pieces collected were organized in reverse order. I went through each magazine, one by one, and then placed them down and cut the pieces out. Ordering the scattered pieces was weird, considering I had never done it before. The final product was composed over the course of two and a half hours. I have never created a piece of work/reflective research in this format. The process was exciting and unnerving, considering I did not have any control over my resources (i.e., magazines). As a result, I went through each magazine and found at least one tidbit instrumental to the overall product created.

Ivan created this collage as part of a researcher reflexivity experience (see Figure 9.5).

(See Lahman, Taylor, et al., 2020, for the course process and each member's representations.)

Source: Lahman M. K. E., Taylor C. M., Beddes L. A., et al. Research Falling Out of Colorful Pages Onto Paper: Collage Inquiry. *Qualitative Inquiry.* 2020; *26*(3-4):262–270. doi:10.1177/1077800418810721

FIGURE 9.5 ● Ivan Blount's Researcher Reflexivity Collage

Source: Lahman M. K. E., Taylor C. M., Beddes L. A., et al. Research Falling Out of Colorful Pages Onto Paper: Collage Inquiry. *Qualitative Inquiry.* 2020; *26*(3-4):262–270. doi:10.1177/1077800418810721

Participant Art Creation and the Mosaic Approach

The Mosaic approach (Clark & Moss, 2001) is a research methodology developed to generate knowledge or research data through a method other than the dominant method, which the authors call *data extraction* (Clark, 2011a). The authors understood that young children are highly skilled at articulating their knowledge through many non-oral-language-oriented mediums that adults may have let fall to the side. The researcher facilitates knowledge generation by providing opportunities for children to actively express themselves through interviews and many types of nonverbal mediums (e.g., bookmaking, photography, walking tours, art, mapmaking). While relying heavily on visuals, the Mosaic approach, as articulated by Clark (2011a; Clark & Moss, 2001), is also a multisensory (Pink, 2020) and multimodal methodology (Leeuwen, 2020), since multiple data collection methods, such as walking interviews, are used. Multisensory research is a natural fit with early-childhood researchers' understanding of young children as researchers of the world around them. The authors created this approach to focus on children under five years of age. It has been adapted for older children and adults too. The authors' original research was with three- and four-year-old children at a child care facility and a homeless family center (Clark & Moss, 2001).

As a former pre-K teacher and laboratory school director with degrees in early-childhood education and development, one of my specialty areas is research methods with young children. I had long been impressed by the Mosaic approach. However, as a methodologist, I primarily consult with researchers of older youth or adults, having little opportunity to connect with those who research children. I began to suggest that researchers of adults use the Mosaic approach. The addition of adult participants has begun to be reflected in Clark's work also (e.g., 2011a).

For an example of the Mosaic approach outside of the original authors researching young children, see Krista Griffin's dissertation (Fiedler, 2012) and subsequent book (Griffin, 2016), representing her in-depth research with third-grade boys regarding their perspectives about their reading ability. Griffin (2016) included a shoulder-to-shoulder interview—a method she studied and developed (Griffin et al., 2014), along with bookmaking—and an open-ended art activity.

Lindsay Beddes's (2017) research is an excellent example of how one can use the Mosaic approach with adults. (See Chapter 4 for images from Beddes's dissertation, which adapted the approach to adults.) Beddes wrote of her research with adults,

> Mosaic is . . . multimethod in that the participants had varied approaches to aesthetic representation, and each brought a unique aesthetic voice to the research.
>
> The traditional mosaic is participatory (Clark, 2005). . . . This participatory approach was present in adult mosaic. The adult

participants were invited to select an artistic medium through which to communicate their experience and . . . to participate in semi-structured interviews to expand on the aesthetic representations of their experience.

The traditional mosaic is reflexive and focuses on lived experience. . . . Adult mosaic is similarly reflexive. . . . Regardless of the age of the individual, when we experience powerful, transformational experience, it can be difficult to convey the meaning of that experience in words. Thus, allowing time for supported, non-verbal processing can help set the stage both for more authentic expression of the essence and emotion surrounding the experience, and deeper overall learning as the participants engage in a richly reflexive process. (p. 55)

Cherjanét Lenzy (2019b) also adapted the Mosaic approach to adults, with powerful outcomes—terming the process and representations "artistic stories." The research participants were given the choice to represent their experiences as race-based activist Black women by engaging through drawing, writing, or image/narrative creation. Lenzy described this process as follows:

Fimo clay,[4] markers, crayons, and pens were provided for use in creating these artistic stories. With participant permission, I took pictures of each woman's hands, creating or holding their art. After a discussion of the participant's artistic story, I shared my own. In so doing, I provided a full sharing of experience while allowing the participants to learn more about me as a Black woman. (p. 63)

Lenzy (2019b) reflected on the artistic stories that emerged and her realization that instead of simply retelling a story the participants seemed to have deepened their reflection about the emotions occurring around their activism through artistic expression.

---

[4] I had the privilege to consult on Lenzy's (2019a, 2019b) work, and I want to take a moment to comment on the use of clay with adults for representing research. As a person whose in-depth training is with young children, I find it hard to say, but for many adults clay that requires the use of water can be off-putting. Most children enjoy getting dirty, and ideally, if a researcher had access to an art studio where clay was used, I am confident it would a powerful experience. However, most adult spaces where we meet to conduct research are meant to be kept clean and do not have running water. This is why polymer clay, of which Fimo is one brand, is ideal. Polymer clay may be modeled without any tools and comes in an array of colors. If the researcher wants to use neutral tones only, they are available also. If the researcher was meeting up with participants over time, the clay could quickly be fired (hardened) in a kitchen oven and then given back to the participants or participants could be given the simple firing instruction, which usually is 275 °F (135 °C) baking for 15 minutes per quarter inch of thickness.

Research Installations

Looking at a clothesline with a range of female diapers and undergarments hanging on it (see Figures 9.6a *and* b)*, I am thrown back in time to a memory of how my family used a long, three-strand clothesline whenever weather permitted. We were outsiders from the North in a southern rural home. During tag or hide-and-seek, any of us children could duck behind the long sheets and bury our face in the fresh fabric, which was starting to stiffen in the sun. The memory wafts over me with soft-as-cotton pleasure. I must have been late to toilet train—or instead let's say, "early to talk"—since a story Mom would often tell is that as she pinned up my cloth diapers I, perhaps sensing her hard work, consoled her by saying, "Don't worry. When I am older, I will hang up my own diapers."*

As I began to be trained on how to hang out the wash, I was instructed to hang all the underwear on the inner clothesline, with larger items such as sheets on the outer rows, so all undergarments were discreetly hidden. We were taught in the South of the United States not to air our family's dirty linen, but for my family, this also included clean linen.

I think about clotheslines and family underwear in my current life, which straddles my children and until recently my parents—the many disposable baby diapers I threw into landfills juxtaposed against the cloth my parents used, the high cost of undergarments for an elderly parent with an eroding memory, and how hard it must be for adult caregivers to change an elderly adult who can be irritable or angry and is undoubtedly no longer cute, as I was when I spoke consolingly to my mother.

FIGURE 9.6A ● Life Lines: The Alzheimer's Project

Note: Photo by Ardra Cole.

Source: Reproduced with permission from Ardra Cole.

FIGURE 9.6B ● Life Lines: The Alzheimer's Project (a Close-Up)

Note: Photo by Ardra Cole.

Source: Reproduced with permission from Ardra Cole.

Installations of art are described as "art made for a specific space exploiting certain qualities of that space" (Delahunt, 2007, in Cole & McIntyre, 2008, p. 289). Research installation artists work to intrigue and engage new audiences, as seen in the following:

> Because one intention of much of installation art-as-research is to make research more accessible to diverse audiences, including but beyond the academy, the work is exhibited in a variety of venues atypical to academic work. The interactive nature of most of the work also renders it responsive and dynamic. Each time it is exhibited in a different venue, the work is changed to suit the space. (Cole & McIntyre, 2008, p. 289)

Ardra Cole and Maura McIntyre (2008) have a highly effective handbook chapter that interested readers should read in full. They send readers along a journey through multiple installations by writing in an active first-person voice. For this brief review, I will heavily condense only one of the installations—Cole and McIntyre's The Alzheimer's Project. This was my first introduction to the powerful presentation genre of research galleries. Now as a child of a recently deceased brilliant professor who was in severe decline due to vascular dementia, the installation spoke to me in new ways—layered on my first experiences viewing the images over 15 years ago—as all meaningful art and research does. Aspects of research installations to consider include creating the exhibit to be interactive; reaching diverse audiences, including those of different ages when appropriate (drawing on children's interactive museum literature here will help); and disrupting conventions about how art is to be viewed. A nonresearch art installation on my campus, Yucca Fountain, was installed by Andrew Bablo and Helen Popinchalk (see a video of the fountain at https://www.youtube.com/watch?v=XDAE-avF4yY [University of Northern Colorado, 2019]). It is a playful, provocative installation set up as a diner open to all in a desert during the atomic era.

The Alzheimer's Project (Cole & McIntyre, n.d.), a research installation, is in a spacious room outside a main museum exhibit hall. Cole and McIntyre (2008) explain that this type of setting for art may be called a *museum intervention*, whereby passersby encounter the art and, intrigued, stop to look closer and may then enter to view the larger, permanent displays. This installation opens with "startling statistics about Alzheimer's disease," designed to pique curiosity while providing valuable information. Fridge doors, each from a different era, are collaged with photos secured by magnets. Time lapses between the mother-daughter images on each fridge move from a mom and a toddler to finally a full role reversal as the toddler, now an adult, feeds and cares for her mother.

Herstory—framed black-and-white photographs of a young girl that capture her developmental span through womanhood, hauntingly displayed with a superimposed image of the child (now a woman with Alzheimer's)—becomes *Yourstory* as the viewer's image is also reflected. Captivatingly and startlingly, the clothesline I reflected on at the outset of this section (Figures 9.6 A, B) runs the length of the exhibit, documenting life changes from a sweet baby diaper pegged on the line to lacey undergarments and practical cotton underwear and ending with the ignoble adult diaper. Other areas, too numerous to detail here, invite attendees to write journal entries, leave memory objects, take a bright clothespin to wear in solidarity, and so on. As people interacted with the instal-lation at the various places it was displayed, more data were gathered in the form of journaling and in-depth interviews. These data were moved into digital formats to be more readily accessible (see Cole & McIntyre, n.d.).

Even a brief foray into Cole and McIntyre's (2008) work has the potential for meaningful impact. The following questions are a starting point for thinking about how an installation research representation might work:

- How do the researchers manage the practical issues of time and portability, not to mention finding materials and actually constructing the pieces?

- What about funding?
  - o What kind of support is available for this kind of research?

- How might we advocate that this is research?
  - o How might a research-based installation "count" in terms of academic merit?

- What might a proposal for one of these projects look like, especially the methodological rationale?

- What about the creative process?

- How did each of the pieces unfold?

- What is it like for the researchers to see their work on public display?
  - o   Is it different from a published article?
  - o   And what about vulnerability?

- Are there particular ethical concerns associated with using installation in research? (Cole & McIntyre, 2008, p. 296)

Galleries

As an enthusiast who has little direct experience with formal art, I see research installations as juxtaposed against galleries. However, this does not mean galleries do not merit a review here. An art gallery, for both the display and at times the sale of art, could be described as a formal viewing space often found in a high-level venue featuring security, climate control for the protection of the pieces, an entry fee, and qualified experts, such as a curator, on the staff. However, a gallery may also simply mean a collection of pictures or an exhibition of items. This latter idea of a gallery has been used in creative and contemporary ways by researchers and teachers.

Pedagogically, a gallery walk is a temporary display of text, images, or end products of an assignment on the walls and in the learning space the course members have shared. Instructions vary, but usually, members of the course are asked to walk around the room and look at each item on display, trying not to stick together in large groups. Negative comments are not welcome out of consideration for the vulnerability of the amateur artist. Members either take the time to write a reflection at their seat or post several sticky notes containing affirming comments or questions offered to extend everyone's learning (Facing History and Ourselves, n.d.). Reflecting on one of the collage gallery walks I facilitated during a course, a student wrote,

> The variation was astounding, and the forms that were created spoke as loudly about the projects as the researchers could have. Those magazines had spoken to each of us in such different ways, and yet we had all heard exactly what we needed to hear while we listened. This activity was simple and yet quite powerful. Those two elements brought together a great teaching opportunity that led to deep reflection and learning. Lahman, Taylor, et al. (2019)

A gallery may be as temporary as Lenzy's (2019b) display during her dissertation defense. Lenzy sought to celebrate and highlight visuals reflecting research with Black women doctoral students and how they experience intersectional identities in race-based activism (see Figures 9.7). By hanging these images on the walls around the table where the dissertation committee and audience were seated, Lenzy highlighted new ways of seeing, beyond the dominant oral presentation form.

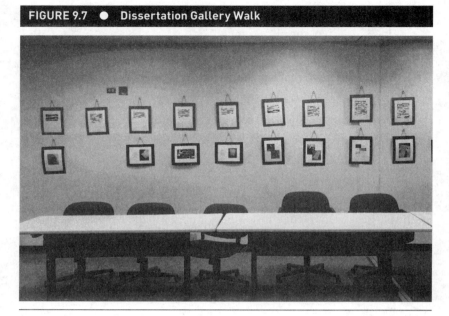

FIGURE 9.7 ● Dissertation Gallery Walk

Note: Photo by Cherjanét Lenzy.

Source: Reproduced with permission from Cherjanét Lenzy.

Beddes (2017), whose dissertation is referenced in Chapter 4, rented a professional art gallery space where the art produced from her dissertation was displayed for several weeks. Ultimately, the actual dissertation defense took place at the gallery. Beddes selected an off-campus gallery to increase community interaction. This choice needed to be negotiated with the graduate school since they wanted to be sure campus constituents could attend the dissertation defense. I offered to drive people in my car; two doctoral students accepted my offer, and Beddes committed to paying for a ride-sharing service for the others. I do not believe anyone took her up on this offer. The graduate school, highlighting the university's commitment to community engagement, agreed to the arrangement and even had the Graduate Student Association represented by a board member who acted as a camera person.

In the preceding sections, I have traced the historical background of visuals in research and current examples of visual research representations that are also considered multisensory and multimodal. In the following section, I discuss the ways in which researchers are navigating issues when publishing visuals.

Representing Visuals

The bulk of this chapter is dedicated to how visual research is expanding and invigorating visual methodological ideas, with little attention given to its representation. The lack of guidance around representing visuals is primarily because visual research is still outside the norm of the way research is thought to function. Still, today's researchers take it on themselves to create videos, blogs, websites, and social/educational media posts to portray and disseminate their visual research. This effort takes a lot of their time and money unless their work is grant funded, and cutting-edge posts can quickly seem technologically dated in a fast-changing world. I ran up against this issue repeatedly as I sought website links to share with readers and found examples that no longer worked correctly or had a dated look, but the research images represented are still relevant. Regarding textual representation outlets, visuals remain primarily black-and-white, static images, as seen in the examples in this book. In the area of visual research representation, I review ETDs, hypermedia articles, and video articles/journals.

The Contemporary ETDs

ETDs have been required as part of a master's or doctoral degree fulfillment in the United States for more than 20 years at some universities (McMillan, 2018). A simple definition of an ETD is a thesis or dissertation prepared as a PDF and emailed or uploaded to the graduate school. A more complex definition is a thesis or dissertation demonstrating a student's research through embedded hypermedia or hyperlinks to external sites where the student has stored digital information.

Virginia Polytechnic Institute and State University was the first to pilot the requirement of ETDs, in 1997, in the United States (McMillan, 2018). As a doctoral student at Virginia Tech, I was among the first group of students piloting ETDs. Overwhelmed, having never received training in this area of research technology, and simultaneously trying to move across the country, find a rental home, and prepare for my first semester as a professor, I recall paying someone to format my work and turn it into a PDF! The PDF reformatted some items, rendering one type of punctuation as another, so I could not even bear to look at the final product. All my literature review research was conducted physically in a library using microfiche and microfilm. The first time I presented using PowerPoint was when I interviewed for professor positions, having previously used only overhead projectors. I do not think I even had a good sense of what a PDF was.

This story most likely seems mind-boggling to today's tech-savvy graduates but illustrates what a jump electronic submission was for some. At the same time, a classmate of mine was inserting digital video clips of participants' actions into their dissertation to illustrate the findings. This type of hypermedia used in the dissertation is the real end goal of ETDs.

ETDs were originally seen as the cutting-edge wave of the future, so when I first arrived at the university where I was to be a professor, I wondered why they were not available. I assumed it was due to the money and infrastructure that would be needed to support the process. Regardless, I still exposed my students to possibilities, but I knew that students could only submit static figures. Sarah Potvin and Santi Thompson (2016) write,

As ETDs moved from theory to practice, the literature emphasized two key areas of promise and innovation in the transition away from print: expression and access. The former considered the possibility that students, now unrestricted by print format requirements, could more fully express their creative and scholarly vision. This hope was wedded to the more pragmatic idea that graduate education would be enhanced by students' mastering those digital production tools necessary to author even a basic ETD. In the latter scenario, the format of ETDs is linked to possibilities of access, and to works distributed, aggregated, and made available worldwide, to wider audiences than bound, shelved volumes had permitted. (p. 101)

When my current university moved to digital dissertations, they also kept the tradition of requiring hard copies to be submitted to the graduate school, the chair of the dissertation, and the university library for quite some time. A few years ago, the university removed the requirement for hard copy submission of the dissertation. When there was a tremendous outcry from some faculty, I realized change had been slow because of tradition and perhaps sentimentality. Faculty members who had worked with ETDs for decades and whose own dissertation was submitted virtually were glad to end the paper process. Eventually, the issue seemed to die down. Students can, of course, still print and bind their dissertation through independent companies.

From a critical perspective, I am a strong proponent of ETDs, agreeing with advocates who point to the heightened ability they create for accessing theses and dissertations. It is also vital for student researchers to be able to feature all aspects of their research through the use of hyperlinks and hypermedia. One advocate, McMillan (2018), was part of the early implementation of ETDs in the United States. She wrote,

While I celebrate the anniversary of the ETD requirement at Virginia Tech, I know that other colleges and universities are still wondering when, not if, they will require ETDs. Unfortunately, the issues surrounding ETDs continue to be more about an institution's political climate than about its technical expertise. I'm still longing for the "innovative" ETDs to evolve into the "typical" ETDs. . . . Although progress is slow, I'm anticipating a time when the norm for a graduate student's legacy will be a *demonstration* of the research, not just words describing it. (p. 59)

Hypermedia Articles

Many research journals are also increasingly developing the ability to support hyperlinks and hypermedia. While this is not a specialty area of mine (as someone who is primarily a user and not a creator), it seems hyperlinks are inserted into the text in the same manner many of us use links in our emails, texts, tweets, and so on. Tom Huston (n.d.) writes about hypermedia,

Ever since the early days of the internet, our brains have been learning to access information in nonlinear ways. . . . Like traditional footnotes or endnotes in a printed book, the digital hyperlinks we encounter throughout the day interrupt an otherwise linear flow of reading, instantly redirecting our attention to another source of information—a pattern that repeats in exponential overdrive, 24/7, as humanity surfs the interconnected array of hyperlinked text, images, audios, databases, games and other applications we call the World Wide Web. (para. 1)

The hyperlink takes the reader to an internet location where the cited information is housed. It often functions as an appendix rather than being integral to the study. (Recall, an appendix is additional matter that is not necessary for a full understanding of the research.) However, for a visual study, a hyperlink may be substantive, such as a video of a research installation discussed in depth in the textual part of the article. Hypertext takes readers to other texts outside the text at hand, whereas hypermedia links take readers to text, graphics, video, sound, and so on. Hypermedia may also be embedded within the document. An issue then arises regarding the maintenance of the website where the research information is housed and the resulting broken hyperlinks when the site has moved or no longer exists.

One of the difficulties I encountered in writing this section is that I, like many other researchers, am only just beginning to understand the digital interface as a creator and not merely a passive consumer. In my case, my children's young ages pull me along because I want to continue to communicate with them in ways that they, as humans born into a digital culture, will appreciate. Writing about this issue within higher education classrooms, where most current students are digitally savvy, Jared Keengwe (2013) says,

One's ability to represent thought digitally with a variety of media is more important than ever. . . . The vast majority of faculty in our institutes are "Digital Immigrants" while the students are "Digital Natives" which in turn has created challenges for both groups.

Students are utilizing media and technologies that are completely foreign to their teachers. (p. 6)

Keengwe (2013) goes on to point out that educators are increasingly embracing technologies and taking advantage of opportunities to learn along with the students they teach. We have seen, and I believe we will continue to see, a substantial increase in the use of these technologies with the heavy virtual emphasis in research in higher education due to the COVID-19 pandemic.

Video Articles and Video Journals

What is a video article or journal? One creator notes that "the idea of video journals is simple as it provides easy access to complex research findings and thereby helps to increase the dissemination and the impact of scientific work" (Sobhani, in Enago Academy, 2018a). Video articles and journals offer some promise for qualitative researchers, however, at the time of writing this section, I primarily see them used in the quantitative physical sciences. The researcher initially publishes the traditional peer-reviewed article. Then, a video version is produced by either the researcher or the publisher. The video article still has most of the sections of a traditional article, such as an abstract, a methods section, and findings.

There is much to consider in this area. Possible pros include making complex material more relatable to readers, enhanced access, easy dissemination across educational (social) media, and video with text reaching many types of learners. Employing tags such as hashtags allows prosumers to find the videos and then add to the discussion. Creative freedom is enhanced by the option to create videos that are graphic, that are focused on the researcher, that only the researcher voices over, or where others' voices and music are utilized. Additionally, videos can provide an audiovisual experience to enhance learners' interaction with the content (De Sousa et al., 2017).

Among the possible cons is that not all aspects of an article make it to the video, yet researchers are already familiar with this type of information restriction from research posters. Second, viewers will need an internet connection unless the video can be downloaded (Enago Academy, 2018b). Third, if the researcher is paying for the video, cost is a definite disadvantage, indicating either the need for a budget or the ability to create a quality video by a member of the research team. Finally, viewers increasingly expect short, captivating videos:

> Data from . . . 6.9 million video watching sessions in math/science showed that median engagement time was . . . 6 minutes, regardless of video length. Median watching time for videos of 9–12 minutes was less than half-way through the video, dropping to less than a quarter for those of 12–40 minutes (Guo et al., 2014). (Carmichael et al., 2018, p. 12)

These data do not reflect scholars' engagement with research videos. We may be inclined to think that scholars would stay tuned for longer segments, but increasingly, I am not sure that is the case. Also, scholars are not the only audience for research videos—students, stakeholders, and the media also watch them. Providing video in segments (e.g., abstract, research design, results) and use of time codes are ways to address length-of-engagement issues (Nielsen, 2020). A question that remains is whether the researcher still needs to write the traditional article. It would seem this will be the case for some time, thus resulting in more work—another disadvantage.

This heading from an internet article, "Change Hurts; Innovation Improves" (Enago, 2018b), sums up the core issue here. Three major points follow:

1. "Researchers must begin to think of themselves as amateur video bloggers, rather than simply opening a new Word/LaTeX file."

2. "The learning curve, from typing to making videos is extremely steep."

3. "Coordination with the journal must be extremely simple, very quick, and responsive." (Enago, 2018b)

The production of some research article videos, where a videographer works in person (physically in close proximity) with the researcher, was suspended due to the COVID-19 pandemic. Still, traditional articles were proceeding at pace because of the prevalence of publishing traditional work entirely through the internet. Putting the video production in the hands of the researcher with ample virtual support seems to be the next step toward continuing production virtually in times when physical proximity is not advisable or is difficult due to geographical restrictions. This model is also more environmentally friendly, with less need for global travel. Video articles and journals are already a useful modern form and will become more prevalent. The adjustment in the short term will be hard for some, but the potential for innovations may well be worth it.

It will be fascinating to see how the area of visual research representations develops over the next decade—much of what I have written about it offers only a glimpse of what is to come. Dannon Cox,[5] who consulted on this chapter says that video production is an additional language that scholars will have to learn to "speak," as video content is accessible to anyone (personal communication, April 24, 2021). In the next and final section, I examine areas necessary for consideration as the field of visual/multisensory research continues to develop.

Considerations for Visual Representations

This is an important section for those considering embarking on visual research and representations. In my experience, I have found that many of us, myself included, have not had enough guidance on the front end of visual research, so we become hampered by important issues in the areas of representation and reproduction of visual research. This is most likely due to visual methodological literature being taught less frequently, given the vast field that constitutes qualitative research. The novice researcher embarking on visual research will want to read up on the literature (e.g., Knowles et al., 2007; Marion & Crowder, 2013; Mitchell, 2011; Mulvihill & Swaminathan, 2019; Pauwels & Mannay, 2020). Dawn Mannay (2020) challenges us to revisualize prose data, the site of the bulk of our training and experience:

> There is a dense, dry, flat prose that forms a "linguistic armour" in much academic writing (Lerum, 2001), which can stifle the affective elements of research findings and distance the reader from the voices of participants (see also Wilson, 2018). Images have the capacity to move us, and by including these in publications there may be an opportunity to better communicate research findings to the reader/viewer and engage them in participants' worlds. (p. 660)

---

[5]See Cox (2020) for Dannon's dissertation on digital media and pedagogy.

Readers will most likely agree about the emphasis of text over visual content. Continuing the discussion regarding lack of training and resources in visual research, Darren Newbury (2020) makes the important point that

> there is a systemic lack of care for images, despite the ostensible focus on the visual. Nowhere is this more evident than in the area of academic publishing. Ask how many volumes have been written on how to publish. Then ask how many of these specifically discuss visual forms of presentation, or the role of images as illustrations. How many even have a chapter devoted to the topic? Even books devoted to visual methods are not always a good advertisement for the use of images in the presentation of research. (p. 670)

In this section, I necessarily briefly cover only a few issues that I chose due to how vital, practical, or cutting edge they are: (a) quality of images for reproduction purposes, (b) copyright, (c) dissemination, (d) ethics, and (e) confidentiality.

Quality of Images for Reproduction Purposes

I was surprised to discover when I wrote a book with a chapter on visual and research ethics that I was not able to use any of the visuals (Lahman, 2017a). If the research revolved around the photos participants took, which was the case in three studies, the images were too poor in quality to be reproduced in a book. Some of these photos were even taken on high-level smartphones but certainly by amateur photographers. These photos had, however, been published in journals and/or dissertations and presented at research conferences, so it didn't occur to me there could be a problem reproducing them in a book. Before embarking on visual research, it is essential to do some investigation around visual reproduction quality requirements. The quality of an image may need to be balanced with the consideration of not overly formalizing the photo process when conducting critical emancipatory research. Still, there are some basic tips researchers can follow around dots per inch (dpi). Check where you plan to publish. SAGE Publishing (n.d.-b) provides guidelines for manuscript submission, a few of which are listed in the next section.

A Few Artwork Guidelines

Illustrations, pictures, and graphs should be of the highest quality and in an electronic format that helps us publish your article in the best way possible. Please follow the guidelines below to enable us to prepare your artwork for the printed issue as well as the online version.

- *Format:* TIFF (Tag Image File Format), JPEG (Joint Photographic Experts Group): Common format for pictures (containing no text or graphs). EPS (Encapsulated PostScript): Preferred format for graphs and line art (retains quality when enlarging/zooming in). (In addition, it was recommended to me to use PNG [Portable Network Graphics], and, in general, raw, uncompressed formats.)

- *Placement:* Figures/charts and tables created in Microsoft Word should be included in the main text rather than at the end of the document. Figures and other files created outside Word (i.e., in Excel, PowerPoint, JPEG, TIFF, EPS, and PDF [Portable Document Format]) should be submitted separately. Please add a placeholder note in the running text (e.g., "insert Figure 1").

- *Resolution:* Raster-based files (i.e., with .tiff or .jpeg extension) require a resolution of at least 300 dpi. Line art should be supplied with a minimum resolution of 800 dpi.

- *Color:* Please note that images supplied in color will be published in color online and in black-and-white in print (unless otherwise arranged). Therefore, it is important that you supply images that are comprehensible in black-and-white as well (i.e., by using color with a distinctive pattern or dotted lines). The captions should reflect this by not using words indicating color.

- *Dimension:* Check that the artworks supplied match or exceed the dimensions of the journal. Images cannot be scaled up after origination.

Copyright

As others have noted, gaining permission to publish preexisting photos or videos or copyrighted images recorded during the research process can be an issue (Knowles & Sweetman, 2004). If a researcher introduces a photo for participants' reflexive reactions and discussion, does the researcher have the right to publish the photo? See Veronica Richard's discussion (Richard & Lahman, 2015) regarding how difficult it was to track down photographers to gain permission to publish photos from a preexisting photobank she had used, where participants created metaphors of their experiences around the images. In this case, the use of images that are free photo stock or created at a high resolution by the researcher seems the best route to follow.

I was also unprepared for copyright issues when publishing a book (Lahman, 2017a). A participant took a photo of a teenager with their skateboard. The backdrop image was a large popular drink logo. This photo was unusable due to the drink's trademark. The trademark needed to be cropped out or blurred, or a different photo had to be substituted. The advice I received from the publisher's lawyer was that this would not have been an issue if the study had been explicitly about logos. It is evident that this is an area where some prereading and planning are essential.

Dissemination

Space is an issue for visual research dissemination. This is clear when we think about research installations. However, space is also an issue in traditional

FIGURE 9.8 ● Sand Tray Visual With Traditional Research Poster

Note: Photo by Claire Critchlow and Michelle Saltis.

Source: Reproduced with permission from Claire Critchlow and Michelle Saltis.

qualitative thematic articles, where the use of visuals takes up much of the space traditionally utilized for prose; that is, the literature review, methodological explanations, and discussions of the findings are often truncated. Here is where hyperlinks and hypermedia are useful to allow readers to move to spaces with more room for visuals.

Research conferences that have not kept up with the times may still primarily offer posters, round tables, and paper sessions. When this is the case, you may need to get creative. Round tables allow researchers to run photos on a continuous slide show on their computer device while they present. The table also allows for visuals that are three-dimensional pieces of art or artifacts to be presented. If the poster space allows, the researcher can set up a small table where these items may be displayed. (See Figure 9.8 for an image from researchers Claire Critchlow and Michelle Saltis, who brought in a counselor's portable sand table and placed it beside their research poster. They reported that attendees were naturally drawn to the sand and, therefore, to the overall research.) Some researchers connect a computer device to their actual poster to run video clips. (See Text Box 9.2, where Dannon Cox describes the use of videos at poster sessions.) We have seen an increase in virtual research conference possibilities during the COVID-19 pandemic. I believe novel virtual and visual research representations will burgeon in the post-pandemic university, allowing for conservation of natural and monetary resources due to reduction of national and global travel.

Given that the traditional journal article and conference presentation are a heavily overemphasized aspect of academic success, it is crucial for journals and publishing houses to continue to find more ways to support researchers' visual representations. This could occur through more publishing groups allowing longer articles with hyperlinks to videos and images in the online version of the publications.

9.2 VISUALS IN POSTER SESSIONS

DANNON COX

If a photograph is worth a thousand words, how do you equate a three-minute video? Every frame could be considered a single photograph—with 30 or 60 frames for every second, that's a lot of words!

As a videographer and a graduate student, I was determined to use each video frame as both a research tool and a product to disseminate data. I found that qualitative research can best showcase both as an artistic expression while incorporating the academic rigor of a doctoral program. My first experience came from an ethnography class where a classmate (now research partner, Dr. Jessica Kirby) and I adapted Lawrence-Lightfoot's (Lawrence-Lightfoot & Davis, 1997) portraiture method by incorporating videos or *vignettes* to coincide with our final research presentation rather than only writing about it. Our university hosts a research evening at the end of the semester, allowing graduate students to showcase their ongoing or completed work. Usually, graduate students would use an application like Microsoft PowerPoint to design and print a large, single-use poster. But

(Continued)

(Continued)

Jess and I wanted to do something different. We wanted to give a more visual glimpse into our data through edited video shots of our participants spliced with interview audio. The three-minute videos were well worth 180,000 words.

Each vignette highlighted aging women (50+ years) who were still competing in sports. The videos were recorded with a DSLR (digital single-lens reflex) camera and ZOOM H4N external microphone. After conducting the interviews, we asked each participant to provide and talk about an item that represented their sport experience, both past and present. We also recorded their participation in their sport—such as a bodybuilder lifting weights, a dancer hula dancing, or a cyclist speeding downhill. Each participant was given their own video while maintaining production continuity (e.g., camera and frame setup and voiceovers; see "Competing and Aging," n.d., to view the final products).

The night of the presentation, we still printed a poster that contained large photographs of our data collection journey. We kept the words to a minimum and had the photographs tell the story. Next to our poster stood four tripods with an iPad. each playing a separate vignette of a participant. Attendees of the poster presentation were welcome to put on a set of headphones and watch the three-minute presentation. Although the approach seemed innovative (we were the only presenters with videos), the attendees seemed slightly hesitant or uncomfortable to put on headphones and stand watching a video for three minutes. Whereas most of the attendees would walk by and nod their heads in approval, few were willing to stop and watch. In fact, only about five people watched an entire video. Perhaps we were too early in developing a visually rich research presentation. Maybe academia is still finding the confidence to step out of the text-heavy reliance of research. But regardless of the coy nature of the researchers at the poster presentation, our rigor in research and video production presentation that night was well worth 720,000 words.

Source: Reproduced with permission from Dannon Cox.

Image as Sacred: Ethics

Researchers (e.g., Allen, 2012; Knowles & Sweetman, 2004; Lahman, 2017a) have identified ethics in visual research as a site of tension and productive thought. A few groups' (e.g., conservative Mennonites, the Amish, and some indigenous groups) understandings of image could be an area of reflection for visual researchers. For instance, a conservative Mennonite might feel they should not pose for a picture since this can be seen as a graven image (e.g., an idol), and an indigenous person who lives traditionally may feel photos are a piece of the soul. In a contemporary context, we might be dismissive of these kinds of beliefs, but when we consider the vast amounts of time, money, and social media attention that occur around one's personal image, we begin to see strands of what these groups' values reflect. Drawing on my background as a Mennonite, where some of the most conservative groups do not allow their picture to be taken, I am comfortable considering image as sacred but will not push this on readers. By this I simply mean that one's image is a part of who you are and should not be given, taken, or reproduced lightly and without thought. The highly sensitive nature of capturing a research participant's image, the permanent nature of images, the perceived privacy (or lack of privacy) of people's actions, and the ever-changing technology utilized in the capturing and reproduction of visuals (e.g., future technologies) contribute to ethical issues in visual research.

Elsewhere, I have written about this subject, considering both minimal procedural ethics, such as research ethics boards (e.g., IRBs), and higher-level relational ethics (Lahman, 2017a). Regarding procedural research ethics, visual research often calls for longer reviews and examinations of both how consent will be obtained for taking visual images of people and how the images will then be stored. Writing on this issue, Mannay (2020) noted, "Restrictions of publishing in many journals, and ethical issues around revealing participants' identities (Clark, 2013), mean that often researchers need to publish their visual research without the pictures" (p. 3). This becomes an awkward situation when one is describing visuals and the reader is not allowed direct access to actually view them.

Drawing on Caroline Wang and Yanique Redwood-Jones (2001), Quaylan Allen (2012) identifies privacy as an ethical issue—public and private spaces, private spaces in public, pointing out that even when we legally can take a photo that does not mean it is ethical—thus calling us to consider a higher aspirational ethic.

In my experience, another area of privacy and safety that we lack understanding of is secure storage. I was a member or chair of the IRB ethics board at my institution for almost two decades and had a technology expert as a member in recent years. This expert helped us negotiate where visuals could be stored on the internet and how. Researchers repeatedly made assumptions about taking and transferring visuals, and storage and reproduction of visuals on multiple computers for group analysis, that were not carefully considered.

Visual research is a rich site for productive thought about what should be considered prior to, during, and after research. The sacredness, permanence, speed of mass reproduction and sharing, and easy manipulation of images heighten methodological and ethical considerations.

The Gist

In this chapter, I reviewed visual research and extended the challenge for researchers to view these methods more accurately as multisensory or multimodal. While the field of visual research is widely accepted and burgeoning, much remains to be done in the area of representation. Static images inserted into prose articles remain the dominant form. While black-and-white photos can be riveting and may be purposefully utilized, research images are often taken by novices, and color reproduction is rare due to the cost, limiting flexibility in representation outlets. The next few years have huge potential in the area of visual research representation.

Reflexive Questions

These questions (Lahman, 2017a) are designed to help you think more deeply about incorporating visual research into your methodology and thus research representations.

Visual Research

1. What are your experiences with images?
    a. Are images something you have considered in depth?
    b. If not, how would you go about identifying your perspective on images and then trouble these perspectives?
2. What do images convince you of, if anything?
3. How have you used or might you use images in research?
4. When is the use of human images an appropriate choice for researchers?
    a. When might human images not be needed? Just one example in this area is an increase in researchers requesting to video record interviews via the internet.
    b. When should this occur?
    c. When should the internet interview occur but with only sound recording?
5. How can potential money issues in photography research be reduced?
    a. Who supplies the cameras?
    b. Who is responsible for a camera loaned to participants if it is damaged or not returned?
    c. How does photo development occur (e.g., instant, film negatives, digital)?
    d. If photography lessons are involved, how is the cost supported?
6. In some countries, such as the United States, mobile phone cameras are seemingly ubiquitous.
    a. What groups may not have access to this resource?
    b. What potential issues might occur with a researcher taking advantage of these types of cameras?

Ethics

7. When is an image private or public?
8. Who does an image belong to (e.g., creator, person in the image)?

Reflexive Activities

Visual Writing Prompts

At the beginning of a course meeting or in your personal writing journal, choose an image or a short video clip as a prompt to write about. For a list of examples (e.g., a door knob, fish in an aquarium, lemons in a bowl), see Appendix E.

For detail on the following activities, see Appendix C.

Technology Share

Alter this activity to have people specifically share technology that supports the use of visuals, such as editing technology.

Guest Panel

Choose a guest or panel of guests to attend class and speak about how they conduct visual research and represent the visuals in their research products.

Resources

Books

Emmison, M., Smith, P., & Mayall, M. (2012). *Researching the visual* (2nd ed.). Sage. https://doi.org/10.4135/9781473913899

Knowles, J. G., Luciani, T., Cole, A. L., & Neilsen, L. (Eds.). (2007). *The art of visual inquiry.* Backalong Books/Centre for Arts-Informed Research.

Mannay, D. (2015). *Visual, narrative and creative research methods: Application, reflection and ethics.* Routledge. https://doi.org/10.4324/9781315775760

Margolis, E., & Pauwels, L. (Eds.). (2011). *The SAGE handbook of visual research methods.* Sage. https://doi.org/10.4135/9781446268278

Mitchell, C. (2011). *Doing visual research.* Sage.

Pauwels, L., & Mannay, D. (Eds.). (2019). *The SAGE handbook of visual research methods.* Sage. https://doi.org/10.4135/9781526417015

Pink, S. (Ed.). (2012). *Advances in visual methodology.* Sage. https://doi.org/10.4135/9781446250921

Prosser, J., & Loxley, A. (2008). *Introducing visual methods.* ESRC National Centre for Research Methods. http://eprints.ncrm.ac.uk/420/

Rose, G. (2016). *Visual methodologies: An introduction to researching with visual materials.* Sage.

Thomson, P. (Ed.). (2008). *Doing visual research with children and young people* (pp. 164–174). Routledge. https://doi.org/10.4324/9780203870525

Book Chapters

Bach, H. (2007). Composing a visual narrative inquiry. In D. J. Clandinin (Ed.), *Handbook of narrative inquiry: Mapping a methodology* (pp, 280–307). Sage. https://doi.org/10.4135/9781452226552.n11

Butler-Kisber, L. (2018). Visual inquiry. In *Qualitative inquiry* (pp. 114–150). Sage. https://doi.org/10.4135/9781526417978

Articles

Butler-Kisber, L. (2008). Collage as inquiry. In J. G. Knowles & A. L. Cole (Eds.), *Handbook of the arts in qualitative research* (pp.265–276). Sage. https://doi.org/10.4135/9781452226545.n22

Websites

Visual Research Methods: https://blogs.brighton.ac.uk/visuallearning/visual-research-methods/

Reflecting Reflexivity in Research Representations

alertness, appreciation, astuteness, attention, awareness, cognizant,
consciousness, experiential, familiarity, insight, keenness, knowing,
mindfulness, perceiving, recognition, understanding, witting

Ms. Sidney is working busily in her preschool classroom as I awkwardly hail her,
clutching my bag while looking around the room with nervous interest. It is my first
official day at this research site.

"Good morning," she sings out. "It is so good to have you here! I am running late this
morning because Jeff (her fiancé) helped me haul this couch to school! Isn't it great?"

As I admire the love seat–size couch and try to get my bearings, Sidney tells me
that her sister had bought new furniture. Sidney and Jeff hauled her old couch from
over three hours away to add a homey element to the classroom. I listen to Sidney talk
about the new couch, feel her pleasure, and remember mine in finding ways to add soft
pieces to a classroom to create a warm, safe haven for children.

The first child I formally meet, Stephen, comes into the room and perches on the
couch, beaming as Sidney greets him.

"Do you see anything new in the room, Stephen?"

"Yeah," he replies, grinning and pointing at the couch he is sitting on.

Always thinking of possibilities for research, I wonder if Sidney's comfortable
couch could be a metaphor for her classroom. It seemed fortuitous that it had shown
up on the same day I arrived to study caring in the classroom.

In this chapter, I explore *reflexivity*, a core aspect of qualitative research,
writing, and representation. While reflexivity is a vital part of the entire research
process, it is a difficult construct to explain, let alone to represent in research
accounts. Note the synonyms for reflexivity at the beginning of the chapter—
none fully captures *research reflexivity*, which is an aspiration, intent, and process

all at once. The inability to easily explain reflexivity speaks to the power of the construct. Some of the most essential aspects of human experience—such as awe or joy—are the hardest to pin down through language. Yet I make this attempt since to a novice the bromide "You will know it when you see it"—experience it, feel it—can be frustrating and does not inspire confidence. However, it is true that the first time a deep reflexive experience washes over you, you will know it. How then might we represent this experience—reflexivity—in research accounts?

To aid this exploration, in this chapter, I

- briefly review researcher reflexivity literature and its role in enhancing research trustworthiness;

- illustrate how reflexivity has traditionally been addressed in research representations through

  o   the researcher resume stance and

  o   the vulnerable researcher stance;

- insert examples throughout of reflexive writings from my own research areas (e.g., the opening vignette to this chapter);

- present contemporary ideas from the field of qualitative research for representing reflexivity—including mindful reflexivity, deep and dangerous reflexivity—and challenge the field to continue to think beyond current conceptions and dominant ways of representing reflexivity;

- introduce an idea I have been mulling over—raw reflexivity—and illustrate this with the research experiences of Tyler Kincaid (2019); I ask if, by honing our reflexive research accounts into seamless, polished versions, we are unwittingly diminishing the raw, intimate vulnerability of reflexive research experiences; and

- close with reflexive questions, activities, and resources.

What Is Reflexivity?

Reflexivity, spanning 100 years of research literature (Dodgson, 2019), is arguably one of the most important constructs in qualitative research. It is referenced in most methodological texts and increasingly in articles across myriad fields (Pillow, 2010). Yet writers rarely demonstrate how reflexivity occurred in their research, beyond a short statement that the research process was reflexive (Pillow, 2010). Rosanna Hertz (1997) defines reflexivity as

an optimistic, active construct that . . . has been said to be an ongoing conversation about experience while simultaneously living in the moment . . . ubiquitous. It permeates every aspect of the research process, challenging us to be more fully conscious of the ideology, culture, and politics of those we study. (p. viii)

Linda Finlay and Brendon Gough (2003) write,

> The root of the word "reflexive" means to "bend back upon oneself." In research terms, this can be translated as thoughtful, self-aware analysis of the intersubjective dynamics between the researcher and the researched. Reflexivity requires critical self-reflection of how researchers' social background, assumptions, positioning and behavior impact on the research process. (p. ix)

If reflection is seen as occurring *after* an experience, reflexivity occurs *before*, *during*, and *after* an experience, such that it "becomes a continuing mode of self-analysis and political awareness" (Callaway, cited in Hertz, 1997, p. viii).

Ann Cunliffe's article (2016), a rich resource for discussion and development of the role of reflexivity in research, describes researcher reflexivity as being

> about having "a heart," it is not a technique but a way of being in relation with others that brings with it moral and ethical considerations. It requires us to be solicitous and respectful of differences. Being reflexive doesn't give us definitive answers to problems but highlights the need to engage in critical questioning and deeper debate around taken for granted issues that have potential moral and ethical implications. (p. 745)

Additionally, Cunliffe (2016) has described self-reflexivity in research as drawing "attention to interpersonal ethics and our relationships with others" (p. 745), highlighting the need to examine our relationship with participants and "how our presence influences and/or changes people and practices and how their presence influences us—intentionally or otherwise" (Cunliffe & Karunanayake, 2013, cited in Cunliffe, 2016, p. 745). This self-examination "can reveal complexities and richer descriptions" (Cunliffe, 2016, p. 745). Critical reflexivity, a construct also developed by Cunliffe (2016), is described as enabling an examination of the "potentially unintended ethical con-sequences of institutional policies and practices. . . . A critically reflexive researcher questions the assumptions underpinning knowledge claims and how they influence research design, research practice, theory generation, and how we write our research accounts" (p. 745). Here and in Cunliffe's earlier thoughts on self-reflexivity, allowing for a more detailed description, we see hints at how reflexivity may affect research representations.

To engage with issues reflexively, researchers are encouraged to keep a researcher journal where they reflect on happenings in the field (Janesick, 1999). These writings may increase transparency, so that researchers' "work can be understood, not only in terms of *what* we have discovered but *how* we have discovered it" (Etherington, 2007, p. 601). "The process of journaling about reflexivity provides the qualitative researcher a heightened awareness of both differences and similarities between the researcher and the participant. In turn, journaling aids in closing the gap between etic and emic perspectives" (Oliphant & Bennett, 2020, p. 600). Researchers have also extended the traditional prose journal into creative arts reflexivity, such as collage (e.g., Janesick, 2015). See Text Box 10.1 for an example of reflexivity in this area.

10.1   RESEARCHER REFLEXIVE COLLAGE SELF-PORTRAITS

I, Maria Lahman (Figure 10.1), have had the privilege to develop and teach an array of qualitative research courses and content over the past two decades, including case study, narrative, portraiture, educational ethnography, culturally responsive research ethics, critical research, autoethnography, family research, research poetry, introduction to qualitative research, visual methods, virtual methods, and more. In each area, I challenge the course members and myself to represent research in ways that are not linear, may be new for us, or may be new within research.

Collage has been a favorite activity for members of the courses in which I've used it—for both the instructor and the students alike. I believe this is

FIGURE 10.1   ●   Maria Lahman

Source: Lahman, M. K. E., De Oliveira, B., Cox, D., Sebastian, M. L., Cadogan, K., Rundle Kahn, A., . . . & Zakotnik-Gutierrez, J. (2020). Own your walls: Portraiture and researcher reflexive collage self-portraits. *Qualitative Inquiry*, 1077800419897699.

because collage allows people who do not perceive themselves as artists to have creative success. Also, the monetary investment for the instructor is minimal—paper, glue, and items from our daily lives that can easily be collected, such as string, food wrappers, magazines, newspapers, wrapping paper, foil, and cards. As the mom of an avid 10-year-old multimedia artist, my home is overflowing with bits that might someday be used in art. Other research art experiences—such as using clay and paints—can be compelling but might be as intimidating for the instructor as for the students.

For a recent course on case study and portraiture, I had been mulling over how the class might create self-portraits, building on the methodology of portraiture, that would empower all of us, including those who did not feel like artists. As a former preschool and kindergarten teacher, I decided to conduct internet research on how self-portrait creation is taught to children and discovered simple ways to trace one's image. Using photocopied images of each person works well for layered self-portraits (*Dali's Mustache*, Halsman & Dali, 1954/1984). Another option is to have participants use a mirror, heavy plastic overhead projector sheets and permanent markers (Beasley, 2012; Magee Donnelly, 2017). My department had not stocked plastic overhead projector sheets for some time, so you can imagine my surprise at how expensive and hard to find they have become. If you have any at work, I suggest hoarding them!

FIGURE 10.2 ● Portrait-Making Process

Source: Lahman, M. K. E., De Oliveira, B., Cox, D., Sebastian, M. L., Cadogan, K., Rundle Kahn, A., . . . & Zakotnik-Gutierrez, J. (2020). Own your walls: Portraiture and researcher reflexive collage self-portraits. *Qualitative Inquiry*, 1077800419897699.

The steps for creating the portrait I shared with the students are as follows:

- Tape a sheet of plastic to a mirror.

- Stand so your face is reflected in the plastic.

- Trace your face using a black permanent marker.

- Create a collage of items reflective of a self-portrait on a piece of paper that is the same size as the plastic sheet.

- Slide both pieces into a sheet protector (with the plastic on top), or tape them together (Figure 10.2).

It was interesting to note how the students altered and added to the directions to streamline the process and increase creativity. There was a queue at the mirrors, so some students, realizing they could see their reflections in windows, taped the plastic sheets there instead. Other students were perceived as "experts" at sketching images and did several of their classmates' outlines. (This is easier also as the person being depicted does not have to move.) One of the course members, Rowen, an artist, looked at their image in a mirror while they sketched (see Figure 10.3 for portraits of the course members).

(Continued)

(Continued)

FIGURE 10.3 ● Portrait of a Class

Source: Lahman, M. K. E., De Oliveira, B., Cox, D., Sebastian, M. L., Cadogan, K., Rundle Kahn, A., . . . & Zakotnik-Gutierrez, J. (2020). Own your walls: Portraiture and researcher reflexive collage self-portraits. *Qualitative Inquiry*, 1077800419897699.

See Lahman, De Oliveira, Cox et al. (2020) for our reflections about the process.

Source: Lahman, M. K. E., De Oliveira, B., Cox, D., Sebastian, M. L., Cadogan, K., Rundle Kahn, A., . . . & Zakotnik-Gutierrez, J. (2020). Own your walls: Portraiture and researcher reflexive collage self-portraits. *Qualitative Inquiry*, 1077800419897699.

Research reflexivity enhances the quality and *trustworthiness* of the inferences made (see Text Box 10.2 for a discussion of trustworthiness). In this sense, reflexivity is related to "knowledge creation" (Guillemin & Gillam, 2004, p. 275). Here, we see *what* we wish to happen in research as related to reflexivity, but the question remains "*How* best do we convey reflexive experiences in research accounts?"

Traditional Reflexivity Representations

Traditionally, reflexivity has been present and vital throughout the research process but is superficially and inconsistently addressed in final research accounts. Of this, Émilie Crossley (2019) wrote, "Published accounts of personal reflexivity vary enormously from intimate, in-depth explorations of the researcher's subjectivity to more modest disclosure statements, which are usually relegated to what are considered 'safe' spaces in the text such as the methodology section" (p. 207). While this superficiality is partly due to space and time restrictions, we must continue to resist the overall research dogma that calls for research "objectivity." Adherence to objectivity is no doubt the underlying reason why the expansive, vulnerable accounts of introspective researchers are often reserved for separate publications from the ones where researchers feature the findings of a research study. It is not surprising then that the dominant way to represent reflexivity in a research account is through what I call a *researcher resume statement* and a more intimate but still truncated entry I refer to here as a *vulnerable researcher stance.*

Researcher Resume Statement

I have not been able to identify a satisfying term for this reflexive stance, so I will use the phrase "researcher resume statement," since it is the way I describe this type of reflexivity statement to introductory qualitative research course members. In this introductory course, I have students from the education sciences, such as chemistry, who have a non-education-related physical scientist as a member of their dissertation committees. In many of these fields and the related journals, writing vulnerably as a researcher is not an option. These courses also include students from the psychologies (e.g., sport, school, counseling), counseling, special education, leadership, music, higher education, physical education, and more. You can imagine what a great learning environment this is for all. As an instructor, it is vital for me to be adept in teaching a range of qualitative representations, from the traditional to the innovative, in varied fields with different expectations. However, as a qualitative methodologist, it is also my responsibility to teach the field's breadth, including reflexive representation possibilities, to all students, regardless of their disciplinary background.

The researcher resume stance reads like a prose version of an entry on a resume and continues to be the dominant form used. It is crafted to allow readers a surface understanding of the researcher's training as well as professional and applied experiences, all of which inform the context and biases surrounding the study. A researcher might write about personal experiences they have had as a coach, teacher, nurse, parent, or educator, as well as their own education in these areas. This statement is a short entry—no more than a scant paragraph—in a journal article.

Examples of a Researcher Resume Statement

These are two examples of researcher resume statements I have used in my own work. They vary according to the type of project I am working on and the level of detail included.

Example 1. *I first met Annette in a graduate introduction to qualitative research course. Annette went on to take other courses with me, and I became a member of her dissertation committee. Since my research area tends to focus on diversity, I was interested in the research topics she studied with my direction as her research professor. As a white woman with U.S. citizenship, my diversity path has been primarily through that of a religious minority, the Mennonites. Traditionally, Mennonite women do not cut their hair, and they wear a head covering, which, while more symbolic in nature than Saudi women's practice of literally covering their hair, still caused me to be profoundly aware of the curiosity, ignorance, and prejudice to which women who wear traditional religious attire are exposed (Peters & Lahman, 2014).*

Example 2. *I, Maria Lahman, am a Caucasian American who has taught children in private and public schools in the United States for 10 years. I met my co-researcher in our doctoral program in child development when we began teaching at the same preschool (Park & Lahman, 2003).*

Vulnerable Researcher Stance

This vulnerable researcher reflexive statement builds on the resume stance but also explicitly tells readers about the direct, intimate relationship the researcher has with the topic of the research. See Text Box 10.2 for questions to ask yourself during the research process that can aid in deepening this reflexive process. It is important to note that not all research has this aspect of reflexivity. Perhaps the study is part of a large grant the researcher has joined, or the researcher has an intellectual idea they have mulled over from the literature but not experienced personally. In these cases, I am in no way advocating for researchers to manufacture a vulnerability that is not real. Also, this kind of vulnerability is not always welcome in all disciplines. I have known students to write a vulnerable researcher statement and have their faculty advisors ask them to withdraw the personal portion from their work. While the student when becoming a professor or professional researcher will have the freedom to make this judgment, I think we must assume that the faculty know the field the student will be applying to professionally. While discomfort with a vulnerable stance is unfortunate, it is important to understand what is at stake when we share intimately in research writing.

The following is an example from my work of a longer researcher statement than the traditional one paragraph we may often see in articles. Note that it starts out as a resume stance, but in the second paragraph it moves to a vulnerable stance as I explain a novice error I made that deeply embarrassed me. I find, pedagogically and methodologically, that the more we can confess mistakes instead of triumphs (triumphs make for easy, uncomplicated accounts), the more people who interact with our work are able to learn.

Examples of a Vulnerable Researcher Stance: Maria's Story

I first became interested in the issue of working with families from diverse cultures when I took a teaching position in a culturally diverse setting. The diversity was exciting yet also confusing and intimidating at times. As a white woman who had the position of "authority" in the classroom, I wanted to understand the parents' hopes and dreams for their child in order to support their efforts. Initially, I turned to the literature and experts' advice to understand how to relate to the families. When I taught a child from a Pakistani Muslim family, I read a book on understanding Islamic culture, talked to other teachers who had worked with Muslim families, and consulted an expert at the local university on Islamic culture. As a novice professional, I was too nervous to ask the parents any specific cultural questions. Respecting the family's culture and causing no conflict was so important to me that I essentially shut off communication. I received a wake-up call when, in another case, a Hindi-speaking family informed me that, contrary to my assumptions, they didn't follow any religious eating customs. I realized that in my effort to understand the families, I was being racist. By not involving the specific family in my quest for understanding, I was lumping them into a vast culture that may not have represented the whole of who they were.

I began to ask questions and initiate dialogue with the families. When I started to treat each family as individuals, I saw increased communication, interactions, and participation from all members of the families. Three years into my new understanding and attempts to implement this value, I had the opportunity to teach with two South Korean teachers. I learned how much a teacher from another country/culture could assist me in widening my perspective as the teacher "host" in the classroom.

10.2 A SUMMARY OF HARRISON ET AL.'S (2001) TRUSTWORTHINESS AND RECIPROCITY
MARIA LAHMAN

Drawing on feminist ideals of reciprocity and the call for deeper understandings of self/researcher and Other/researched, Jane Harrison et al. (2001) put forward the idea that reflexive attention to reciprocity in research will enhance research trustworthiness. The bullet points given here are reflexive points to consider quoted from the authors. I believe that if we pay attention to questions such as those that follow, we will be attuned to moments in research that when represented in our accounts will allow readers to access our reflexive experiences, thus enhancing reflexivity for all.

(Continued)

(Continued)

- What new questions about trustworthiness arise when qualitative research is viewed through the lens of reciprocity?

- Every stage of the research process relies on negotiating complex social situations.

- Participants are active in this process.

- Through judicious use of self-disclosure, interviews become conversations, and richer data may be possible.

- By asking participants to examine field notes and early analyses, researchers might be able to give back something to their participants and engage in member checks to enhance trustworthiness.

- Reciprocity may also "be employed to build more useful theory"; through collaborative theorizing with participants, it may be possible to "both advance emancipatory theory and empower the researched" (p. 324).

- What relationship(s) do we wish to have with our participants? Why?

- What strategies are we using to establish, maintain, alter, or end a relationship? Why?

- When we claim a collaborative relationship with research participants, who determines it's a collaborative relationship?

- Whose stories are we telling?

- Why have we chosen to tell a particular story, at a particular time, in a particular place?

- When did we give too little—or patronized the participants who talked and listened with us?

Contemporary Reflexivity: Undergirding Representations

Invigorating writing around contemporary conceptions of research reflexivity is occurring. These areas include *feminist reflexivity* (Pillow, 2010), *self-reflexivity* (e.g., Bettez, 2015), *critical reflexivity* (e.g., Hastings, 2010), *queer reflexivity* (McDonald, 2013), and *ethical reflexivity* (Gewirtz & Cribb, 2006). The conversation in these areas has long been fruitful (e.g., Cunliffe, 2016; Hertz, 1997), but as seen in the previous section, when reflexivity filters out from more extended complex discussion to questions of exactly *how* we should represent reflexivity in our writing, resources and models are scant, with little discussion. Therefore, a dominant form, the *truncated researcher stance*, which reads much like a researcher resume statement, remains accepted and often uncontested. This short form is driven by a lack of space in manuscripts and, more problematically, the likelihood that a lingering sense of being judged by objectivists still causes researchers to pull back from examining their own subjectivities within research accounts. In this section, I trace conversations in the literature that researchers may wish to tap into as we begin to create and advocate for richer and deeper reflexive accounts within our research. I also review cutting-edge ideas in reflexivity—*mindful, dangerous, deep*—and advocate for a stance I have come to think of as *raw reflexivity*.

Mindful Reflexivity

Mindful reflexivity draws on the spiritual and religious practices of mindfulness and builds intentionally on researcher reflexivity by calling for deep reflection on our personal biases. Of mindful reflexivity, Michael Baranski & Christopher Was (2019) write,

> Mindfulness . . . is a centuries-old practice intended to stabilize and calm the mind and is the focus of a growing number of empirical studies. It refers to a broad variety of attentional processes, practices, and states with differing features and functions (Lutz et al., 2015; Van Dam et al., 2017). Commonly . . . mindfulness meditation is defined as attending to one's present moment experience in a non-judgmental and non-elaborative way (Chiesa, Calati, & Serretti, 2011; Isbel & Summers, 2017). (p. 188)

Mindful reflexivity is a natural fit for researchers who practice mindfulness in their lives and/or research mindfulness in their work. Mindfulness is discussed and researched in contexts as diverse as higher education classrooms (e.g., Baranski & Was, 2019), music (e.g., Chang et al., 2019), and early-childhood education (e.g., Taylor, 2018).

> By being mindful of the "I" identity or "we" identity cultural value assumptions, we may be able to monitor our snapshot ethnocentric evaluations reflexively. . . . Beyond mindful reflexivity, we also need to be open to novelty or unfamiliar behavior. . . . We also need to develop multiple visions in understanding the stylistic and substantive levels of the communication process. Integrating new ideas or perspectives into one's value system requires mental flexibility. Mental flexibility requires one to rethink assumptions about oneself and the world. (Ting-Toomey, 1999, as quoted in Yorks et al., 2003, p. 110).

In a more recent version of mindful reflexivity, the authors "draw upon the principles and practices of Buddhist mindfulness and Quaker discernment to elaborate how spiritual practice encourages mindful reflexivity to facilitate a process of self-transformation" (Vu & Burton, 2020, p. 208).

While fascinating and full of potential, it remains unclear how mindful reflexivity might be represented in final research accounts. I had the privilege to consult about research conducted by Christy Taylor (2018), who explored a mindful preschool. I believe mindful reflexivity as crafted by Vu and Burton (2019) is seen in Taylor's (2018) final research account, which included sound drawings, research poetry, and photos of children's daily sand tray creations. It would make sense if this sort of reflexivity was explicitly nested within qualitative contemplative research methods (e.g., Janesick, 2016). Still, as of this writing, I am only seeing implicit ties in the literature.

Relatedly, Arthur Bochner (2017) has written about *raising reflexive consciousness*—"a mind-set embodied in the ethical commitments, methodological pluralism, and reflexive self-consciousness to which qualitative researchers . . . adhere" (p. 363). Given Bochner's standing in qualitative research and his being in a position to reflect back over a career that spanned both quantitative and qualitative research, his perspective resounds with me as deeply profound. Bochner created a series of statements that challenge qualitative researchers to an increased level of "reflexive self-consciousness." Each one is well worth our consideration. I directly quote Bochner's ideas about the qualitative mind-set in the following bullet points:

- Where once we saw subjects, now we see participants and co-collaborators.

- Where once we sought to predict and control, now we seek to learn, to talk with, to empower, to transform, and to empathize.

- Where once we were concerned with the accuracy of our descriptions, now we ask how useful they are and what we can do with them.

- Where once we thought research ethics meant debriefing before leaving, now we see ethics as a relational obligation to stay awhile, return, and give something back.

- Where once we conceived of our readers as passive receivers of our knowledge, now we construe them as active co-constructors of meaning.

- Where once we focused on what they can learn about themselves from us, now we also stress what we can learn about ourselves from them.

- Where once we thought the right thing to do was to ensure that we composed texts that were scientific, detached, and valid, now we want to make our research performances artful, urgent, and believable.

- Where once we worried about how we would be judged as scientists (by other scientists), now we concern ourselves with whether our work will be applicable and meaningful and for whom.

- Where once we considered it sufficient to show that our voice as researchers had authority, now we insist that the voices of the people we study be put on an equal plane to our own.

- Where once we thought we were exclusively talking about them, now we sense that we are talking about ourselves as well.

- Where once we elevated ourselves to the position of confident theorists in pursuit of rigorously produced knowledge, now we more humbly understand ourselves as vulnerable storytellers with moral imagination in pursuit of social justice.

- Where once we saw ourselves as apart from, now we see ourselves as part of those people we study.

- Where once we were preoccupied with scientific rigor, now we feel liberated to use our poetic imagination and literary license. (pp. 363–364)

Bochner's (2017) words point out paths to other ways of reflexively enhancing knowing:

> The rigor by which we abide is one that obliges us to turn our lives inside out and upside down to investigate what it means to be alive, as Shields (2013) puts it, "a bare body housed in a mortal cage" (p. 97), dizzied and liberated by a vigorous confrontation with existence. (p. 366)

Source: Bochner, A. P. (2017). Unfurling rigor: On continuity and change in qualitative inquiry. *Qualitative Inquiry*, 1077800417727766.

Dangerous and Deep Reflexivity

Wanda Pillow (2010, p. 270), writing in response to critiques that feminist research may be "dangerous" because it is "too confessional" and therefore "not rigorous" research, developed the idea of *dangerous reflexivity*. This type of reflexivity while seemingly playful is in fact profoundly challenging. Pillow may be saying that while deep self-reflection can lead to personal danger, the *real* danger is in the complacent manner we state, in account after account, that reflexivity has occurred, believing that this somehow validates our research, with no evidence as to *how* reflexivity occurred. Pillow challenges researchers to read and discuss deeply to begin developing an understanding of our own subjectivities and the vast and growing field of qualitative research. While much of Pillow's advice is for novice researchers, the rest of us should heed her words and not stand on what we know now but continue to learn and grow.

Recently, Crossley (2019), building on Pillow's (2010) work, developed the idea of *deep reflexivity*. She did so to extend conversations and assumptions around self-reflexivity.

The current climate is . . . conducive to challenging conventional approaches to reflexivity in the pursuit of disrupting and advancing methodological practice. . . . I introduce the notion of "deep reflexivity," a radical approach to positional and intersectional reflexivity developed through psychosocial research, which implies that reflexive practice should be extended to include critical reflections on the researcher's emotions, embodiment and unconscious processes that may impact on research. (Crossley, 2019, p. 206)

Crossley (2019) identified three levels of reflexivity in the field of tourism research, which apply broadly to qualitative research in all areas:

1. *Reflexive disclosure statements* (which I termed *researcher resume statements*)

2. *Ongoing conscious reflexive practice* woven through the entirety of the text

3. *Deep reflexivity*, which builds on the previous level through the inclusion of the researcher's embodied, emotional, and unconscious meanings.

Crossley draws on Pillow's (2010) work to highlight the idea that as reflexivity has become standard in qualitative research, qualitative researchers may have also become complacent. Does the resume reflexivity statement reflect an active commitment to the reflexive process? We are in danger of becoming "complicit in reproducing the social structures and power relations that many researchers seek to challenge" (Crossley, 2019, p. 209). Crossley (2019) extends Pillow's (2010) exhortation for researchers to embrace a reflexivity of discomfort and points out that what she terms *deep reflexivity* may be uncomfortable and difficult for the researcher to confront in themselves. I have combined Pillow's and Crossley's (2019) work here since I see considerable overlap in the ideas of dangerous and deep reflexivity. I close with a quote from Pillow (2010) that exemplifies this overlap:

The discomfort of the unfamiliar may to some seem too dangerous, unruly and not rigorous enough. . . . Reading, re-reading, writing, rewriting, sharing, and discussing our work; diligently keeping and reviewing field notes and a researcher journal, and giving time and more time to reflexivity can work to counter comfortable research practices of reflexivity and interrupt too easy and neat usages of reflexivity. This work will be rigorous, responsible and dangerous. (p. 280)

Raw Reflexivity

exposed, helpless, naked, open, powerless, pregnable, raw, unarmed, unguarded, vulnerable

Inspired by a research study I was privileged to supervise, I began to consider the idea of what I came to term *raw reflexivity*. Kincaid's (2019) research included in-depth interviews with members of a homeless shelter and observations conducted during a National Point-in-Time homeless survey. His research was the culmination of personal experiences as a youth who had been homeless, research he conducted with homeless individuals, and deep engagement with scholarship in research ethics with respect to the homeless (see Text Box 10.3).

During the writing stage of his study, I was struck yet again by what I came to think of as the rawness of Kincaid's (2019) reflexive entries. I wondered out loud about the powerful level of intimacy, vulnerability, and even confusion he allowed into his reflections, which were portrayed in the final research representation. Listen as Kincaid considers the Point-in-Time survey.

Reflection From Researcher

> I can't believe that I feel like a failure for not finding homeless people. . . . There was a weird sense of competition . . . like "Did you find anyone"? . . . "I found 3 homeless people!"—feelings of jealousy and anger . . . so weird. This other person, this other volunteer, this other researcher, somehow beat me at this? They win because they found more people who are suffering? (Kincaid, 2019, p. 65)

As we spoke about his journaling process, Kincaid (2019) mentioned that the field reflections were all recorded by dictating into a voice-to-text application in his smartphone. This meant that his researcher reflexivity notes were transcriptions, just as participant interviews are. This gives the researcher reflexivity entries a clear sense of immediacy—you are listening to Kincaid talk to himself because, indeed, he is doing so. There is something about this rawness that increases vulnerability as compared with written reflexive journal entries, where we can hide our vulnerability behind the academic ease of writing.

This is a process Kincaid (2019) had first developed when researching punk rock bands. Kincaid's research venues and participants are not conducive to computer use. The settings call for extensive driving, walking, and just hanging out, so dictating into a smartphone app was ideal. What I came to see, based on the hundreds of written researcher journal and reflexive entries I have read or written, is that Kincaid's researcher journal entries had a deep sense of rawness because they were his *spoken thoughts* at the time in the field. These entries were not written, thoughtful prose composed at a later time and crafted with consideration of audience and writing style. Trying to think of how this might apply to my own work, it reminded me most of an autoethnography based on my outpourings of grief into a word-processed journal at the time of my pregnancy loss (Lahman, 2009). I never thought of using the writings professionally since they were so personal. I can picture how intimate and vulnerable the entries would have been if orally dictated rather than frantically typed.

This brings about consideration of how the voices of research participants are handled in research representations compared with how our own researcher voices are handled. The convention is to record participants' voices and use direct quotes to convey their experience. Let's challenge ourselves to do the same with our raw reflexive moments—audio record or dictate—these moments of revelation, confusion, and relational connection to the larger picture of humanity that is the context of our research. I am not trying to undermine the forays we make into reflexive writing in our work but to challenge us to continue to identify the moments of *raw reflexivity* we experience and to recount them in our research. I have pushed—required—many a novice researcher to write in the first person, develop a paragraph about who they are as related to their research, and place themselves beside the participants to the extent possible in a conventional research article. While this is a great starting place, it has too often become the stopping place. We can and must do better.

10.3 "HOW IN THE HELL DOES THIS ANSWER MY RESEARCH QUESTION!?": REPRESENTING RESEARCHER RAW REFLEXIVITY IN WRITING

TYLER KINCAID

As part of an in-depth qualitative exploration of the role of sampling (Kincaid, 2019) with hard-to-reach or hidden groups, I interviewed members of a shelter for the homeless and participated in a federal count of homeless individuals. Due to limited space, I only highlight a few brief examples here. I wrote,

> Reflexivity was integral to this research in two distinct ways: first, as a process of trustworthiness and triangulation of the findings, and second, as a data analysis tool to help examine the methodological process of the reflexivity in research. In this research, reflexivity findings were overlaid and recorded during the data analysis. A careful reflection of the researcher's role in the study provides an opportunity for the researcher to cross-reference their findings. It also offers potential readers an opportunity to consider the findings within the opinions, thoughts, feelings, and social-cultural interactions of the researcher. During the research, a self-reflexive examination of my history as a homeless teenager, my work as a homeless advocate, and as a graduate student researching homeless populations were employed.

Reflection:

The first time Texas (person experiencing homelessness) started crying in our interview, my very first interview, I was like "What the hell is happening"?! I'm not ready for this. We're supposed to be talking about sampling considerations and best practices to consider their role in the outcome of research. . . . What is this all of a sudden?

I'm sitting in a strange office inside of a homeless shelter I just walked into for the first time a couple of hours ago, and now Texas is in full-blown crying mode about how they became homeless!

I didn't even ask that question!

We were talking about pseudonyms two seconds ago. How am I supposed to handle this now?

Are there tissues in this office?

Should I say something?

Should I ignore it?

Should I respond with something generic like "I'm sorry you're crying, here's a Kleenex"?!

How in the hell is this going to help me? . . . Already, I've separated myself from the crying person in front of me. . . .

How in the hell does this answer my research question!?

Ok, never mind, just shut up and listen. . . .

Reflection From Researcher: A Flashback

I hated panhandling. I hated it so much. I know that I'll sit here all day, and yeah, I'm kind of having fun with these kids. I mean, it's San Francisco, this is insane! But I'm not like them, they're not like me. We're going to make some money today, but what am I going to get? I'm still going to be eating leftovers out of the trash can. They're buying dope. All our money and it's gone. Why am I even here? I'm not fucked up like these guys . . . am I? I'm here. . . . I'm stuck here, but I'm here. I'm just the same.

Reflection From Researcher

"Hey! Check it out. . . . I found one, let's go." We had all but given up on finding anyone to survey that day. Three hours walking through the woods, up and down the bike trail by the river, and nothing. But there he was—an old man, limping, disheveled, covered in years of dirt—but he's pushing a bike, with two flat tires, that has a makeshift shopping cart trailer hitched to the back. He's our guy. We did it. Let's pull over, and . . . I don't know. Should we park down the street . . .

(Continued)

(Continued)

```
should we pull over right here . . . do we follow him?
. . . I'm kind of a big guy, over 6 feet tall and big
frame. . . . This feels weird, really weird. Let's park
a couple of blocks away, calmly walk down the street,
and say Hi. This still feels wrong, like we're hunting
this guy. Those tires are flat. Let's go ask him if he
needs a hand.

Let's start there.
```

Source: Reproduced with permission from Tyler Kincaid.

The Gist

As we have seen, "Being reflexive is about having a heart" (Cunliffe, 2016, p. 745). Reflexivity is a fascinating area of qualitative research that, when permeating the entire process, enriches research by heightening our awareness of the experience. Yet only hints of how reflexivity might best be represented in research accounts are found in the literature (Cunliffe, 2016). Therefore, I sought to review the *researcher resume stance* and the *vulnerable researcher stance* as two dominant short forms of representation. I reviewed mindful, deep, dangerous reflexivity from the literature, with suggestions for how researchers might advocate for it. I ended by advocating for and giving examples of *raw reflexivity*, where our research experience and the voice we use to present it are as ragged and seamless as the participants' research accounts we record. The process of representing reflexivity in research accounts has much room for development, and I look forward to reading future ideas. The position of this chapter, the last in the book, was deliberate, since all strands of qualitative research writing come together through reflexive accounts.

Reflexive Questions

Researcher Self-Reflexivity

- What do you know about the idea of reflexivity in qualitative research?

- How can you learn more, read, and discuss at a deeper level?

- What is your reflexivity plan for the research process (e.g., researcher journal, oral dictation, peer processing)?

- Considering the many types of reflexivity referenced or detailed in this chapter, which appeal to you most and why?

- What might you add to the literature on reflexivity? For instance, how might you use images or art in researcher reflexivity?

Considering the Research Participants

(Questions From Lahman, 2017)

- What are the participants' social and cultural identities?

- How do the participants' social and cultural identities inform their unique communication and/or relationship characteristics that are important for me to acknowledge within this research?

- What are the naturally occurring environments the participants already share?

- How can I create and/or join a context that feels comfortable and affirming to the participants?

- How do I best acknowledge my own social and cultural identities and minimize the distance between myself and the participants?

- How do I best elicit the rich information these participants can share about their storied lives, which in turn will make the research story very rich and representative of their experience?

- It has been posited that by first knowing our own identities, we may know others better. Why might this be?

Final Representation

(Questions Adapted From Ellis, 2000; Richardson, 2000a, 2000b, in Piercy & Benson, 2005)

- Does the representation have aesthetic merit?

- Has the researcher made it clear how they sought to understand the standards of the genre they are working in?
  - Relatedly, does the representation meet some of the expectations in the area of the representation (e.g., art, writing, or drama)?

- Is the representation convincing?

- Is the representation culturally responsive to and respectful of those studied?

- Does the audience become more sensitive to the participants?

- Is the work contextually situated?

- Did the researcher locate self in the representation?

- Is the researcher transparent in the representation?

- Does the work support reflexivity and co-construction on the part of the audience?

Reflexive Activities

The following reflexive activities are written up in detail in Appendix C. Some additional activities follow:

How Do We Write?

Personal Writing: A Reflexivity Experience

What's in Your Writing Space?

Doodle It

Image Writing

Reflexive Self-Portrait Collage

Read Text Box 10.1 of this chapter. Consider how you want to create your image. Be sure to trace the major lines of your face in a dark color so it can still be seen when you create the collage. Assemble collage items reflecting who you are. This assembling should be done over the course of a few weeks. Layer these items onto one side of the image using a clear-drying glue. As you work, check to see how your image alters when you add different items. Consider captioning your image. When your image is completed, write a journal entry about the experience, considering how the collage reflects you as a researcher.

Possible collage items: wrapping paper, magazine/newspaper words and images, food wrappers, candy wrappers, yarn, string, twine, ribbon, art papers, and so on.

Researcher Journal

1. Read Janesick's (1999, 2015) work in this area. Consider how you prefer to journal—with a notebook, on an application, on a computer or other electronic device, by voice dictation, or using multidimensional books where you can add clippings, drawings, and so on, almost like a scrapbook.

2. *Comparing reflexive researcher entries*

   a. Experiment with different ways of creating reflexive entries about research. For example, you could identify one experience you wish to consider in depth and create any of the following (and more):

      i. Dictated voice-to-text memo

      ii. Research journal entry

      iii. Sketch, doodle, or drawing

      iv. Collage (see Text Box 9.1 in Chapter 9)

      v. Reflexive self-portrait collage (see preceeding activity)

   b. Consider the richness and questions your creations generate for further exploration.

Resources

Books

Finlay, L., & Gough, B. (Eds.). (2003). *Reflexivity: A practical guide for researchers in health and social sciences*. Blackwell. https://doi.org/10.1002/9780470776094

Hertz, R. (1997). *Reflexivity and voice*. Sage.

Book Chapters

Arvay, M. J. (2003). Doing reflexivity: A collaborative narrative approach. In L. Finlay & B. Gough (Eds.), *Reflexivity: A practical guide for researchers in health and social sciences* (pp. 163–175). Blackwell.

Mruck, K., & Mey, G. (2007). Grounded theory and reflexivity. In A. Bryant & K. Charmaz (Eds.), *The SAGE handbook of grounded theory* (pp. 515–538). Sage.

• Epilogue •

I'm crouched under a favorite tree in my yard—a catalpa—massive green leaves, punctuated with heady scented white flowers, which develop into an improbable two-foot bean. Impatient at not finding gardening gloves at first glance, I have shoved my hands deep into the fertile earth, working around spent early-spring bulbs. I peer up from time to time at the still skeletal branches. The scarred bark causes me to wonder if the catalpa has become too damaged from hail. As I weed, my mind drifts to Mom's death; she loved trees many see as messy—mulberry, mimosa, and bean trees. With each pull and tug at the weeds, a poem starts to add to the rhythm. My deep pain takes on words that sprout, bud, and then flower in the fertile ground. I stumble toward my home, brushing dirt from my hands and knees, needing to record the poetry pulsing in my mind.

I have been able to create a safe space in my life and work for qualitative research, methodology, poetry, and autoethnography. It is a space of *becoming*, an *ish* space with room for *good enough* work, which at times when revisited seems solidly good. I know this safe space is not available for everyone and grieve for the loss of diverse perspectives and ways of knowing. Through this book, I offer both an invitation and a wish. An invitation to create an ish space—where you can create good enough research accounts that, while you are ever becoming, grow better—and a wish for you to publish and persevere.

• Appendix A •

A Sample Syllabus From a Graduate-Level Qualitative Research Writing Course

Course Syllabus

SRM 688 Writing as Analysis of Qualitative Research

Instructor: Maria Lahman

Credits: Three

Course Description

This course is an in-depth study of the role writing plays in qualitative research data collection, analysis, and representation. Students will use data in a variety of writing activities.

Objectives

Through reading others' writing, peer critiquing, reviewing the literature, writing, reflecting, exploring a variety of published research, and actively inquiring into the process of writing qualitative research, the students will

- understand and evaluate the writing of others;

- be exposed to an array of possible ways of representing qualitative data, such as a research article, poetry, multimedia, narratives, and so on;

- understand the connection between reading, writing, data collection, and analysis in relation to the emergent nature of qualitative research;

- represent and "write up" original research with some assistance;

- participate in writing support groups and critique peers' work; and

- experience and understand the importance of representing themselves as a researcher in qualitative research writing.

Course Requirements

- Attend all classes unless an excuse for leave of absence for professional reasons or illness is given in advance.

- Complete and turn in all assignments on time.

- Complete all readings.

- Participate in class activities.

Assignments

1. Writers' group

    Students will be part of a writers' group that will meet in class to critique one another's work in a supportive and encouraging fashion. Students will have the opportunity to give the instructor feedback regarding the group process. One data set will be used to develop three different representations of the data. The following are all components of the writers' group assignments that need to be given to the instructor at the end of the semester in a *three-ring binder* or *electronically* in an easily readable fashion—not a massive MS Word document (e.g., a portfolio, LiveBinders).

    a. A one-page explanation of the three representation projects you created. Present these representations to your writers' group and instructor for critique. Revise accordingly. Turn in the final draft of what you agreed on with the instructor.

    b. Choose a journal you will write a traditional qualitative article for, and obtain the author guidelines and evaluation criteria.

    c. As a group, develop criteria for evaluating members' work.

    d. Apply to be a reviewer for a journal, supply evidence that you already are a reviewer, or review with a professor.

    e. Read your group members' representations, and provide a critique in a professional and supportive manner. Include all the critiques you do for others in your binder. Conduct critiques using the Word or Google Track Changes and Comment functions. Copy the instructor on emails that are submissions of your work to your group for critique.

    f. Turn in all three representations.

    g. Revise one of the representations according to the critiques, and post on Canvas for the instructor as a Word document.

    Possible representations of the data set include, but are not limited to, a traditional qualitative journal article, a model, a research poster, autoethnography, research poetry, a narrative essay, a fictionalized article, readers' theater, a play, a multimedia display, a website, music, brochures, and artwork. One of the representations you choose *must be* a traditional qualitative article.

2. Book talk

Read the book you choose from the textbook choice section, and come to class on the book chat evening prepared to discuss the book. Develop a 45-minute presentation of the book with your group. The presentation should emphasize how the book was written and how it represents the data. Use the following questions for reflection:

- What type of research does this book describe?
- How does the author use existing texts and interviews to support the findings?
- How could you use this book's method to conduct research?
- What writing techniques were used in this representation?
- How could you use these techniques?
- Consider the social, cultural, and historical implications of the book. Did it convince you? If so, of what? If not, how could it have done so?

3. Participation, attendance, readings, and in-class assignments

Participation is defined as speaking for an appropriate amount of time during class discussions, attending class prepared, completing all the readings, and doing in-class and out-of-class assignments. For each reading, bring a written comment and question to class for discussion.

Assignment of Grades

All assignments are part of the class experience and therefore cannot be submitted late. Extreme situations should be discussed with the instructor in advance, and in these exceptional cases, assignments may be handed in late. Otherwise, all late assignments will be reduced to a B before grading begins and will receive minimal written feedback. Grades are assigned as follows:

A	94% and above	A–	90% to 93%
B+	86% to 89%	B	83% to 85%
B–	80% to 82%	C+	76% to 79%
C	70% to 75%	C–	69%
20%	Book presentation		
60%	Final notebook, final representation		
20%	Participation, attendance, submitting representations to your group at the time agreed on, readings, homework, writers' group, and in-class assignments		

Readings

The texts in this section are required reading for students in all of the qualitative courses as a basic shared reference point.

Program Texts

Crotty, M. (1998). *The foundations of social research. Meaning and perspective in the research process.* Sage.

Merriam, S. B., & Tisdell, E. J. (2016). *Qualitative research: A guide to design and implementation.* Jossey-Bass.

Course Texts

Lahman, M. K. E. (2021). *Writing and representing qualitative research.* Sage.

Wolf, M. (1992). *A thrice-told tale: Feminism, postmodernism, and ethnographic responsibility.* Stanford University Press. https://doi.org/10.1515/9780804788243

Choose One to Read

Angrosino, M. (1998). *Opportunity house: Ethnographic stories of mental retardation.* Alta Mira.

Lather, P., & Smithies, C. (1997). *Troubling the angels: Women living with HIV/AIDS.* Westview Press.

Liebow, E. (1993). *Tell them who I am: The lives of homeless women.* Free Press.

Recommended Texts

American Psychological Association. (2020). *Publication manual of the American Psychological Association* (7th ed.).

Lamott, A. (1994). *Bird by bird: Some instructions on writing and life.* Anchor Books.

Rankin, E. (2001). *The work of writing: Insights and strategies for academics and professionals.* Jossey-Bass.

Schwandt, T. J. (2001). *Dictionary of qualitative inquiry* (2nd ed.). Sage.

Wolcott, H. (2008). *Writing up qualitative research* (3rd ed.). Sage. https://doi.org/10.4135/9781452234878 (This text was used in past courses)

Articles for Course Readings

Banks, S. P. (2000). Five holiday letters: A fiction. *Qualitative Inquiry, 6*(3), 392–405. https://doi.org/10.1177/107780040000600307

Bowen, G. A. (2010). From qualitative dissertation to quality articles: Seven lessons learned. *Qualitative Report, 15*(4), 864–879.

Caulley, D. N. (2008). Making qualitative research reports less boring: The techniques of writing creative nonfiction. *Qualitative Inquiry, 14*(3), 424–449. https://doi.org/10.1177/1077800407311961

Colyar, J. (2009). Becoming writing, becoming writers. *Qualitative Inquiry, 15*(2), 421–436. https://doi.org/10.1177/1077800408318280

Council of Graduate Schools. (2016). Imagining the dissertation's many futures. *Grad Edge, 5*(3), 1–5.

Ellis, C. (2000). Creating criteria: An ethnographic short story. *Qualitative Inquiry, 6*(2), 273–277. https://doi.org/10.1177/107780040000600210

Eisner, E. W. (1997). The promise and perils of alternative forms of data representation. *Educational Researcher, 26*(6), 4–10. https://doi.org/10.3102/00131 89X026006004

Grant, M. J., Munro, W., McIsaac, J., & Hill, S. (2010). Cross-disciplinary writers' group stimulates fresh approaches to scholarly communication: A reflective case study within a higher education institution in the north west of England. *New Review of Academic Librarianship, 16*(S1), 44–64. https://doi.org/10.1080/13614533 .2010.509481

Lewis, P. J. (2011). Storytelling as research/research as storytelling. *Qualitative Inquiry, 17*(6), 505–510. https://doi.org/10.1177/1077800411409883

Mitchell, G. J., Dupuis, S., Jonas-Simpson, C., Whyte, C., Carson, J., & Gillis, J. (2011). The experience of engaging with research-based drama: Evaluation and explication of synergy and transformation. *Qualitative Inquiry, 17*(4), 379–392. https://doi.org/10.1177/1077800411401200

Richardson, L. (1993). Poetics, dramatics, and transgressive validity: The case of the skipped line. *The Sociological Quarterly, 34*(4), 695–710. https://doi.org/10.1111/ j.1533-8525.1993.tb00113.x

Tracy, S. J. (2010). Qualitative quality: Eight "big-tent" criteria for excellent qualitative research. *Qualitative Inquiry, 16*(10), 837–851. https://doi.org/10.1177/1077800410 383121

Zeller, N., & Farmer, F. M. (1999). "Catchy, clever titles are not acceptable": Style, APA, and qualitative reporting. *International Journal of Qualitative Studies in Education, 12*(1), 3–19. https://doi.org/10.1080/095183999236303

Course Calendar (subject to change)

Date	Theme	Readings	Assignment due
Mon. Aug. 21	Introduction to Writing Qualitative Research	Text: Chapter 1, Lahman Article: "Becoming Writers"	Three representations plan due in Canvas on Fri. Aug. 25 at 5 p.m. Include what data set (topic, size) you are working with.
Aug. 28	Writers' Groups Writing Criteria	Articles: "Creating Criteria: An Ethnographic Short Story," "Qualitative Quality," "Cross Disciplinary Writers' Group" Text: *A Thrice-Told Tale*, Chapters 1–3, Wolf; Chapter 2, Lahman	Organizational meeting with writers' group
Sep. 4	No class, Labor Day		
Sep. 11	Writing Basics	Text: *A Thrice-Told Tale*, Chapters 4, 5, Wolf; Chapter 3, Lahman Articles: "The Promise and Perils of Alternative Forms," "Making Qualitative Research Reports Less Boring"	Meet for critique in writers' groups for the first time.
Sep. 18	Writing and Publishing Articles 1	Text: Chapter 5, Lahman	1st rep., Sep. 18 end of day on Canvas
Sep. 25	Writing and Publishing Articles 2	Article: "Catchy Clever Titles Are Not Acceptable"	
Oct. 2	Dissertations	Text: Chapter 4, Lahman Articles: "Qualitative Dissertation to Article . . . ," "Imagining the Dissertation's Many Futures"	
Oct. 9	Textbooks	Instructor's textbook prospectus Internet resources	

Date	Theme	Readings	Assignment due
Oct. 16	Alternative Forms: Poetics	Text: Chapter 8, Lahman Articles: "Poetics, Dramatics, and Transgressive Validity: The Case of the Skipped Line"	2nd rep., end of day on Canvas
Oct. 23	Autoethnography, Performance, and Other Forms	Text: Chapter 7, Lahman Articles: "The Experience of Engaging With Research Based Drama," "Storytelling as Research," "Five Holiday Letters"	
Oct. 30	Choice Book Chats		Meet in small groups with the instructor at a coffee house.
Nov. 6	Book Presentations		Book talks
Nov. 13	Book Presentations: Reliability of Alternative Forms of Representation		Book talks 3rd rep., end of day on Canvas
Nov. 20	Visuals	Text: Chapter 9, Lahman	In class, organize for research evening.
Nov. 27	Publishing/ Marketing Reflexivity in Research Accounts	Text: Chapters 6 & 10, Lahman	Writer binder due in class or virtual Rewrite of traditional qualitative article on Canvas
Wed., Dec. 6 5:00–7:00 (required) Research Evening 7:00–7:30 (not required) Awards	Attendance this evening is required in lieu of an exam unless you make arrangements with the instructor due to exam conflicts.	Our class will present posters or virtual slide shows on writing/ representation topics.	

• Appendix B •

An Example of a Doctoral Student Representing the Same Data Set in Three Different Ways

Erin Patchett, at the time a doctoral student in sport administration, represented the observational and interview data she collected on the topic of the experiences of campus recreation student employees with diversity and inclusion training. The representations were (a) a manuscript with a thematic analysis—a case study, (b) a research poster, and (c) black out poetry.

The following is an excerpt from Erin's course manuscript.

"Eye Opening": Exploring the Experiences of Campus Recreation Student Employees Participating in Diversity and Inclusion Training

Erin M. Patchett

Abstract

To welcome shifting demographics in the United States higher education system, many institutions are attempting to be more intentional in the creation of supportive campus environments for students with marginalized identities. Programs, facilities, policies, and training have all been explored as instruments for inclusion. Through an instrumental case study, the author explored the staff training component of creating a welcoming campus. The research questions included (a) how do campus recreation student employees who attend diversity and inclusion training make meaning of their experience and (b) what aspects of diversity and inclusion training inform understanding of diversity and inclusion? The themes included personal growth, engaged and ongoing learning methods, and creating a welcoming recreation environment.

Keywords: case study, campus recreation, inclusivity, staff training, student employees

As the demographics of the United States shift and become even more diverse, so do the demographics of U.S. college students (Snyder & Dillow, 2015). To welcome and celebrate this diversity, institutions of higher education are focusing efforts toward making their campuses inclusive to all students, especially those holding marginalized identities. Programs, facilities, policies, and staff training have all been explored as tools to foster inclusion (Butcher, Taylor, & Wallace, 2012; King, 2012; Patchett & Foster, 2015). Despite recent calls for research to back current diversity and inclusion efforts within campus recreation (e.g., Kaltenbaugh, Parsons, Brubaker, Bonadio, & Locust, 2017), seemingly little research has been performed on the impact diversity and inclusion trainings have on campus recreation employees. A deeper understanding of student employees' experiences with diversity and inclusion trainings may provide guidance to campus recreation practitioners and administrators working to provide more meaningful and affirming environments for participants of all identities.

Through this instrumental case study (Stake, 1995), I explored the experiences of students employed by a campus recreation department who participated in diversity and inclusion training. Bell (2016) identified *diversity* to be "differences among social groups such as ethnic heritage, class, age, gender, sexuality, ability, region, or nationality" (p. 1). Miller (1998) described *inclusion* to be the full participation and contribution of all individuals in a group. Given these definitions, for the purpose of this study I identified *diversity and inclusion training* to be any professional development which included concepts related to social identities and/or how to create opportunities for historically marginalized groups to participate in recreation. The research questions included (a) how do campus recreation student employees who attend diversity and inclusion training make meaning of their experience and (b) what aspects of diversity and inclusion training inform understanding of diversity and inclusion?

Theoretical Perspective

A paradigm offers "a way to think about our world and how to gain and interpret knowledge about it" (Guido, Chávez, & Lincoln, 2010, p. 3), and the use of an explicitly stated paradigm can provide readers with additional information to understand and appraise research. In this study, I utilized a constructivist paradigm (Creswell, 2013; Crotty, 1998). Given my research goal was to understand "the world in which they [study participants] live and work" (Creswell, 2013, p. 24), the research setting was central in my study. While some researchers have examined social justice training for college students (e.g., Evans, Reason, & Broido, 2001; King, 2012), seemingly there has been no investigation of how student employees in campus recreation make meaning of those types of trainings. Additionally, in my role as an administrator in campus recreation, this type of training has been a priority for me as a supervisor of staff members. This belief has shaped my interest in this topic, and I bring this value and priority into the research (Guido et al., 2010).

Consistent with the constructivist paradigm, the co-construction of knowledge performed by the participants and researcher can help shape progression in how social justice messages are delivered in a campus recreation student employment setting (Plano, Clark, & Creswell, 2008). My role as both a researcher and a campus recreation practitioner is reciprocal, and the constructivist paradigm suits both of these roles.

(Due to limited space, the literature review was removed.)

Methodology

This instrumental case study (Stake, 1995) was conducted following a constructivist paradigm (Creswell, 2013). An instrumental case study design was chosen in order to allow for in-depth understanding of a topic that has little prior research specific to the campus recreation setting (Creswell, 2013). The constructivist worldview is appropriate given the goal of "understanding the world in which they [study participants] live and work" and specifically how the participants make meaning of the diversity and inclusion trainings they attend (Creswell, 2013, p. 24). A transformative paradigm tangentially directed aspects of this study given the action-oriented goal of better understanding how employees are shaped by diversity and inclusion trainings and then applying this knowledge to better prepare individuals to understand and change the role they play in systemic oppression (Creswell, 2013). The study was approved by the Institutional Review Board.

Data Collection

This study was conducted using one case: a campus recreation department at a large, four-year, predominantly white, research one institution of higher education in the Western U.S. In line with case study methodology, data were collected from a variety of sources including interviews, observation, and artifact review (Stake, 1995). Purposeful sampling was used to obtain participants for the interview portion of the study (Creswell, 2013). Criteria used to sample participants included being a student, being employed by the campus recreation department, and being in attendance at the training observed as part of this study. Participants were intentionally recruited to have representation among staff new to the organization (under six months of employment) and among those more experienced within the organization (over one year of employment).

The study had two participants, Sam and Jordan. Each participant was interviewed before a diversity and inclusion training and approximately one week after the training for a total of four in-person interviews, two per participant. The digitally recorded interviews were semi-structured to allow for topics of interest to be explored while also permitting additional topics to emerge. At the beginning of the first interview for both participants, they were given a handout to share their social identities. Sam shared the identities of Hispanic, female, 21 years old, English as first language, and Christian. She was a senior and had worked 2.5 years in the recreation center. Jordan shared the identities of white, upper middle class, male, heterosexual, 20 years old, English as first language, physically able, and Catholic. Jordan was a junior and had worked at the recreation center for two months.

In addition to the interviews, I observed a mandatory, 60-minute staff training for the facility operations student staff, which was held at the recreation center during the middle of a fall semester. The training topics included content on the definition of diversity and how to show respect for others. The training also included an activity asking staff to share the backstory on their given names and two different activities for raising awareness and self-reflection around the social identities they may take for granted, of self and others. One awareness activity involved the use of M&M candy pieces, where each color of candy represented a different race or ethnicity. Employees were given prompts regarding what was the race or ethnicity of their co-workers at the recreation center as well as their friends, family, professors, etc. At the end of the prompts, they reflected about what color of candy was most represented on their plate. The second activity was similar but used a chart, instead of candy, as the means for documenting social identities. The second activity also went beyond race or ethnicity to include gender, sexuality, ability, and religion. Observations were recorded via detailed field notes taken by the researcher in order to document the training environment. Finally, the full-time supervisor of the participating staff provided access to documents utilized for new employee training as well as the department's policies, handbooks, and marketing materials. Artifact review was performed on all of the documents in order to better understand the organization employing the study participants.

Data Analysis

Following transcription and member checking of the recorded interviews, open coding followed by axial coding was performed in NVivo to uncover and distill themes (Creswell, 2013). The triangulation of multiple sources of data, such as observations, interviews, and artifact review, was used to confirm themes and enhance the study's credibility (Merriam & Tisdell, 2015). The researcher's familiarity with the campus recreation field assisted with making "decisions about what is salient to the study" (Creswell, 2013, p. 251).

Findings

During the interviews, the participants discussed their experiences with diversity and inclusivity trainings, which aspects of the trainings they were most impacted by, and their perceptions of the role of campus recreation within diversity and inclusion efforts. From these interviews, an initial list of 17 codes were created. From those codes, seven subthemes emerged and were grouped into three overarching themes. The three themes were personal growth, engaged and ongoing learning methods, and creating a welcoming environment.

The first theme of *personal growth* included the subthemes of raised awareness, empathy, and applying learning beyond the recreation center. The participants shared how the observed training as well as prior trainings or conversations had resulted in increased awareness of the social identities of their family, friends, and peers. Participants also articulated more empathy in how they viewed many participants within the recreation center. Finally, the students indicated the learning they had experienced at the recreation center around issues of diversity and inclusion had impacted them beyond their job, such as in academic and personal spaces. Participant quotes for this theme are presented in Table B1.

TABLE B1 ● Personal Growth Quotes		
Subtheme	**Jordan's Quotes**	**Sam's Quotes**
Raised Awareness	Most people's plates had generally the blue M&Ms representing most people in their lives are white.	I feel like it's [training] really helped me understand that not everybody is the same.
Empathy	A lot of people at the Rec Center, they're surrounded by a bunch of people that are different from them, and that might be hard for them.	If you are the one with different colored M&Ms, then you're one out of many, and you kind of stand out a little bit more.
Applying Learning Beyond the Rec Center	I'm like more keen to notice anti-inclusive language, behavior—it stands out a little bit more now, and I'm more actively aware of it. So I can do something about it now.	Now teachers say things that aren't appropriate and I'm just like, "Oh stop, that's not okay."

The second theme was *engaged and ongoing learning methods* and included subthemes of using activities and stories as well as continued conversations. The impact of activities was mentioned by all participants in numerous ways. Some comments indicated the activities were impactful simply from the perspective of getting a chance to have interactions rather than listening to content in a more lecture-based format. The activities were also impactful in how they required the participants to reflect on their own social identities and identities of their close friends, family, etc. The training facilitators encouraged engagement, with frequent prompts for participants to engage deeper with their reflections and comments.

The importance of continuing the conversation outside of the training environment was noted by all participants. The newer employee indicated how staff reflected on the training activities almost immediately after leaving the meeting room, while the more experienced staff member noted how her learning around diversity and inclusion was a cumulative effect of discussing the topics with peers and supervisors over her 2+ years of employment. Participant quotes for this theme are presented in Table B2.

TABLE B2 ● Engaged and Ongoing Learning Quotes		
Subtheme	**Jordan's quotes**	**Sam's quotes**
Use of Activities and Stories	I thought the activities really help, like emphasize what they [presenters] were talking about.	Because it was engaging, people took more out of it rather than it just being a lecture.
Continued Conversations	You're all kinda talking about how it is a little bit eye opening, how diverse everybody thinks they are, but then you get asked all these questions and you realize you can do better.	So the conversations that I've had throughout this last two-and-a-half years or so has just like reminded me that there's a lot more out there than just the people that surround me.

(Due to limited space the conclusion was removed.)

References

Bell, L. A. (2016). Theoretical foundations for social justice education. In M. Adams & L. A. Bell (Eds.), *Teaching for diversity and social justice* (3rd ed.). New York, NY: Routledge.

Butcher, M., Taylor, F., & Wallace, W. (2012). Developing multiculturally competent staff members in higher education. *Journal of Student Affairs, 21*, 40–48.

Creswell, J. W. (2013). *Qualitative inquiry & research design: Choosing among five approaches* (3rd ed.). Thousand Oaks: Sage.

Crotty, M. (1998). *The foundations of social research: Meaning and perspective in the research process*. London: Sage.

Evans, N. J., Reason, R. D., & Broido, E. M. (2001). Lesbian, gay, and bisexual students' perceptions of resident assistants: Implications for resident assistant selection and training. *College Student Affairs Journal, 21*(1), 82–91.

Guido, F. M., Chávez, A. F., & Lincoln, Y. S. (2010). Underlying paradigms in student affairs research and practice. *Journal of Student Affairs Research and Practice, 47*(1), 1–22.

Kaltenbaugh, L. P., Parsons, J., Brubaker, K., Bonadio, W., & Locust, J. (2017). Institutional type and campus recreation department staff as a mediating factor for diversity/multicultural training. *Recreational Sports Journal, 41*(1), 76–86.

King, A. R. (2012). A social-justice-based Resident Assistant (RA) training program on a midsized rural community college campus. *Community College Journal of Research and Practice, 36*(12), 982–993.

Merriam, S. B., & Tisdell, E. J. (2016). *Qualitative research: A guide to design and implementation* (4th ed.). San Francisco, CA: Jossey-Bass.

Miller, F. A. (1998). Strategic culture change: The door to achieving high performance and inclusion. *Public Personnel Management, 27*(2), 151.

Patchett, E., & Foster, J. (2015). Inclusive recreation: The state of campus policies, facilities, trainings, and programs for transgender participants. *Recreational Sports Journal, 39*(2).

Plano Clark, V. L., & Creswell, J. W. (2008). *The mixed methods reader.* Thousand Oaks: Sage.

Snyder, T. D., & Dillow, S. A. (2015). *Digest of education statistics, 2013* (NCES 2015-011). *National Center for Education Statistics.* Retrieved from http://nces.ed.gov/pubs2015/2015011.pdf

Stake, R. E. (1995). *The art of case study research.* London: Sage.

Representation 2A Research Poster

(See Text Box 5.3 and Figure 5.5 in Chapter 5 for Erin's research poster representation of this data set.)

Representation 3: Black Out Poetry

The following black out poems represent a style of research poetry called *data poems*. With data poems, the researcher utilizes the participants' own words to create poetry; thus, both poems below are verbatim transcriptions with selected words redacted. Researcher reflexivity is paramount in the creation of the poetry to ensure the data's new form is authentic—not unlike any other qualitative data analysis process.

Blue M&Ms

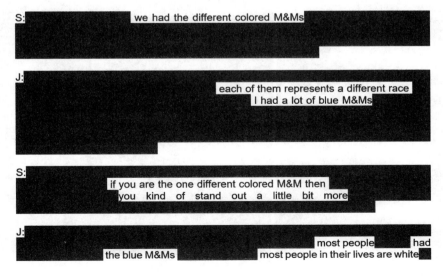

• Appendix C •

Reflexive Activities for
Novice and Sage Writers

At the end of each chapter in the book, I make a suggestion on which of these activities might be most suited for that chapter. Detailed description of each of the activities is provided here.

1. **How Do We Write?** Take a moment and consider what the writing process resembles for you. Look at the reflexive questions at the end of Chapter 2 to help with this process. For example, do you feel you write best when up against a deadline? A strength of this type of writing is the ability to keep writing under pressure. While this writing style works for course deadlines and some areas of academic writing in general, initial submission of journal manuscripts does not have a deadline—an exception to this is the call for special journal issues. The thought that writing under pressure brings about great results may be a habit that has been formed in deadline-intense contexts or by people who tend to procrastinate. It is hard to believe that extra time to read over a writing multiple times and for polishing is not beneficial. Once you have identified the different ways you write, question these ways, and look for areas that are strengths and areas that are potential weaknesses.

2. **Writers' Scavenger Hunt** The description I am providing here is for a physical scavenger hunt with some online items, but this can easily be changed to be solely online. Split up into groups. Set a time frame. Each group should receive a list of items and stay together as they search.

   a. Identify famous writers who have been employed at your university or have been a student there. Identify three things qualitative research writers might learn from their writing. (For example, James Michener was a graduate student at my university.)

   b. Go to the university library stacks, and check out one book on writing or qualitative research writing. Identify three things qualitative writers might learn from this book.

   c. Find out what writers' groups exist on campus, in the community the university you attend resides within, or online. Which of these groups, if any, might be supportive of the qualitative writing experience?

d. Meet with or examine your scholarly librarian's resources for qualitative research and writing.

e. Identify what writing resources exist on your campus. How might these resources become resources for qualitative research writing? (For example, my university holds an annual writers' conference and poetry slams. My doctoral degree–granting university has a famous poet who is a faculty member.)

3. **A Writers' Group** Create or join a writers' group. See Chapter 2 for details on how to do this. Having writers' groups as part of a course also works well. The group could focus specifically on dissertation writing or on journal manuscripts. Groups work just as effectively in person as virtually.

4. **Top Tips** Have group members brainstorm, on their own or as a group, a list of their top tips for productive writing. This can be strategies they use or ones they have heard of. Critically examine the ideas generated in pairs or small groups. What do the strategies have in common? How do they differ? How might each strategy support writers in different or similar ways?

5. **Technology Share** What new technologies have course members been using that help with their writing process? Sharing these could be done as a virtual post, in person during a class, or as part of a writers' group.

6. **Manuscript Review** Students identify a professor who is willing to conduct a review of a qualitative manuscript with the student. If you are in a course or writers' group, the group members could review a manuscript together. For example, in my writing course, we gain permission from an editor and split into three groups: One group is Reviewer 1, the next is Reviewer 2, and so on. Course members read the manuscript and review it outside of class and then meet during class to discuss the manuscript and write up one reviewer's voice and decision. I then review the reviews and submit them to the editor.

7. **Research Poetry Group** I formed a group of researchers who were interested in representing poetry. We committed to reading poetry, emailing in a round-robin fashion between face-to-face meetings about what we were reading, and trying to represent research as poetry. Members took notes of the process, and three publications were a direct result of the process. *Round robin* means the first person writes something and emails it to the second, who responds and adds other information and then emails all of the text to the next person, and so on. Subsequent groups have worked in a Google Doc, alerting each other as they add entries.

8. **Poem-a-Day** Buy a poem-a-day book, or sign up for one of the poem-a-day email lists referenced in Chapter 8 of this text. Then take five minutes a day to read the poem, and make a few notes to yourself in a poem-a-day journal.

9. **Personal Writing: A Reflexivity Experience** Choose one of the following writing topics. If you are in a course, after these are completed, meet in a small group to discuss what you wrote about.

   a. What is the first writing experience you recall?

   b. Write about a time when you had a negative writing experience.

   c. Write about a time when you had a wonderful writing experience.

   d. What are your short-term writing goals for the next three months?

      i. What are your long term goals for the year?

      ii. How does writing about these make you feel, and why?

10. **Professional Writers Panel or Guest Speaker** Assemble a panel of experts on the topic you are considering; be sure to include as many members with different identities and professional backgrounds as possible. Each course member should come prepared with questions for the panel, and the course instructor may wish to email some questions ahead of time for members to consider. The discussion would center on advice for how to write in the area being represented.

    • Instructor: Consider assigning groups of students to identify and invite a guest speaker or panel.

    • Possible topics include journalism, poetry, writing in the ethnographic present, writing about art experiences, writing for a journal, visual creation, interpretation, or writing a textbook.

11. **Flip-Flop Debate** Members of the course should choose a position on a writing topic. Members are put in two groups according to their decision. I typically have to ask some students just to choose the side they align with most for the purpose of the activity since they are able to see both sides of the issue or take a middle position on the issue. The groups are then told they must debate the opposite of the position they chose. Possible debate topics follow.

    a. Is the traditional dissertation valuable, and if so, why?

    b. Should alternative forms of representation be allowed for dissertations?

12. **What's in Your Writing Space?** This activity helps people to think about their writing identity. Ask course members to bring photos of where they write and a few items from the space or to share

their writing space virtually. Be sensitive to people who may not want to share. Sharing photos could be optional. Given limitations of time, space, and money, what are the ways graduate students could make their writing space more conducive to writing?

Consider reading the book (Hill, 1967) or watching the film adaptation of *Evan's Corner* (reelblack, 2017) to help people think about creative spaces for privacy and the need for company.

13. **Speed Discussion** I created this activity from the idea of speed dating. Form two circles one within the other. Course members each share their perspective on a topic, and then the outer circle rotates one person clockwise, and they do so again. Use a timer, and keep the time short—one to three minutes. Virtually, this would occur in break-out rooms. Possible topics follow.

     a. What research areas are you considering writing about?

     b. What challenges do you have to successful writing?

     c. What is your top tip for successful writing?

14. **Doodle It** Doodling[1] (informal drawing) may be seen as "making spontaneous marks with your mind and body to help yourself think" (Brown, 2014, p. 11).

     Doodling involves three senses (Brown, 2014): (1) listening to the lecture (auditory learning), (2) drawing (kinesthetic learning), and (3) creating a picture (visual learning).

     Possible doodle time topics—choose a time when you will be lecturing about writing, and ask the students to do the following:

     a. Doodle your writing plan for this week.

     b. Doodle about what may be keeping you from writing.

     c. Doodle about how you feel when you have had a day of writing.

Doodle time directions

a. Clear your workspace, and doodle instead of taking notes during this portion of the class.

b. Pair up with one person, and share about your doodle. Identify one concept that is not clear from the lecture, and see if you can clarify it between the two of you.

---

[1] I would like to thank Alaa Zeyab (2017) for introducing me to the idea of formally doodling in education. Alaa was studying the concept as part of a pilot study in a qualitative research course I teach. When a student is studying a pedagogical idea, I like to try it out in class when appropriate to the course content. Alaa helped me develop the activity and pilot it in two of my courses. I was then able to use it in a textbook on ethics and this text. Doodling as a learning tool may also be referred to as visual note recording. See Alaa Zeyab et al. (2020) for more information.

    c.   Prepare a question for the instructor if there is any remaining confusion.

15. **Interview a Writer** Choose a seasoned writer from your discipline or one who teaches research writing to interview.

    a.   Decide together if you will record the interview. I suggest doing so for the purpose of reviewing and in case the two of you want to teach a session or give a conference talk on writing someday.

    b.   What is the writer's writing process?

    c.   What writing stories does the writer share? Beginning stories, good stories, negative stories, and so on.

    d.   Consider presenting a research poster or writing an article, perhaps with the writer, on the information gained.

16. **Image Writing** Choose an image or have group members choose an image to write about. If each person chooses an image, consider having each person write about their image and then pass the image two people over and have each person write about the new image. Get in small groups, and share the writing that resulted. Images could be from members' research topics.

17. **Many Voices** For all of the suggested activities, if the class or group forms one voice of thought, thus achieving consensus quickly, provide opportunities for the course members to think from other perspectives. For example, if the class quickly decides that dissertation should allow artistic forms, ask them what detractors would say and what merit there is in those points.

• Appendix D •

Tips for Writing and Presenting
a Research Poster

Templates

- Search the internet for poster templates (e.g., https://www.makesigns.com/SciPosters_Templates.aspx).

- Review the computer programs you use for templates (e.g., PowerPoint, Prezi).

- Does your university have a template? Mine does, and it is also professionally laid out with the university logo and colors. This is not a choice I prefer for campus since it blends in too much, but it works well for off-campus conferences.

Poster Layout

Write in Short Word Chunks (Phrases)

- Three columns

- Bulleted short phrase

- Speech bubbles

- Figures, images, and charts

Content

- Abstract

- Research questions

- Literature (just highlights)

- Theory

- Methodology

- Findings

- Recommendations
- References
  - Consider having these in a QR code to save space.

Readability

- Serif fonts (e.g., Helvitica)
- Should be readable from 10 to 15 feet away
- Catchy, clear title in 60- to 90-point font

Weed Out Words

- Have someone else cut word amount
- Use phrases.
- Avoid all transition phrases and words (e.g., *therefore, additionally*).

Harness the Power of Blank Space

- Ideally, 40% of the poster will be blank.
- Blank space makes the poster seem more accessible.
- More blank space may help draw more views.

Before You Print

Pilot the poster with others—family, friends, other students, colleagues.

But don't believe everything you are told. There are a lot of text-dense posters at conferences. If you are not sure, read or view some of the resources at the end of this section, or see Erin Patchett's poster (Figure 5.5 in Chapter 5) as an example.

At the Conference

- Think of yourself as the host of your poster.
- How would a host engage others?
- Questions to ask poster guests:
  a. Do you study in the research area of the poster?
  b. May I give you a short overview?
     - If they say yes, be sure to keep this to an "elevator ride–length overview," and only speak more if they ask questions.
  c. Are you presenting at the conference?
     - If so, what are you presenting?

- If you have to leave the poster station,
  - leave your business card beside your poster,
  - provide a QR code,
  - leave your email address, or
  - have someone stand at the poster station for you.

Resources

Better Posters: http://betterposters.blogspot.ca/

Tips on Writing a Research Poster: https://bitesizebio.com/13599/10-tips-on-writing-a-research-poster/

Qualitative Data & Research Posters: https://michellekrieger.wordpress.com/2015/08/09/qualitative-data-research-posters/

Ways to Create a Powerful Research Poster: https://www.aje.com/en/arc/ways-to-create-great-research-poster/

Designing Conference Posters: http://colinpurrington.com/tips/poster-design/protips

Making a Better Research Poster: https://www.youtube.com/watch?v=AwMFhyH7_5g

• Appendix E •

Writing Prompts

All of these prompts have been used in the qualitative writing course I teach. Most of the prompts are sensory in nature, with a few focused on considering past writing experiences and planning for future writing. After sharing the prompt with the class, everyone writes for five minutes and then breaks into groups and shares their writing.

If you are doing this by yourself you may want to try several different ways of writing, such as a description, what the prompt reminded you of from your life stories, and a poem.

Face-to-Face

a. *Lemon:* Cut a lemon in the class, and pass around the slices for people to smell.

b. *Chocolate:* Each person has a piece of chocolate they can let melt on their tongue as they write. My favorite type of chocolate for this activity has pop rocks in it. I warn the students they will have a small surprise in the chocolate. Always keep the wrapper to pass around so people with food restrictions can read it and see if they can participate.

Firecracker Chocolate Free-Write Example

Becky De Oliveira

Pop rocks! My childhood in the 1970s. Climbing trees. Digging holes. I would never eat pop rocks now except embedded in chocolate. This is my favorite chocolate by Chuao, a California chocolate company. The bar is called Firecracker, I'm pretty sure. It even comes in minis that I used to pick up at airports when I felt like a treat. I rewarded myself with this chocolate the summer I did French, several times. My husband brought me two bars when he came out to visit, and I portioned them slowly over days, weeks, along with other rewards like pedicures and naps. The popping, I can't decide if I even really like it or whether it stresses me out like fizzy drinks do. I like hot things but not necessarily explosive things, but this chocolate is so good. And it makes me think of trees, of French, of Washington and Michigan, of all the places I've ever loved. It makes me think of watching the fireworks alone in the parking lot of my apartment in Kalamazoo in between learning French verbs.

c. *Slime:* My daughter makes a lot of slime. Some of the slime have additions in them such as glitter, googly eyes, and buttons. I took enough jars into class that each student could have one while the wrote. Some just poked it with one finger and others squeezed it the whole time they were writing.

Slime Free-Write Example

Becky De Oliveira

My slime is less slimy than I expected—more like silly putty. I like playing with things like this, not that I do so very often these days. It's very zen: balling the slime, flattening the slime, rolling the slime into a sausage, bouncing the slime back and forth between my hands. If it were more socially acceptable, I'd hurl the slime at one of these classroom whiteboards to see if it would stick. My slime has sparkles. Some of them have ended up on my hands. It has a weird smell, not particularly pleasant, but my hands haven't picked up the scent the way they do when I've been handling, for instance, a snake. I wonder if the slime can make copies of newsprint the way silly putty does. I have no newspaper to experiment with. I wonder if it bounces. It does—I just tried it! How many things could I do with the slime if left alone in this room all day? How long would it take me to get bored, how long before I'd want some productive work to do? I can't even imagine. Right now, I'd like nothing more than a few mindless hours, staring into space and seeing nothing, casting my mind elsewhere, back in time, forward in time, suspended in the present.

d. *Peppermint candy:* Each person opens a peppermint candy from a wrapper and sucks on it while they write. If they don't want to do that, they can just smell it.

e. *Peppermint oil:* Put peppermint oil or another distinctive essential oil on a cotton ball in a container and have each person sniff it and then write.

Potato Writing

1. Put enough potatoes on a table so that each person will have one. The potatoes should be of the same variety.

2. Place a stack of notecards on the table.

3. Each person takes a potato and an index card.

4. Describe your potato in detail. You may not trace or sketch it.

5. Put all the potatoes back on the table, and mix them up in a pile.

6. Take up the notecards, mix them up, and redistribute them. No one should keep the card that was theirs.

   Can you find the potato that matches your description? This has worked every time I have used this activity!

   This descriptive writing activity can also be done with oranges (Word for Word, 2011).

Virtual or Face-to-Face

- Underwater video of fish in a coral reef

- Video of fireworks

- Picture of a doorknob

- Picture of peppermint candy

- Sound of a doorbell ringing

- Sound of an old-time car horn

- Sound of a motor revving

- Sound of metal being sanded

- Sound of waves

The worst experience with writing

The best experience with writing

An early experience in life about writing

What writing do you want to accomplish this semester? At the end of the semester—what writing do you want to accomplish next semester?

• References •

Academy of American Poets. (2015). *Poem-a-day: 365 Poems for every occasion*. Harry N. Abrams.

Academy of Poets. (n.d.). *Abecedarian*. https://poets.org/glossary/abecedarian

Adams, D. (2002). *The salmon of doubt: Hitchhiking the universe one last time* (Vol. *3*). Harmony.

Adams, T. E. (2006). Seeking father: Relationally reframing a troubled love story. *Qualitative Inquiry, 12*(4), 704–723. https://doi.org/10.1177/1077800406288607

Adams, T. E. (2017). Critical autoethnography, education, and a call for forgiveness. *International Journal of Multicultural Education, 19*(1), 79–88. https://doi.org/10.18251/ijme.v19i1.1387

Adams, T. E., & Herrmann, A. F. (2020). Expanding our autoethnographic future. *Journal of Autoethnography, 1*(1), 1–8. https://doi.org/10.1525/joae.2020.1.1.1

Adams, T. E., Jones, S. H., & Ellis, C. (2015). *Autoethnography*. Oxford University Press.

Ainsworth, M. D. S. (1978). The Bowlby-Ainsworth attachment theory. *Behavioral and Brain Sciences, 1*(3), 436–438. https://doi.org/10.1017/S0140525X00075828

Ali-Khan, C. (2015). Writing, dancing and navel gazing: Examining the ins and outs of autoethnography. In K. Tobin & S. R. Steinberg (Eds.), *Doing educational research: A handbook* (2nd ed., pp. 293–320). Sense.

Allen, M. (2016). *Essentials of publishing qualitative research* (Vol. 12). Routledge. https://doi.org/10.4324/9781315429298

Allen, Q. (2012). Photographs and stories: Ethics, benefits and dilemmas of using participant photography with Black middle-class male youth. *Qualitative Research, 12*(4), 443–458. https://doi.org/10.1177/1468794111433088

Allerton, C. (Ed.). (2016). *Children: Ethnographic encounters* (Vol. 1). Bloomsbury.

Alvear, M. (2017). *The bulletproof writer. How to overcome constant rejection to become an unstoppable writer*. Woodpecker Media.

Anderson, T., Saunders, G., & Alexander, I. (2021). Alternative dissertation formats in education-based doctorates. *Higher Education Research & Development*. Advance online publication. https://doi.org/10.1080/07294360.2020.1867513

Anzul, M., Downing, M., Ely, M., & Vinz, R. (2003). *On writing qualitative research: Living by words*. Routledge. https://doi.org/10.4324/9780203451427

Archibald, M. M., & Onwuegbuzie, A. J. (2020). Poetry and mixed methods research. *International Journal of Multiple Research Approaches, 12*(2), 153–165. https://doi.org/10.29034/ijmra.v12n2editorial3

Armstrong, J. S. (1997). Peer review for journals: Evidence on quality control, fairness, and innovation. *Science and Engineering Ethics, 3*(1), 63–84. https://doi.org/10.1007/s11948-997-0017-3

Asimov, I. (1964). *Adding a dimension: Seventeen essays on the history of science.* Doubleday.

Badley, G. (2009). Publish and be doctor-rated: The PhD by published work. *Quality Assurance in Education, 17*(4), 331–342. https://doi.org/10.1108/0968 4880910992313

Baker, M. J., & Saren, M. (Eds.). (2016). *Marketing theory: A student text.* Sage.

Banks, M. (2001). *Visual methods in social research.* Sage. https://doi.org/10.4135/9780857020284

Baranski, M. F., & Was, C. A. (2019). Can mindfulness meditation improve short-term and long-term academic achievement in a higher-education course? *College Teaching, 67*(3), 188–195. https://doi.org/10.1080/87567555.2019.1594150

Bartholomew, R. E. (2014). Science for sale: The rise of predatory journals. *Journal of the Royal Society of Medicine, 107*(10), 384–385. https://doi.org/10.1177/0141076814548526

Beall, J. (2017). What I learned from predatory publishers. *Biochemia Medica, 27*(2), 273–278. https://doi.org/10.11613/BM.2017.029

Beasley, C. (2012, December 1). *Traced portraits.* Indietutes. http://indietutes.blogspot.com/2012/01/traced-portraits.html

Beddes, L. (2017). *Increasing reflexivity in service learning through arts based research* (Publication No. 10638640) [Doctoral dissertation, University of Northern Colorado]. ProQuest Dissertations and Theses Global.

Beer, L. E. (2012). *"It was beautiful, but it wasn't supposed to be there": Spirituality in the work lives of higher education administrative leaders* (Publication No. 3523413) [Doctoral dissertation, University of Northern Colorado]. ProQuest Dissertations and Theses Global.

Behar, R. (1993). *Translated woman: Crossing the border with Esperanza's story.* Beacon Press.

Behar, R. (1996). *The vulnerable observer: Anthropology that breaks your heart.* Beacon Press.

Benson, M. J., & Piercy, K. W. (1997). Multiple approaches to developing research: A flexible framework for students and advisors. *Family Science Review, 10,* 121–135.

Bernal, Delgado. D. (1998). Using a Chicana feminist epistemology in educational research. *Harvard educational review, 68*(4), 555–583.

Bernstein, C. (n.d.). *Dear Mr. Fanelli.* Poetry Foundation. https://www.poetryfoundation.org/poems/50750/dear-mr-fanelli

Berry, K. S. (2011). Embracing radical research: A commentary on "To the Next Level: Continuing the Conceptualization of the Bricolage." In J. L. Kincheloe, K. Hayes, S. Steinberg, & K. Tobin (Eds.), *Key works in critical pedagogy* (pp. 279–284). Sense.

Bettez, S. C. (2015). Navigating the complexity of qualitative research in postmodern contexts: Assemblage, critical reflexivity, and communion as guides. *International Journal of Qualitative Studies in Education, 28*(8), 932–954. https://doi.org/10.1080/09518398.2014.948096

Bhattacharya, K. (2020). Understanding entangled relationships between un/interrogated privileges: Tracing research pathways with contemplative art-making, duoethnography, and Pecha Kucha. *Cultural Studies ↔ Critical Methodologies, 20*(1), 75–85. https://doi.org/10.1177/1532708619884963

Bird, C. M. (2005). How I stopped dreading and learned to love transcription. *Qualitative Inquiry, 11*(2), 226–248. https://doi.org/10.1177/1077800404273413

Bloomberg, L. D., & Volpe, M. (2018). *Completing your qualitative dissertation: A road map from beginning to end.* Sage.

Boyatzis, R. E. (1998). *Transforming qualitative information: Thematic analysis and code development.* Sage.

Bochner, A. P. (1997). It's about time: Narrative and the divided self. *Qualitative Inquiry, 3*(4), 418–438. https://doi.org/10.1177/107780049700300404

Bochner, A. P. (2012). Suffering happiness: On autoethnography's ethical calling. *Qualitative Communication Research, 1*(2), 209–229. https://doi.org/10.1525/qcr.2012.1.2.209

Bochner, A. P. (2017). Unfurling rigor: On continuity and change in qualitative inquiry. *Qualitative Inquiry, 24*(6), 359–368. https://doi.org/10.1177/1077800417727766

Bohannon, J. (2016). Hate journal impact factors? New study gives you one more reason. *Science.* https://www.sciencemag.org/news/2016/07/hate-journal-impact-factors-new-study-gives-you-one-more-reason

Borland, K. (1991). "That's not what I said": Interpretative conflict in oral narrative research. In S. B. Gluck & D. Patai (Eds.), *Women's words: The feminist practice of oral history* (pp. 63–75). Routledge.

Bowlby, J. (2008). *Attachment.* Basic Books.

Bragg, R. (1997). *All over but the shoutin'.* Vintage Books.

Braun, V., & Clarke, V. (2006). Using thematic analysis in psychology. *Qualitative Research in Psychology, 3*(2), 77–101. https://doi.org/10.1191/1478088706qp063oa

Brown, K. C. (2018). *A performative autoethnography on the irruption of a healing assemblage* (Publication No. 10839324) [Doctoral dissertation, University of Memphis]. ProQuest Dissertations and Theses Global.

Brown, S. (2014). *The doodle revolution.* Penguin Group.

Burdick, M. (2011). Researcher and teacher–participant found poetry: Collaboration in poetic transcription. *International Journal of Education & the Arts, 12*(Special issue 1.10). https://files.eric.ed.gov/fulltext/EJ937081.pdf

Burnard, P., Gill, P., Stewart, K., Treasure, E., & Chadwick, B. (2008). Analysing and presenting qualitative data. *British Dental Journal, 204*(8), 429–432. https://doi.org/10.1038/sj.bdj.2008.292

Butler-Kisber, L. (2002). Artful portrayals in qualitative inquiry: The road to found poetry and beyond. *Alberta*

Journal of Educational Research, *48*(3), 229–239.

Butler-Kisber, L. (2008). Collage as inquiry. In J. G. Knowles & A. L. Cole (Eds.), *Handbook of the arts in qualitative research: Perspectives, methodologies, examples, and issues* (pp. 265–276). Sage. https://doi.org/10.4135/9781452226545.n22

Butler-Kisber, L. (2010). *Qualitative inquiry: Thematic, narrative and arts-informed perspectives*. Sage. https://doi.org/10.4135/9781526435408

Butler-Kisber, L., & Poldma, T. (2010). The power of visual approaches in qualitative inquiry: The use of collage making and concept mapping in experiential research. *Journal of Research Practice*, *6*(2), Article M18.

Butt, M. (2013). One I made earlier: On the PhD by publication. *Text–Australasian Association of Writing Programs Journal of Writing and Writing Courses*, *22*, 1–14.

Cahnmann, M. (2003). The craft, practice, and possibility of poetry in educational research. *Educational Researcher*, *32*(3), 29–36. https://doi.org/10.3102/0013189X032003029

California Poets. (2019). *Three-dimensional poetry*. https://www.californiapoets.org/post/three-dimensional-poetry

Campbell, E. (2017). "Apparently being a self-obsessed c**t is now academically lauded": Experiencing Twitter trolling of autoethnographers. *Forum: Qualitative Sozialforschung/Forum: Qualitative Social Research*, *18*(3), 1–19. https://doi.org/10.17169/fqs-18.3.2819

Cann, C. N., & DeMeulenaere, E. J. (2012). Critical co-constructed autoethnography. *Cultural Studies ↔ Critical Methodologies*, *12*(2), 146–158. https://doi.org/10.1177/1532708611435214

Carmichael, M., Reid, A., & Karpicke, J. D. (2018). *Assessing the impact of educational video on student engagement, critical thinking and learning* (A SAGE white paper). Sage.

Carr, J. M. (2003). Poetic expressions of vigilance. *Qualitative Health Research*, *13*(9), 1324–1331. https://doi.org/10.1177/1049732303254018

Carson, A. D. (2017). *Owning my masters: The rhetorics of rhymes and revolutions* (Publication No. 10267305) [Doctoral dissertation, Clemson University]. ProQuest Dissertations and Theses Global.

Caulley, D. N. (2008). Making qualitative research reports less boring: The techniques of writing creative nonfiction. *Qualitative Inquiry*, *14*(3), 424–449. https://doi.org/10.1177/1077800407311961

Chang, J., Lin, P., & Seiden, H. M. (2019). Music performance and education: A case presentation of mindfulness approach in higher education. *Journal of Performance & Mindfulness*, *2*(2), 1. https://doi.org/10.5920/pam.617

Charmaz, K. (2014). *Constructing grounded theory*. Sage.

Chenail, R. J. (1995). Presenting qualitative data. *The Qualitative Report*, *2*(3), 1–9. https://doi.org/10.46743/2160-3715/1995.2067

Chieu, P. K. (2005). *An examination of the coach/athlete relationship using leader-member exchange theory* (Publication

No. 3171922) [Doctoral dissertation, University of Northern Colorado]. ProQuest Dissertations and Theses Global.

Choi, A. J., Stotlar, D. K., & Park, S. R. (2006). Visual ethnography of on-site sport sponsorship activation: LG Action Sports Championship. *Sports Marketing Quarterly, 15*(2), 71–79.

Chu-i, P. (n.d.). *The flower market.* http://bs.dayabook.com/poetry/po-chu-i-selected-poems/the-flower-market

Cirillo, F. (n.d.). *The Pomodoro® technique.* https://francescocirillo.com/pages/pomodoro-technique

Clark, A. (2004). The Mosaic approach and research with young children. In M. Lewis, C. Kellett, S. Robinson, S. Fraser, & S. Ding (Eds.), *The reality of research with children and young people* (pp. 142–161). Sage.

Clark, A. (2011a). Breaking methodological boundaries? Exploring visual, participatory methods with adults and young children. *European Early Childhood Education Research Journal, 19*(3), 321–330. https://doi.org/10.1080/1350293X.2011.597964

Clark, A. (2011b). Multimodal map making with young children: Exploring ethnographic and participatory methods. *Qualitative Research, 11*(3), 311–330. https://doi.org/10.1177/1468794111400532

Clark, A. (2017). *Listening to young children: A guide to understanding and using the Mosaic approach* (3rd ed.). Jessica Kingsley.

Clark, A., & Moss, P. (2001). *Listening to young children: The Mosaic approach.* National Children's Bureau.

Clark, J., & Smith, R. (2015). Firm action needed on predatory journals. *British Medical Journal, 350.* https://doi.org/10.1136/bmj.h210

Code of Ethics: American Educational Research Association. (2011). *Educational Researcher, 40*(3), 145–156. https://doi.org/10.3102/0013189X11410403

Coelho, P. (2011, November, 1). *@paulocoelho.* https://twitter.com/paulocoelho/status/131440521116790784

Cole, A. L., & McIntyre, M. (n.d.). *The Alzheimer's project.* https://legacy.oise.utoronto.ca/research/mappingcare/alzproject_publications.shtml

Cole, A. L., & McIntyre, M. (2008). Installation art as research. In J. G. Knowles & A. L. Cole (Eds.), *Handbook of the arts in qualitative research: Perspectives, methodologies, examples, and issues* (pp. 287–298). Sage.

Cole, N. (n.d.). *Seven skills you need to practice to become a successful writer in the digital age.* https://www.inc.com/nicolas-cole/the-7-skills-you-need-to-practice-to-become-a-successful-writer-in-digital-age.html

Colegrove, M. (2004). *Be a last-minute leader, not a procrastinator.* iUniverse.

Collier, J. J. (1957). Photography in anthropology: A report on two experiments. *American Anthropologist, 59*(5), 843–859. https://doi.org/10.1525/aa.1957.59.5.02a00100

Collier, J. J. (1967). *Visual anthropology: Photography as a research method.* Holt.

Collier, M. (2001). Approaches to analysis in visual anthropology. In T. Van Leeuwen & C. Jewitt (Eds.), *Handbook of visual analysis* (pp. 35–60). Sage. https://doi.org/10.4135/9780857020062.n3

Collins, B. (1988). *Introduction to poetry.* https://www.loc.gov/programs/poetry-and-literature/poet-laureate/poet-laureate-projects/poetry-180/all-poems/

Collins, B. (2011, March, 19). Twitter poem. *New York Times.* http://www.nytimes.com/2011/03/20/weekin review/20twitterature-poems.html

Competing and Aging. (n.d.). *Challenging the cultural narrative of women and sports.* www.competingandaging.com

Cordell, R. (2014, February 10). Writing 20 minutes every. Single. Day. *The Chronicle of Higher Education.* https://www.chronicle.com/blogs/profhacker/writing-20-minutes-every-single-day/55459

Council of Graduate Schools. (2016). Imagining the dissertation's many futures. *GradEdge: Insights and Research on Graduate Education, 5*(3), 1–6. https://cgsnet.org/sites/default/files/March%20FINAL2.pdf

Cox, A. R., & Montgomerie, R. (2019, December, 16). The cases for and against double-blind reviews. *PeerJ, 7,* e6702. http://dx.doi.org/10.7717/peerj.6702

Cox, D. G. (2020). *Implementing digital media as a pedagogical tool in university physical activity courses* (Publication No. 27959078) [Doctoral dissertation, University of Northern Colorado]. ProQuest Dissertations and Theses Global.

Crane, S. C. M. (2005). *Child-centered play therapy and parent–child interaction therapy: A practice-based case study exploration of two play therapies as trauma treatment* (Publication No. 3183577) [Doctoral dissertation, University of Northern Colorado]. ProQuest Dissertations and These Global.

Creswell, J. W. (2013). *Qualitative inquiry and research design: Choosing among five approaches.* Sage.

Creswell, J. W., & Poth, C. N. (2018). *Qualitative inquiry and research design: Choosing among five approaches.* Sage.

Cripps, C. (2013, July, 17). Twihaiku? Micropoetry? The rise of Twitter poetry. *Independent.* http://www.independent.co.uk/arts-entertainment/books/features/twihaikumicropoetry-the-rise-of-twitter-poetry-8711637.html

Crossley, É. (2019). Deep reflexivity in tourism research. *Tourism Geographies, 23*(1–2), 206–227. https://doi.org/10.1080/14616688.2019.1571098

Crotty, M. (1998). *The foundations of social research: Meaning and perspective in the research process.* Sage.

Cunliffe, A. L. (2016). "On becoming a critically reflexive practitioner" redux: What does it mean to be reflexive? *Journal of Management Education, 40*(6), 740–746. https://doi.org/10.1177/1052562916668919

Czarniawska, B. (2008). Organizing: How to study it and how to write about it. *Qualitative Research in Organizations and Management: An International Journal, 3*(1), 4–20. https://doi.org/10.1108/17465640810870364

Daigh, R. (1977). *Maybe you should write a book.* Prentice Hall.

Dane, E. (2011). Changing the tune of academic writing: Muting cognitive entrenchment. *Journal of Management*

Inquiry, 20(3), 332–336. https://doi
.org/10.1177/1056492611408267

Darmer, P. (2006). Poetry as a way
to inspire (the management of) the
research process. *Management Decision,
44*(4), 551–560. https://doi.org/10.1108/
00251740610663072

Davidson, D. (Ed.). (2016). *The tattoo
project: Commemorative tattoos, visual
culture, and the digital archive.* Canadian
Scholars.

Davis, B. (n.d.). *Dimensional poetry.*
http://www.math.brown.edu/~
banchoff/STG/ma8/papers/mimber/
final.html

Davis, D., & Butler-Kisber, L. (1999,
April 19–23). *Arts-based representation in
qualitative research: Collage as a contextualizing analytic strategy* [Conference
presentation]. American Educational
Research Association Annual Meeting,
Montreal, Quebec, Canada.

Delgado, R., & Stefancic, J. (Eds.).
(1997). *Critical white studies: Looking
behind the mirror.* Temple University
Press.

Delich, J. R. (2004). *A qualitative case
study on the implementation of a priority
seating program at an NCAA Division I
school* (Publication No. 3139608) [Doc-
toral dissertation, University of Northern Colorado]. ProQuest Dissertations
and Theses Global.

Deller, R. A. (2018). Ethics in fan studies
research. In P. Booth (Ed.), *A companion
to media fandom and fan studies* (pp.
123–142). Wiley. https://doi.org/10.1002/
9781119237211.ch8

Denzin, N. K. (2010). On elephants and
gold standards. *Qualitative Research,*
10(2), 269–272. https://doi.org/10.1177/
1468794109357367

DeRoche, K. K., & Lahman, M. K. (2008).
Methodological considerations for
conducting qualitative interviews with
youth receiving mental health services.
*Forum Qualitative Sozialforschung/Forum:
Qualitative Social Research, 9*(3), Article 17.
https://doi.org/10.17169/fqs-9.3.1016

De Sousa, L., Richter, B., & Nel, C.
(2017). The effect of multimedia use
on the teaching and learning of social
sciences at tertiary level: A case study.
Yesterday and Today, 17, 1–22. https://
doi.org/10.17159/2223-0386/2017/
n17a1

Deutsch, B. (1974). *Poetry handbook:
A dictionary of terms* (4th ed.). Harper
Collins.

De Vecchi, N., Kenny, A., Dickson-
Swift, V., & Kidd, S. (2017). Exploring the process of digital storytelling
in mental health research: A process
evaluation of consumer and clinician
experiences. *International Journal of
Qualitative Methods, 16*(1). https://doi
.org/10.1177/1609406917729291

DiCarlo, A. (n.d.). *The power hour: How
to beat procrastination.* https://www
.lifehack.org/articles/productivity/the-
power-hour.html

Dictionary.com. (n.d.). *Cliché.* https://
www.dictionary.com/browse/cliche

Dinesen, I. (1937). *Out of Africa.*
Random House.

Dodgson, J. E. (2019). Reflexivity in
qualitative research. *Journal of Human
Lactation, 35*(2), 220–222. https://doi
.org/10.1177/0890334419830990

Dostoyevsky, F. (1950). *Crime and punishment*. Modern Library. (Original work published 1866)

Drew, S. E., Duncan, R. E., & Sawyer, S. M. (2010). Visual storytelling: A beneficial but challenging method for health research with young people. *Qualitative Health Research, 20*(12), 1677–1688. https://doi.org/10.1177/1049732310377455

Duhamel, D. (2004). I've been known. *MARGIE: The American Journal of Poetry, 2*. https://www.loc.gov/programs/poetry-and-literature/poet-laureate/poet-laureate-projects/poetry-180/all-poems/item/poetry-180-065/ive-been-known/

Dunbar, P. L. (1899). *Sympathy*. Poetry Foundation. https://www.poetryfoundation.org/poems/46459/sympathy-56d22658afbc0

Durand, F. (2019, June, 4). *Good question: What does "short" mean in a recipe?* http://www.thekitchn.com/good-question-what-does-short-50169

Durst, R. K. (1992). A writer's community: How teachers can form writing groups. In K. L. Dahl (Ed.), *Teacher as writer: Entering the professional conversation* (pp. 261–271). National Council of Teachers of English.

ECFR. (2018). *Electronic code of federal regulations*. https://www.ecfr.gov/cgi-bin/retrieveECFR?gp=&SID=83cd09e1c0f5c6937cd9d7513160fc3f&pitd=2018071 9&n=pt45.1.46&r=PART&ty=HTML#se45.1.46_1102

The Ectopic Pregnancy Trust. (n.d.). *Trying to conceive after an ectopic pregnancy*. https://ectopic.org.uk/patients/trying-to-conceive/

Edwards, R., & Weller, S. (2012). Shifting analytic ontology: Using I-poems in qualitative longitudinal research. *Qualitative Research, 12*(2), 202–217. https://doi.org/10.1177/1468794111422040

Eisenbach, B. (2013). Finding a balance: A narrative inquiry into motherhood and the doctoral process. *The Qualitative Report, 18*(17), 1–13.

Eisner, E. W. (2017). *The enlightened eye: Qualitative inquiry and the enhancement of educational practice*. Teachers College Press.

Elbow, P. (1973). *Writing without teachers*. Oxford University Press.

Ellingson, L. L. (2011). Introduction to crystallization. In *Engaging crystallization in qualitative research*. Sage.

Ellis, C. (1997). Evocative ethnography: Writing emotionally about our lives. In W. G. Tierney & Y. S. Lincoln (Eds.), *Representation and the text: Re-framing the narrative voice* (pp. 114–142). State University of New York Press. https://doi.org/10.1177/104973299129122153

Ellis, C. (1999). Heartful autoethnography. *Qualitative Health Research, 9*(5), 669–683. https://doi.org/10.1177/104973299129122153

Ellis, C. (2000). Creating criteria: An ethnographic short story. *Qualitative Inquiry, 6*(2), 273–277. https://doi.org/10.1177/107780040000600210

Ellis, C. (2004). *The ethnographic I: A methodological novel about autoethnography*. AltaMira.

Ellis, C., Adams, T. E., & Bochner, A. P. (2011). Autoethnography: An overview. *Historical Social Research/Historische*

Sozialforschung, 36(4), 273–290. https://doi.org/10.2307/23032294

Ellis, C., & Bochner, A. (2000). Autoethnography, personal narrative, reflexivity: Researcher as subject. In N. K. Denzin & Y. S. Lincoln (Eds.), *The SAGE handbook of qualitative research* (2nd ed., pp. 733–768). Sage.

Elliston, F. A. (1982). Anonymity and whistleblowing. *Journal of Business Ethics, 1*, 167–177. https://doi.org/10.1007/BF00382768

Elsevier. (2018). *Get noticed: Promoting your article for maximum interest.* https://www.elsevier.com/__data/assets/pdf_file/0013/201325/Get-Noticed_Brochure_2018.pdf

Ely, M. (2007). In-forming re-presentations. In D. J. Clandinin (Ed.), *Handbook of narrative inquiry: Mapping a methodology* (pp. 567–598). Sage. https://doi.org/10.4135/9781452226552.n22

Enago Academy. (2018a, May 21). *Exploring video journals: An interview with Latest Thinking.* https://www.enago.com/academy/exploring-video-journals-an-interview-with-latest-thinking/

Enago Academy. (2018b, September 21). *Video research: Open access academic video journals.* https://www.enago.com/academy/video-research-open-access-academic-video-journals/

Esquivel, L. (1995). *Like water for chocolate* (C. Christensen & T. Christensen, Trans.). Random House.

Etherington, K. (2007). Ethical research in reflexive relationships. *Qualitative Inquiry, 13*(5), 599–616. https://doi.org/10.1177/1077800407301175

Evans, L., & Blair, J. (2016, February 9). Listening to self: An appeal for autoethnography in art museum education. *Medium.* https://medium.com/viewfinder-reflecting-on-museum-education/listening-to-self-an-appeal-for-autoethnography-in-art-museum-education-c9903db25bc9

Facing History and Ourselves. (n.d.). *Gallery walk.* https://www.facinghistory.org/resource-library/teaching-strategies/gallery-walk

Faulkner, S. L. (2016). *Poetry as method: Reporting research through verse.* Routledge.

Faulkner, S. L. (2017). Poetic inquiry. In P. Leavy (Ed.), *Handbook of arts-based research* (pp. 208–230). Guilford Press.

Fiedler, K. M. (2012). *Listening to the voices of boys: A Mosaic approach to exploring the motivation to engage in reading* (Publication No. 3550041) [Doctoral dissertation, University of Northern Colorado]. ProQuest Dissertations and Theses Global.

Fine Dictionary. (n.d.). *Manuscript.* http://www.finedictionary.com/manuscript.html

Finlay, L., & Gough, B. (2003). *Reflexivity: A practical guide for researchers in health and social sciences.* Blackwell. https://doi.org/10.1002/9780470776094

Finley, M. (2003). Fugue of the street rat: Writing research poetry. *International Journal of Qualitative Studies in Education, 16*(4), 603–604. https://doi.org/10.1080/0951839032000135010

Flick, U. (2018). *Designing qualitative research.* Sage.

Foss, S. K. (2015). *Destination dissertation: A traveler's guide to a done dissertation*. Rowman & Littlefield.

Four Arrows, aka Jacobs, D. T. (2008). *The authentic dissertation: Alternative ways of knowing, research and representation*. Routledge.

Freeman, S., Jr. (2018). The manuscript dissertation: A means of increasing competitive edge for tenure-track faculty positions. *International Journal of Doctoral Studies, 13*, 273–292. https://doi.org/10.28945/4093

Frost, R. (1922). *Stopping by woods on a snowy evening*. Poetry Foundation. https://www.poetryfoundation.org/poems/42891/stopping-by-woods-on-a-snowy-evening

Furman, R. (2006). Poetic forms and structures in qualitative health research. *Qualitative Health Research, 16*(4), 560–566. https://doi.org/10.1177/1049732306286819

Furman, R., Lietz, C., & Langer, C. L. (2006). The research poem in international social work: Innovations in qualitative methodology. *International Journal of Qualitative Methods, 5*(3), 24–34. https://doi.org/10.1177/160940690600500305

Garcia, C. S. (2018). *Borderlands art practice: Performing borderlands spaces through art/food/performative/writing/pedagogy* (Publication No. 13803956) [Doctoral dissertation, Pennsylvania State University]. ProQuest Dissertations and Theses Global.

Gardiner, M., & Kearns, H. (2011). Turbocharge your writing today. *Nature, 475*, 129–130. https://doi.org/10.1038/nj7354-129a

Geertz, C. (1973). *The interpretation of cultures* (Vol. 5019). Basic Books. https://doi.org/10.1177/1049732306297884

Gewirtz, S., & Cribb, A. (2006). What to do about values in social research: The case for ethical reflexivity in the sociology of education. *British Journal of Sociology of Education, 27*(2), 141–155. https://doi.org/10.1080/01425690600556081

Gibbs, G. R., Friese, S., & Mangabeira, W. C. (2002, May). The use of new technology in qualitative research: Introduction to Issue 3(2) of FQS. *Forum Qualitative Sozialforschung/Forum: Qualitative Social Research, 3*(2), Article 8. https://www.qualitative-research.net/index.php/fqs/article/view/847/1841

Gilligan, C., & Eddy, J. (2017). Listening as a path to psychological discovery: An introduction to the Listening Guide. *Perspectives on Medical Education, 6*(2), 76–81. https://doi.org/10.1007/s40037-017-0335-3

Gilligan, C., Spencer, R., Weinberg, M. K., & Bertsch, T. (2003). On the Listening Guide: A voice-centered relational model. In P. M. Camic, J. E. Rhodes, & L. Yardley (Eds.), *Qualitative research in psychology: Expanding perspectives in methodology and design* (pp. 157–172). American Psychological Association. https://doi.org/10.1037/10595-009

Giordano, J., O'Reilly, M., Taylor, H., & Dogra, N. (2007). Confidentiality and autonomy: The challenge(s) of offering research participants a choice of disclosing their identity. *Qualitative Health Research, 17*, 264–275. https://doi.org/10.1177/1049732306297884

Glaser, B. G., & Strauss, A. L. (1999). *Discovery of grounded theory: Strategies for qualitative research*. Routledge.

Glaw, X., Inder, K., Kable, A., & Hazelton, M. (2017). Visual methodologies in qualitative research: Autophotography and photo elicitation applied to mental health research. *International Journal of Qualitative Methods, 16*(1). https://doi.org/10.1177/1609406917748215

Glesne, C. (1997). That rare feeling: Re-presenting research through poetic transcription. *Qualitative Inquiry, 3*(2), 202–221. https://doi.org/10.1177/107780049700300204

Gold, R. L. (1958). Roles in sociological field observation. *Social Forces, 36*(3), 217–223. https://doi.org/10.2307/2573808

Goldberg, N. (1985). *Writing down the bones: Freeing the writer within.* Shambhala.

Golden-Biddle, K., & Locke, K. (1997). *Composing qualitative research.* Sage.

Golden-Biddle, K., & Locke, K. (2007). *Composing qualitative research* (2nd ed.). Sage.

Gomez, R., & Vannini, S. (2015). *Fotohistorias: Participatory photography and the experience of migration.* CreateSpace.

Gonzalez, M. (2013). *¡Si se puede! First-generation, Latino immigrant college success stories: A transformative autoethnographic study* (Publication No. 3588557) [Doctoral dissertation, University of Northern Colorado]. ProQuest Dissertations and Theses Global.

Goodreads. (n.d.). *William Faulkner.* https://www.goodreads.com/quotes/39009-read-read-read-read-everything-trash-classics-good-and

Goodyear, S. (2018, June, 11). *B.C. art teacher submits thesis in the form of a comic book.* CBC Radio. https://www.cbc.ca/radio/asithappens/as-it-happens-monday-edition-1.4700930/b-c-art-teacher-submits-thesis-in-the-form-of-a-comic-book-1.4700932

Grahame, K. (1908). *The wind in the willows.* Methuen.

Grant, M. J., Munro, W., McIsaac, J., & Hill, S. (2010). Cross-disciplinary writers' group stimulates fresh approaches to scholarly communication: A reflective case study within a higher education institution in the North West of England. *New Review of Academic Librarianship, 16*, 44–64. https://doi.org/10.1080/13614533.2010.509481

Greve, W., Bröder, A., & Erdfelder, E. (2013). Result-blind peer reviews and editorial decisions: A missing pillar of scientific culture. *European Psychologist, 18*(4), 286–294. https://doi.org/10.1027/1016-9040/a000144

Griffin, K. M. (2016). *Listening to the voices of boys: Exploring the motivation of primary boys to engage in reading.* Information Age.

Griffin, K. M., Lahman, M. K., & Opitz, M. F. (2014). Shoulder-to-shoulder research with children: Methodological and ethical considerations. *Journal of Early Childhood Research, 14*(1), 18–27. https://doi.org/10.1177/1476718X14523747

Grinyer, A. (2002). The anonymity of research participants: Assumptions, ethics and practicalities. *Social Research Update, 36*, 1–4. http://sru.soc.surrey.ac.uk/SRU36.pdf

Guenther, K. M. (2009). The politics of names: Rethinking the methodological and ethical significance of naming people, organizations, and places. *Qualitative Research*, *9*(4), 411–421. https://doi.org/10.1177/1468794109337872

Guest, G., MacQueen, K. M., & Namey, E. E. (2012). *Applied thematic analysis*. Sage. https://doi.org/10.4135/97814833 84436

Guillemin, M., & Gillam, L. (2004). Ethics, reflexivity, and "ethically important moments" in research. *Qualitative Inquiry*, *10*(2), 261–280. https://doi.org/10.1177/1077800403262360

Hadjistavropoulos, T., & Smythe, W. E. (2001). Elements of risk in qualitative research. *Ethics & Behavior*, *11*(2), 163–174. https://doi.org/10.1207/S15327019 EB1102_4

Halsman, P., & Dali, S. (1984). *Dalis' mustache*. Simon & Schuster. (Original work published 1954)

Hamilton, B. (2011). *"I think of myself as a talented writer": Understanding fifth and sixth grade students' self-concepts in writing* (Publication No. 3464865) [Doctoral dissertation, University of Northern Colorado]. Proquest Dissertations and Theses Global.

Harmon, W., & Holman, C. H. (1996). *A handbook to literature* (7th ed.). Prentice Hall.

Harper, D. (1994). On the authority of the image: Visual methods at the crossroads. In N. K. Denzin & Y. S Lincoln (Eds.), *Handbook of qualitative research* (pp. 403–412). Sage.

Harper, D. (2000). Reimagining visual methods: Galileo to Neuromancer. In N. K. Denzin & Y. S. Lincoln (Eds.), *Handbook of qualitative research* (2nd ed., pp. 717–732). Sage.

Harper, D. (2005). What's new visually? In N. K. Denzin & Y. S. Lincoln (Eds.), *Handbook of qualitative research* (3rd ed., pp. 747–762). Sage.

Harrison, J., MacGibbon, L., & Morton, M. (2001). Regimes of trustworthiness in qualitative research: The rigors of reciprocity. *Qualitative Inquiry*, *7*(3), 323–345. https://doi.org/10.1177/1077 80040100700305

Harrison, K. (n.d.). *What is visual literacy?* Visual Literacy Today. https://visual literacytoday.org/what-is-visual-literacy/

Hartnett, S. J. (2003). *Incarceration nation: Investigative prison poems of hope and terror*. AltaMira Press.

Hastings, W. (2010). Research and the ambiguity of reflexivity and ethical practice. *Discourse: Studies in the Cultural Politics of Education*, *31*, 307–318. https://doi.org/10.1080/01596301003786902

Heisley, D. D., & Levy, S. J. (1991). Autodriving: A photo elicitation technique. *Journal of Consumer Research*, *18*(3), 257–272. https://doi.org/10.1086/209258

Herbert, G. (n.d.). *Easter wings*. Poetry Foundation. https://www.poetryfoundation .org/poems/44361/easter-wings

Hertz, R. (1997). *Reflexivity and voice*. Sage.

Highfield, T., & Leaver, T. (2016). Instagrammatics and digital methods: Studying visual social media, from selfies and GIFs to memes and emoji. *Communication Research and Practice*, *2*(1), 47–62. https://doi.org/10.1080/220414 51.2016.1155332

Hill, E. S. (1967). *Evan's corner*. Holt, Rinehart, & Winston.

Hodder, I. (2000). The interpretation of documents and material culture. In N. K. Denzin & Y. S. Lincoln (Eds.), *The SAGE handbook of qualitative research* (2nd ed., pp. 703–715). Sage.

Hoffman, G. (1997). *Adios, Strunk and White*. Verve Press.

Holliday, A. (2007). *Doing and writing qualitative research*. Sage. https://doi.org/10.4135/9781446287958

Holloway, I., & Todres, L. (2003). The status of method: Flexibility, consistency and coherence. *Qualitative Research, 3*(3), 345–357. https://doi.org/10.1177/1468794103033004

Holm, G. (2008). Visual research methods: Where are we and where are we going? In S. N. Hesse-Biber & P. Leavy (Eds.), *Handbook of emergent methods* (pp. 325–341). Guilford Press.

Holman, B., & Muske-Dukes, C. (Eds.). (2011). *Crossing state lines: An American renga*. Farrar, Straus & Giroux.

Holman Jones, S. (2005). Autoethnography: Making the personal political. In N. K. Denzin & Y. S. Lincoln (Eds.), *Handbook of qualitative research* (3rd ed., pp. 763–791). Sage.

Holman Jones, S. (2016). Living bodies of thought: The "critical" in critical autoethnography. *Qualitative Inquiry, 22*(4), 228–237. https://doi.org/10.1177/1077800415622509

Holman Jones, S. L., Adams, T. E., & Ellis, C. (2013). *Handbook of autoethnography*. Left Coast Press.

Hoonaard, W. C. van den. (2003). Is anonymity an artifact in ethnographic research? *Journal of Academic Ethics, 1*, 141–151. https://doi.org/10.1023/B:JAET.0000006919.58804.4c

Howard, P. (2014). *A poppy*. http://www.bbc.co.uk/arts/poetry/ondisplay/poppy.html

Hughes, J. (Ed.). (2012). *SAGE visual methods*. Sage.

Hughes, L. (1966). *From the archive: Langston Hughes's 1966 letter*. poets.org. https://poets.org/text/archive-langston-hughess-1966-letter

Hult, C. A. (2015). *The handy English grammar answer book*. Visible Ink Press.

Hurst, A. L. (2008). A healing echo: Methodological reflections of a working-class researcher on class. *Qualitative Report, 13*(3), 334–352.

Hurworth, R. (2003). Photo interviewing for research. *Social Research Update, 40*, 1–4. http://sru.soc.surrey.ac.uk/SRU40.html

Husserl, E. (1999). *The essential Husserl: Basic writings in transcendental phenomenology*. Indiana University Press.

Huston, T. (n.d.). *What is hypermedia?* Smartbear. https://smartbear.com/learn/api-design/what-is-hypermedia/

Janesick, V. J. (1998). *"Stretching" exercises for qualitative researchers*. Sage.

Janesick, V. J. (1999). A journal about journal writing as a qualitative research technique: History, issues, and reflections. *Qualitative Inquiry, 5*(4), 505–524. https://doi.org/10.1177/107780049900500404

Janesick, V. J. (2015). Journaling, reflexive. In G. Ritzer (Ed.), *Blackwell encyclopedia of sociology* (2nd ed., pp. 3387–3389). Blackwell. https://doi .org/10.1002/9781405165518.wbeosj007 .pub2

Janesick, V. J. (2016). *Contemplative qualitative inquiry: Practicing the zen of research.* Routledge. https://doi.org/ 10.4324/9781315431697

Janzen, J. (1995). *Snake in the parsonage.* Simon & Schuster.

Janzen, J. (2008). *Paper house: Poems.* Good Books.

Jemielniak, D. (2014). *Common knowledge? An ethnography of Wikipedia.* Stanford University Press. https://doi .org/10.11126/stanford/9780804789448 .001.0001

Jensen, J. V. (1987). Ethical tension points in whistleblowing. *Journal of Business Ethics, 6,* 321–328. https://doi .org/10.1007/BF00382941

Jerolmack, C., & Murphy, A. K. (2019). The ethical dilemmas and social scientific trade-offs of masking in ethnography. *Sociological Methods & Research, 48*(4), 801–827. https://doi.org/10.1177/0049 124117701483

Johns, R. D. (2014). *Narratives of competency, creativity, and comfort: Religion and spirituality in counselor education* (Publication No. 3687922) [Doctoral dissertation, University of Northern Colorado]. ProQuest Dissertations and Theses Global.

Johns, R. D. (2017a). A spiritual question. *Qualitative Inquiry, 23*(8), 631–638. https://doi.org/10.1177/1077 800417692362

Johns, R. D. (2017b). Stories matter: Narrative themes of counselor educators'

religious and spiritual competency. *Counseling and Values, 62*(1), 72–89. https://doi.org/10.1002/cvj.12050

Johnson, T. H. (1961). *The complete poems of Emily Dickinson.* Back Bay Books, Little, Brown.

Kaiser, K. (2009). Protecting respondent confidentiality in qualitative research. *Qualitative Health Research, 19*(11), 1632–1641. https://doi.org/10.1177/104973 2309350879

Kamler, B., & Thomson, P. (2008). The failure of dissertation advice books: Toward alternative pedagogies for doctoral writing. *Educational Researcher, 37*(8), 507–514. https://doi .org/10.3102/0013189X08327390

Kamler, B., & Thomson, P. (2014). *Helping doctoral students write: Pedagogies for supervision.* Routledge. https://doi.org/ 10.4324/9781315813639

Keats, J. (1820). *Ode on a Grecian urn.* poets.org. https://poets.org/poem/ode-grecian-urn

Kėdra, J., & Žakevičiūtė, R. (2019). Visual literacy practices in higher education: What, why and how? *Journal of Visual Literacy, 38*(1–2), 1–7. https://doi .org/10.1080/1051144X.2019.1580438

Keengwe, J. (Ed.). (2013). *Literacy enrichment and technology integration in preservice teacher education.* IGI Global. https://doi.org/10.4018/978-1-4666-4924-8

Kidder, T. (1989). *Among schoolchildren.* Houghton Mifflin.

Kincaid, T. W. (2019). *Methodological considerations for researching hidden populations with an emphasis on homeless research sampling methods* (Publication No. 27669684) [Doctoral dissertation, University of Northern Colorado]. Pro-Quest Dissertations and Theses Global.

Kincheloe, J. (2006). Critical ontology and indigenous ways on being: Forging a postcolonial curriculum. In Y. Kanu (Ed.), *Curriculum as cultural practice: Postcolonial imaginations* (pp. 179–195). University of Toronto Press. https://doi.org/10.3138/9781442686267-010

King, S. (2000). *On writing: A memoir of the craft.* Charles Scribner.

Kleon, A. (2014). *Newspaper blackout.* HarperCollins.

Knowles, C., & Sweetman, P. (2004). Introduction. In *Picturing the social landscape: Visual methods and the sociological imagination* (pp. 1–17). Routledge. https://doi.org/10.4324/9780203694527

Knowles, J. G., Luciani, T., Cole, A. L., & Neilsen, L. (Eds.). (2007). *The art of visual inquiry.* Backalong Books; Centre for Arts-Informed Research.

Koelsch, L. E. (2015). I poems: Evoking self. *Qualitative Psychology, 2*(1), 96–107. https://doi.org/10.1037/qup0000021

Kristin. (2011). *Relief society "new dimension" ball.* https://www.pinterest.com/pin/98657048065606238/

Ku, H. Y., Lahman, M. K., Yeh, H. T., & Cheng, Y. C. (2008). Into the academy: Preparing and mentoring international doctoral students. *Educational Technology Research and Development, 56*(3), 365–377. https://doi.org/10.1007/s11423-007-9083-0

Kuttner, P. J., Sousanis, N., & Weaver-Hightower, M. B. (2017). How to draw comics the scholarly way: Creating comics-based research in the academy. In P. Leavy (Ed.), *Handbook of arts-based research* (pp. 396–422). Guilford Press.

Kuttner, P. J., Weaver-Hightower, M. B., & Sousanis, N. (2020). Comics-based research: The affordances of comics for research across disciplines. *Qualitative Research, 21*(2), 195–214. https://doi.org/10.1177/1468794120918845

Ladenheim, M. (2014). Engaging honors students through newspaper blackout poetry. *Honors in Practice, 10*, 45–54. https://core.ac.uk/download/pdf/20266768.pdf

Lahman, M. (2017b). Mother hood. *Qualitative Inquiry, 23*(8), 639–640. https://doi.org/10.1177/1077800416684875

Lahman, M. K. E. (2008). Always othered: Ethical research with children. *Journal of Early Childhood Research, 6*(3), 281–300. https://doi.org/10.1177/1468794120918845

Lahman, M. K. E. (2009). Dreams of my daughter: An ectopic pregnancy. *Qualitative Health Research, 19*(2), 272–278. https://doi.org/10.1177/104973230832 9484

Lahman, M. K. E. (2011). I am ALL woma[e]n! *Qualitative Inquiry, 17*(2), 126–129. https://doi.org/10.1177/1077 800410392330

Lahman, M. K. E. (2013). Dear Doctor and our (my/your) ectopic pregnancy. *Qualitative Inquiry, 19*(7), 538–541. https://doi.org/10.1177/1077800413489517

Lahman, M. K. E. (2015). Peckernite poetry (zwei). *Qualitative Inquiry, 21*(5), 407–409. https://doi.org/10.1177/1077 800415569786

Lahman, M. K. E. (2017a). *Ethics in social science research: Becoming culturally responsive*. Sage.

Lahman, M. K. E. (2018). *Social science research ethics: Becoming culturally responsive*. Sage.

Lahman, M. K. E. (2019a). Big beautiful heart. *Qualitative Inquiry*, *25*(9–10), 834. https://doi.org/10.1177/1077800418808538

Lahman, M. K. E. (2019b). Blacking out. *Qualitative Inquiry*. Advance online publication. https://doi.org/10.1177/1077800419883318

Lahman, M. K. E. (2019c). The dead chick. *Qualitative Inquiry*, *25*(9–10), 835. https://doi.org/10.1177/1077800419857753

Lahman, M. K. E. (2019d). Email with the dead. *Qualitative Inquiry*, *25*(9–10), 831–832. https://doi.org/10.1177/1077800418784324

Lahman, M. K. E. (2019e). Hail. *Qualitative Inquiry*, *25*(9–10), 833. https://doi.org/10.1177/1077800418792017

Lahman, M. K. E. (2020). Beneath the lemon tree: An interrupted family story. *Qualitative Inquiry*, *27*(1), 86–89. https://doi.org/10.1177/1077800419897680

Lahman, M. K. (2021). A loss of innocence: Infertility. *Qualitative Inquiry*, *27*(1), 125–128. https://doi.org/10.1177/1077800419883305

Lahman, M. K. E., & De Oliveira, B. (2020). Poetry spheres, flower poems: A dimensional poetry experience. *Qualitative Inquiry*. Advance online publication. https://doi.org/10.1177/1077800420941050

Lahman, M. K. E., De Oliveira, B., Cox, D., Sebastian, M. L., Cadogan, K., Rundle Kahn, A., Lafferty, M., Morgan, M., Thapa, K., Thomas, R., & Zakotnik-Gutierrez, J. (2020). Own your walls: Portraiture and researcher reflexive collage self-portraits. *Qualitative Inquiry*, *27*(1), 136–147. https://doi.org/10.1177/1077800419897699

Lahman, M. K. E., De Oliveira, B., Fan, X., Hodges, J., Moncivais, I., & Royse, E. (2020). Pandemic poetry. *Qualitative Inquiry*. Advance online publication. https://doi.org/10.1177/1077800420948099

Lahman, M. K. E., Geist, M. R., Rodriguez, K. L., Graglia, P. E., Richard, V. M., & Schendel, R. K. (2010). Poking around poetically: Research, poetry, and trustworthiness. *Qualitative Inquiry*, *16*(1), 39–48. https://doi.org/10.1177/1077800409350061

Lahman, M. K. E., Hancock, E., Alhudithi, A., Kincaid, T., Lafferty, M., Patchett, E., Loften, L., & Couch, C. (2019). Renga, research, reflexivity: Poetic representation. *Qualitative Inquiry*, *25*(9–10), 826–829. https://doi.org/10.1177/1077800418788108

Lahman, M. K. E., & Park, S. (2004). Understanding children from diverse cultures: Bridging perspectives of parents and teachers. *International Journal of Early Years Education*, *12*(2), 131–142. https://doi.org/10.1080/0966976042000225525

Lahman, M. K. E., & Richard, V. M. (2014). Appropriated poetry: Archival poetry in research. *Qualitative Inquiry*, *20*(3), 344–355. https://doi.org/10.1177/1077800413489272

Lahman, M. K. E., Richard, V. M., & Teman, E. D. (2019). Ish: How to write poemish (research) poetry. *Qualitative Inquiry, 25*(2), 215–227. https://doi.org/10.1177/1077800417750182

Lahman, M. K. E., Rodriguez, K. L., Moses, L., Griffin, K. M., Mendoza, B. M., & Yacoub, W. (2015). A rose by any other name is still a rose? Problematizing pseudonyms in research. *Qualitative Inquiry, 21*(5), 445–453. https://doi.org/10.1177/1077800415572391

Lahman, M. K. E., Rodriguez, K. L., Richard, V. M., Geist, M. R., Schendel, R. K., & Graglia, P. E. (2011). (Re)forming research poetry. *Qualitative Inquiry, 17*(9), 887–896. https://doi.org/10.1177/1077800411423219

Lahman, M. K. E., Teman, E. D., & Richard, V. M. (2017). IRB as poetry. *Qualitative Inquiry, 25*(2), 200–214. https://doi.org/10.1177/1077800417744580.

Lahman, M. K. E., Taylor, C. M., Beddes, L. A., Blount, I. D., Bontempo, K. A., Coon, J. D., Fernandez, C., & Motter, B. (2019). Research falling out of colorful pages onto paper: Collage inquiry. *Qualitative Inquiry, 26*(3–4), 262–270. https://doi.org/10.1177/1077800418810721

Lail, A. J., & Lahman, M. K. (2019). Mascots, metaphor, methodology: Counter poetics. *Qualitative Inquiry, 25*(2), 154–159. https://doi.org/10.1177/1077800417745918

Lakoff, G., & Johnson, M. (1980). *Metaphors we live by.* University of Chicago Press.

Lamott, A. (1994). *Bird by bird: Some instructions on writing and life.* Anchor Books.

Landram, S. V. (2018). *A methodological review of the cross-cultural ethical dilemmas that exist within the informed consent process: When ethical considerations in human research differ* (Publication No. 10928371) [Doctoral dissertation, University of Northern Colorado]. ProQuest Dissertations and Theses Global.

Lasker, J. N., & Toedter, L. J. (1994). Satisfaction with hospital care and interventions after pregnancy loss. *Death Studies, 18*(1), 41–64. https://doi.org/10.1080/07481189408252642

Lasker, J. N., & Toedter, L. J. (2003). The impact of ectopic pregnancy: A 16-year follow-up study. *Health Care for Women International, 24*(3), 209–230. https://doi.org/10.1080/07399330390178486

Lather, P. (2012). *Getting lost: Feminist efforts toward a double(d) science.* SUNY Press.

Lawrence-Lightfoot, S. (2016). Commentary: Portraiture methodology: Blending art and science. *LEARNing Landscapes, 9*(2), 19–27. https://doi.org/10.36510/learnland.v9i2.760

Lawrence-Lightfoot, S., & Davis, J. H. (1997). *The art and science of portraiture.* Jossey-Bass.

Leavy, P. (2008). *Method meets art: Arts based research practice.* Guilford Press.

Lee, C. (2015). *Contractions in formal writing: What's allowed, what's not.* https://blog.apastyle.org/apastyle/2015/12/contractions-in-formal-writing-whats-allowed-whats-not.html

Lee, H. (1960). *To kill a mockingbird.* J. B. Lippincott.

Leeuwen, T. (2020). Multimodality and multimodal research. In L. Pauwels & D. Mannay (Eds.), *The SAGE handbook of visual research methods* (pp. 464–483). Sage. https://doi.org/10.4135/9781526417015

Le Guin, U. K. (2017). *Dancing at the edge of the world: Thoughts on words, women, places.* Open Road+ Grove Atlantic.

L'Engle, M. (1962). *A wrinkle in time.* Farrar, Straus & Giroux.

Lenzy, C. D. (2019a). Navigating the complexities of race-based activism. In S. Y. Evans, A. D. Domingue, & T. D. Mitchell. (Eds.), *Black women and social justice education: Legacies and lessons* (pp. 261–274). SUNY Press.

Lenzy, C. D. (2019b). *We were asked to deny a part of ourselves—and did: How Black women doctoral students experience their intersectional identities in race-based activism* (Publication No. 22619176) [Doctoral dissertation, University of Northern Colorado]. ProQuest Dissertations and Theses Global.

Lester, J. (2007, January, 24). *Found Poem #6: A commonplace book.* http://acommonplacejbl.blogspot.com/2007/01/found-poem-6.html

Levin, P. (1996). End of April. In *The Afterimage.* Copper Beech Press.

Lewis, C. (2013). *Once, twice, thrice told tales: Three mice full of writing advice.* Atheneum Books.

Lewis, C. S. (1978). *The lion, the witch, and the wardrobe* (The Chronicles of Narnia). Collier Books.

Lexico. (n.d.). Medley. https://www.lexico.com/en/definition/medley

Liamputtong, P. (2007). *Researching the vulnerable: A guide to sensitive research methods.* Sage. https://doi.org/10.4135/9781849209861

Lightfoot, S. L. (1985). *Good high school.* Basic.

Lim, J. (2016, November 16). *Editor's pick: Top qualitative research blogs.* Qualitative 360. https://qual360.com/editors-pick-top-qualitative-research-blogs/

Lincoln, Y. S. (2007). Authenticity criteria. In *The Blackwell encyclopedia of sociology.* Wiley. https://doi.org/10.1002/9781405165518.wbeosa076

Lincoln, Y. S., & Guba, E. G. (1985). *Naturalistic inquiry.* Sage. https://doi.org/10.1016/0147-1767(85)90062-8

Lisle, H. (n.d.). *The good, the bad, and the ugly, or how to choose a writers' group.* https://hollylisle.com/the-good-the-bad-and-the-ugly-or-how-to-choose-a-writers-group/

Literary Devices. (n.d.). *Style.*

Lucock, C., & Yeo, M. (2006). Naming names: The pseudonym in the name of the law. *University of Ottawa Law and Technology Journal, 3*(1), 53–108.

Luke, P. (2017). *Master creative writing quickly.* Be a Better Writer. http://www.be-a-better-writer.com/cliches.html

Magee Donnelly, M. (2017, March, 11). *Clear frame portrait paintings.* http://homegrownfriends.com/home/clear-frame-portrait-paintings/

Magolda, P. M. (2016). *The lives of campus custodians: Insights into corporatization and civic disengagement in the academy.* Stylus.

Majmudar, A. (Ed.). (2017). *Resistance, rebellion, life: 50 Poems now*. Alfred A. Knopf.

Malott, K. M. (2005). *Ethnic self-labeling in the Latina population* (Publication No. 3171930) [Doctoral dissertation, University of Northern Colorado]. ProQuest Dissertations and Theses Global.

Mannay, D. (2010). Making the familiar strange: Can visual research methods render the familiar setting more perceptible? *Qualitative Research, 10*(1), 91–111. https://doi.org/10.1177/1468794109348684

Mannay, D. (2020). Revisualizing data: Engagement, impact and multimodal dissemination. In L. Pauwels & D. Mannay (Eds.), *The SAGE handbook of visual research methods* (pp. 659–669). Sage. https://doi.org/10.4135/9781526417015

Margolin, I. (2014). Collage as a method of inquiry for university women practicing Mahavakyam meditation: Ameliorating the effects of stress, anxiety, and sadness. *Journal of Religion & Spirituality in Social Work: Social Thought, 33*, 254–273. https://doi.org/10.1080/15426432.2014.930632

Marion, J. S., & Crowder, J. W. (2013). *Visual research: A concise introduction to thinking visually*. A & C Black.

McAdoo, T. (2009). *Use of first person in APA style*. APA Style Blog. https://blog.apastyle.org/apastyle/2009/09/use-of-first-person-in-apa-style.html

McBride, J. (1996). *The color of water: A Black man's tribute to his white mother*. Riverhead Books.

McCosker, K., & Albery, N. (1998). *Poem a day* (Vol. *1*). Natural Death Center.

McDonald, J. (2013). Coming out in the field: A queer reflexive account of shifting researcher identity. *Management Learning, 44*(2), 127–143. https://doi.org/10.1177/1350507612473711

McMillan, G. (2018). ETDs in the 21st century. *Educause Review, 70*(1), 21–29. https://doi.org/10.1111/erev.12329

Meeks, C. (2017). *Poetic sense: Sound and imagery*. Christopher's Blog. http://www.chrismeeks.com/blog/poetic-sense-sound-and-imagery

Merriam, S. B. (1998). *Qualitative research and case study applications in education: Revised and expanded from "Case Study Research in Education."* Jossey-Bass.

Merriam, S. B. (2009). *Qualitative research: A guide to design and implementation* (pp. 39–54). Jossey-Bass.

Merriam, S. B., & Tisdell, E. J. (2016). *Qualitative research: A guide to design and implementation*. Jossey-Bass.

Merriam-Webster. (n.d.-a). Fair use. In *Merriam-Webster.com dictionary*. Retrieved March 24, 2021, from https://www.merriam-webster.com/dictionary/fair%20use

Merriam Webster. (n.d.-b). Hone. In *Merriam-Webster.com dictionary*. Retrieved May 2, 2021, from https://www.merriam-webster.com/dictionary/hone

Merriam-Webster. (n.d.-c). Hotchpotch. In *Merriam-Webster.com dictionary*. Retrieved March 24, 2021, from https://www.merriam-webster.com/dictionary/hotchpotch

Merriam Webster. (n.d.-d). Kaleidoscope. In *Merriam-Webster.com dictionary*.

Retrieved April 27, 2021, from https://www.merriam-webster.com/dictionary/kaleidoscope

Meyer, D. (2008). *Why we hate us: American discontent in the new millennium.* Crown.

Meyer, M. (2017). Concrete research poetry: A visual representation of metaphor. *Art/Research International: A Transdisciplinary Journal, 2*(1), 32–57. https://doi.org/10.18432/R2KS6F

Millar, J. (n.d.) *Poem 056: Red wing.* Library of Congress. https://www.loc.gov/programs/poetry-and-literature/poet-laureate/poet-laureate-projects/poetry-180/all-poems/item/poetry-180-056/red-wing/?loclr=lsp1_rg0001

Miller, N. (2017). *Lemon tart mystery.* S&G.

Milne, A. A. (1956). *The house at Pooh Corner.* Dutton Children's Books.

Milne, E.-J., & Muir, R. (2020). Photovoice: A critical introduction. In L. Pauwels & D. Mannay (Eds.), *The SAGE handbook of visual research methods* (pp. 15–36). Sage. https://doi.org/10.4135/9781526417015.n17

Mitchell, C. (2011). *Doing visual research.* Sage.

Morgan, D. L. (2018). *Basic and advanced focus groups.* Sage. https://doi.org/10.4135/9781071814307

Morse, J. M. (2002). Writing my own experience [Editorial]. *Qualitative Health Research, 12*(9), 1159–1160. https://doi.org/10.1177/1049732302238241

Mosak, H., & Maniacci, M. (2013). *Primer of Adlerian psychology: The analytic-behavioural-cognitive psychology of Alfred Adler.* Routledge. https://doi.org/10.4324/9780203768518

Moss, J., & Pini, B. (Eds.). (2016). *Visual research methods in educational research.* Springer. https://doi.org/10.1057/9781137447357

Moustakas, C. (1994). *Phenomenological research methods.* Sage. https://doi.org/10.4135/9781412995658

Mukungu, K. (2017). "How can you write about a person who does not exist?" Rethinking pseudonymity and informed consent in life history research. *Social Sciences, 6*(3), 86. https://doi.org/10.3390/socsci6030086

Mulkerrins, J. (2017, June 10). Elisabeth Moss on *The Handmaid's Tale*: "It is a feminist story." *The Guardian.* https://www.theguardian.com/tv-and-radio/2017/jun/10/elisabeth-moss-handmaids-tale-feminist-story

Mulvihill, T. M., & Swaminathan, R. (2019). *Arts-based educational research and qualitative inquiry: Walking the path.* Routledge. https://doi.org/10.4324/9781315143361

Naylor, A., & Wood, A. (2012). *Teaching poetry: Reading and responding to poetry in the secondary classroom.* Routledge. https://doi.org/10.4324/9780203139240

Neruda, P. (n.d.). *I'm explaining a few things.* https://www.poetryinternational.org/pi/poem/22618/auto/0/0/Pablo-Neruda/Im-Explaining-a-Few-Things/en/tile

Nesbitt, K. (2014, May, 18). *Forced rhymes: What they are and how to avoid them*. https://forum.rhymezone.com/articles/963-forced-rhymes-what-they-are-and-how-to-avoid-them

Nespor, J. (2000). Anonymity and place in qualitative inquiry. *Qualitative Inquiry, 6*(4), 546–569. https://doi.org/10.1177/107780040000600408

The New York Times. (2016, June, 7). *The eternally quotable Dorothy Parker*. https://www.nytimes.com/interactive/projects/cp/obituaries/archives/dorothy-parker

Newbury, D. (2020). Making arguments with images: Visual scholarship and academic publishing. In L. Pauwels & D. Mannay (Eds.), *The SAGE handbook of visual research methods* (pp. 670–681). Sage. https://doi.org/10.4135/9781526417015

Nichols, T. R., Biederman, D. J., & Gringle, M. R. (2015). Using research poetics responsibly: Applications for health promotion research. *International Quarterly for Community Health Education, 35*(1), 5–20. https://doi.org/10.2190/IQ.35.1.b

Nielsen, K. L. (2020). Students' video viewing habits during a flipped classroom course in engineering mathematics. *Research in Learning Technology, 28*. https://doi.org/10.25304/rlt.v28.2404

Oliffe, J. L., & Bottorff, J. L. (2007). Further than the eye can see? Photo elicitation and research with men. *Qualitative Health Research, 17*(6), 850–858. https://doi.org/10.1177/1049732306298756

Oliphant, S. M., & Bennett, C. S. (2020). Using reflexivity journaling to lessen the emic–etic divide in a qualitative study of Ethiopian immigrant women. *Qualitative Social Work, 19*(4), 599–611. https://doi.org/10.1177/1473325019836723

Ong, P. A. L. (2020). Visual research methods: Qualifying and quantifying the visual. *Beijing International Review of Education, 2*(1), 35–53. https://doi.org/10.1163/25902539-00201004

Paley, V. G. (2009). *You can't say you can't play*. Harvard University Press.

Park, S., & Lahman, M. K. (2003). Bridging perspectives of parents, teachers and co-researchers: Methodological reflections on cross-cultural research. *Reflective Practice, 4*(3), 375–383. https://doi.org/10.1080/1462394032000112264

Parker, M. (2017). *Art teacher in process: An illustrated exploration of art, education and what matters* [Master's thesis, Simon Fraser University]. Education—Theses, Dissertations, and Other Required Graduate Degree Essays. https://summit.sfu.ca/item/17806

Parr, A. (2017). *The poetry of resistance*. https://lareviewofbooks.org/article/the-poetry-of-resistance/

Pauwels, L., & Mannay, D. (2020). *The SAGE handbook of visual research methods*. Sage. https://doi.org/10.4135/9781526417015

Peres, T. S. (2016). *Stigma management in waste management: An investigation into the interactions of "waste pickers" on the streets of Cape Town and the consequences for agency* [Doctoral dissertation, University of Cape Town]. OpenUCT—Theses/Dissertations. http://hdl.handle.net/11427/24492

Peters, A. S., & Lahman, M. (2014). "Am I at peace"? A deeper look into identity formation and integration. *Journal of Educational Research and Innovation*, 3(1), Article 3.

Phoenix, C. (2010). Seeing the world of physical culture: The potential of visual methods for qualitative research in sport and exercise. *Qualitative Research in Sport and Exercise, 2*(2), 93–108. https://doi.org/10.1080/19398441.2010.488017

Phoenix, C., & Rich, E. (2016). Visual research methods. In B. Smith & A. C. Sparkes (Eds.), *Routledge handbook of qualitative research in sport and exercise* (pp. 161–173). Routledge.

Piercy, F. P., & Benson, K. (2005). Aesthetic forms of data representation in qualitative family therapy research. *Journal of Marital and Family Therapy, 31*(1), 107–119. https://doi.org/10.1111/j.1752-0606.2005.tb01547.x

Pillow, W. S. (2010). Dangerous reflexivity: Rigour, responsibility, and reflexivity in qualitative research. In P. Thomson & M. Walker (Eds.), *The Routledge doctoral student's companion* (pp. 270–282). Routledge.

Pink, S. (Ed.). (2007). *Visual interventions: Applied visual anthropology* (Vol. 4). Berghahn Books.

Pink, S. (2013). *Doing visual ethnography.* Sage.

Pink, S. (2020). A multisensory approach to visual methods. In L. Pauwels & D. Mannay (Eds.), *The SAGE handbook of visual research methods* (pp. 523–533). Sage. https://doi.org/10.4135/9781526417015

Plath, S. (n.d.). *Tulips.* Poetry Foundation. https://www.poetryfoundation.org/poems/49013/tulips-56d22ab68fdd0

Plessis, C. du. (2019). Prosumer engagement through story-making in transmedia branding. *International Journal of Cultural Studies, 22*(1), 175–192. https://doi.org/10.1177/1367877917750445

Plimpton, G. (Interviewer). (1986). E. L. Doctorow, the art of fiction No. 94. *The Paris Review,* Winter(101). https://www.theparisreview.org/interviews/2718/the-art-of-fiction-no-94-e-l-doctorow

Plimpton, G. (Interviewer). (1990). Maya Angelou, the art of fiction No. 119. *The Paris Review,* Fall(116). https://www.theparisreview.org/interviews/2279/the-art-of-fiction-no-119-maya-angelou

Poe, E. A. (1969). Elizabeth [Rebecca]. In T. O. Mabbott (Ed.), *The collected works of Edgar Allan Poe: Vol. 1. Poems* (pp. 147–149). https://www.eapoe.org/works/mabbott/tom1p039.htm

Poetry Foundation. (n.d.). *Glossary of poetic terms: Found poem.* https://www.poetryfoundation.org/learn/glossary-terms/found-poem

poets.org. (n.d.-a). *Epistolary poem.* https://www.poets.org/poetsorg/text/epistle-poetic-form

poets.org. (n.d.-b). *Erasure.* https://poets.org/text/erasure-or-blackout-poetry-poetic-form

poets.org. (n.d.-c). *Found poem.* http://www.poets.org/viewmedia.php/prmMID/5780

poets.org. (n.d.-d). *Renga.* https://www.poets.org/poetsorg/text/renga-poetic-form

Poland, B. D. (2002). Transcription quality. In J. F. Gubrium & J. A. Holstein (Eds.), *Handbook of interview research, context and method* (pp. 629–649). Sage.

Potvin, S., & Thompson, S. (2016). An analysis of evolving practices in electronic theses and dissertations. *Library Resources & Technical Services, 60*(2), 99–114. https://doi.org/10.5860/lrts.60n2.99

Pratt, M. G. (2008). Fitting oval pegs into round holes: Tensions in evaluating and publishing qualitative research in top-tier North American journals. *Organizational Research Methods, 11*(3), 481–509. https://doi.org/10.1177/1094428107303349

Prendergast, M. (2004). "Shaped like a question mark": Found poetry from Herbert Blau's *The Audience. Research in Drama Education, 9*(1), 73–92. https://doi.org/10.1080/1356978042000185920

Prendergast, M. (2006). Found poetry as literature review: Research poems on audience and performance. *Qualitative Inquiry, 12*(2), 369–388. https://doi.org/10.1177/1077800405284601

Prendergast, M., Leggo, C., & Sameshima, P. (Eds.). (2009). *Poetic inquiry: Vibrant voices in the social sciences.* Brill. https://doi.org/10.1163/9789087909512

Pretorius, M. (2016). Paper-based theses as the silver bullet for increased research outputs: First hear my story as a supervisor. *Higher Education Research & Development, 36*(4), 823–837. https://doi.org/10.1080/07294360.2016.1208639

The Punctuation Guide. (n.d.). Em dash. https://www.thepunctuationguide.com/em-dash.html

QuoteFancy. (n.d.). *Kamand Kojouri quotes.* https://quotefancy.com/quote/2359876/Kamand-Kojouri-Oh-how-scary-and-wonderful-it-is-that-words-can-change-our-lives-simply-by

Reavey, P. (2011). *Visual methods in psychology: Using and interpreting images in qualitative research.* Routledge. https://doi.org/10.4324/9780203829042

Reed, J. (2006). *Appreciative inquiry: Research for change.* Sage. https://doi.org/10.4135/9781412983464

reelblack. (2017). *Evan's corner (1969).* YouTube. https://www.youtube.com/watch?v=Jm-x_QX9fJM

Reilly, S. (2019). Stick 'em up! A surprising history of collage. *The Economist 1843.* https://www.1843magazine.com/culture/look-closer/stick-em-up-a-surprising-history-of-collage

Rennie, D. L., Watson, K. D., & Monteiro, A. M. (2002). The rise of qualitative research in psychology. *Canadian Psychology/Psychologie Canadienne, 43*(3), 179–189. https://doi.org/10.1037/h0086914

ReproductiveFacts.org. (n.d.). *Age and fertility.* https://www.reproductivefacts.org/news-and-publications/patient-fact-sheets-and-booklets/documents/fact-sheets-and-info-booklets/age-and-fertility/#:~:text=Fertility%20gradually%20declines%20in%20the,20%25%20chance%20of%20getting%20pregnant

Reynolds, P. (2004). *ish.* Candlewick Press.

Richard, V. M. (2010). *Using (re)valuing methodology to understand content area literacy immersion (CALI): A journey with preservice secondary content area teachers* (Publication No. 3448547) [Doctoral dissertation, University of Northern Colorado]. Proquest Dissertations and Theses Global.

Richard, V. M., & Lahman, M. K. (2015). Photo-elicitation: Reflexivity on method, analysis, and graphic portraits. *International Journal of Research & Method in Education, 38*(1), 3–22. https://doi.org/10.1080/1743727X.2013.843073

Richardson, L. (1990). Literary devices in social science writing. In *Writing strategies* (pp. 18–20). Sage. https://www.doi.org/10.4135/9781412986526

Richardson, L. (1993). Poetics, dramatics, and transgressive validity: The case of the skipped line. *The Sociological Quarterly, 34*(4), 695–710.

Richardson, L. (1994). Writing: A method of inquiry. In N. K. Denzin & Y. S. Lincoln (Eds.), *The SAGE handbook of qualitative research* (pp. 516–529). Sage.

Richardson, L. (1999). Feathers in our CAP. *Journal of Contemporary Ethnography, 28*(6), 660–668. https://doi.org/10.1177/089124199129023767

Riordan, H. (2019, June, 30). 13 Clever jokes only literature lovers will appreciate. *All Women's Talk.* https://funny.allwomenstalk.com/clever-jokes-only-literature-lovers-will-appreciate/

Roberts, C. M. (2010). *The dissertation journey: A practical and comprehensive guide to planning, writing, and defending your dissertation.* Corwin Press.

Rodriguez, K. L. (2004). *Las comadres: Cuentame su historia: Latina college students make meaning of the body politic* [Las comadres: Tell me your story:

Latina college students make meaning of the body politic] (Publication No. 3130541) [Doctoral dissertation, University of Northern Colorado]. ProQuest Dissertations and Theses Global.

Rodriguez, K. L., Schwartz, J. L., Lahman, M. K., & Geist, M. R. (2011). Culturally responsive focus groups: Reframing the research experience to focus on participants. *International Journal of Qualitative Methods, 10*(4), 400–417. https://doi.org/10.1177/160940691101000407

Rose, G. (2007). *Visual methodologies. An introduction to the interpretation of visual materials.* Sage.

Rossman, G. B., & Rallis, S. F. (2016). *An introduction to qualitative research: Learning in the field.* Sage. https://doi.org/10.4135/9781071802694

Roulston, K. (2001). Data analysis and "theorizing as ideology." *Qualitative Research, 1*(3), 279–302. https://doi.org/10.1177/146879410100100302

Rukeyser. M. (n.d.). *The speed of darkness.* Poetry Foundation. https://www.poetryfoundation.org/poems/56287/the-speed-of-darkness

Russ, J. (1983). *How to suppress women's writing.* University of Texas Press.

Rutledge, T. M. (2020). Visual–verbal redundancy and college choice: Does the level of redundancy in student recruitment advertisements affect high school students' decision-making process? In S. Josephson, J. Kelly, & K. Smith (Eds.), *Handbook of visual communication* (pp. 71–86). Routledge. https://doi.org/10.4324/9780429491115-6

SAGE Publishing. (n.d.-a). *Fair use.* https://us.sagepub.com/en-us/nam/copyright-and-permissions#fairuse

SAGE Publishing. (n.d.-b). *Manuscript submission guidelines.* https://us.sagepub.com/en-us/nam/manuscript-submission-guidelines

Sampson-Cordle, A. V. (2001). *Exploring the relationship between a small rural school in northwest Georgia and its community: An image based study using participant-produced photographs* [Unpublished doctoral dissertation]. University of Athens, Georgia.

Samuels, J. (2004). Breaking the ethnographer's frames: Reflections on the use of photo elicitation in understanding Sri Lankan monastic culture. *American Behavioral Scientist, 47*(12), 1528–1550. https://doi.org/10.1177/0002764204266238

Särmä, S. (2016). "Congrats, you have an all-male panel!" A personal narrative. *International Feminist Journal of Politics, 18*(3), 470–476. https://doi.org/10.1080/14616742.2016.1189671

Sawyer, R. D., & Norris, J. (2009). Duoethnography: Articulations/(re)creation of meaning in the making. In W. S. Gershon (Ed.), *The collaborative turn* (pp. 127–140). Brill Sense. https://doi.org/10.1163/9789087909604_008

Schapiro, M., & Meyer, M. (1977). Waste not want not: An inquiry into what women saved and assembled: FEMMAGE (1977–78). *Heresies, 1*(4), 66–69.

Schwandt, T. A. (2014). *The SAGE dictionary of qualitative inquiry.* Sage.

Sharmini, S., Spronken-Smith, R., Golding, C., & Harland, T. (2015). Assessing the doctoral thesis when it includes published work. *Assessment & Evaluation in Higher Education, 40*(1), 89–102. https://doi.org/10.1080/02602938.2014.888535

Sherry, J. F., Jr., & Schouten, J. W. (2002). A role for poetry in consumer research. *Journal of Consumer Research, 29*(2), 218–234. https://doi.org/10.1086/341572

Shit Academics Say [@AcademicsSay]. (2018, April 19). Reviewer 2 walks into a bar complaining immediately of this not being the joke they would have written. [Tweet]. Twitter. https://twitter.com/AcademicsSay/status/986963490513543168

Shosha, G. A. (2012). Employment of Colaizzi's strategy in descriptive phenomenology: A reflection of a researcher. *European Scientific Journal, 8*(27), 31–43. https://core.ac.uk/download/pdf/236417203.pdf

Showalter, M. E. (1950). *Mennonite community cookbook: Favorite family recipes by Mary Emma Showalter.* Herald Press. (Original work published 1709)

Silvia, P. J. (2007). *How to write a lot: A practical guide to productive academic writing.* American Psychological Association.

Smartt Gullion, J. (2016). *Writing ethnography.* Sense.

Solórzano, D. G., & Yosso, T. J. (2002a). A critical race counterstory of race, racism, and affirmative action. *Equity & Excellence in*

Education, *35*(2), 155–168. https://doi.org/10.1080/713845284

Solórzano, D. G., & Yosso, T. J. (2002b). Critical race methodology: Counter-storytelling as an analytical framework for education research. *Qualitative Inquiry*, *8*(1), 23–44. https://doi.org/10.1177/107780040200800103

Sorsoli, L., & Tolman, D. (2008). Hearing voice: Listening for multiplicity and movement in interview data. In S. N. Hesse-Biber & P. Leavy (Eds.), *Handbook of emergent methods* (pp. 495–515). Guilford Press.

Sousanis, N. (2012). Comics as a tool for inquiry. *Juniata Voices*, *12*, 162–172.

Sousanis, N. (2015). *Unflattening*. Harvard University Press.

Sparkes, A. C., (2009). Ethnography and the senses: Challenges and possibilities. *Qualitative Research in Sport and Exercise*, *1*(1), 21–35. https://doi.org/10.1080/19398440802567923

Sparkes, A. C., & Smith, B. (2013). *Qualitative research methods in sport, exercise and health: From process to product*. Routledge. https://doi.org/10.4324/9780203852187

Spicer, A. (2015, May, 21). Explainer: What is an h-index and how is it calculated? *The Conversation*. https://theconversation.com/explainer-what-is-an-h-index-and-how-is-it-calculated-41162

Spizer, J. (2003). *Rejections of the written famous*. Joshua Tree.

Stake, R. E. (1995). *The art of case study research*. Sage.

Stein, J. (1956). William Faulkner: The art of fiction. *The Paris Review*, Spring(12). https://www.theparisreview.org/interviews/4954/the-art-of-fiction-no-12-william-faulkner

Stoller, P. (1989). *The taste of ethnographic things: The senses in anthropology*. University of Pennsylvania Press. https://doi.org/10.9783/9780812203141

Strunk, W., Jr., & White, E. B. (2007). *The elements of style*. Penguin Books. (Original work published 1918)

Sue-Chan, C., Chen, Z., & Lam, W. (2011). LMX, coaching attributions, and employee performance. *Group & Organization Management*, *36*(4), 466–498. https://doi.org/10.1177/1059601111408896

Taylor, C. M. (2018). *Alaya preschool: A culture of care and meaningful work in contemplative early childhood education* (Publication No. 10830500) [Doctoral dissertation, University of Northern Colorado]. ProQuest Dissertations and Theses Global.

Taylor, J. (2014). Poetry, cosmology, cosmogony. *Interdisciplinary Science Reviews*, *39*(1), 85–98. https://doi.org/10.1179/0308018813Z.00000000067

TED-Ed. (2019, September). *Ode to the only Black kid in class*. https://www.ted.com/talks/clint_smith_ode_to_the_only_black_kid_in_the_class?language=en

Teman, E. D., & Lahman, M. K. E. (2012). Broom closet or fish bowl? Using educational ethnography to explore the culture of a university queer youth center. *Qualitative Inquiry*, *18*(4), 341–354. https://doi.org/10.1177/1077800411433548

Teman, E. D., & Lahman, M. K. (2019). Coming out (as a poststructuralist): A rant. *Qualitative Inquiry*, *25*(1), 57–68.

Thomas, J. R., Nelson, J. K., & Magill, R. A. (1986). A case for an alternative format for the thesis/dissertation. *Quest, 38*(2), 116–124. https://doi.org/10.1080/0033 6297.1986.10483846

Thompson, B. (1995). Publishing your research results: Some suggestions and counsel. *Journal of Counseling & Development, 73*(3), 342–345. https://doi .org/10.1002/j.1556-6676.1995.tb01761.x

Thomson, P. (Ed.). (2008). *Doing visual research with children and young people* (pp. 164–174). Routledge. https://doi .org/10.4324/9780203870525

Tillmann-Healy, L. M. (2003). Friendship as method. *Qualitative Inquiry, 9*(5), 729–749. https://doi.org/10.1177/1077 800403254894

Tonner, A. (2019). Consumer culture poetry: Insightful data and methodological approaches. *Consumption Markets & Culture, 22*(3), 256–271. https://doi.org/ 10.1080/10253866.2018.1474110

Tsang, K. K., & Besley, T. (2020). Visual inquiry in educational research. *Beijing International Review of Education, 2*(1), 2–10. https://doi.org/10.1163/ 25902539-00201002

Typewriter Poetry. (n.d.). *About.* http:// www.typewriterpoetry.com/about/

Ulmer, J. B. (2017). Writing slow ontology. *Qualitative Inquiry, 23*(3), 201–211. https:// doi.org/10.1177/1077800416643994

Ulmer, J. B. (2018). Composing techniques: Choreographing a postqualitative writing practice. *Qualitative Inquiry, 24*(9), 728–736.

University of Northern Colorado. (2019, November, 12). *UNC Galleries spotlight: Yucca fountain.* YouTube. https://www .youtube.com/watch?v=XDAE-avF4yY

Vagle, M. D. (2018). *Crafting phenomenological research.* Routledge. https:// doi.org/10.4324/9781315173474

Vanderbuilt, A. T. (1999). *The making of a bestseller: From author to reader.* McFarland.

Vannier, M. (2018). The power of the pen: Prisoners' letters to explore extreme imprisonment. *Criminology & Criminal Justice, 20*(3), 249–267. https://doi.org/ 10.1177/1748895818818872

Vaughan, K. (2005). Pieced together: Collage as an artist's method for interdisciplinary research. *International Journal of Qualitative Methods, 4*(1), 27–52. https://doi.org/10.1177/ 160940690500400103

Vick, J. (2018). *Classic jokes for writers.* https://brevity.wordpress.com/2018/ 06/13/classic-jokes-for-writers/

Vidal, L., Ares, G., & Jaeger, S. R. (2016). Use of emoticon and emoji in tweets for food-related emotional expression. *Food Quality and Preference, 49,* 119–128. https://doi.org/10.1016/j.food qual.2015.12.002

Vu, M. C., & Burton, N. (2020). Mindful reflexivity: Unpacking the process of transformative learning in mindfulness and discernment. *Management Learning, 51*(2), 207–226. https://doi .org/10.1177/1350507619888751

Walker, A. (1982). *The color purple.* Harcourt Brace Jovanovich.

Wallach, L. (2012). *A cut-down history of collage.* http://www.artspace.com/ magazine/art_101/art_market/art_101_ collage-5622

Wa-Mbaleka, S. (2014). *Publish or perish: Fear no more.* CentralBooks.

Wang, C. (2003). Using photovoice as a participatory assessment and issue selection tool: A case study with the homeless in Ann Arbor. In M. Minkler & N. Wallerstein (Eds.), *Community-based participatory research for health* (pp. 179–196). Jossey-Bass/Wiley.

Wang, C., & Burris, M. A. (1994). Empowerment through photo novella: Portraits of participation. *Health Education & Behavior, 21*(2), 171–186. https://doi.org/10.1177/109019819402100204

Wang, C., & Burris, M. A. (1997). Photovoice: Concept, methodology, and use for participatory needs assessment. *Health Education & Behavior, 24*(3), 369–387. https://doi.org/10.1177/109019819702400309

Wang, C., & Redwood-Jones, Y. (2001). Photovoice ethics: Perspectives from Flint Photovoice. *Health Education & Behavior, 28*(5), 560–572.

Weaver-Hightower, M. (2014, March, 17). *Writing Tip #3: Writing qualitative findings paragraphs.* YouTube. https://www.youtube.com/watch?v=mmKuvwk8x84

White, E. B. (1952). *Charlotte's web.* Harper.

Whitman, W. (1865). *Oh, Captain! My, Captain.* Poetry Foundation. https://www.poetryfoundation.org/poems/45474/o-captain-my-captain

Wiles, R., Prosser, J., Bagnoli, A., Clark, A., Davies, K., Holland, S., & Renold, E. (2008). *Visual ethics: Ethical issues in visual research* (NCRM Working Paper). National Centre for Research Methods. http://eprints.ncrm.ac.uk/421/

Wolcott, H. F. (1994). *Transforming qualitative data: Description, analysis, and interpretation.* Sage.

Wolcott, H. F. (2009). *Writing up qualitative research* (3rd ed.). Sage. https://doi.org/10.4135/9781452234878

Wolf, M. (1992). *A thrice-told tale: Feminism, postmodernism, and ethnographic responsibility.* Stanford University Press.

Word for Word. (2011, February, 9). *One potato, two potato: The art of describing characters.* http://wordforwords.blogspot.com/2011/02/one-potato-two-potato-art-of-describing.html

Wordsworth, W. (n.d.). *I wandered lonely as a cloud.* Poetry Foundation. https://www.poetryfoundation.org/poems/45521/i-wandered-lonely-as-a-cloud

The Writing Center. (n.d.). *Dissertations.* University of North Carolina at Chapel Hill. https://writingcenter.unc.edu/tips-and-tools/dissertations/

Yorks, L., Marsick, V. J., Kasl, E., & Dechant, K. (2003). Contextualizing team learning: Implications for research and practice. *Advances in Developing Human Resources, 5*(1), 103–117. https://doi.org/10.1177/1523422302239185

Yin, R. K. (2017). *Case study research and applications: Design and methods.* Sage.

Young, A., & Martin, M. (2017, July, 15). *Music interviews: After rapping his dissertation, A. D. Carson is UVa's new hip-hop professor.* All Things Considered: National Public Radio. https://www.npr.org/2017/07/15/537274235/

after-rapping-his-dissertation-a-d-carson-is-uvas-new-hip-hop-professor

Zeller, N., & Farmer, F. M. (1999). "Catchy, clever titles are not acceptable": Style, APA, and qualitative reporting. *International Journal of Qualitative Studies in Education, 12*(1), 3–19. https://doi.org/10.1080/0951839 99236303

Zeyab, A. (2017). *Educational technology and visual literacy: The effect of using doodling on student learning performance* [Unpublished doctoral dissertation]. University of Northern Colorado.

Zeyab, A., Almodaires, A., & Almutairi, F. (2020). Thinking differently: A visual note recording strategy to improve learning. *Journal of Education and Practice, 11*(2). https://doi.org/10.7176/JEP/11-2-02

Ziehl, K., & Jerz, D. G. (2020). *Poetry writing hacks: 10 Tips on how to write a poem.* https://jerz.setonhill.edu/writing/creative1/poetry-writing-tips-how-to-write-a-poem/

Zinsser, W. (2006). *On writing well: The classic guide to writing nonfiction* (7th ed.). HarperCollins.

• Index •